T0291433

ENTREPRENEURSHIP AND GLOBAL ECONOMIC GROWTH

Series editor: Bruno S. Sergi, Harvard University, USA

Entrepreneurship and Global Economic Growth is Emerald's cutting-edge Global Economic Growth book series, presenting modern examinations of economic growth at national, regional and global levels. Each book in this series discusses different dimensions of the changing economic and industrial contexts, and examines in detail their impact on the nature of growth and development. For academics and senior practitioners, this series puts forward significant new research in the global economic growth field, opening discussions regarding new topics and updating existing literature.

Published Titles in This Series

Modeling Economic Growth in Contemporary Russia, edited by Bruno S. Sergi

Modeling Economic Growth in Contemporary Belarus, edited by Bruno S. Sergi

Modeling Economic Growth in Contemporary Malaysia, edited by Bruno S. Sergi and Abdul Rahman Jaaffar

Modeling Economic Growth in Contemporary Greece, edited by Vasileiois Vlachos, Aristidis Bitzenis and Bruno S. Sergi

Modeling Economic Growth in Contemporary Poland, edited by Elżbieta Bukalska, Tomasz Kijek and Bruno S. Sergi

Forthcoming Titles in This Series

Modeling Economic Growth in Contemporary India, edited by Bruno S. Sergi, Aviral Kumar Tiwari and Samia Nasreen

Modeling Economic Growth in Contemporary Czechia

EDITED BY

DANIEL STAVÁREK

Silesian University in Opava, Czechia

AND

MICHAL TVRDOŇ

Silesian University in Opava, Czechia

United Kingdom – North America – Japan – India – Malaysia – China

Emerald Publishing Limited
Emerald Publishing, Floor 5, Northspring, 21-23 Wellington Street, Leeds LS1 4DL

First edition 2024

British Library Cataloguing in Publication Data
A catalogue record for this book is available from the British Library

ISBN: 978-1-83753-841-6 (Print)
ISBN: 978-1-83753-840-9 (Online)
ISBN: 978-1-83753-842-3 (Epub)

Printed and bound by CPI Group (UK) Ltd, Croydon, CR0 4YY

Contents

List of Tables and Figures

Chapter 2

Chapter 3

Chapter 4

Chapter 5

Chapter 6

Chapter 7

Chapter 9

Chapter 10

Chapter 11

Chapter 12

Chapter 14

Chapter 15

Chapter 17

Chapter 18

About the Editors

Daniel Stavárek is a Professor and Head of the Department of Finance and Accounting at the Silesian University in Opava, School of Business Administration in Karviná. His research interest focuses on international finance and banking with a strong emphasis on the process of convergence and European monetary integration. Daniel has published extensively in scholarly journals and authored and edited several books published by renowned international publishers. He currently serves as the Vice Rector for Science and International Relations of the Silesian University in Opava.

Michal Tvrdoň is an Associate Professor at the Department of Economics and Public Administration at the Silesian University in Opava, School of Business Administration in Karviná. As a macroeconomist, his main research fields are related to business cycles, economic integration processes and the labour market. Michal participated in several international and domestic research projects focused on macroeconomic and labour market performance in the countries of the European Union.

About the Contributors

Liběna Černohorská is an Associate Professor at Faculty of Economics and Administration, University of Pardubice, Czechia. She has written book about banking and two chapters in books related to public private cooperation and is co-author of two chapters in books *Credit Risk and Financial Crises a Systematic Risk in Post-Crisis Financial Markets*. Her research mainly deals with various issues of banking.

Jan Černohorský is an Associate Professor at Faculty of Economics and Administration, University of Pardubice, Czechia. He has written the book *Finance – From Theory to Reality*, two chapters in books related to public–private cooperation and co-authored the book *Fundamentals of Finance* (all in Czech) and two chapters in book *Credit Risk and Financial Crises*. His research interests focus on macroeconomics and banking.

Petr David is a Professor at the Department of Accounting and Taxes, Faculty of Business and Economics, Mendel University in Brno, Czechia. For many years, he has systematically been working on the issues of externalities, road transport and the related tax policies. He has carried out research projects in this field and cooperated with public sector institutions.

Aleš Franc is an Assistant Professor at Department of Economics, Faculty of Business and Economics, Mendel University in Brno, Czechia. In his publication activities, Aleš focuses on labour market and particularly on labour market institutions, structural changes of employment, the impact of infrastructure on unemployment.

Tomáš Heryán is an Assistant Professor at the School of Business Administration in Karvina, Silesian University in Opava, Czechia. She has authored or co-authored numerous papers published in reputable scientific journals, focusing his research on corporate finance, financial markets and monetary policy. He holds certificates from attending several courses on applied statistics using STATA software by Timberlake, London. Hence, as a statistician, he has also participated in medicinal research.

Roman Hlawiczka is an Assistant Professor at the Department of Finance and Accounting at Silesian University in Opava, School of Business Administration in Karviná, Czechia. He has nearly 30 years of experience in management positions in retail banking with a focus on the small and medium-sized enterprise (SME) and entrepreneur sectors. His research interests have focused on the SME sector. His area of expertise is in the banking sector.

Ladislava Issever Grochová is a Researcher and Instructor in the field of economics at Mendel University in Brno, Czechia. She specializes in environmental economics, macroeconomic and environmental policies, with a focus on the interplay between the economy and the environment addressing institutional context, and productivity and efficiency analysis. She actively involves in a number of international research projects; the outputs being published in scientific journals indexed by the Web of Science and Scopus.

Jana Janoušková is an Associate Professor at the School of Business Administration in Karvina, Silesian University in Opava, Czechia. She has authored or co-authored numerous papers published in reputable scientific journals, focusing her research on taxes, tax policy and international tax harmonization.

Vojtěch Koňařík is a doctoral student at the VSB-Technical University in Ostrava, Czechia. His focus includes behavioural economics, altruism and philosophy in economics.

Tetiana Konieva is an Assistant Professor at the School of Business Administration in Karvina, Silesian University in Opava, Czechia. She has authored and co-authored several journal articles focused on financing management and corporate finance. Her research activities analyse various aspects of financing policy and cost management.

Ivana Košturíková is an Assistant Professor at the School of Business Administration in Karvina, Silesian University in Opava, Czechia. Her previous publications in journals focused mainly on various issues of accounting and accounting education. She is currently engaged in research in the field of working capital management.

Eva Kotlánová is an Assistant Professor at the Silesian University in Opava, School of Business Administration in Karviná, Czechia. She is a member of Department of Economics and Public Administration. She focuses on economic policy, institutional environment, corruption and its impact on macroeconomic environment and variables.

Radmila Krkošková is an Assistant Professor at the Department of Informatics and Mathematics at the Silesian University in Opava, School of Business Administration in Karvina, Czechia. She successfully completed her doctoral studies in Applied Mathematics at the University of Ostrava, Faculty of Science. Her scientific research is focused on econometric analysis and analysis of time series.

Zuzana Kučerová is an Associate Professor at the VSB-Technical University in Ostrava and Mendel University in Brno, Czechia. Her research interests include monetary theory and policy, crowdfunding, exchange rates, monetary and financial integration, economic policy and cryptocurrencies.

Marek Litzman is an Assistant Professor at Department of Economics, Faculty of Business and Economics, Mendel University in Brno, Czechia. The main interest of his research is in the impact of formal institutional environment on macroeconomic indicators. He also participated in research in the field of the introduction of EU's Common Consolidated Corporate Tax Base and estimation of its impacts on state budgets.

Aleš Melecký is an Associate Professor and Senior Researcher at the Department of Economics, VSB-Technical University of Ostrava, Czechia. He was Head of the Department of Economics at VSB-TUO during the period 2016–2020. His research topics include macroeconomic modelling, credit risk modelling, government debt management and quantitative literature review.

Radek Náplava is an Assistant Professor at the Department of Economics of Mendel University in Brno in Czechia. His research and publications focus primarily on structural changes in the European labour markets and its socio-economic consequences.

Dennis Nchor received his PhD in Economics and Management in 2016 from Mendel University in Brno, Czechia. He joined the research team of the Department of Economics, Faculty of Business and Economics and has been instrumental in organizing research activities and publishing their outcomes. He has been involved in many collaborative research projects that are financed by renown institutions such as the Internal Grant Agency, European Union and Civil Society Institutions. Dennis is author and co-author of 25 journal papers and conference proceedings that are indexed by the Web of Science and Scopus.

Jan Nevima is an Associate Professor in the field of International Trade and a doctor in the field of Economics at the School of Business Administration in Karvina, Silesian University in Opava, Czechia. His research interest is in econometric and statistical analysis for assessment of competitiveness and convergence. He deals with the issue of smart cities and brownfields.

Daniel Pakši is a doctoral student at the VSB-Technical University in Ostrava, Czechia. His research interests include monetary economics, inflation expectations, housing prices, migration and social exclusion.

Iveta Palečková is an Associate Professor at the Department of Finance and Accounting at Silesian University in Opava, School of Business Administration in Karviná, Czechia. She is the author and co-author of several publications in scientific journals on the stability, performance, efficiency and competition in the banking sector. She was a member of the research team of the projects funded by the Czech Science Foundation.

Lenka Přečková is an Assistant Professor at the Department of Finance and Accounting at Silesian University in Opava, School of Business Administration in Karviná, Czechia. She has authored or co-authored several publications in scientific journals on financial stability, performance and development of the insurance market. She was a member of the research team of the projects funded by the Czech Science Foundation.

Petr Rozmahel is an Associate Professor in the Department of Economics, Faculty of Business and Economics, Mendel University in Brno, Czechia. Previously, he also led the Research Center of Mendel University. As a macroeconomist, his main research fields are related to business cycles, economic and monetary integration processes and macroeconomic policy. Petr led and participated in many international research projects focused, for example, on the adoption of the euro in Czechia and other Central and Eastern European countries and on processes of macroeconomic convergence in Europe.

Petra Růčková is an Associate Professor at the School of Business Administration in Karvina, Silesian University in Opava, Czechia. She has authored or co-authored numerous papers published in reputable scientific journals, focusing her research on corporate finance, financial analysis and capital structure. Petra is a member of the Academic council of School of Business Administration in Karviná and she is also a member of the editorial board of Acta academica Karviniensia.

Jiří Rusnok is a Czech Politician and Economist who served as the Prime Minister of the Czech Republic between June 2013 and January 2014. From 2016 to 2022 he served as the governor of the Czech National Bank. During his time at the helm of the central bank, he received the international awards Central Bank Governor for Central and Eastern Europe 2017 and Central Bank Governor in Europe 2018. He advocated transparent central bank communication, for which the CNB under his leadership was awarded the international Central Banking Transparency Award 2022.

Jana Šimáková is an Assistant Professor at the School of Business Administration in Karvina, Silesian University in Opava, Czechia. She has authored or co-authored numerous papers published in reputable scientific journals, focusing her research on exchange rates, foreign trade and international financial management. Jana also lends her expertise as a member of the control and advisory body in the multifunctional coworking center for business support known as Business Gate. Currently, she holds the role of Vice Dean for international relations.

Michal Škára completed his master's degree at Mendel University. Since then, he has been working at the Financial Market Supervision Department II of the Czech National Bank where he contributed to the development and implementation of the reporting framework for financial services intermediaries.

Markéta Skupieňová is an Assistant Professor at the School of Business Administration in Karvina, Silesian University in Opava, Czechia. She has authored and co-authored several journal articles focused on managerial and cost accounting. Her current research interests include decision-making processes based on outputs of managerial accounting.

Šárka Sobotovičová is an Assistant Professor at the School of Business Administration in Karvina, Silesian University in Opava, Czechia. She regularly publishes papers in scholarly journals with interest in direct and indirect taxes, national and international tax policy.

Irena Szarowská is an Assistant Professor at the Department of Finance and Accounting of the Silesian University in Opava, School of Business Administration in Karvina, Czechia. She is the author of many articles published in scientific journals included in the Web of Science and Scopus databases. Her scientific interests refer to the field of public finance and fiscal policy as well as municipal and regional finance.

Zuzana Szkorupová is an Assistant Professor at the Department of Finance and Accounting of the Silesian University in Opava, School of Business Administration in Karvina, Czechia. Her research is focused on foreign direct investment and monetary policy.

Petr Teplý is a Professor at Prague University of Economics and Business, Czechia. He has written or co-authored 10 books in the field of banking and finance. His top publications include a *Czech-English Bilingual Book Banking in Theory and Practice*, *Consumer Lending in Theory and Practice* and *Financial Disintermediation: The Case of Peer to Peer Lending*. His research focuses mainly on the area of banking and financial services.

Foreword

Czechia is a medium-sized country in the middle of Europe. Next year, together with the other new EU Member States, we will mark the 20th anniversary of our accession to the European Union. In 2021, Czechia reached 91% of the EU27 average, measured by GDP per capita in purchasing power parity standards. While this level is higher than Portugal or Spain (75% and 84%, respectively) and close to Italy (95%), Czechia has been growing at the slowest average rate in recent years in almost the entire EU and by far the slowest in the group of Central and Eastern European countries. Between 2005 and 2021, this indicator increased by 63% in Czechia, while it increased by 119% in Poland, 75% in Hungary and 65% in Slovakia. Most recently, between 2021 and 2019, the growth gap is even more pronounced with Czechia +1%, Poland +10%, Hungary +7% and Slovakia +2%. During this period a number of developed Member States (e.g. all Nordic countries, Benelux, Germany, France, Ireland) also grew faster than Czechia.

It is therefore clear that economic convergence towards more advanced countries has stalled. And the Czech economy is losing its ability to catch up, let alone overtake more advanced economies. The medium-term perspective is burdened with a number of complex challenges. Therefore, we must think hard about what the future of the Czech Republic in general and its economy in particular should look like.

This book undeniably comes at the right time and provides us with a lot of inspiration for this thinking. The right therapy in medicine as well as in economic policy cannot be established without a good diagnosis, i.e. an analysis of the state of affairs and the previous developments that have brought us to our current state. In this methodologically correct approach, I find the greatest contribution of this publication. This book provides a professional analysis of many key areas of the economy and the economic policy applied in recent years, using the example of a medium-sized and medium-developed open economy such as Czechia.

The existing model of the Czech economy has been largely based on massive inflows of foreign investment since the second half of the 1990s, which continued de facto throughout the first decade of the current century. This capital has been directed mainly towards industrial capacities, often linked to automobile production. In addition to a long industrial tradition, targeted government support, a favourable geographical location and a well-equipped infrastructure, these investments also found a cheap and high-quality workforce in Czechia.

However, over the last 5–7 years, the situation in Czechia, as well as worldwide, has changed dramatically. The COVID-19 pandemic and the subsequent disruption of global value chains, as well as the ongoing European energy crisis and Russia's subsequent aggression in Ukraine, symbolise the end of the 'golden' era of globalisation that has shaped world development for the last 30 years.

Labour has long been a scarce commodity in Czechia. We have had the lowest unemployment rate in the EU for a long time, and similarly, the employment rate exceeds 80% and is also well above-average EU standards. The share of foreigners in the labour market is around 15%. The Czech economy is highly energy intensive. Too many companies operate in a subcontracting position so that they do not have the full opportunity to exploit the added value from, for example, research and development and from the sale of their own products. These are perhaps the key structural problems of the Czech economy.

In a certain sense, the Czech economy is facing the challenge of overcoming the so-called middle income trap. That is to say, finding a way to move from the level of a medium-developed EU country to the desirable position of approaching the above-average developed countries. I believe that whether we succeed or not will be determined by how successful Czech society is in making a fundamental qualitative shift in the key areas of our country's governance, which are institutions, innovation and infrastructure.

Economic policy in the narrow sense cannot deliver these priorities. However, its successful management, which in the end means, above all, maintaining the overall macroeconomic balance, is a necessary condition for any positive shift in these priorities. Finding the appropriate monetary and fiscal policy settings appears to be the biggest challenge for the period ahead. This will lead to a sustainable restoration of price and fiscal balance while maintaining adequate growth potential of the Czech economy.

Jiří Rusnok

Governor of Czech National Bank (2016–2022)

Prime Minister of Czechia (2013–2014)

Acknowledgment

Publication of this book was supported by the Ministry of Education, Youth and Sports of the Czech Republic within the Institutional Support for Long-term Development of a Research Organization in 2023.

Chapter 1

The Czech Economy in the Last Decade: Determinants and Obstacles to Economic Growth

Daniel Stavárek and Michal Tvrdoň

Silesian University in Opava, Czechia

Abstract

Czechia is a small open economy and a member state of the European Union. Several important trends and episodes that have determined economic growth can be identified over the last two decades. This chapter deals with some macroeconomic features like macroeconomic and labour market performance within the business cycle, the Czech National Bank (CNB) exchange rate commitment and interest rate policy, increasing indebtedness and budget deficits, foreign trade and the international investment position. We applied publicly available data from Eurostat, the Organisation for Economic Co-operation and Development and CNB databases. The data show that the Czech economy was significantly converging to the average economic level of the European Union. We also identified key turning points in business cycles. Macroeconomic data on economic development of the economy indicate an atypical course of the business cycle between 2020 and 2022, which can be evaluated as different from the one that followed the global financial crisis.

Keywords: Macroeconomic performance; gross domestic product; output gap; unemployment rate; external economic balance; exchange rate; business and consumer surveys

1.1 Introduction

Czechia has been a member state of the European Union (EU) for more than 18 years. During this time, the Czech economy underwent a significant

Modeling Economic Growth in Contemporary Czechia, 1–16

Published under exclusive licence by Emerald Publishing Limited
doi:10.1108/978-1-83753-840-920241001

transformation. In the past two decades, the Czech economy had to cope with several external and internal shocks, the effects of the global financial crisis and the subsequent crisis of the real economy, the internal recession and subsequent significant economic growth interrupted by the COVID-19 pandemic. The main goal of this chapter is to identify the main macroeconomic trends of the last two decades in the context of the business cycle, the COVID-19 pandemic, disruption of global supply chains and high inflation rates. The last decade brought several situations that disrupted traditional mechanisms of using economic policy instruments to achieve economic growth. We employed key macroeconomic indicators for analysis of the macroeconomic environment, both traditional indicators of a quantitative nature (gross domestic product [GDP], industrial production index [IPI], unemployment rate) and qualitative indicators (economic sentiment indicator [ESI] or the Organisation for Economic Co-operation and Development [OECD] business and consumer confidence indicators). Special attention is also paid to the external economic position as Czechia is an open economy with strong international economic relations. We present development of external balances, the international investment position and exchange rates. We focus on the period between the years 2000 and 2022. We used data from publicly available Eurostat, the Czech National Bank (CNB) and the OECD databases.

1.2 Development of the Key Quantitative Macroeconomic Indicators

The most widely used macroeconomic indicator that represents the general economic activity is the GDP. Fig. 1.1 shows the growth rate of real GDP between the years 2000 and 2022. As can be seen in the figure, the Czech economy recorded two full business cycles, which consist of phases of conjuncture and phases of contraction. In addition, it is clear from the development of the time series that four turning points (two peaks and two troughs) can be identified during this period. If we focus on the significant contractions in 2009 and 2020, these sudden changes were caused by (i) the consequences of the 2008 global financial crisis and (ii) the 2020 COVID-19 pandemic. In the context of the 2009 crisis, Czechia experienced a sharp drop in real GDP growth to negative values. After a period of time, the Czech economy returned to significant economic growth, which is particularly visible between 2016 and 2019. The main contributors to growth were strong domestic demand and exports. Such strong economic growth enabled convergence to the GDP level. On the other hand, it caused a shortage of labour supply, leading to a very low unemployment rate, even below the natural rate of unemployment. Another accompanying feature of rapid growth was the enormous rise in prices in the real estate market. Although there were signs of the economy overheating in 2018 and 2019 that were similar to those of the years 2007 and 2008, the same scenario did not repeat itself. A significant drop in GDP level occurred in 2020 due to the COVID-19 pandemic, which subsequently affected economic development not only in the V4 countries but also

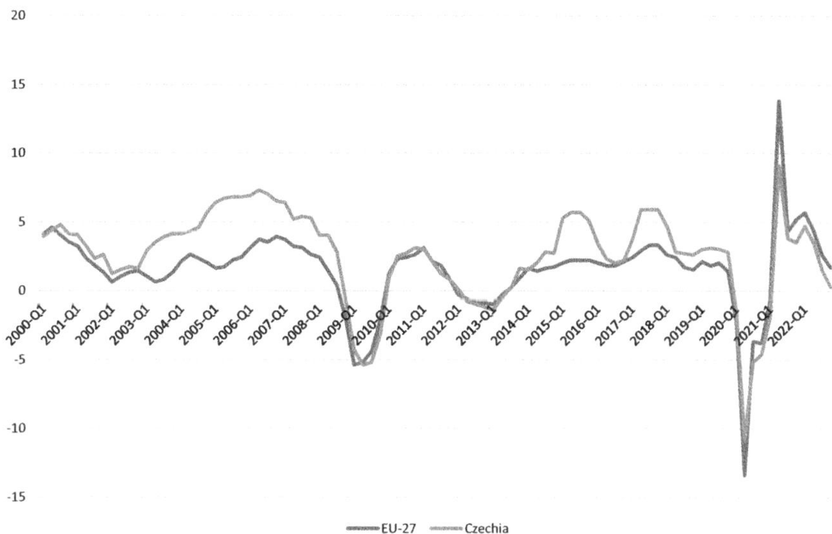

Fig. 1.1. Real GDP Growth in Years 2000–2022 (Quarterly Data, Seasonally and Calendar Adjusted). *Source:* Eurostat.

in the EU and the global economy. The development of real GDP was very volatile during 2020, mainly due to the pandemic situation and the resulting government measures against the spread of the virus. The most prominent measures were the lockdowns applied in the first, second and fourth quarter – these lockdowns led to a decline in household consumption and enterprise investment. The impact on individual sectors of the economy was also different. The following sequence of events can be demonstrated using the example of the Czech economy: (i) there is a noticeable slowdown of the economy in the first quarter of 2020 and a subsequent sharp drop in real GDP level during the second quarter of 2020 (by 10.8% year-on-year); (ii) year-on-year declines in real GDP continued until the first quarter of 2021, with year-on-year changes gradually decreasing; (iii) real GDP growth was recorded from the second quarter of 2021, but with the fact that the base for calculating was the year 2020; and (iv) further developments in the V4 countries indicated inception of a recovery phase after the end of the pandemic; however, the sharp rise in energy and commodity prices reversed this trend during 2022. In addition to this factor, the slower growth of the global economy, the ongoing disruption of global supply chains and greater uncertainty were also influential. These factors, together with weak household demand, led to a remarkable economic slowdown.

During the monitored period, a gradual convergence of the Czech economy to the average economic level (expressed by GDP per capita in PPS) is evident (see Fig. 1.2). However, this convergence process was disrupted during the economic

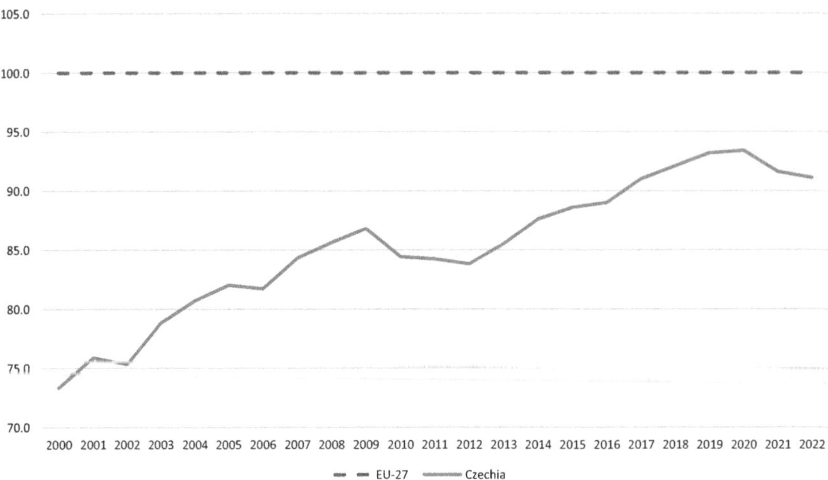

Fig. 1.2. Development of Czech GDP per Capita 2000–2022 (Annual Data, EU-27 = 100). *Source:* Eurostat.

recession (years 2009 and 2010) and subsequently during the internal recession in 2012. The second disruption of this process occurred in the pandemic and post-pandemic period (2020–2022). Overall, the development of the Czech economy can be positively assessed, as there was an increase in the economic level from 73% of the EU-27 average in 2000 to 91% in 2022.

Since there were significant fluctuations in economic development during the observed period, it is also appropriate to focus on the estimation of the output gap. This indicator measures the difference between the estimated potential output and the actual product (real GDP). Subsequently, it can be determined whether demand pressures appear in the economy. If current real GDP is above the level of potential output, then the economy is in an inflationary gap, which means that the prices of goods and services tend to rise, leading to an increase in the price level. Conversely, if current output is below the potential one, then the economy is not fully utilising the factors of production and the economy is in a recessionary gap, or in other words, a negative output gap occurs.

The most common approaches to estimate the output gap include either the method based on the Cobb–Douglas production function or various procedures based on the estimation of trend. We have employed the Hodrick-Prescott filter (HP filter), which is often used for trend estimation. According to Hloušek and Polanský (2007), we applied the time series of real GDP for the potential output estimation (Eurostat's quarterly data between 2000 and 2022). It was also important to determine the value of the smoothing constant λ, which is defined as the ratio variance of the shock causing cyclical fluctuations and the shock affecting trend growth – according to the recommendations in previous studies, it is appropriate to set the value of the smoothing constant to 1,600 for quarterly data and 100 for annual data (see Gerlach & Yiun, 2004; Hájek & Bezděk, 2001; Němec, 2008; Zimková & Barochovský, 2007). As mentioned above, the only variable needed is real GDP at constant prices (year 2015) and seasonally adjusted.

According to Hájek and Bezděk (2001), the disadvantage of estimating the potential product using the HP filter is the fact that its results are slightly skewed at the beginning and end of the time series, if the beginning and end of the time series do not capture a similar phase of the cycle. Since the key observed period is not located at the beginning and end of the time series, this problem is not a major reason for us not to apply this method.

Fig. 1.3 shows the development of the estimated output gap for the Czech economy between 2000 and 2022. Looking at the development of real GDP and the estimated trend, it can be stated that during the monitored period, the Czech economy reached a significant positive output gap twice (from 2006 to 2007 and from 2017 to 2019).

The disadvantage of GDP is its time lag, and therefore it is used for ex post evaluation of economic development. If we want to describe the current economic situation more accurately or predict future development, it is necessary to use other indicators, usually on a monthly basis. For this purpose, Eurostat created short-term business statistics (STS). In spirit of the above, STS are the first published statistics that show current trends in the economies of the EU. These short-term indicators can be divided into (i) quantitative indicators, which reflect past macroeconomic performance or employment developments, and (ii) qualitative indicators, that is, those that reflect the subjective assessment of the cyclical situation by entrepreneurs or households. Sub-indices measure trends in a time series (e.g. industrial production). The average of the index is equal to 100 for the

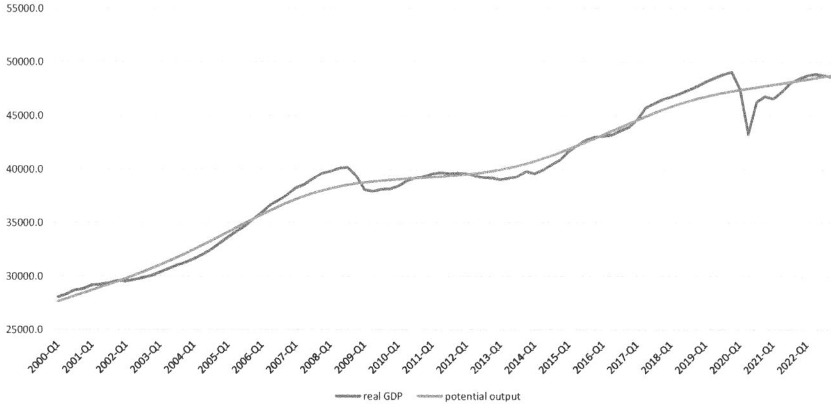

Fig. 1.3. Output Gap in Czechia (Quarterly Data, Seasonally and Calendar Adjusted). *Source:* Eurostat.

base year (usually 2015). Index movements can be expressed in index points (as the difference between two index levels) or as a percentage change. Index points are sensitive to the level of the index itself, whereas percentage changes are not and are therefore suitable for comparison with other variables on a single chart. In addition, it must be added that short-term business statistics do not provide information on the level of prices or turnover, but only information on how prices or turnover have increased or decreased in the previous month, the previous quarter or the previous 12 months.

Fig. 1.4 shows the development of IPI in the manufacturing sector from 2000 to 2022. The manufacturing sector is one of the key sectors of the Czech economy that is strongly pro-export orientated. The figure shows that the manufacturing industry grew quite dynamically in the years preceding the global financial and economic crisis. During the crisis, the manufacturing industry significantly declined, and after a relatively quick recovery during 2010 and 2011, another decline is seen during the years 2012 and 2013 due to internal recession. The precrisis level of IPI in the manufacturing sector was reached in 2014. During the COVID-19 pandemic in 2020, the decline in IPI in the manufacturing sector was sharper compared to the 2009 crisis. On the other hand, it can be stated that the recovery was more dynamic, which resulted from the nature of this shock.

When evaluating the macroeconomic situation, it is important to consider the household sector. Household consumption expenditure accounts for more than half of the GDP measured by the expenditure method in most countries of the EU. Taking into account that households divide their disposable income into two main components, namely consumption and savings, the gross savings rate of households (GSRH) appears as an important indicator in this context. It can be defined as gross saving divided by gross disposable income, with the latter

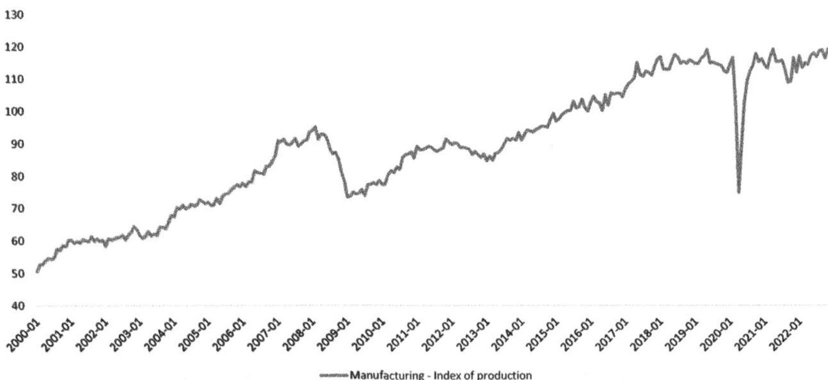

Fig. 1.4. Production in Industry – Manufacturing in Years 2000–2022 (Monthly Data, Seasonally and Calendar Adjusted). *Source:* Eurostat.

adjusted for the change in the net equity of households in pension funds reserves. Gross savings is the part of the gross disposable income, which is not spent as final consumption expenditure. GSRH increases if gross disposable income grows faster than final consumption expenditure. Statistics show that household savings rates increase during periods of increased uncertainty as purchases of essential goods are postponed.

Fig. 1.5 shows the development of household consumption (chain-linked volumes, index 2005 = 100, left axis) and the GSRH (in %, right axis) between 2000 and 2022 (quarterly data). Household consumption increased in the periods of expansion, especially in the years 2005–2008 and 2015–2019. In the case of the global financial crisis and subsequent real economy crisis, household consumption stagnated as a result of the deterioration of consumer confidence in the economy and the growth of the unemployment rate. On the contrary, the decrease in consumption in the second quarter was the result of restrictive measures of governments (lockdown). The specificity of this period also lies in the very rapid recovery of consumption, which reached the pre-COVID level already in the third quarter of 2021. If we look at the development of GSRH, it can be seen from the figure that, while in the case of Czechia, this indicator is relatively stable in the monitored period and varies between 5% and 15%.

Macroeconomic performance subsequently has an impact on another important part of the macroenvironment, namely the labour market performance. In general, the unemployment rate is a key indicator of labour market performance. It increases during a contraction, while it decreases during an expansion. These movements are mainly related to fluctuations in economic activity and the resulting changes in labour demand. The reaction of the labour market to changes in economic activity occurs with a certain time delay, but historical data show

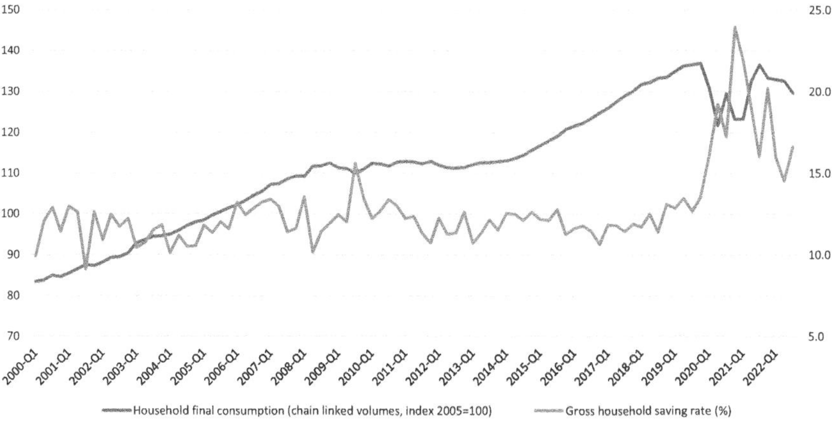

Fig. 1.5. Household Sector (Quarterly Data, Seasonally and Calendar Adjusted). *Source:* Eurostat.

that, while the unemployment rate increases quickly and sharply, its decrease occurs very slowly and over a longer period of time (e.g. the situation before and after the 2008 global financial crisis). In this context, however, it is important to distinguish between the cyclical and structural nature of unemployment. The first is closely related to the development of the business cycle and the second is linked to the structure of the economy and often represents a serious problem, especially from a regional point of view. To analyse the labour market from a macroeconomic point of view, the unemployment rate is the most often used. However, with regard to the above, it is necessary to decompose the unemployment rate into a cyclical and structural component for a more precise assessment of the macroenvironment in the context of the labour market performance. First, it is necessary to seasonally adjust the given time series; then the trend component can be estimated using the HP filter. The difference between the trend thus estimated and the original seasonally adjusted series represents the cyclical component of unemployment (if we reverse the sign). The structural component of unemployment can be determined as the residual part of total unemployment after deducting the seasonal and cyclical components. Fig. 1.6 shows the decomposition of the unemployment rate between the years 2000 and 2022. The figure shows that this important aspect of the overall macroenvironment changed dynamically in Czechia during the monitored period. The initial phase was associated with transition problems that led to higher unemployment rates. As mentioned above, the situation on the labour market is closely related to the overall macroeconomic performance (measured by GDP). In the context of the business cycle, there is an important link between the actual unemployment rate and the natural rate of unemployment. In other words, if the actual unemployment rate is lower than the

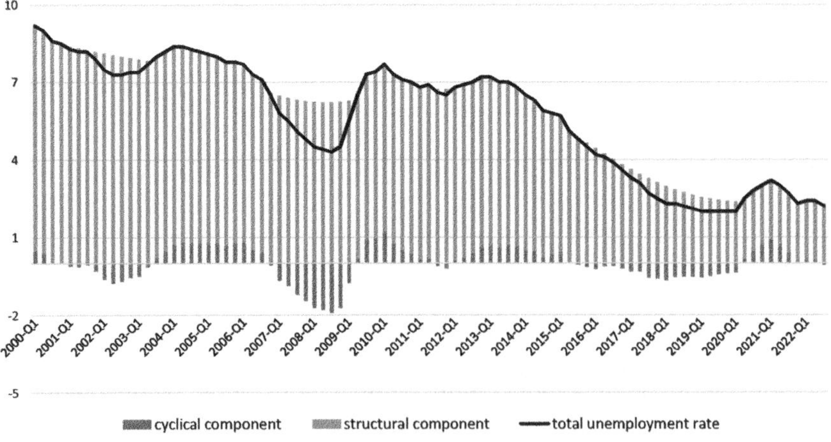

Fig. 1.6. Decomposition of Unemployment (Quarterly Data, Seasonally and Calendar Adjusted). *Source:* Eurostat.

natural one, then the situation on the labour market is difficult, especially for employers who find it very difficult to find labour force. Finally, it can have an impact on macroeconomic performance in the sense of a barrier to further growth. As is clear from Fig. 1.6, Czechia has recently faced a very low unemployment rate, which was significantly lower compared to the EU average. On the one hand, it shows satisfactory macroeconomic performance that is able to generate enough jobs. On the other hand, such low unemployment rate represents a brake on further growth, and, last but not least, it is a significant pro-inflationary factor in the economy, as this situation affects the household sector in their wage demands. The unemployment rate indicator also has an impact on households' decisions about their consumption or the purchase of real estate, which in turn is closely related to the sector of financial institutions.

1.3 Development of the Key Qualitative Macroeconomic Indicators

In the previous section, traditional macroeconomic indicators were presented. These indicators have the ability to describe the macroeconomic situation very well, but their disadvantage is a certain delay. In contrast, the so-called confidence indicators are indicators that are available with a shorter delay and are able to provide information about the future development of the economy and the behaviour of economic entities. However, these are so-called soft indicators because they are not able to indicate exactly how extensive changes are occurring, but rather capture the trend of macroeconomic performance, that is, whether the situation is improving or worsening. These conjunctural surveys are important mainly because they can record the mood in the business sector and provide information ahead of time. Therefore, they can be helpful in identifying turning points within the business cycle.

For the purpose of economic supervision, short-term forecasts and economic research, Eurostat has developed indicators of a qualitative nature. These business and consumer surveys can be divided into (i) business sector (industry, construction, trade and services) and (ii) consumer sector. As part of these surveys, the opinions of relevant subjects on the recently observed economic situation as well as future expectations in areas such as production, employment, sales and price developments are recorded.

ESI is a composite indicator consisting of the five above-mentioned sectoral confidence indicators with different weights: confidence indicator in industry, confidence indicator in services, confidence indicator in construction, confidence indicator in retail trade and consumer confidence indicator. The ESI is constructed on the basis of the following weighting system: the confidence indicator in industry is assigned a weight of 40%, the indicator in construction and trade 5% each, the indicator in selected service sectors 30%, and the consumer confidence indicator has a weight of 20% in the aggregate ESI.

Surveys within ESI provide important information about the probable development of business activity. Furthermore, these surveys include information known to the survey respondents, but not yet reflected in aggregate economic variables. Sub-indicators of confidence can also reveal important information about optimistic or pessimistic expectations, which are important factors influencing the business cycle (although these surveys usually do not provide information about the level of production, sales, prices or employment, information about expectations can be suitable for monitoring and business cycle forecasting).

Based on research in eurozone countries, Van Aarle and Kappler (2012) believe that shocks in economic sentiment have an impact on important macroeconomic variables, such as GDP, retail sales or the unemployment rate. However, the authors also point to the finding that the macroeconomic situation or economic shocks simultaneously affect economic sentiment, or in other words, a two-way relationship applies.

Fig. 1.7 shows the development of ESI and the real GDP growth (quarterly data between 2000 and 2022). The figure shows a similar development of both variables – there can be seen reactions to the shocks during the monitored period (global financial crisis or COVID-19 and subsequent energy–economic turbulences). It is clear from the figure that before 2008, confidence in the economy had grown strongly as a result of significant economic growth.

Fig. 1.8 shows the development of OECD business and consumer confidence indices from 2000 to 2022. In addition, grey columns represent time periods in which the Czech economy was in recession. As seen from the figure, there was a tendency for greater optimism regarding further developments in the household sector before the COVID-19 pandemic. However, confidence in the economy

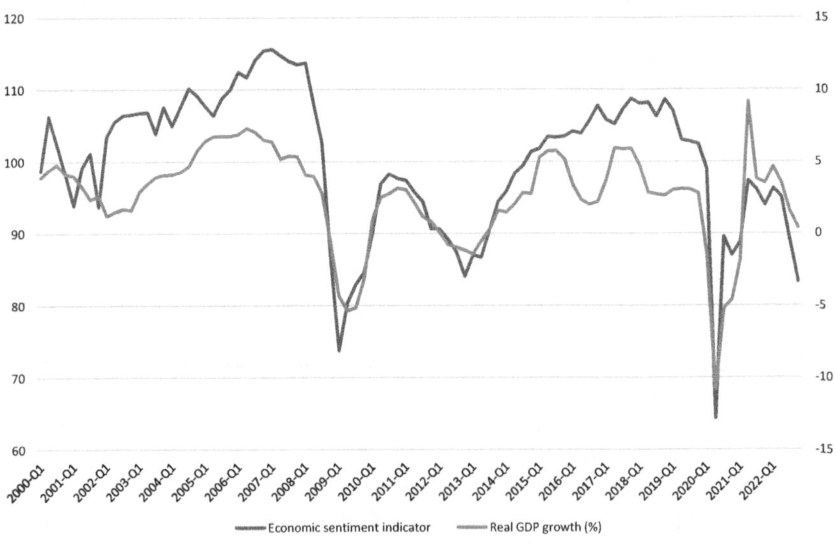

Fig. 1.7. Economic Sentiment Indicator (Left Axis) and Real GDP Growth in % (Right Axis) Development in Czechia. *Source:* Eurostat.

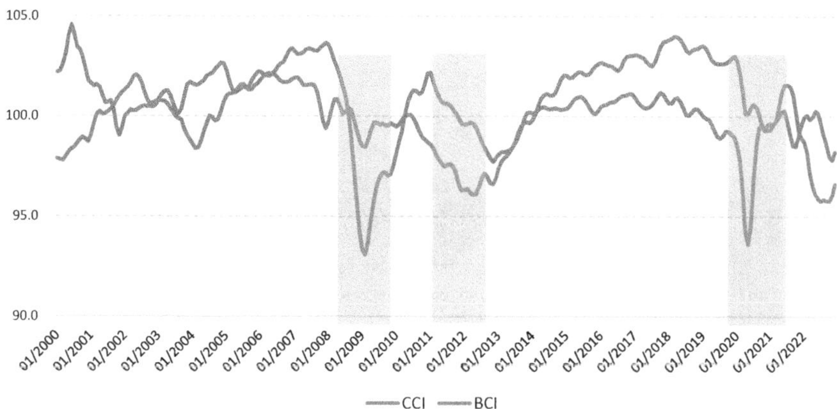

Fig. 1.8. Business Cycle Indicator (BCI) and Consumer Cycle Indicator (CCI) Development in Czechia. *Source:* Eurostat.

deteriorated significantly in the corporate sector compared to the household sector during COVID-19, which may ultimately be the result of government measures to support household incomes. The previous economic crisis caused by the global financial crisis already showed that, in the case of the contraction phase of the business cycle, confidence in the economy falls more significantly in the business sector.

1.4 Development of External Economic Position

Czechia is an open economy that is intensively involved in international economic transactions such as foreign trade, investment or the repatriation of profits. Thus, non-domestic transactions significantly affect the size and growth of the Czech economy. According to the World Openness Index, Czechia was the 16th most open economy in the world in 2020. Moreover, the degree of openness has been increasing over time, as in 2008, Czechia was ranked 27th in the same international comparison (Institute of World Economics and Politics, 2023, p. 235). Therefore, a description of the development of the external economic position should be an essential part of the general overview of the Czech economy presented in this chapter.

First, we focus on the external balance. The external balance is defined as the sum of the goods and services balance with income balances (current account) and the capital account balance. These accounts cover all transactions between residents and non-residents related to international trade in goods and services, payments for capital and labour (primary income), unilateral transfers (secondary income) and transactions of other nature (capital account). The evolution of the external balance and its individual components since 2000 is shown in Fig. 1.9. The chart reveals several long-term trends.

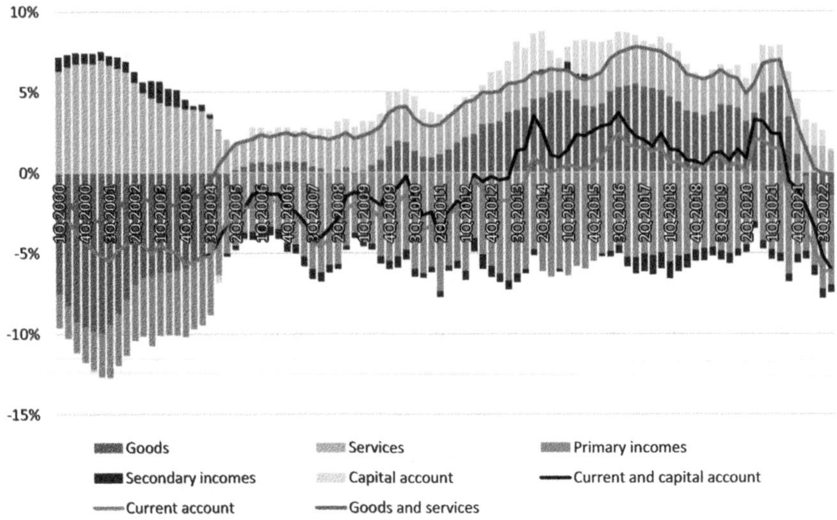

Fig. 1.9. Partial External Balances of Czechia (2000–2020, in % of GDP). *Source:* Authors' calculations based on data from Czech National Bank and Czech Statistical Office. *Note:* Data are cumulative values of last four quarters.

Czechia became a net exporter of goods and services in 2005. Since then, the export performance of the Czech economy has been growing and peaked in 2017, when the trade balance reached almost 8% of GDP. By mid-2021, it was still around 7% of GDP. Czechia is traditionally a recipient country in terms of foreign investment. This fact has been reflected in the development of the primary income balance over the long term, as profits from investments in Czechia flow abroad to a large extent. Marková (2017) points out that repatriated profits largely exceed reinvested profits in Czechia. The high export competitiveness of Czech businesses and the outflow of dividends abroad are interrelated phenomena, as approximately three quarters of Czech exports are generated by foreign-owned companies. The opposite effects of these factors explained the relatively balanced current account in previous years. During the period 2012–2021, the current account balance ranged from −2% to 2% of GDP, with a surplus from 2014 to mid-2021.

However, in 2021, significant changes that ended many long-term trends and put the external balance into a different perspective occurred. For the first time after 7 years of surpluses, the current account of the balance of payments ended 2021 with a deficit of 0.8% of GDP. The deterioration continued in 2022 when the deficit fell to 6.1% of GDP. The main cause of this collapse was the significant increase in the price of imported raw materials, in particular fuels, after the Russian invasion of Ukraine. Production problems related to global supply chains after the COVID-19 pandemic also continued to affect exporters. These factors along with other influences returned Czechia, after almost 20 years as a net exporter, to being a net importer of goods and services (Czech National Bank, 2023, p. 3). However, the sequence of crises has not yet affected the profitability of Czech businesses in foreign ownership. The revenues generated for foreign owners roughly correspond to the levels before the pandemic and contributed to the deepening of the current account deficit.

Another way to analyse a country's external economic situation is to look at its international investment position. Czechia has long been characterised by a negative international investment position. While in 2009–2012, the position was about −45% of GDP, at the beginning of the millennium and in recent years it was less than −20% of GDP. The negative investment position reflects the extensive ownership interests of foreign investors in the Czech economy, which are regarded materially less risky from a macroeconomic vulnerability point of view than indebtedness related to debt instruments. Excluding direct investment, Czechia has a significant net creditor position of around 30% of GDP (Fig. 1.10). Positive implications of this constellation are discussed by Lisický and Maleček (2012), among others.

The deepening of the debtor position in 2022 reflects the external imbalance. The current account deficit was financed by selling the reserve assets of the CNB and an increase in the foreign debt of the general government and non-financial businesses. The volume of CNB foreign exchange reserves fell during the

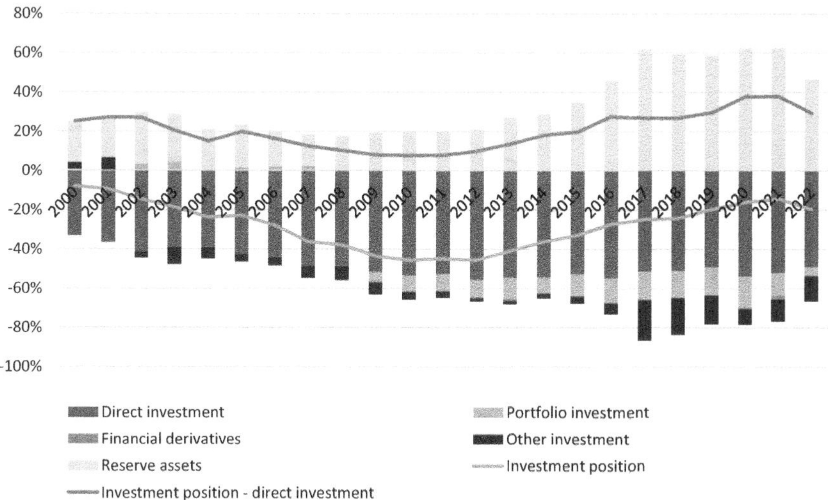

Fig. 1.10. Investment Position of Czechia (2000–2020, in % of GDP). *Source:* Authors' calculations based on data from Czech National Bank and Czech Statistical Office.

exchange rate interventions in 2022 but remains high in an international comparison and comfortably exceeds all prudential indicators for reserve adequacy (Czech National Bank, 2023, p. 4).

The last variable we use to describe the external economic situation of Czechia is the exchange rate. One of the main channels through which the exchange rate affects economic conditions is through its impact on prices. The effect occurs directly through import prices or indirectly through the impact of price changes on real incomes, customer spending and trade flows, with feedback effects on the overall price level. The second important way in which the exchange rate affects the economy is through its impact on international trade flows through the effect of switching expenditures. An appreciation in domestic currency implies a reduction in exports and an increase in imports, resulting in an overall deterioration in the trade balance, thus reducing the net trade contribution to GDP growth. Third, a crucial channel through which exchange rates influence the economy is by their effect on the total volume of foreign direct investment and the allocation of investment spending across a range of countries. When a currency appreciates, it increases that country's wages and production costs relative to those of its foreign counterparts. If all else is equal, the attractiveness of the country experiencing real appreciation therefore decreases, and the country is likely to receive less productive capacity investment (Stavárek & Miglietti, 2015, p. 158).

Fig. 1.11 shows the evolution of the nominal bilateral exchange rate of the euro against the Czech koruna (CZK) and the real effective exchange rate (REER) of CZK. The nominal exchange rate is expressed both as an index and in

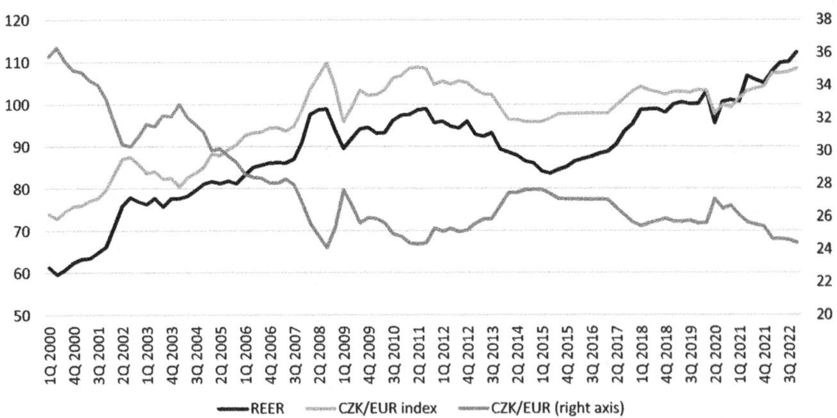

Fig. 1.11. Nominal Bilateral and Real Effective Exchange Rate (REER) of Czech Koruna (CZK). *Source:* Authors' calculations based on data from Czech National Bank. *Note:* REER and CZK/EUR index on left axis and CZK/EUR in standard quotation on right axis.

standard quotations. An increase in both the REER and CZK/EUR index values is indicative of an appreciation of CZK. In contrast, in the standard quotation, which is shown on the right-hand axis, a rise in the value of the exchange rate indicates depreciation of the koruna and vice versa.

Although the chart started in 2000, it can be seen that since the calming of the situation after the 1997 financial crisis, the CZK has undergone a period of intense nominal and real appreciation, which lasted until mid-2008. The total rate of nominal and real appreciation during the 8-year period was around 40%. The period of the global financial crisis and subsequent stabilisation was characterised by development without a clear trend, followed by a roughly 3-year period of depreciation of the CZK lasting until mid-2015. Exchange rate developments were significantly affected by the CNB's exchange rate commitment, which was in force from November 2013 to November 2017. During this period, the CNB committed to maintaining the exchange rate close to CZK 27 to the euro. The exchange rate commitment is analysed in detail in a separate chapter of this book. Following the easing of the exchange rate commitment, the koruna began to appreciate again, with the rate of appreciation accelerating especially in recent years. From mid-2020 to the end of 2022, the CZK appreciated by 10% in nominal terms, and due to high inflation, the real appreciation was as high as 15%.

1.5 Conclusion

The analysis carried out shows that the Czech economy went through several turning points within the business cycle during the observed period between the years 2000 and 2022, just as most countries of the EU. During this period, the Czech economy remarkably converged to the average economic level of the EU. As part of the analysis, quantitative and qualitative data were used. As conventional quantitative statistics are often published with a delay, it seems very important to include indicators of a qualitative nature in addition to short-term statistics of a quantitative nature (e.g. business and consumer surveys). Empirical data show that these indicators have the character of a leading indicator, which, with a certain time advance, can indicate the future development of the reference series, usually real GDP. On the other hand, these indicators could also be regarded as delayed indicators if we focus on evaluation of the situation in the past. Therefore, the system of qualitative short-term indicators developed by Eurostat or the OECD can be considered a valuable enrichment to the system of quantitative statistics. These surveys (business or consumer) demonstrate the important connection between decision-making at the micro- and macro-level. The mutual influence of these two levels is evident in several indicators that were mentioned in this chapter, and this only underlines the complexity of the economic system, which is also constantly developing dynamically.

Macroeconomic data on economic development of the economy indicate an atypical course of the business cycle between 2020 and 2022, which can be evaluated as different from the one that followed the global financial crisis. The period during the pandemic is characterised by sharp changes and relatively deep declines, but also increases, which, however, did not last long. In addition, several phenomena occur at the same time (supply and demand shocks, energy crisis or disruption of global supply chains), which ultimately complicates the choice of appropriate economic policy measures.

The external economic position could be characterised as stable for a long period. Long-term trends such as the ability to be a net exporter, a significant recipient of foreign direct investment and a country whose currency has a predominantly appreciating trend were manifested. Recently, however, there has been a significant deterioration in the trade balance, current account balance and external debt. Given the high degree of openness of the Czech economy, a prolonged deterioration in external economic parameters would have a negative impact on overall economic development.

References

Czech National Bank. (2023). *Balance of Payments Report 2022*. Czech National Bank. https://www.cnb.cz/export/sites/cnb/en/monetary-policy/.galleries/balance-of-payments-reports/balance_of_payments_report_2022.pdf

Gerlach, S., & Yiun, M. (2004). Estimating output gaps in Asia: A cross-country study. *Journal of Japanese and International Economies*, *18*(1), 115–136.

Hájek, M., & Bezděk, V. (2001). Odhad potencionálního produktu a produkční mezery v České republice. *Politická ekonomie*, *50*(4), 473–491.

Hloušek, M., & Polanský, V. (2007). Produkční přístup k odhadu potenciálního produktu – aplikace pro ČR. *Národohospodářský obzor*, *7*(4), 3–12.

Institute of World Economics and Politics. (2023). *World Openness Report 2022*. Paths International. https://www.ciie.org/resource/upload/zbh/202211/281044112s1b.pdf

Lisický, M., & Maleček, P. (2012). The Czech Republic's net international investment position. *ECFIN Country Focus*, *9*(1), 1–10.

Marková, J. (2017). Vnější rovnováha z pohledu investiční pozice vůči zahraničí. *Český finanční a účetní časopis*, *2017*(1), 17–40. https://doi.org/10.18267/j.cfuc.490

Němec, D. (2008). Brno: ESF MU, Centrum výzkumu konkurenční schopnosti české ekonomiky. Working Paper č. 22/2008. Kvantitativní analýza mezery nezaměstnanosti a výstupu v České republice.

Stavárek, D., & Miglietti, C. (2015). Effective exchange rates in Central and Eastern European countries: Cyclicality and relationship with macroeconomic fundamentals. *Review of Economic Perspectives*, *15*(2), 157–177. https://doi.org/10.1515/revecp-2015-0015

van Aarle, B., & Kappler, M. (2012). Economic sentiment shocks and fluctuations in economic activity in the euro area and the USA. *Intereconomics*, *47*(1), 44–51.

Zimková, E., & Barochovský, J. (2007). Odhad potencionálného produktu a produkčnej medzery v slovenskych podmienkach. *Politická ekonomie*, *55*(4), 473–489.

Chapter 2

Nominal and Real Convergence of Czechia With the Euro Area

Zuzana Szkorupová, Radmila Krkošková and Irena Szarowská

Silesian University in Opava, Czechia

Abstract

The aim of this chapter is to examine the nominal and real convergence of Czechia. The importance of the convergence of Czechia with the euro area is linked to the future intention of joining the Economic and Monetary Union after the Maastricht criteria are met. This chapter covers the period from 2004 to 2021. We argue that nominal convergence is relative to the Maastricht criteria, when real convergence focuses on different areas: the Maastricht criteria, gross domestic product (GDP) per capita in purchasing power standards and real GDP growth rate, labour market (minimum labour costs and unemployment rates. Findings suggest that Czechia has reported the strongest real convergence in the area of relative economic level, moderate convergence of labour costs and divergence of unemployment. The nominal convergence analysis suggests that Czechia will not meet the Maastricht benchmarks in the near future and is not ready to join the euro area given its high inflation rate and the state of public finances.

Keywords: Nominal convergence; euro area; Maastricht convergence criteria; real convergence; economic performance; labour market

2.1 Introduction

The aim of this chapter is to examine the nominal and real convergence of Czechia. Postiglione et al. (2020) state economic convergence refers to the process by which regions or countries with lower levels of economic development catch up with those with higher levels of development. This can be measured through sigma convergence, which looks at the reduction in the dispersion of income levels, and beta convergence, which looks at the speed at which less developed

Modeling Economic Growth in Contemporary Czechia, 17–34

doi:10.1108/978-1-83753-840-920241002

regions catch up with more developed ones. The importance of the convergence of Czechia with the euro area (EA) is linked to the future intention of joining the Economic and Monetary Union (EMU) after the Maastricht criteria are met. Therefore, one of the main challenges for Czechia is to achieve a high degree of nominal convergence with the EA, which is assessed by four criteria: price stability, sound public finances, exchange rate stability and convergence of long-term interest rates. These criteria are designed to ensure that a country is ready to participate in a single monetary policy and to cope with possible shocks without resorting to exchange rate adjustments.

Equally important is real convergence, which means the process of narrowing the gap between the income levels of different economies over time. European Commission (2012) defined real convergence as endogenous process at national and regional level and a key for improving European cohesion and increasing the competitiveness and efficiency of the single market. Therefore, real convergence was one of the main objectives of the European Union (EU) Cohesion Policy in the period 2007–2013, which focused on the poorest regions of the EU. According to the European Central Bank (ECB), real convergence can be primarily measured by indicator gross domestic product (GDP) per capita. The relationship between real and nominal convergence, that is, the relationship between the achieved economic level and the price level, is bilateral, mutually influencing and determinant (Ingianni & Žd'árek, 2009; Janáčková, 2000; Suciu et al., 2021; Žd'árek & Šindel, 2007). This chapter will examine the changes in nominal and real convergence in Czechia in the last 20 years, with a focus on its progress towards meeting the Maastricht criteria for adopting the euro.

2.2 Nominal Convergence

Czechia committed to adopting the euro with its entry into the EU in 2004. According to ECB (2022), one of the conditions that every member state must meet in the process of joining the eurozone is achieving a high degree of sustainable convergence, which is assessed in relation to the degree of fulfilment of the so-called Maastricht convergence criteria. In addition to the compatibility of legal regulations with Articles 130 and 131 of the Treaty on the Functioning of the European Union (TFEU) and the Statute of the European System of Central Banks and of the ECB, achieving a high degree of sustainable convergence is a condition for a member state of the EU to enter the eurozone. Criteria (also known as Maastricht criteria) are used to determine this, including the achievement of a high degree of price stability, a long-term sustainable state of public finances, adherence to the normal fluctuation range of the national currency exchange rate against the euro and stability of convergence, which is reflected in long-term interest rate levels. These criteria are anchored in Article 140 of the TFEU and are elaborated in Protocol No. 13 to the Treaties on convergence criteria. This chapter characterizes each criterion and analyzes its fulfilment.

2.2.1 Criterion of Price Stability

Article 1 of the Protocol (No. 13) on the convergence criteria referred to in Article 140(1) of the Treaty stipulates: the criterion of price stability assesses the level of consumer inflation, which must not exceed by more than 1.5 percentage points the average of the three EU countries with the best results in regard to price stability (Czech National Bank, 2022).

In the observed period, Czechia did not fulfil this criterion in the years 2007, 2008, 2012, 2017 and 2019–2021. The increase in inflation in 2008 was caused by the same factors as in 2007, namely rising commodity prices, especially for energy and food. Another factor was the increase in regulated prices and indirect taxes (Ministry of Finance of the Czech Republic, 2009). Paleta (2012) describes that the beginning of 2008 marked a turning point associated with a significant increase in inflation above the reference value, where inflation remained until September 2009. The sharp rise in inflation was caused by factors beyond the reach of monetary policy. The slowdown in economic activity and recession subsequently led to a decrease in inflation. In January 2012, the development of prices was mainly affected by the increase in the reduced VAT rate from 10% to 14%, which was reflected particularly in the categories of food and non-alcoholic beverages, health care and partially in housing and transportation. According to an approximate calculation by the Czech Statistical Office, the impact of this change on the month-on-month increase in the consumer price index in January represented an increase of 1.1 percentage points. In 2017, the largest impact on the price level growth in Czechia was caused by an increase in prices of food and non-alcoholic beverages, which were influenced primarily by an exceptional drought and fluctuations in prices of agricultural commodities on world markets. The growth of the price level was also influenced by an increase in prices of housing (rent), transportation (fuels) and catering and accommodation (catering services). Overall, inflation in 2017 was around 2.5%, which exceeded the set limit for fulfiling the Maastricht criterion of price stability (Czech National Bank, 2018). According to Ministry of Finance of the Czech Republic (2022), Czechia did not meet the price stability criterion in 2020 and 2021, also due to the low reference value of the criterion. Inflation in Czechia in 2021 was influenced by supply-side factors compounded by relaxed fiscal and monetary policies and a tight labour market. This was reflected in accelerated growth in wages and prices of production inputs and energy. In connection with the relaxation of anti-epidemic measures, there was also a very rapid growth in household consumption. For these reasons, in 2021, Czechia was among the countries in the EU with higher inflation. The fulfilment of the price stability criterion in the observed period is shown in Fig. 2.1.

2.2.2 Criterion on Long-Term Interest Rates

Article 4 of the Protocol (No. 13) on the convergence criteria referred to in Article 140(1) of the Treaty stipulates: convergence of interest rates is considered to be achieved if the yields on bonds with an average residual maturity of 10 years do

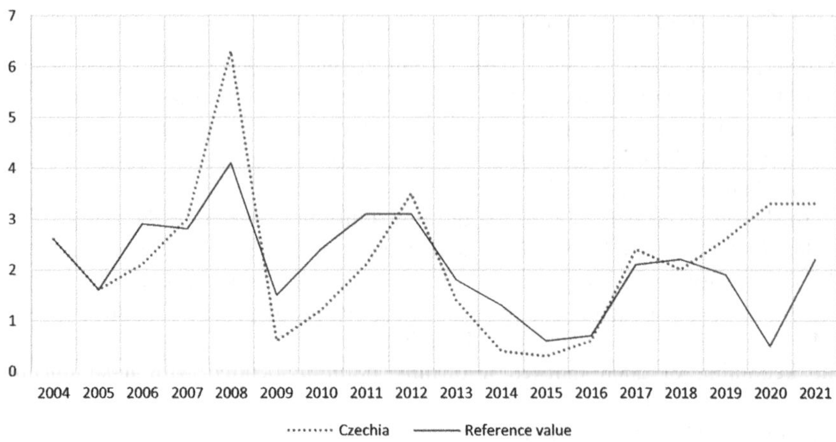

Fig. 2.1. Country Comparison Czechia vs Euro Area: Consumer Prices. *Source:* Eurostat.

not exceed by more than 2 percentage points the average yield on bonds in three EU countries that have achieved the best results in the field of price stability (Czech National Bank, 2022). In the past, this criterion was always met. However, from the middle of 2021, the Czech National Bank responded to rapidly increasing inflationary pressures by significantly increasing the key interest rates. This subsequently contributed to the increase in yields of government bonds. In contrast, the ECB kept its key interest rates at zero until July of this year and only then began to increase them significantly. The situation regarding the fulfilment of the long-term interest rate criterion is captured by the Fig. 2.2. The expected persistence of a negative differential between the ECB and the CNB in the coming years will likely hinder the fulfilment of this criterion (Ministry of Finance of the Czech Republic, 2022).

2.2.3 The Criterion on Sustainability of the Government Financial Position

Fiscal criterion is defined as: the general government deficit must not exceed 3% of GDP and the general government debt should not exceed 60% of GDP. Fulfiling these criteria is strongly influenced by government policies, but it is also susceptible to crises and recessions (Czech National Bank, 2022). Paleta (2012) claims that if a country attempts to enter the eurozone and does not meet the fiscal criteria, political will to reduce the budget is necessary. As a result of a sharp slowdown in economic growth in 2008 and an economic recession in 2009, there was a significant deterioration in the government sector balance after 2007. The government sector faced an unprecedented decline in tax revenue, both due to an exceptionally unfavourable economic situation and due to approved legislative

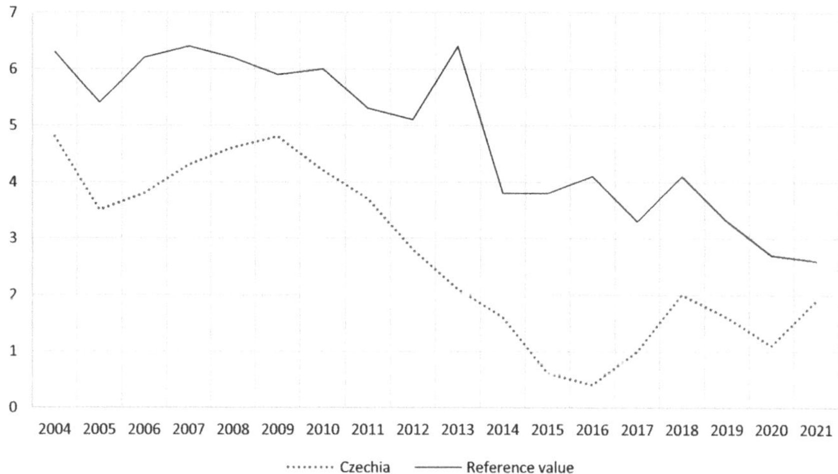

Fig. 2.2. Country Comparison Czechia vs Euro Area: Long-Term Interest Rates on Government Bonds. *Source:* Eurostat.

changes, especially on the revenue side of public budgets (Ministry of Finance of the Czech Republic, 2009).

From 2010 to 2013, the government carried out budget consolidation, and the deficit of the government sector gradually decreased. An exception was the deepening of the deficit in 2012, which reflected significant one-time effects, mainly the financial compensation for the state's property settlement with churches and religious societies (Ministry of Finance of the Czech Republic, 2014).

In June 2014, the excessive deficit procedure against Czechia, which had been in place since 2009, was terminated. In 2014, there was an increase in the deficit of the government sector to 1.9% of GDP, which was caused by a one-off accrual shortfall in consumption taxes, a significant increase in investment and a redefinition of the government sector.

In 2016, the government sector in Czechia achieved a surplus for the first time after years of running a deficit, which amounted to 0.7% of GDP. In 2017, the surplus of the government sector increased to 1.5% of GDP. On the revenue side, this was due to the growth of tax revenues, including social security contributions, and most expenditures grew at a moderate pace.

Between 2016 and 2019, Czechia achieved a surplus in the government sector (Fig. 2.3). However, in 2020 and 2021, there was a decline in the balance below the value of −5% of GDP. The sharp deterioration in the government sector's performance was due to the decrease in economic activity during the COVID-19 epidemic and the related government stabilization, support and redistributive policies (Ministry of Finance of the Czech Republic, 2022).

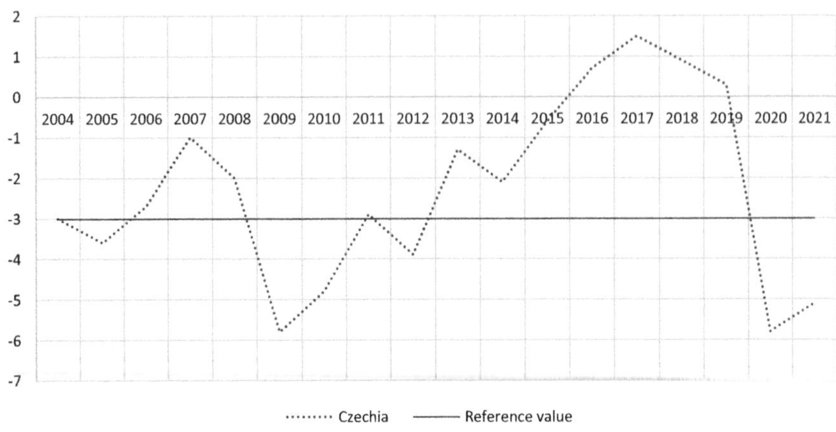

Fig. 2.3. Country Comparison Czechia vs Euro Area: Government Balance. *Source:* Eurostat.

Given that Czechia had a low initial level of general government debt, it has no problems in this component of the criterion. As a result of the global financial and economic crisis (2009–2012), debt increased from 30% of GDP to around 45% of GDP in 2013 (Fig. 2.4). This was driven by higher general government budget

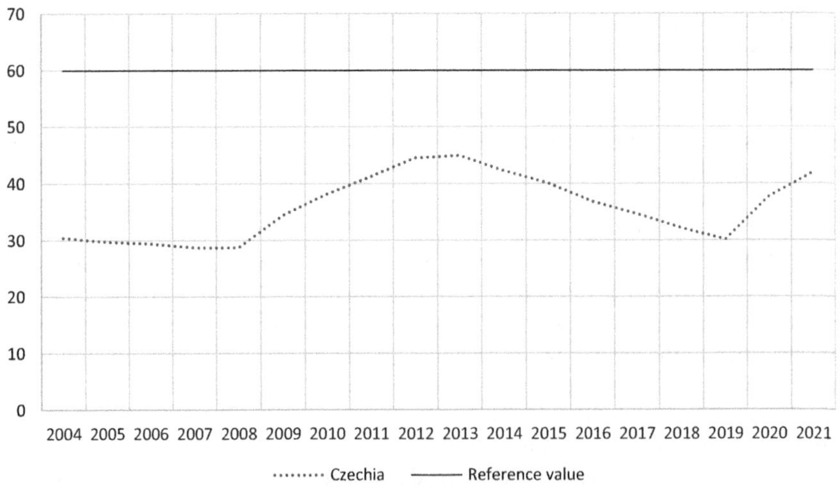

Fig. 2.4. Country Comparison Czechia vs Euro Area: General Government Debt. *Source:* Eurostat.

deficits and low nominal GDP growth rates. The significant increase in debt in 2012 was due to the creation of a reserve to finance the deficit and the refinancing of government debt, the gradual dissolution of which led to a decline in debt in 2014. A renewed increase in the debt burden occurs in 2020 and 2021 as a result of COVID-19. Despite this, Czechia fulfils the debt criterion over the long term (Ministry of Finance of the Czech Republic, 2022).

According to the assessment of nominal convergence and the conclusions of the Ministry of Finance of the Czech Republic and the Czech National Bank (2022), Czechia is very unlikely to meet the benchmarks in 2022 or 2023. The Czech economy is among the EU countries with the highest inflation, which is driven by strong supply and demand pressures as well as elevated inflation expectations. Differences in the intensity of price level increases and in the monetary policy approaches of the Czech National Bank and the ECB also led to differences in interest rates. Public finances are burdened by high structural deficits following a series of support measures introduced during the COVID-19 epidemic, to which are added further measures aimed at reducing the impact of the energy crisis on households and businesses. Last but not least, the exchange rate fluctuation criterion is not formally fulfiled as Czechia does not participate in the mechanism.

2.3 Real Convergence

Since 2004, Czechia has been trying to converge in real terms towards the EU average, which is considered the reference point for economic integration and convergence. Real convergence of Czechia is a process that reduces the gap between the level of economic development and living standards between Czechia and EA. In the case of real convergence (the so-called absolute convergence concept), the theoretical background is based on neoclassical growth theory, which assumes convergence to a steady state (the same for all economies) is influenced by a number of factors (e.g. savings, population growth, degree of depreciation of the capital goods used). However, this concept does not provide a satisfactory explanation of the trends observed in empirical studies. Empirical analyzes have produced a number of different and contradictory results (e.g. Barro, 1991; Barro & Sala i Martin, 2004; Todorov & Boneva, 2022). The results suggest that in many cases less developed countries remain at their lower level and there is no convergence or even widening differences between developed and less developed countries. On the other hand, Ingianni and Žd'árek (2009) mention that rapid convergence has been observed in some countries, which contradicts the theoretical assumptions of neoclassical growth theory. This has led to the formulation of alternative conceptions of convergence and several approaches have emerged to explain the observed real economic developments. Modern conceptions of endogenous growth have emerged, which include hitherto neglected factors such as the education of the population and the quality of institutions. These models can provide a theoretical description of empirically documented development of economies with greater differences in economic levels that grow faster.

Real convergence is primarily measured in terms of GDP per capita in purchasing power parity (PPP), which reflects the economic output and income of a country or region relative to its population size. This indicator reflects differences in prices and the cost of living between countries and allows for better comparisons of their real performance and welfare. Other possible indicators are labour productivity, nominal labour costs, employment and poverty rates or income inequality. Slavík (2005) also understands real convergence as structural approaching between economies or technologies used. Real convergence is also a condition for successful nominal convergence, that is, meeting the Maastricht criteria, which are necessary for joining the EA.

2.4 Real Convergence of Relative Economic Level

Since joining the EU, Czechia has shown remarkable progress in real convergence with the EA. To compare GDP per capita across countries or regions with different price levels, it is necessary to adjust for differences in purchasing power by using PPPs. PPPs are exchange rates that equalize the price of a basket of goods and services across countries or regions. According to Eurostat data, the relative economic level of Czechia expressed by GDP per capita at purchasing power standards (PPS) in 2004 was 69% of the EA average as can be seen in Table 2.1.

In the following years, this ratio gradually increased due to faster GDP per capita growth in Czechia than in the EA as shown in Fig. 2.5. In 2008, it peaked at 80% of the EA average. However, due to the global financial crisis and the subsequent economic recession, real convergence slowed down and even turned into a slight divergence. In 2012, relative GDP per capita in the Czechia fell to 79% of the EA average. Since 2013, real convergence has recovered and accelerated again.

Rapid growth in the following years led to substantial convergence and an increase to 91% of the EA average in 2019. This development was supported by strong GDP per capita growth in the Czechia, which outpaced that of the EU. Although the COVID-19 pandemic had an adverse effect with a deep drop in GDP per capita, the relative economic level of Czechia reached 92% of the EA average in 2020 (the latest available data), surpassing some of the older EA members such as Portugal and Greece. This development was mainly driven by strong growth in total factor productivity, which reflects the improvement in the quality and efficiency of production factors (European Commission, 2022).

Czechia's economic convergence can be attributed to its sound macroeconomic policies, flexible exchange rate regime, diversified export structure, strong innovation capacity and low public debt. On the contrary, the EA's economic performance has been hampered by several factors, such as the sovereign debt crisis, structural rigidities, fiscal consolidation, low inflation and political uncertainty. Moreover, Czechia has also achieved a significant structural transformation of its economy, shifting from low value-added sectors such as agriculture and mining to high value-added sectors such as manufacturing and services. Based on data from OECD

Table 2.1. Relative Economic Level of Czechia in Relation to the Euro Area (GDP per Capita in PPS, EA = 100%).

	2004	2005	2006	2007	2008	2009	2010	2011	2012	2013	2014	2015	2016	2017	2018	2019	2020	2021
CZ	69	73	75	77	80	78	79	78	79	79	80	82	83	85	86	91	92	88

Source: Eurostat.

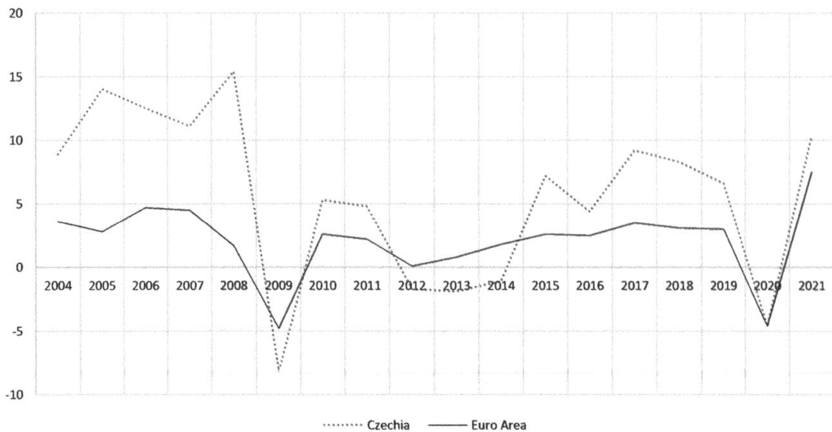

Fig. 2.5. Country Comparison Czechia vs Euro Area: Annual Real GDP Growth (in %). *Source:* Eurostat.

Trade in Value Added database, the share of manufacturing in gross value added decreased from 28.9% in 2004 to 25.8% in 2021, while the share of services increased from 56.8% to 66.5% over the same period. These changes reflect Czechia's integration into global value chains and its specialization in export-oriented industries such as automotive, machinery and electrical equipment.

Real economic growth is also crucial for real convergence. Real GDP measures the value of goods and services produced in an economy, adjusted for inflation. Czechia's real GDP growth averaged 2.5% per year from 2004 to 2021, while the EA's real GDP growth averaged 1.0% per year over the same period. This means that Czechia's economy grew faster than the EA's economy by 1.5 percentage points per year on average. Fig. 2.5 summarizes the real GDP growth rates for both regions from 2004 to 2021, based on the World Bank and ECB's data.

The data show that Czechia's real GDP growth was higher than the EA's real GDP growth in every year from 2004 to 2021, except for 2008 and 2020, when both regions experienced negative growth due to the global financial crisis and the COVID-19 pandemic, respectively. Czechia has achieved a higher and more stable real growth than the EA over the past two decades, despite being a small open economy that is highly integrated with the EU single market.

To understand the convergence or divergence of real GDP growth between Czechia and the EA, it is useful to look at some factors that may explain their different economic performance. These factors include:

- The degree of containment measures in response to the varying intensity of the health crisis as countries with stricter lockdowns and more severe outbreaks tended to experience larger declines in economic activity.

- The different sectoral compositions and economic structures. The ECB (2022) points out that countries with a larger share of tourism or non-tradable sectors were more affected by international travel bans and social distancing measures.
- Institutional quality as countries with better governance, rule of law, innovation and human capital tend to have higher potential growth and resilience to shocks.
- Fiscal and monetary policy support. The ECB stresses that fiscal and monetary policies have played a crucial role in mitigating the impact of the pandemic and supporting the recovery, but they also imply different effects on public debt and inflation across countries.

Based on these factors, it is possible to claim that Czechia and the EA have some similarities and some differences that may account for their convergence or divergence of real GDP growth. For example, Czechia has a relatively high share of manufacturing and exports in its economy, which makes it vulnerable to external shocks but also benefits from global trade recovery. Czechia ranks above the EU average in terms of governance quality, innovation performance and human capital development, which may enhance its potential growth and resilience. Last but not least, Czechia had a relatively mild first wave of COVID-19 infections in 2020, but a severe second wave in early 2021, which required strict lockdown measures that affected economic activity.

2.5 Real Convergence of Labour Market

The labour market in Czechia has undergone significant changes since its accession to the EU. Analysis of real convergence of the labour market is focused on two key indicators: labour costs and unemployment.

Labour costs are an important determinant of competitiveness and inflation, as well as a reflection of productivity and attractiveness of a region for businesses and workers. They include wages and salaries, as well as non-wage costs such as social security contributions and taxes. According to Eurostat data, the average hourly labour cost in Czechia increased from 6.3 euros in 2004 to 15.3 euros in 2021 as Fig. 2.6 shows, which corresponds to an annual growth rate of 5.6%. This was higher than the EA average growth rate of 2.3% over the same period, implying a real convergence of labour costs between Czechia and the EA. However, despite this convergence, there is still a significant gap between the two regions, as the average hourly labour cost in the EA was 32.8 euros compared to 15.3 euros in Czechia in 2021.

In comparison with the EU average, Czechia's labour costs remained relatively low, although the gap has been closing over time. In 2004, Czechia's labour costs were 28% of the EU average; by 2021, they reached 47%. The convergence was faster in some sectors than others. For instance, in manufacturing, Czechia's labour costs rose from 30% of the EU average in 2004 to 57% in 2021; in construction, they increased from 25% to 46%; and in services, they grew from 26% to 44%. The convergence of labour costs reflects the increasing productivity and quality of Czech workers, as well as the rising demand for skilled labour in a tight labour market. Fig. 2.7 provides an overview of the level of minimum wages in EUR per month between 2004 and 2021.

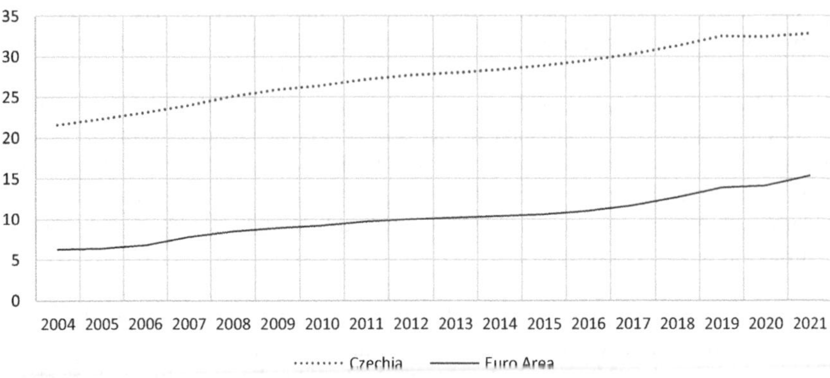

Fig. 2.6. Country Comparison Czechia vs Euro Area: Minimum Labour Costs in EUR per Hour. *Source:* Eurostat.

The COVID-19 pandemic has posed unprecedented challenges to both Czechia and the EA labour markets, but with different implications for wages. As shown by recent data, both regions have experienced a decline in employment and hours worked, as well as an increase in job retention schemes and teleworking. However, while compensation per employee declined significantly in the EA during the pandemic, reflecting lower average hours worked and wage moderation, it increased slightly in Czechia, reflecting higher minimum wages and collective bargaining agreements. This suggests that wage pressures are more visible in Czechia than in the EA, which could pose a risk to inflation and competitiveness.

Unemployment is another key indicator of labour market performance and social welfare. According to Eurostat data, the unemployment rate in Czechia decreased from 8.3% in 2004 to 2.8% in 2021, which was the lowest among all EU

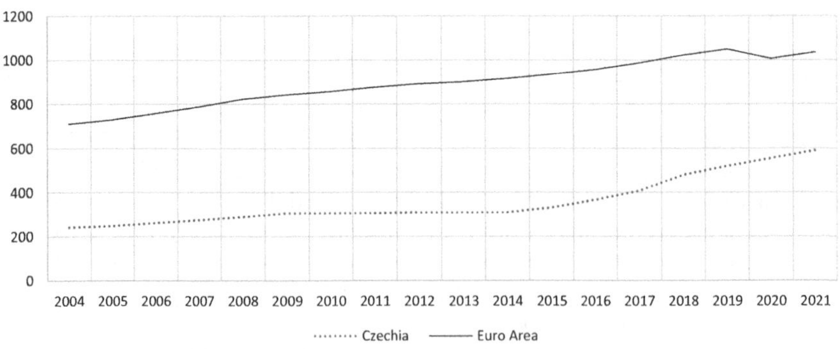

Fig. 2.7. Country Comparison Czechia vs Euro Area: Minimum Wages in EUR per Month. *Source:* Eurostat.

countries. Fig. 2.8 shows the trend of unemployment rate in Czechia and the EA from 2004 to 2021.

Czechia's unemployment rate has followed a downward trend, with some fluctuations due to external shocks such as the global financial crisis of 2008–2009 and the COVID-19 pandemic of 2020–2021. The lowest value was reached in 2019, with an unemployment rate of 2% compared to 7.6% in the EA. This improvement was driven by strong economic growth, structural reforms and favourable demographic trends. In contrast, the unemployment rate in the EA increased from 8.9% in 2004 to 10% in 2013, due to the impact of the global financial crisis and the sovereign debt crisis, and then gradually declined to 7.6% in 2021, still above its pre-crisis level.

Fig. 2.8 shows that the gap between countries is widening – the minimum difference was 1.1 percentage point upon joining the EU in 2004. A more pronounced divergence of the curves is evident in the post-financial crisis period, that is, since 2010. The maximum difference in unemployment was recorded in 2017 at 6.2 percentage points (2.9% in Czechia and 9.1% in the EA). This implies a real divergence of unemployment rates between Czechia and the EA, as well as a lower sensitivity of the Czech labour market to external shocks.

Over the period 2004–2021, the unemployment rate in the EA was on average higher than in Czechia. The reasons for this situation are diverse and include factors such as the economic cycle, structural problems, the institutional framework and demographic changes. Some of the main causes of higher unemployment in the EA are:

- the financial and debt crisis that hit some EA member states after 2008, leading to recession, cuts in public spending, tax increases and loss of investor and consumer confidence;

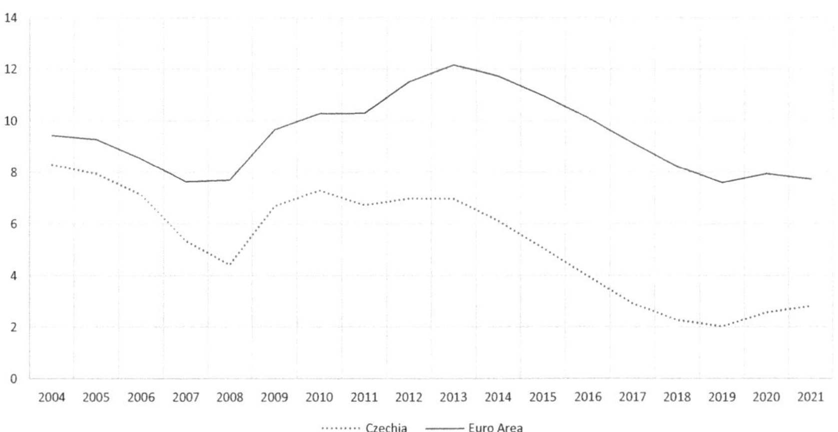

Fig. 2.8. Country Comparison Czechia vs Euro Area: Unemployment Rate (in %). *Source:* Eurostat.

- labour market rigidities that limit labour mobility and adaptability and increase the cost of firing and hiring;
- insufficient harmonization of economic policies and fiscal rules between EA member states, which makes coordination and convergence of macroeconomic indicators and targets difficult; and
- population ageing, which reduces the share of working age people in the total population and also affects the supply of and demand for certain types of labour and skills.

On the contrary, in Czechia, the unemployment rate in the period 2004–2021 was lower than in the EA due to the several factors. One factor is the economic growth and flexibility in the labour market, supported by a strong export sector, low inflation, a stable exchange rate of the Czech koruna and a favourable external environment. Rapid economic growth has led to job creation, rising wages and consumption and poverty reduction and strong demand for labour from employers, especially in industries such as automotive, engineering or electrical engineering. These sectors drive the Czech economy and are highly productive and competitive on international markets. As a result, they need skilled and flexible workers who are able to adapt to changes in technology and demand. In some regions and industries, there are even shortages of workers, which increases pressure on wage growth and improving working conditions.

Another factor is demographic trends, which affect labour supply. Czechia has an ageing population with a low birth rate and long-life expectancy. This means that the number of people of working age is falling, and the number of pensioners is rising. While in 2005 the share of people aged 15–64 in the total population was 70%, in 2020 it was only 64%. This trend reduces pressure on the labour market and increases the need to keep as many people as possible active and employed.

The third factor is labour migration, which helps to partially offset the imbalance between supply and demand in the labour market. Czechia is both a destination and a transit country for migrants from other EU countries and third countries. According to the Czech Statistical Office, as of 31 December 2020, a total of 654,000 foreigners with a residence permit lived in Czechia, representing 6.1% of the population. Most of the foreigners worked in industry, construction or services.

However, despite these achievements, Czechia still faces some challenges in terms of unemployment, such as:

- the shortage of skilled workers in some sectors, such as information technology, engineering and health care;
- the regional disparities in unemployment rates, which reflect different levels of economic development and infrastructure across regions;
- the impact of technological change and globalization, which require constant adaptation and innovation from workers and firms; and
- an ageing population that will reduce labour supply in the future.

Therefore, to sustain its low unemployment rate and achieve real convergence with the EU average, Czechia needs to continue its structural reforms and invest in education, innovation and social protection.

2.6 Fiscal Situation in Czechia and the EA

The COVID-19 pandemic and associated stabilization measures have led to a noticeable deterioration in public finances across EA countries. According to the Ministry of Finance of the Czech Republic (2022), the deficit of the general government sector in the EA reached 5.1% of GDP in 2021, with 12 countries seeing the debt of their general government sector exceed 60% of GDP. In Czechia, the state budget deficit has risen to 5.1% of GDP, making budget consolidation important. However, the energy crisis has severely hampered budget consolidation efforts in Czechia and other EA countries. Czechia currently complies with the Maastricht criteria regarding government debt, but public debt is increasing. Currently, public debt stands at 42% of GDP, compared to 28% in 2004 when Czechia joined the EU (Figs. 2.9 and 2.10).

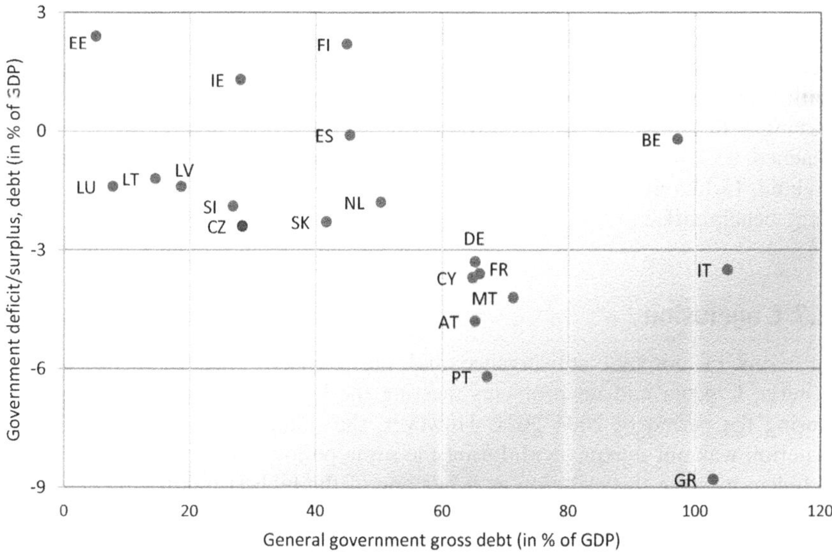

Fig. 2.9. Fiscal Situation in Czechia and the Euro Area in 2004.
Source: Eurostat.
Note: AT – Austria, BE – Belgium, BG – Bulgaria, CY – Cyprus, CZ – Czechia, DE – Germany, DK – Denmark, EE – Estonia, ES – Spain, FI – Finland, FR – France, GR – Greece, HR – Croatia, HU – Hungary, IE – Ireland, IT – Italy, LT – Lithuania, LU – Luxembourg, LV – Latvia, MT – Malta, NL – Netherlands, PL – Poland, PT – Portugal, RO – Romania, SE – Sweden, SI – Slovenia, SK – Slovakia.

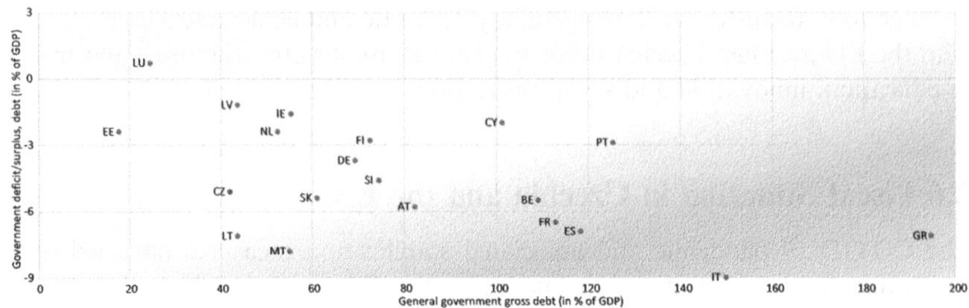

Fig. 2.10. Fiscal Situation in Czechia and the Euro Area in 2021.
Source: Eurostat.
Note. AT – Austria, BE – Belgium, BG – Bulgaria, CY – Cyprus, CZ – Czechia, DE – Germany, DK – Denmark, EE – Estonia, ES – Spain, FI – Finland, FR – France, GR – Greece, HR – Croatia, HU – Hungary, IE – Ireland, IT – Italy, LT – Lithuania, LU – Luxembourg, LV – Latvia, MT – Malta, NL – Netherlands, PL – Poland, PT – Portugal, RO – Romania, SE – Sweden, SI – Slovenia, SK – Slovakia.

According to the Ministry of Finance of the Czech Republic (2022), the general government debt exceeded the 60% of GDP threshold in 12 countries, with 7 of them (Belgium, France, Italy, Cyprus, Portugal, Greece and Spain) having a debt-to-GDP ratio above 100%. The average debt ratio in the EA reached 95.4% of GDP. In 2021, only 5 out of 19 EA countries (Estonia, Ireland, Lithuania, Luxembourg and the Netherlands) met both the deficit and debt benchmarks.

2.7 Conclusion

In terms of nominal convergence and meeting the Maastricht convergence criteria, Czechia had no problems meeting the long-term interest rate criterion during the period of 2004–2021. However, the fulfilment of the price stability criterion was not unequivocal during the same period. Currently, Czechia has a problem meeting this criterion as it has one of the highest inflation rates among EU countries. Additionally, it fails to meet the fiscal criterion on government budget deficit. Although the public debt has been fulfiled throughout the period, it has shown an increase in debt-to-GDP ratio in recent years. The last prescribed convergence condition, the criterion on the stability of the exchange rate of the national currency, cannot be evaluated from the perspective of Czechia without ERM II membership. However, according to developments on the foreign exchange market, the volatility of the CZK exchange rate is not a significant problem for the Czech currency.

The real convergence of Czechia towards the EA is supported by the government's economic policy, which emphasizes structural reforms, investment in infrastructure, education, research and innovation, social cohesion and sustainability of public finances. Czechia is also cooperating with other EU member states and aims to achieve full real convergence towards the EA and to meet the conditions for adopting the euro as the single currency.

However, despite these impressive achievements, Czechia still faces some challenges and risks in its real convergence process. One of them is the ageing of its population, which could hamper its potential growth and fiscal sustainability in the long run. Another one is the dependence on foreign direct investment, which could expose Czechia to external shocks and reduce its domestic innovation capacity. The third one is the need to further improve its institutional quality and governance, which could enhance its business environment and attractiveness for investors.

In conclusion, Czechia has made significant strides in real convergence with the EA since its EU accession in 2004, but it still needs to address some remaining gaps and vulnerabilities to ensure a smooth and sustainable integration into the EMU.

References

Barro, R. J. (1991). Economic growth in a cross section of nations. *Quarterly Journal of Economics*, *2*, 407–433.

Barro, R. J., & Sala i Martin, X. (2004). *Economic growth*. MIT Press.

Czech National Bank. (2018). *Assessment of the fulfilment of the Maastricht convergence criteria and the degree of economic alignment of the Czech Republic with the Euro Area*.

Czech National Bank. (2022). *Convergence criteria*.

European Central Bank. (2022). *Convergence report*.

European Commission. (2012). Directorate-General for Economic and Financial Affairs. *Convergence report 2012*. Publications Office. https://data.europa.eu/doi/10.2765/18844

European Commission. (2022). *Convergence report 2022*.

Ingianni, A., & Žd'árek, V. (2009). Real convergence in the new member states: Myth or reality? *Journal of Economic Integration*, *24*(2), 294–320. http://www.jstor.org/stable/23000882

Janáčková, S. (2000). Price convergence and the readiness of the Czech economy for accession to the European Union. *Eastern European Economics*, *38*(4), 73–91.

Ministry of Finance of the Czech Republic. (2009). *Assessment of the Maastricht convergence criteria and the degree of economic alignment of the Czech Republic with the Euro Area*.

Ministry of Finance of the Czech Republic. (2014). *Assessment of the Maastricht convergence criteria and the degree of economic alignment of the Czech Republic with the Euro Area*.

Ministry of Finance of the Czech Republic. (2022). *Assessment of the Maastricht convergence criteria and the degree of economic alignment of the Czech Republic with the Euro Area*.

Paleta, T. (2012). Maastricht criteria of … divergence? *Review of Economic Perspectives*, *12*(2), 92–119. https://doi.org/10.2478/v10135-012-0005-7

Postiglione, P., Cartone, A., & Panzera, D. (2020). Economic convergence in EU NUTS 3 regions: A spatial econometric perspective. *Sustainability*, *12*(17). https://doi.org/10.3390/su12176717

Slavík, C. (2005). *Reálná konvergence České republiky k EU v porovnání s ostatními novými členskými zeměmi.* CESES UK.

Suciu, M. C., Petre, A., Istudor, L. G., Mituca, M. O., Stativa, G. A., Mardarovici, D., Tofan, O. R., & Cotescu, R. G. (2021). Testing real convergence as a prerequisite for long run sustainability. *Sustainability*, *13*(17), 9943. https://doi.org/10.3390/su13179943

Todorov, I., & Boneva, S. (2022). The real convergence of THE NMS-10 to THE EU-15. *Economic Alternatives*, *1*, 5–16. https://doi.org/10.37075/EA.2022.1.01

Žd'árek, V., & Šindel, J. (2007). Real and nominal convergence and the new EU member states – Actual state and implications. *Prague Economic Papers*, *16*(3), 195–219. https://doi.org/10.18267/j.pep.305

Chapter 3

International Trade and the Competitiveness of Czechia as the Fundamental Determinants of Economic Growth

Jan Nevima

Silesian University in Opava, Czechia

Abstract

The aim of this chapter is to draw attention to the changes that have taken place in Czechia in the last 20 years in the field of foreign trade, focussing on the key milestones of 2002, 2012 and 2022. The chapter also explains the important link between the performance of foreign trade and economic growth; this link has its support in theory, and above all in empiricism. The importance of foreign trade for economic growth is key, especially from the point of view of changes in the territorial and commodity structure, which saw several important changes in the observed period 2002–2022, so we can relevantly explain the effects on the economic growth of Czechia. However, the chapter finds a connection with yet another economic category, which is competitiveness. The method of measuring and subsequent ranking of competitiveness is also of utmost importance. If the economy is to be competitive, it must have its own strategy, and this directly concerns the key instruments of pro-export policy.

Keywords: International trade; systemic competitiveness; economic growth; ranking; commodity structure; territorial structure

3.1 Introduction

The ever-increasing interconnectedness of economies within the economic and political system creates a natural pressure to seek competitive advantages not only

Modeling Economic Growth in Contemporary Czechia, 35–49

Published under exclusive licence by Emerald Publishing Limited
doi:10.1108/978-1-83753-840-920241003

for national economies but especially in the context of international competitiveness. The origins of competitiveness can be identified in the increasing international mobility of factors of production and their links to international trade flows. The theoretical and empirical links between international trade and economic growth are historically determined; this chapter will demonstrate this context in the case of Czechia, among others. Due to the ambiguous definition of competitiveness, we are looking for the building blocks of competitiveness in the concept of systemic competitiveness. Systemic competitiveness offered a relevant and practical way of formulating and implementing local initiatives in a predefined territorial space. This has had a very positive impact on development trends especially in developing and transition economies. A significant role in this is also played by the diversity of views in the concept of historical schools of economics, especially the pioneers of competitiveness – M. Porter and P. Krugman. The aim of this chapter is mainly to highlight the changes that have occurred in Czechia in the field of international trade over the last 20 years, with key milestones in 2002, 2012 and 2022. These changes were subsequently reflected in a time lag in the development of economic growth and were also reflected in the performance rankings of Czechia's international competitiveness. In this sense, the chapter seeks to provide a unique synthesising conception of international trade, economic growth and competitiveness. The interconnection of these three areas creates the prerequisites for a comprehensive assessment of a rather complex issue, which is a permanent subject of economic research. The chapter thereby provides the reader with a fairly comprehensive overview of interconnected economic categories that are still at the forefront of economic research.

3.2 Competitiveness Paradigm

Sometimes it is easier to view the issue of competitiveness as an ambiguous economic category. This is very close to the concept of Clark and Tracey (2004) and Spulber (2007). Although competitiveness has no well-defined place in economics, it has become a natural foundation of the modern theory of international trade. The level at which we define, measure and then compare competitiveness is crucial. Competitiveness has changed significantly over the last 30 years or so of economic research, not only in terms of its content and the subsequent impact on economic growth but also in terms of its focus for researchers. A certain trend today is to analyse the smallest possible territorial units. Indeed, we are reaching a point where competitiveness remains a concept that is still not well understood because of its relatively broad scope of meaning. The topic itself is so vast and interconnected that it can never be comprehensively covered.

There have been efforts in the past to develop the concept of the so-called systemic competitiveness. Here, the most prominent pioneers in this area include Esser et al. (1995). In simple terms, the idea is to create a model of competition that is based on contemporary knowledge and technological possibilities and does not rely on inherited factors that are gradually losing their importance. Only then can we identify the relevant factors that will put an end to the expert and often controversial debate about what is best for economic development, and at the same time we can move away from the question of whether a state-led or market-led approach to the economy is better. The key to achieving systemic competitiveness is to strike an appropriate balance (though one cannot predetermine its initial conditions) between market mechanisms on the one hand and government intervention on the other.

Systemic competitiveness emphasises that it is the interconnection of the economy in four important systemic areas. These include the meta, macro, meso and micro levels (Fig. 3.1).

(1) The meta level is the imaginary culmination of systemic competitiveness, as it is here that visions are formulated, strategies are subsequently developed and the framework for competitive integration is formed.
(2) The macro level represents a triumvirate of political, legal and economic frameworks.
(3) The meso level is to a certain extent based on mesoeconomics in the concept of Stuart Holland (1987), who sees the main reason for the divergent development of regions in the failure of neoclassical assumptions and, above all, in the absence of perfect competition. In the context of systemic competitiveness, we are focussing here on sectoral competitiveness in the

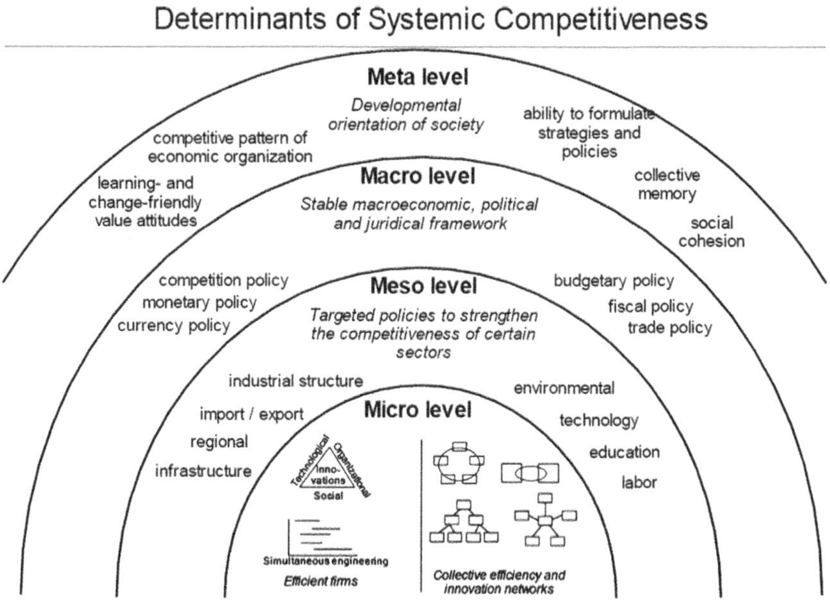

Fig. 3.1. Comprehensive Concept of Systemic Competitiveness Including Its Determinants. *Source:* Esser et al. (1995, p. 3).

context of institutions that are the carriers of regional policy. Here, for the first time, we could systematically underpin the competitiveness of territories (especially cities and municipalities). Esser et al. (1995) also discuss here the evolutionary definition of mesopolicy, it is one of the rare theoretically oriented works that deal in detail with this relatively seldom covered topic.

(4) The micro level is about the ability of the corporate environment to respond to constant changes in fluctuations in the available quantity of production factors and linking firms into clusters in the form of cluster initiatives that transform into further clusters or remain only on the level of intentions.

The complex concept of systemic competitiveness raises the pertinent question of whether this concept can be used in today's dynamically evolving economy. The answer to this question is yes. This is primarily due to the fact that there was a clear lack of methodological support for a systemic approach to competitiveness in the past. Since the concept of systemic competitiveness was defined, various modifications of the categorisation of competitiveness have appeared, but there is a lack of a strong theoretical basis and, above all, a link to economic reality.

3.3 Contemporary Economic Theories

As an economic category, competitiveness was understood as a synonym for the export performance of a country at first, which is the reason why it was known as external economic competitiveness. Subsequently, with the influence of evolution, competitiveness started to be approached from the point of view of aggregate indicators. In this sense, it is possible to view competitiveness from the point of view of economic growth and international trade. Within the category of economic growth, particular alternative approaches to this issue can be divided into three basic groups.

The first group consists of the so-called *traditional models of economic growth* based on Solow's model. The perception of technology as a public good and the exogenous character of technological changes are their main presumptions. An effort for convergence of neoclassical theory towards real economic development represents the result of a particular modification. Three issues are related to that: underestimation of the size of international differences regarding the levels of income per inhabitant, overestimation of convergence pace towards steady state and overestimation of differences between capital revenue rates between poor and rich countries.

The second group of growth theories is represented by the concept of a *technology gap* and closing derived from Schumpeter's tradition. These theories are based on the assumption that technological transmission is possible but rather complicated and expensive. All this is determined by the fact that technology, as a production factor, is incorporated into particular organisational structures and is characterised by various combinations of companies' inner abilities and strategies. In the case of this particular group, we need to take into consideration that individual countries are considered to have independent technological systems with their own development dynamics in these models. A certain modification lies in the fact that regions, which are the holders of these technological systems since they are equipped in a different way, have a much more important role. The differences between regions are observed within closing and retreating. The convergence process, or more precisely, the divergence process, is directly dependent on the social, political, environmental and economic dispositions of the regions.

The third group is represented by a new growth theory, or the so-called *endogenous growth theory*. In this case, technological advance is understood as a result of the market activity of economic subjects in a particular economy. Important pioneers of this theory are Paul Romer and Robert Lucas. The first contributions dealing with the endogenous growth theory are based on the assumption of perfect competition, and the theory is based on the capital expansion approach, which enables a country to continue its economic growth even when exogenous technological change is not present. To sustain the assumption of perfect competition, it is important that capital profits grow at an aggregate level; however, for individual companies, they remain constant. Under the influence of evolution, the assumption of perfect competition was abandoned, and Romer started working on his own theory dealing with endogenous technological gaps with monopolistic competition. The motive of profit when investing in innovations represented further advancement.

In case of international trade, two groups are recognised. The first group is formed by traditional models of international trade, and the second one encompasses models based on a created comparative advantage or technological change, or possibly production cycles.

International trade static models deal with the explanation regarding the specialisation of individual countries based on the principle structures of autarky prices. The differences between countries are caused by different equipment of production factors, and technologies remain exogenous. The relation to regional equipment of production factors can be noted again. These theories split into the one represented by Ricardo, emphasising the importance of international technological differences in combination with various levels of real wages. The second theory is derived from the Heckscher–Ohlin theorem, which stresses the differences in factor equipment between countries based on the assumption of identical consumers' preferences and technologies.

The second category dealing with international trade is formed by *technologically oriented theories* stressing the importance of technological change and new product trading. Due to the influence of innovative activities, countries gain a temporary comparative advantage in international trade. Specialisation depends on the pace of the emergence of innovations and the ability to imitate these innovations (Turečková, 2016).

3.4 International Competitiveness Strategy of Czechia

The international competitiveness strategy of Czechia has undergone several changes and developments over the years, particularly in the periods of 2002, 2012 and 2022. Here's an overview of each period and its evaluation:

2002: Czechia became a member of the European Union (EU) in May 2004, and in the period leading up to its accession, the country implemented a range of economic reforms to improve its international competitiveness. These reforms included liberalising the economy, reducing the role of the state and promoting foreign investment. As a result, the country experienced a period of economic growth, with gross domestic product (GDP) per capita increasing from 57% of the EU average in 1995 to 73% in 2002. However, the country still faced several challenges, such as high levels of corruption, an underdeveloped infrastructure and a shortage of skilled workers.

2012: In the years following the global financial crisis, Czechia faced a period of economic stagnation, with GDP growth averaging only around 2% per year. The country also faced problems such as high levels of youth unemployment, a lack of investment in research and development and an ageing population. To address these challenges, the Czech government launched a new competitiveness strategy in 2012, which focused on boosting innovation, increasing investment in education and training and improving infrastructure. The strategy also emphasised the importance of supporting small- and medium-sized enterprises and improving the business environment.

2022: In recent years, Czechia has continued to make progress in improving its international competitiveness. The country's strengths include its strong institutions, high-quality health care and well-developed infrastructure. However, the country is still dealing with issues such as a shortage of skilled workers and a low level of investment in research and development.

In 2023, Czechia can be expected to focus on issues such as pension reform, revision of the tax system, support for defence in the context of the crisis in Ukraine, fighting inflation and extreme differences in regional and higher education salaries. The sooner these issues are dealt with, the sooner Czechia can be expected to move forward in terms of international competitiveness and begin to achieve at least moderate economic growth.

The trend of Czechia in the rankings of international organisations is evident in the last 20 years – the country is moving upwards (Table 3.1). There may be a temporary decline in the sub-rankings, but the final ranking also reflects to some extent the internal economic policy implemented, which is manifested with a

Table 3.1. IMD and WEF Ranking of Czechia (2002, 2012, 2022).

Period/ Index	**IMD World Competitiveness Ranking**	**WEF Global Competitiveness Index**
2002	32	40
2012	33	33
2022	26	N/A

Source: Own Processing According to IMD and WEF.

IMD: International Institute for Management Development (World Competitiveness Yearbook). WEF: World Economic Forum.

certain time lag and is also a manifestation of external economic policy. In terms of measuring and ranking competitiveness, the comparison needs to be made in a context that takes into account the degree of similarity of the country in terms of the size and structure of the economy. However, what is crucial in this respect is the methodology of the measurement carried out. Due to its complexity and the attempt to comprehensively capture even partial phenomena, it generates the following problems:

- The number of criteria and the associated sub-criteria is constantly changing and, as a result, the relevance in measuring the competitiveness and ranking of individual countries in the international context is de facto decreasing.
- The number of countries included in the evaluation is also not stable. This significantly undermines the relevance of the measurement, as it de facto negates the comparability of countries over time.
- Although the International Institute for Management Development (IMD) and the World Economic Forum present a methodological framework for measurement, the problem is that in the case of IMD, two thirds of the criteria are hard statistical data from national statistics and one third is represented by the survey itself.
- The weighting of each criterion is determined through expert estimates, but there is no general agreement on the value of the weighting criterion. If the weights are subsequently changed, there may be a more significant change that will lead to a shift in the final ranking achieved by the country.
- What is the relevance of measurement if there is a permanent change in input characteristics and this is reflected in the final ranking of countries? There is no exact answer to this question, but we can make some generalisations. From a methodological point of view, this distorts the issue of international comparison.

Impact of international evaluation results:

- rating of the country;
- foreign investors' interest in entering or leaving the country;
- tourism;
- continuing evaluation of international organisations;
- development of the stock market and rating of bonds; and
- the economic policy of the government – with respect to the policy statement of the government.

3.5 Linking Competitiveness, International Trade and Economic Growth

As mentioned in the previous section, the concept of competitiveness, due to its ambiguity, has no clearly defined place in economics. This is mainly due to the levels (methodologically it is the area of systemic competitiveness, see earlier) at which competitiveness is analysed and able to be measured and compared.

In addition, purely from the point of view of the resulting competitiveness of firms, it is only natural in a market environment that firms that fail in the long term leave the market. It does not matter whether it is a monopoly, oligopoly or monopolistic competitiveness. The key is always market success or failure. Failure results in the closure of a firm, whether as a result of zero economic profit over a long period or as a result of the closure of production. This is not the case in a national economy; a national economy does not end. Let us now abstract from the situation where states concentrate large amounts of foreign debt.

From the perspective of international trade, trade deficits can build up over a long period, which the government then covers with loans, which in turn has a negative impact on the balance of payments. On the other hand, the economy can use foreign funds to promote exports, which in turn will be reflected in a boost to economic growth. So here we have a clear link between international trade, economic growth and the competitiveness of the national economy.

In this context, however, it is necessary to draw attention to this link from the other perspective. In the case of national economies, the main focus is on increasing aggregate labour productivity. However, the question naturally arises: How could a relative increase in a country's competitiveness (in relation to a potentially rival economy) lead to an increase in living standards, employment and corporate welfare when economies consume each other's exports and then employ each other's workers through foreign direct investment? Again, this all links back to the topic of labour productivity, which is therefore a subject of economic research and in some cases a clear source for increasing competitiveness from the firm level and then through the regions to the national level.

Naturally and to some extent unconsciously, we look for a correlation between foreign trade and economic growth, and hence the competitiveness of the economy. There have been several papers that have looked for both theoretical and empirical correlations between foreign trade and economic growth. It should be noted, however, that even in this area no clear conclusions can be drawn.

Economic theory generally regards foreign trade liberalisation as a positive contribution to economic growth. At the empirical level, this assumption has been supported by, for example, Frankel and Romer (1999). This verified the positive correlation between the ratio of trade to GDP and the growth of income per capita of 0.5–2.0%. In this context, the authors used linear, logarithmic and semi-logarithmic equations to show that this correlation does exist. However, it is a matter of not only demonstrating a direct link between foreign trade and economic growth but also capturing the estimated effect of international trade on income generated. Frankel and Romer conclude by stating that their paper was primarily intended to answer the question of how international trade affects living standards. Thus, the authors see the impact not only on the economy as a whole but also on individuals. A crucial finding arising from the empirical analyses is: 'The point estimates suggest that increasing a country's size and area by one per cent raises income by one-tenth of a per cent or more', Frankel and Romer (1999, p. 394). Another finding is that international trade raises income through capital accumulation and through income for given levels of capital. All of these findings ultimately have a direct impact on economic growth.

A positive correlation between export growth and economic growth has been demonstrated in earlier studies, for example, Balassa (1978). This study, in empirical verification, confirms that export growth positively affects the rate of economic growth beyond the contributions of domestic and foreign capital and labour, and it is also confirmed that an export-oriented economy is more beneficial compared to policies oriented towards import or labour substitution. In addition, the authors Lewer and Berg (2003) conducted an extensive empirical analysis of the relationship between international trade and economic growth. In that context, they confirmed that a number of published studies have produced fairly consistent results. According to existing empirical research, a 1% increase in exports increases economic growth by about 0.2%.

More recent studies empirically confirm the conclusions of Lewer and Berg. One of them, for example, is a time series analysis of 1970–2009 from Luxembourg, where it is confirmed that an increase in export volume results in a 0.17-times increase in economic growth. In addition, increasing government spending by one unit increases economic growth by a factor of 2.7; in the case of government expenditure on education, it is almost 10 times.

Many of the empirical studies presented here use either a simple linear regression model or a panel data model. The dependent variable is economic growth. From the perspective of economic interpretation, assuming a well conducted econometric verification, it can be concluded that the impact on the explanatory variable should be interpreted as changes in the average level of expected economic growth, ceteris paribus.

In Czechia, a collection of works by Radiměřský (2011) dealing with competitiveness and growth performance has been published in this regard. Here, the authors confirmed that, with the exception of the 1997–1998 recession and the subsequent 2008–2009 recession, there is a correlation between economic growth and foreign trade growth. Moreover, empirically, they confirmed that foreign trade reached its minimum about a quarter prior to economic growth. This was de facto a logical advance indicator of an economic downturn. This finding makes it all the more important to pay attention to foreign influences on the Czech economy.

If we make a quarterly analysis for the 2002–2022 period regarding the evolution of the current account balance of payments and the seasonally adjusted GDP in constant prices (Fig. 3.2), we find that in the case of Czechia, GDP is lagging behind the evolution of the current account balance of payments by about one quarter. It can therefore be deduced that net exports play a key role in the balance of the current account balance of payments, where it acts as a leading aggregate ahead of GDP. This development is of course to be expected, as the Czech economy is export-led in many sectors, which is subsequently reflected in the value of economic growth achieved.

This finding corroborates previous empirical studies on the impact of exports on economic growth that have been reported above. In this regard, however, it should still be noted that what matters in terms of the quality of economic growth

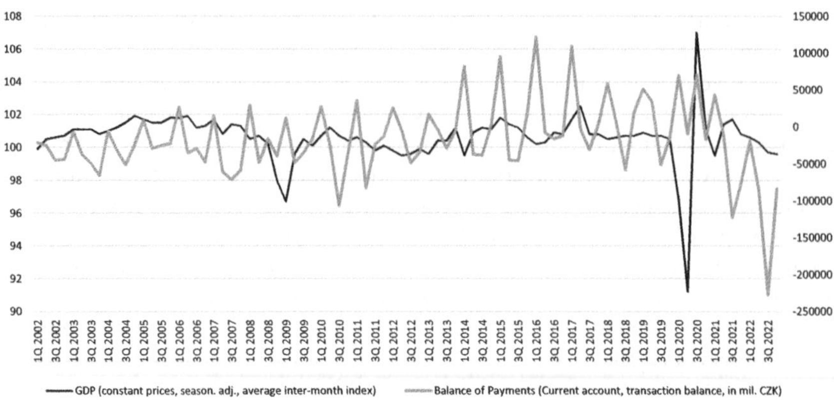

Fig. 3.2. Balance of Current Account, Balance of Payments and Seasonally Adjusted GDP Index. *Source:* Own Processing and Adjustments According to ARAD Statistics (ČNB, 2023).

is the long-run growth in labour productivity and, in particular, the growth in the share of value added in exports. This in turn will have a positive impact on the international competitiveness of the Czech economy. The share of value added in exports will be discussed in the next part of the chapter.

3.6 Changes in the Territorial and Commodity Structure of Foreign Trade

The changes in the territorial structure between 2002 and 2022 are clear. Firstly, in the case of imports (Table 3.3), it is the growing dynamics of China and Poland (in the case of Poland, we were only able to stimulate exports before EU accession). In addition, due to turbulence in world markets, the conflict in Ukraine and the energy crisis, imports in 2022 from the Russian Federation were significant in the field of oil and gas, while for 2023, a drop in the statistics can be expected specifically in the field of imports due to the adopted sanction measures against the Russian Federation.

As far as other trading partners are concerned, Germany and Slovakia are the most important trading partners of Czechia, where the trend of export growth (Table 3.2) is clearly in the lead. Czechia is also exporting to France and Austria, while Italian imports slightly exceed exports.

In terms of statistical reporting, there have been significant methodological changes over the 20 years. First, the methodology for reporting the commodity structure of foreign trade has changed. This was partly due to Czechia's accession to the EU in 2004 and then the methodology for reporting goods movements in 2020 changed, which makes it difficult to make relevant comparisons of the reporting of the commodity structure of Czechia in foreign trade when comparing

Table 3.2. Territorial Structure of Foreign Trade of Czechia (2002, 2012, 2022) – Export of Goods.

Export of Goods/Period	2002	2012	2022
Total (in mill. CZK, current prices)	1,254,860	3,072,598	5,637,099
– Of which:			
France	58,445	134,605	213,567
Italy	50,774	98,880	187,035
Germany	457,020	853,802	1,329,611
Austria	69,424	132,034	200,786
Slovakia	96,651	272,317	445,217
Poland	59,248	175,750	309,270
Russian Federation	16,795	106,166	32,318
United Kingdom	72,791	119,445	168,905
China	N/A	28,601	45,444

Source: Own Calculations from CSO and MIT Data, Own Adjustments.

Table 3.3. Territorial Structure of Foreign Trade of Czechia (2002, 2012, 2022) – Imports of Goods.

Import of Goods/Period	2002	2012	2022
Total (in mill. CZK, current prices)	1,325,671	2,776,888	5,515,780
– Of which:			
France	63,544	85,717	142,446
Italy	70,604	106,037	196,885
Germany	430,510	686,134	993,712
Austria	57,540	87,615	137,303
Slovakia	69,324	167,272	223,602
Poland	53,179	193,894	407,958
Russian Federation	59,988	154,961	265,830
United Kingdom	41,606	51,152	73,977
China	N/A	263,179	594,842

Source: Own Calculations from CSO and MIT Data, Own Adjustments.

2002, 2012 and 2022. The fundamental change brought about by the changes reporting from 2020, building on the changes adopted in 2014, is based on more detailed recording, especially for non-resident units. The elaboration of the previous reporting method consists mainly of detailed analyses of the links of global trade chains, the identification of basic business models for the most important non-resident units operating in the territory of Czechia, the detection of quasi-transit movements of goods across the territory of Czechia and the capture of real sales and purchases made between non-residents and residents. The advantage of the updated calculation method is that it allows for better determination of foreign trade in goods at a higher level of detail and also allows for a more detailed analysis of trade flows and linkages between residents and non-residents. This provides a significant improvement in the calculation of foreign trade in goods and allows for a more detailed analysis in this area. At the same time, the current method can respond quickly to changes in the trading behaviour of non-residents. The updated methodology for statistics on foreign trade in goods and its outputs has an impact on the National Accounts data. The quarterly GDP estimates work with the refined data of the external trade statistics immediately after their publication. The National Accounts plan to carry out a backward revision up to 2020 in 2024. The data remain consistent with the balance of payments of Czechia, which is published by the Czech National Bank in conjunction with the National Accounts (CSO, 2023a, 2023b).

As mentioned above, from the perspective of international comparison, a change in methodology is a problem in the case of the commodity structure. However, to illustrate, let us consider what major changes in the commodity structure have taken place.

It is evident that we can see much more significant changes in the commodity structure in terms of the volumes of imports (Table 3.5) and exports (Table 3.4) than in the territorial structure. The dynamics of change is particularly evident in

Table 3.4. Commodity Structure of Foreign Trade of Czechia (2002, 2012, 2022) – Export of Goods.

Export of Goods/Period	**2002**	**2012**	**2022**
Total (in mill. CZK, current prices)	1,254,860	3,072,598	5,637,099
– Of which according to SITC, rev. 3:			
0 Food and live animals	31,136	108,057	203,444
1 Beverages and tobacco	8,558	19,873	37,587
2 Crude materials, inedible	35,094	86,439	140,233
3 Mineral fuels, lubricants	35,952	118,705	204,697
4 Animal and vegetable oils	978	9,177	13,861
5 Chemical products	74,741	189,474	409,903
6 Manufactured goods by material	294,000	532,504	827,400
7 Machinery, transport equipment	622,998	1,663,416	3,127,478
8 Manufactured articles	149,507	340,363	646,465
9 Commodities not classified	1,896	4,591	26,029

Source: CSO (2023a, 2023b) and MIT (2023), Own Modifications.

Note: SITC = Standard International Trade Classification.

Table 3.5. Commodity Structure of Foreign Trade of Czechia (2002, 2012, 2022) – Import of Goods.

Import of Goods/Period	2002	2012	2022
Total (in mill. CZK, current prices)	1,325,671	2,776,888	5,515,780
– Of which according to SITC, rev. 3:			
0 Food and live animals	54,168	136,784	240,630
1 Beverages and tobacco	6,598	18,539	37,004
2 Crude materials, inedible	38,189	79,306	112,610
3 Mineral fuels, lubricants	100,248	307,576	522,398
4 Animal and vegetable oils	3,028	5,430	14,636
5 Chemical products	148,406	307,017	637,930
6 Manufactured goods by material	272,974	493,687	842,140
7 Machinery, transport equipment	561,745	1,143,512	2,490,779
8 Manufactured articles	140,042	267,494	589,353
9 Commodities not classified	272	7,545	28,300

Source: CSO (2023a, 2023b) and MIT (2023), Own Modifications.

Note: SITC = Standard International Trade Classification.

exports of machinery and transport equipment, which is linked to the significant growth of the automotive sector. In addition, the dependence of the Czech economy on imports of fuels and chemicals is not overlooked, which is determined both historically and with regard to the factor endowment of the economy.

Overall, there is a noticeable shift in the total volume of exports and imports. In the case of exports, there has been a 4.5-fold multiplication over 20 years compared to 2002, and a fourfold multiplication in imports. However, this trend could be even stronger. The transformation of the structure of the Czech economy and, at the same time, the prospects for foreign trade have one more major challenge ahead. This is increasing the share of value added in Czech exports. According to a Deloitte analysis (Ekonom, 2020, vol. 45), which was based on long-term research, the share of the Czech economy in exports in 2020 was only 61%. While the share of value added in the optical sector is around 50%, in the case of the automotive industry, which is the dominant driver of the Czech economy, it is only 20%. Of course, it is questionable whether this will change with the gradual transition to electromobility when carmakers will have to carry out their own research and development activities. It is by no means to be expected that the value added to exports will increase by leaps and bounds, but it is to be expected that this development will only affect selected sectors of the Czech economy that are most suited to it. One solution is to change the law on investment incentives, which should stimulate research and development itself.

3.7 Conclusion

In the context of the role of competitiveness in economic growth, we need to consider two important aspects. The first aspect is the fact that competitiveness is now a kind of integral standard in modern theories of international trade, and the second aspect is the fact that a country can be competitive even if it does not achieve economic growth. This is due to the relatively wide range of areas that competitiveness is able to cover.

Empirical studies show that there is a demonstrably positive correlation between the development of foreign trade and economic growth, which was also confirmed in the case of the Czech Republic, we can identify a clear causality in this. In addition, pro-export measures are also essential to the Czech Republic over the long term. It is about free trade agreements and investment incentives. The Czech government has implemented various investment incentives, such as tax incentives and subsidies, to encourage foreign investors to establish operations in the country. These incentives have also helped Czech companies to expand their exports by investing in new technologies and production capacity. Other measures include, for example, infrastructure development and education and training programs.

Overall, these pro-export tools have played an important role in supporting the growth of the Czech Republic's exports over the past 20 years, and they will likely continue to be important in the country's efforts to remain competitive in the global market.

However, the vague perception of competitiveness remains a fundamental problem – it means something different to everyone. One can identify with this because the ambiguity of the concept still applies. This is also evident in the approach of the historical schools of economics and their perception of competitiveness.

References

Balassa, B. (1978). Exports and economic growth: Further evidence. *Journal of Development Economics*, *5*, 181–189.

Clark, L. G., & Tracey, P. (2004). *Global competitiveness and innovation: An agent – Centred perspective*. Palgrave Macmillan. ISBN 1-4039-1889-9.

ČNB. (2023). *ARAD systém časových řad*. https://www.cnb.cz/arad/#/cs/home

CSO. (2023a). *Aktualizace metody propočtu – Zahraniční obchod se zbožím*. Czech Statistical Office. https://www.czso.cz/csu/czso/aktualizace-metody-propoctu-zahranicni-obchod-se-zbozim

CSO. (2023b). *Zahraniční obchod se zbožím*. Czech Statistical Office. https://www.czso.cz/csu/czso/zo_se_zbozim_podle_zmeny_vlastnictvi_narodni_pojeti

Ekonom. (2020). Ekonomika bez přidané hodnoty. *Ekonom*, *45*, 2020.

Esser, K., Hillebrand, W., Messner, D., & Meyer-Stamer, J. (1995). *Systemic competitiveness. New governance patterns for industrial development*. Frank Cass (GDI Book Series. No. 5).

Frankel, J. A., & Romer, D. (1999). Does trade cause growth? *The American Economic Review*, *89*(3), 379–399.

Holland, S. (1987). *The market economy: From micro to mesoeconomics*. Wiedenfeld & Nicolson. ISBN 978-0312013240.

Lewer, J. J., & Berg, H. (2003). How large is international trade's effect on economic growth? *Journal of Economic Surveys*, *17*(3), 363–396.

MIT. (2023). *Ministry of industry and trade. Statistiky zahraničního obchodu*. https://www.mpo.cz/cz/zahranicni-obchod/statistiky-zahranicniho-obchodu/

Radiměřský, M. (2011). Vnější vztahy – zahraniční obchod In Slaný a kol. *Konkurenceschopnost, růstová výkonnost a stabilita české ekonomiky*. Masarykova univerzita. 184 strany. ISBN 978-80-210-5656-5.

Spulber, D. F. (2007). *Global competitive strategy*. Cambridge University Press. ISBN 978-0-521-88081-7.

Turečková, K. (2016). Sectoral specialization as a source of competitiveness: Case study on ICT sector in V4+ countries. In *Proceedings of the 3rd International Conference on European Integration 2016* (pp. 1023–1029). VŠB-TU Ostrava. ISBN 978-80-248-3911-0.

Chapter 4

The Role of Exchange Rate in Contemporary Czechia's Foreign Trade

Jana Šimáková

Silesian University in Opava, Czechia

Abstract

Czechia's economic growth is substantially dependent on foreign trade. An independent monetary policy in a managed floating exchange rate regime gives a unique perspective on the effects of the exchange rate on foreign trade. This chapter evaluates the effects of exchange rate development on different sectors of Czechia's foreign trade. Using disaggregated data based on trading partner and product category, the period from 1999 to 2020 is analyzed. Czechia's 10 major trading partners are included in the estimation. The relationship between exchange rates and foreign trade is assessed through a Johansen cointegration approach and modified vector error correction model. The results of the Johansen cointegration test indicate that the majority of the aggregate bilateral trade balances are in a long-term relationship with Czechia's gross domestic product (GDP), foreign GDP and exchange rate movements. The J-curve is proved only in chemicals and related products traded with France, manufactured goods traded with Italy and Slovakia and mineral fuels and lubricants traded with the Netherlands.

Keywords: Exchange rate; industry-level data; international trade; managed floating exchange rate regime; small open economy; trade balance

4.1 Introduction

Czechia's transition to a market economy has significantly impacted its economic and monetary specifics, including its involvement in international economic activities and exchange rate regime. The recent interventions in the foreign exchange market by the Czech National Bank (CNB) have served as an unconventional monetary policy tool under the managed floating exchange rate regime.

Modeling Economic Growth in Contemporary Czechia, 51–69

Published under exclusive licence by Emerald Publishing Limited
doi:10.1108/978-1-83753-840-920241004

However, both directions of interventions were adopted in the last decade. On the one hand, the first interventions (2013–2017) were initiated to avoid deflation or falling short of the long-term inflation target. These interventions led to a depreciation of the Czech koruna (CZK) against the euro (EUR), the currency of Czechia's most important trading partners. On the other hand, the interventions adopted in 2022 aimed to appreciate the CZK value against the EUR. The protection of the koruna and making it more stable should have led to support steps to decrease the high rates of inflation hurting the whole economy. In both cases, the exchange rate transmission mechanism is the crucial element of the CNB's monetary policy, with exports and imports development serving as the main drivers of the inflation target fulfilment.

In Czechia, which is a small, very open economy, the exchange rate channel is expected to have a signicant position. As stated by Mishkin (1996), the influence of monetary policy through the exchange rate channel is of fundamental importance and is especially strong in the environment of small, very open economies (2022). Nevertheless, recent studies have raised doubts about the effectiveness of this monetary tool. Only a few studies found a rarely significant low effect of the exchange rate on inflation (e.g. Caselli, 2017; Hájek & Horváth, 2016; Opatrný, 2017). Furthermore, Baxa and Šestorád (2019) point out that exchange rate pass-through to prices has been rather low and gradually decreasing since the early 2000s, suggesting limited potential effects of the exchange rate on inflation. Therefore, in line with Morales and Raei (2013), it is important to focus on the particular macroeconomic conditions of the country. This chapter focuses on one of the essential parts of the overall mechanism – on the effects of the exchange rate on international trade. The aim is to evaluate the effects of exchange rate development on different sectors of Czechia's foreign trade. The unique perspective on international trade that the Czech open economy offers with its managed floating exchange rate regime allows for an in-depth analysis. By undertaking this research, we hope to shed light on the complex relationship between exchange rates and international trade in Czechia. We believe that this research is of great significance to policymakers, academics and business professionals interested in understanding the impact of exchange rate movements on foreign trade in Czechia.

4.2 Literature Review

Monetary policy operates on the assumption that currency depreciation stimulates exports and curtails imports, while currency appreciation has the opposite effect. When the domestic currency depreciates, it makes imports more expensive in domestic currency terms but exports cheaper in foreign currency terms. As a result, the volume of exports and imports can change in response to exchange rate movements. The exchange rate plays a critical role in the profitability of both export-oriented and import-competing industries and can affect foreign trade, ultimately impacting the overall market conditions in the economy.

An influential theory in this area is Magee's J-curve theory, introduced in 1973 (Magee, 1973). According to this approach, a positive effect of currency depreciation on the trade balance is conditioned by the validity of the Marshall–Lerner condition, which states that the sum of export and import demand elasticity must be at least one (see Lerner, 1944; Machlup, 1939; Marshall, 1923; Robinson, 1937). This condition is usually not met in the short run. The initial negative effect of home currency depreciation is followed by a positive effect on the trade balance, forming a J-shaped curve in the long term.

Extensive research has been conducted on this theory. Based on the current state of knowledge, data and econometric development, there has been a clear shift from an aggregation analysis approach (e.g. Bahmani-Oskooee, 1986; Mahdavi & Sohrabian, 1993; Rose & Yellen, 1989) to a bilateral analysis approach (e.g. Bahmani-Oskooee & Brooks, 1999; Bahmani-Oskooee & Ratha, 2004) and, most recently, a disaggregated approach (e.g. Bahmani-Oskooee & Hegerty, 2011; Bahmani-Oskooee et al., 2014; Šimáková & Stavárek, 2015). Therefore, the current methodology uses exchange rates and industry-level data on a bilateral level to accurately assess the relationship between the exchange rate and trade balance. The disaggregation of industry-level data allows for a decrease in bias derived from grouping products with different price elasticities into one basket and more reflects the assumptions of the Marshall–Lerner condition.

On the Czech aggregated level, Gürtler (2019) using aggregate quarterly data for the period 2000–2014 found that the real effective exchange rate has a strongly negative effect on trade balance in the short run. This effect was found to be replaced with a positive trade balance development in the long run, thus confirming the J-curve phenomenon. However, different conclusions are present in studies reflecting the aggregation biases. Several studies have investigated the presence of the J-curve effect in Czechia's trade with other countries on the bilateral levels. Extensive studies were performed by Bahmani-Oskooee and Kutan (2009) based on data from 12 countries covering the period 1990–2005 and by Nusair (2013) based on data from 17 emerging and transitioning countries over the period 1991–2012. Although the J-curve effect was present in several countries, Czechia remained free of the J-curve effect. Even Hsing (2009) found no evidence of the J-curve effect in the bilateral trade of six Central European countries, including Czechia, with the United States. On the other hand, Hacker and Hatemi-J (2004) found evidence of the effect in Czechia's bilateral trade with Germany. They concluded that the trade balance deteriorates within a few months after depreciation and then rises to a long-term equilibrium value higher than the initial exchange rate. Similarly, Šimáková (2016) confirmed the J-curve in Czechia's trade with Poland and Germany.

Additionally, few product-level studies were conducted for Czech trade flows. Šimáková and Stavárek (2015) using Johansen's cointegration test demonstrated the beneficial effects of depreciation on most of the product categories studied in Czechia's trade from 1993 to 2013. Šimáková (2017) proved the long-term relationship between exchange rates and foreign agrifood trade with food, live animals, beverages and tobacco commodities in all Visegrád countries, Czechia included. However, directions of the domestic currency's effects were found to be inconsistent. Although the majority of particular trade balances were positively affected by currency depreciation, the J-curve for Czechia itself was estimated only in the foreign trade of food and live animals with Italy and Poland. Šimáková (2021) assumes in her study that the ambiguous effects can be caused by the different reactions of producers and consumers to the opposite movement of the exchange rates. Therefore, assumed asymmetries were incorporated into the model of the J-curve of foreign trade in agrifood in Czechia, Hungary and Poland. Šimáková (2021) found there the difference not only in the direction but also in the intensity of the effects of exchange rate changes on the trade balances of food and live animals, dairy products and birds' eggs and animal oils and fats in Czechia; meat and preparations in Hungary; and sugar, sugar preparations and honey and beverages in Poland.

Overall, the literature suggests that exchange rates play an important role in shaping international trade in Czechia. Exchange rate stability is crucial for promoting international trade, and exchange rate fluctuations can have both positive and negative impacts on the volume and competitiveness of international trade in specific industries. However, more research is needed to fully understand the complex relationship between exchange rates and international trade, particularly at the industry level.

4.3 Methodology

Following Magee's (1973) distinction between long-term and short-term effects, we apply a two-step procedure. To address the main criticism of earlier studies, which were susceptible to spurious regression issues due to nonstationary data, we employ the cointegration procedure developed by Johansen (1997). This approach allows us to evaluate the long-term relationships between exchange rates and international trade, specifically by analyzing bilateral trade balances at the industry level. In accordance with Bahmani-Oskooee et al.'s (2014) work, we apply the following model (4.1):

$$\ln TB_{p,t} = \alpha + \beta \ln Y_{d,t} + \gamma \ln Y_{f,t} + \lambda \ln ER_{f,t} + \delta FXI + \varepsilon_t \quad (4.1)$$

where TB_p is a measure of the trade balance in time period t, defined as the ratio of Czechia's exports to country f over Czech imports from country f in a selected industry. Y_d represents domestic income, a proxy for Czechia's demand for foreign goods, and is measured as gross domestic product (GDP). As an increase in domestic income Y_d is assumed to result in increased imports, the estimate for β is expected to be negative. Y_f represents the income of trading partner f, serving as a proxy for foreign demand for Czechia's exported goods. As an increase in foreign income Y_f is expected to lead to increased exports to the respective country, the estimate for γ is expected to be positive. GDPs are expressed in index form to make them unit-free. ER_f represents the nominal bilateral exchange rate. The exchange rate is defined in direct quotation, meaning that an increase reflects a depreciation of the domestic currency. FXI represents the dummy variable for the period, when CNB conducts foreign exchange interventions, and δ represents its effects. ε_t represents the error term. Hence, the parameter λ is expected to be positive, as the trade balance of the respective industry should improve due to domestic currency depreciation.

In order to test the short-run relationship, a short-term dynamic is incorporated into the long-run model. According to Hsing (2009), we apply the following error correction model (4.2):

$$\Delta \ln TB_{p,t} = \alpha + \sum_{k=1}^{n} \omega_k \Delta \ln TB_{t-k} + \sum_{k=1}^{n} \beta_k \Delta \ln Y_{d,t-k} + \sum_{k=1}^{n} \gamma_k \Delta \ln Y_{f,t-k} + \sum_{k=1}^{n} \lambda_k \Delta \ln ER_{f,t-k} + \vartheta_k EC_{t-1} + \varepsilon_t \tag{4.2}$$

where EC is the disequilibrium term and $\vartheta_k EC_{t-1}$ represents the error correction mechanism.

4.4 Data

The data used for estimation are on a quarterly frequency and cover the period from 1999 to 2020. The GDP data, bilateral exchange rates and import and export flows were obtained from the Organisation for Economic Co-operation and Development iLibrary statistical database. The data for exchange rate development are based on the direct quotation. It means that appreciation of CZK against the currency of the foreign partner is reflected by the decrease of the exchange rate. Fig. 4.1 depicts the development of CZK against relevant currencies set in index form in the sample period of 1999–2020.

CZK has generally demonstrated long-term appreciation against the EUR, British pound (GBP), Hungarian forint (HUF) and Polish zloty (PLN). However,

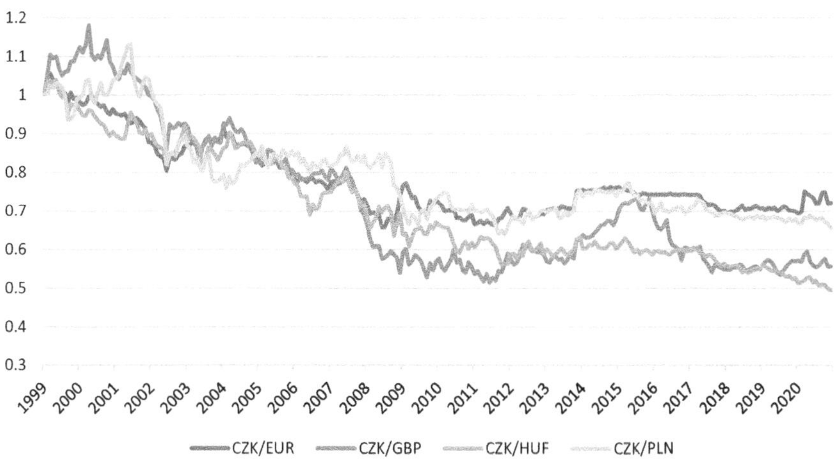

Fig. 4.1. Development of CZK Against HUF, EUR, PLN and GBP (Index, 1999 = 100). *Source:* Own Processing Based on Data from OECD iLibrary Statistical Database.

there have been different periods characterized by various fluctuations and trends. It is worth noting that the CZK experienced the highest appreciation against the Polish zloty, while the appreciation against EUR was relatively lower during the period under consideration. One can see clear effects of general factors affecting the exchange rates, such as European Union accession in 2004, global financial crisis, European debt crisis, interest rates and inflation differentials, BREXIT and COVID-19. The specific is that Czechia operates under a floating currency regime, but the central bank has the authority to intervene in the foreign exchange market to manage volatility or adjust monetary policy. From 2013 to 2017, the country maintained a de facto exchange rate anchor to the euro, with the central bank aiming to keep the exchange rate close to 27 CZK/EUR. These interventions not only affected the CZK/EUR exchange rate but also had an impact on the bilateral exchange rates of CZK/PLN and CZK/HUF, given the high correlation between them.

After abandoning the interventions in April 2017, the appreciation of the CZK was lower than market expectations. The most significant wave of interventions by the CNB occurred in the first quarter of 2017. As the exchange rate commitment was nearing its end, exporting companies started hedging against potential future exchange rate appreciation. Concurrently, financial investors were building substantial long positions in the koruna (Franta et al., 2018). Several factors, as derived by Mehrotra and Schanz (2020), contributed to this development. Firstly, before the central bank intervention, the exchange rate was slightly overvalued, preventing a significant undervaluation of the koruna. Secondly, the effects of the depreciated exchange rate extended to other domestic nominal variables, including wages and inflation. The real equilibrium appreciation was achieved through inflation differentials compared to major trading partners, particularly the euro area. Thirdly, the pace of the koruna's real equilibrium appreciation has slowed compared to the pre-crisis trend. Lastly, exporters had pre-hedged their future euro-denominated revenues while the exchange rate commitment was in effect. Since then, there have been no foreign exchange interventions in Czechia, and the exchange rate exhibited smooth developments until the negative shock caused by the COVID-19 pandemic.

The analysis focuses on the 10 major trading partners, which collectively account for an average of 67% of Czechia's overall foreign trade between 1999 and 2020. Therefore, analysis is applied to Austria, France, Germany, Hungary, Italy, the Netherlands, Poland, Slovakia, Spain and the United Kingdom. Fig. 4.2 provides an overview of the territorial structure of Czechia's foreign trade. It is evident from the presented indices that Germany stands out as the most significant trading partner, representing an average share of 30% of the total trade. Furthermore, Germany's share has been consistently increasing over time. Slovakia and Poland hold the positions of Czechia's second and third largest partners, with respective shares of 7% and 6%. However, both countries experienced a significant decline in their trade volumes during the period from 1993 to 2013. The remaining partners have shares ranging from 2% to 4%.

The industry levels of international trade used in the estimations are determined based on the Standard International Trade Classification (SITC):

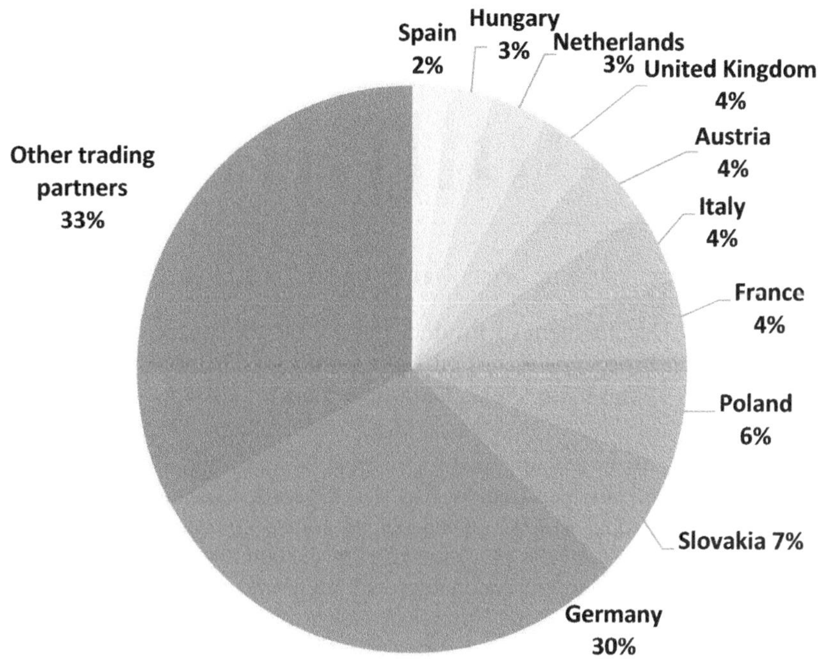

Fig. 4.2. Territorial Structure of Foreign Trade of Czechia (1999–2020). *Source:* Own Processing Based on Data from OECD iLibrary Statistical Database.

- T0: Food and live animals;
- T1: Beverages and tobacco;
- T2: Crude materials, inedible, except fuels;
- T3: Mineral fuels, lubricants and related materials;
- T4: Animal and vegetable oils, fats and waxes;
- T5: Chemicals and related products;
- T6: Manufactured goods;
- T7: Machinery and transport equipment;
- T8: Miscellaneous manufactured articles; and
- T9: Commodities and transactions not classified elsewhere in the SITC.

Fig. 4.3 highlights the substantial variations in trade balances across different product categories. It is evident that certain sectors consistently operate at a deficit over the long term, such as food and live animals, mineral fuels, lubricants and related materials and chemicals and related products. On the other hand, there are sectors where exports exceed imports, leading to a trade surplus in those specific industries.

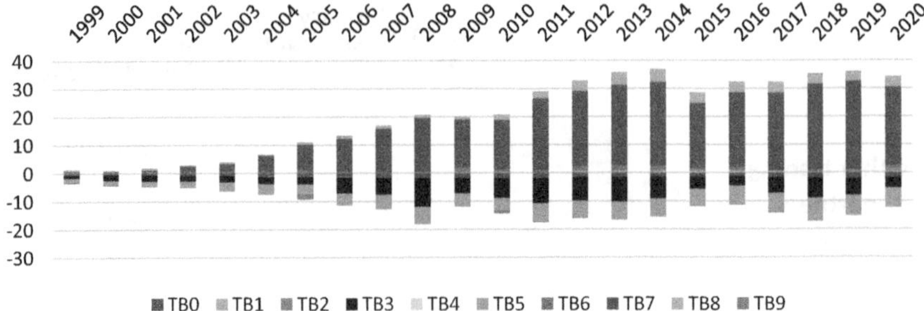

Fig. 4.3. Development of Product-Level Trade Balances of Czechia. *Source:* Own Processing Based on Data from OECD iLibrary Statistical Database. *Note:* Data in Billions of CZK.

The average shares of individual sector-level foreign trade of Czechia within the sample period are depicted in Fig. 4.4. Overall, Czechia's foreign trade demonstrates a strong presence in machinery, transport equipment and manufactured goods. These sectors play vital roles in the country's export and import activities, contributing to its economic growth and industrial development.

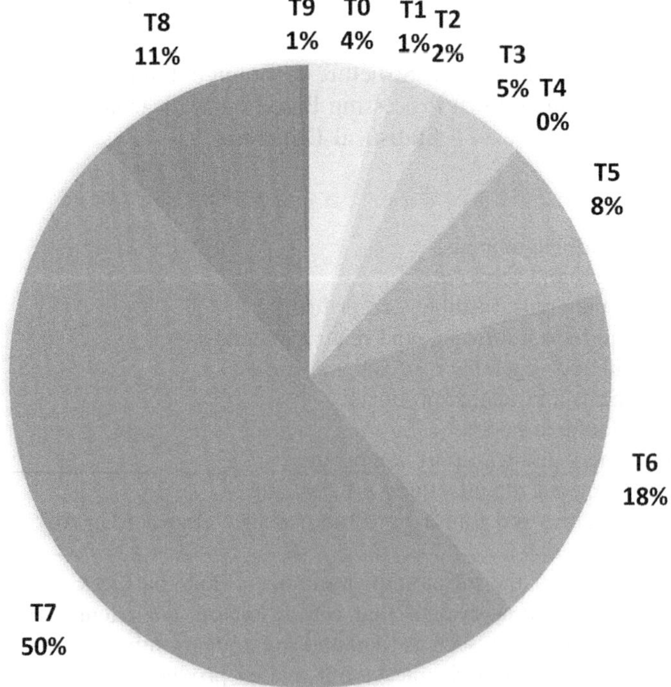

Fig. 4.4. Product Structure of Foreign Trade of Czechia (1999–2020). *Source:* Own Processing Based on Data from OECD iLibrary Statistical Database.

4.5 Results

The effects of exchange rates on Czechia's foreign trade are assessed using bilateral data between Czechia and its 10 major trading partners. To estimate the long-term relationship between exchange rates and the respective product-level trade balances, we apply the Johansen cointegration approach to the Eq. (4.1). In order to address skewness and heteroscedasticity and to stabilize variability, a logarithmic transformation is performed. Empirical estimation requires stability in the regressors, which is assessed using the augmented Dickey–Fuller test for integration of time series. Unit root tests are conducted for each individual time series, and it is found that all variables exhibit first-difference stationarity. The determination of lag orders in the vector error correction model specification is crucial for accurate inferences drawn from the model. We sequentially determine the appropriate lag length for each variable, considering that the specific numbers vary across trading partners and trading categories, ranging from 2 to 4 quarters. The optimal lags in this analysis are determined by maximizing the Schwarz information criterion. The choice of lag difference is assumed to be influenced by differences in the nature and elasticity of traded goods, as well as time lags in consumers' search for more affordable alternatives. The results for long-term relationships from each product-level model are reported in Table 4.1.

The results of the Johansen cointegration test indicate that the aggregate bilateral trade balances are in a long-term relationship with Czechia's GDP, foreign GDP and exchange rate movements, except for certain product categories. Specifically, no cointegration is estimated for product categories involving animal and vegetable oils, fats, waxes as well as a heterogeneous category of commodities and transactions not classified elsewhere. These categories, such as animal and vegetable oils, fats and waxes, account for a relatively small share in the total foreign trade of Czechia, only 0.2% during the sample period. The presence of a long-term relationship is also limited in the product categories of mineral fuels, lubricants and related products (5% share on total trade) and beverages and tobacco (0.7% share on total trade). When considering the territorial structure, a lower number of statistically significant coefficients is observed in trade with Austria, France and Italy. Therefore, it can be concluded that individual trade balances are mostly characterized by a long-term joint development of Czechia's GDP, GDP of trading partners and bilateral exchange rates.

The analysis of long-term coefficients of domestic GDP for Czechia reveals variations across different product categories and trading partners. The expected negative effects of domestic GDP on the trade balance are confirmed in the majority of individual trade balances, although there are some exceptions. Notably, the opposite effects, contrary to expectations, are observed primarily in trade with Poland and Germany from a territorial perspective. From a sectoral perspective, the opposite effects are predominantly found in the categories of food and live animals, as well as machinery and transport equipment. However, in most cases, an increase in Czechia's GDP results in an increase in the quantity demanded for goods from foreign trading partners, leading to a rise in imports.

Table 4.1. Estimated Long-Run Coefficients of Trade Models.

Austria	**TT**	**T0**	**T1**	**T2**	**T3**	**T4**	**T5**	**T6**	**T7**	**T8**	**T9**
Y_d	**−4.85**	5.12	−0.54	−1.12	–	–	**5.82**	−9.61	−8.33	**−4.00**	–
Y_f	1.09	1.31	**0.13**	3.89	–	–	0.43	3.42	1.97	**0.72**	–
ER	0.47	–	**0.09**	−0.09	–	–	–	–	–	0.03	–
FXI	–	–	0.38	0.75	–	–	–	–	–	−0.06	–
France	**TT**	**T0**	**T1**	**T2**	**T3**	**T4**	**T5**	**T6**	**T7**	**T8**	**T9**
Y_d	−4.27	3.94	–	**−7.59**	−0.68	–	–	−8.77	0.13	−3.94	–
Y_f	3.13	**−1.08**	–	15.04	–	–	9.45	5.09	15.51	–	–
ER	–	**1.12**	–	–	–	–	**0.79**	1.20	–	–	–
FXI	–	0.13	–	–	–	–	**1.08**	–	–	–	–
Germany	**TT**	**T0**	**T1**	**T2**	**T3**	**T4**	**T5**	**T6**	**T7**	**T8**	**T9**
Y_d	9.45	**−0.81**	–	−1.37	0.09	–	−8.05	−7.55	**7.48**	**3.42**	–
Y_f	0.23	**2.10**	–	8.14	7.64	–	−0.99	1.96	**8.31**	**1.18**	0.08
ER	0.19	0.49	–	0.72	–	–	**0.91**	**0.04**	−0.02	−0.17	–
FXI	–	0.05	–	–	–	–	0.06	–	–	–	–
Hungary	**TT**	**T0**	**T1**	**T2**	**T3**	**T4**	**T5**	**T6**	**T7**	**T8**	**T9**
Y_d	**−0.55**	–	**−6.76**	1.52	−6.12	–	−1.34	**−9.08**	1.42	**−10.01**	–
Y_f	2.48	–	4.93	9.72	2.04	–	5.39	2.14	5.25	**0.26**	–
ER	**0.37**	–	0.47	–	–	–	**0.75**	**3.16**	–	**−0.07**	–

Italy	**TT**	**T0**	**T1**	**T2**	**T3**	**T4**	**T5**	**T6**	**T7**	**T8**	**T9**
Y_d	**−9.12**	−4.08	–	−3.16	2.91	–	**−8.44**	**−8.43**	3.64	1.12	–
Y_f	–	−3.20	–	4.49	**0.01**	–	1.28	0.89	2.45	10.98	–
ER	1.05	1.41	–	–	–	–	0.59	**0.03**	−0.92	−0.02	–
FXI	–	–	–	–	1.81	–	–	0.12	–	–	–
Netherlands	**TT**	**T0**	**T1**	**T2**	**T3**	**T4**	**T5**	**T6**	**T7**	**T8**	**T9**
Y_d	−2.02	−9.17	–	−9.10	−0.03	–	−1.84	−4.35	**−3.78**	3.17	–
Y_f	1.98	−8.89	–	**1.16**	−7.57	–	1.91	6.69	5.01	0.16	–
ER	0.56	–	–	**2.63**	–	–	–	−0.19	0.04	0.21	–
FXI	–	–	–	–	–	–	–	–	–	–	–
Poland	**TT**	**T0**	**T1**	**T2**	**T3**	**T4**	**T5**	**T6**	**T7**	**T8**	**T9**
Y_d	11.09	1.18	–	2.92	0.26	–	**−7.41**	−2.45	**2.39**	−6.42	–
Y_f	7.42	**−9.55**	–	6.13	0.75	3.01	−0.57	4.48	8.94	**1.89**	–
ER	1.02	–	–	4.32	–	–	**0.09**	−0.00	0.42	–	–
Slovakia	**TT**	**T0**	**T1**	**T2**	**T3**	**T4**	**T5**	**T6**	**T7**	**T8**	**T9**
Y_d	**−7.28**	1.96	–	–	−4.85	8.92	−2.77	**7.56**	−0.08	−5.99	–
Y_f	**1.63**	**7.06**	–	5.53	**9.89**	3.96	3.18	**10.73**	−1.05	8.19	–

(Continued)

Table 4.1. *(Continued)*

ER	0.37	1.14	–	−0.05	0.15	–	–	**0.32**	**−1.71**	1.54	–
FXI	–	–	–	–	−0.04	–	–	0.00	–	–	–
Spain	**TT**	**T0**	**T1**	**T2**	**T3**	**T4**	**T5**	**T6**	**T7**	**T8**	**T9**
Y_d	**1.24**	0.97	–	0.94	–	–	**−2.77**	**−1.82**	**−5.10**	−0.29	–
Y_f	5.81	6.62	–	**9.91**	**4.06**	–	9.47	5.12	9.03	2.48	–
ER	**−0.07**	0.82	–	0.78	–	–	1.65	−0.29	0.73	1.16	–
FXI	–	–	–	–	–	–	–	0.15	–	–	–
United Kingdom	**TT**	**T0**	**T1**	**T2**	**T3**	**T4**	**T5**	**T6**	**T7**	**T8**	**T9**
Y_d	–	**−3.06**	–	−2.94	1.57	–	−1.59	−2.25	−9.62	**3.37**	–
Y_f	10.18	2.48	–	6.13	–	–	6.00	**3.36**	8.14	1.74	–
ER	−0.45	–	–	–	−0.06	–	1.72	0.02	0.00	–	–

Source: Own Processing Based on Data from OECD iLibrary Statistical Database.
Note: We Report Only Coefficients Statistically Significant at the 5% (Bold) and 10% Level, Respectively.

This subsequently worsens the trade balance and is reflected in the negative effect on the total bilateral trade balance.

The estimation of coefficients for foreign partners' GDP yields more definitive conclusions. In all cases, the GDP of trading partners has a positive effect on the total bilateral trade balances of Czechia. An increase in GDP in foreign economies can thus be associated with an expansion in the purchasing power of foreign entities, an increase in the quantity demanded for domestic goods abroad and consequently, an increase in exported goods. The highest impact is observed for the GDP of Poland and the United Kingdom. Rare instances of opposite effects at the commodity level can be found, predominantly in the food and live animals product category.

The results presented in Table 4.1 reveal a predominantly positive effect of CZK depreciation on the total bilateral trade balances, particularly with Germany, Hungary, Italy, the Netherlands, Poland and Slovakia. However, upon disaggregating the trade flows, the impact of CZK depreciation becomes less clear. The opposite effect is primarily observed in product categories such as manufactured goods, machinery and transport equipment and miscellaneous manufactured goods, which represent a significant portion of Czechia's foreign trade. This analysis demonstrates that while depreciation of the CZK against the euro promotes exports and reduces imports in the overall bilateral trade balance, it yields varied outcomes at the disaggregated level. These findings align with the assertions made by Bahmani-Oskooee et al. (2014), emphasizing the importance of analyzing industry-level data to mitigate biases resulting from grouping products with differing price elasticities and to align more closely with the assumptions of the Marshall–Lerner condition. Foreign exchange interventions were found to have a minimal impact, as only a few cases exhibited a positive effect.

As mentioned earlier, the chapter investigates the short-run effects of depreciation by analyzing the coefficient estimates of the lagged value of the first differenced exchange rate variable (Table 4.2). The J-curve framework allows for a distinction between short-run and long-run effects. The traditional J-curve pattern is confirmed if the coefficient estimate for the exchange rate is significantly negative at shorter lags and transitions to a significantly positive coefficient at longer lags. Alternatively, it can be observed as negative short-run coefficients followed by a positive long-run coefficient. In this research, only certain short-term coefficients show statistical significance. The significant negative coefficient in chemicals and related products traded with France, manufactured goods traded with Italy and Slovakia and mineral fuels and lubricants traded with the Netherlands indicates a positive long-run relationship, providing evidence for the J-curve pattern. However, for the other cases examined, the estimated coefficients of exchange rates do not support the existence of the J-curve phenomenon. These findings align with the conclusions of previous studies on Czechia, such as those conducted by Bahmani-Oskooee and Kutan (2009), Nusair (2013), Šimáková and Stavárek (2015) and Šimáková (2017).

Table 4.2. Estimated Short-Run Coefficients of Exchange Rates.

Austria	TT	T0	T1	T2	T3	T4	T5	T6	T7	T8	T9
Δ1	0.08		0.11								
Δ2	0.04										
Δ3											
Δ4											
France	**TT**	**T0**	**T1**	**T2**	**T3**	**T4**	**T5**	**T6**	**T7**	**T8**	**T9**
Δ1							−0.18				
Δ2							**0.02**				
Δ3							0.65				
Δ4											
Germany	**TT**	**T0**	**T1**	**T2**	**T3**	**T4**	**T5**	**T6**	**T7**	**T8**	**T9**
Δ1	**−0.01**								0.78	0.05	
Δ2	0.03								−0.12	0.08	
Δ3	−0.18									−0.12	
Δ4	**0.17**										
Hungary	**TT**	**T0**	**T1**	**T2**	**T3**	**T4**	**T5**	**T6**	**T7**	**T8**	**T9**
Δ1	0.05			0.22						−0.14	
Δ2				−0.04						−0.56	
Δ3				0.00							
Δ4											

Italy	**TT**	**T0**	**T1**	**T2**	**T3**	**T4**	**T5**	**T6**	**T7**	**T8**	**T9**
Δ1								**−0.01**	*0.02*		
Δ2								−0.21	0.41		
Δ3								0.15			
Δ4											
Netherlands	**TT**	**T0**	**T1**	**T2**	**T3**	**T4**	**T5**	**T6**	**T7**	**T8**	**T9**
Δ1				0.16	−0.02						
Δ2				0.03							
Δ3					**0.09**						
Δ4											
Slovakia	**TT**	**T0**	**T1**	**T2**	**T3**	**T4**	**T5**	**T6**	**T7**	**T8**	**T9**
Δ1	0.02							−0.04	0.22		
Δ2	0.00							−0.17	−0.06		
Δ3	0.14								−0.15		
Δ4											
Spain	**TT**	**T0**	**T1**	**T2**	**T3**	**T4**	**T5**	**T6**	**T7**	**T8**	**T9**
Δ1				0.00							
Δ2				0.01							

(Continued)

Table 4.2. *(Continued)*

Spain	**TT**	**T0**	**T1**	**T2**	**T3**	**T4**	**T5**	**T6**	**T7**	**T8**	**T9**
Δ3											
Δ4											
United Kingdom	**TT**	**T0**	**T1**	**T2**	**T3**	**T4**	**T5**	**T6**	**T7**	**T8**	**T9**
Δ1	−0.02						0.15				
Δ2	0.12						0.09				
Δ3	**−0.46**						0.11				
Δ4							0.23				

Source: Own Processing Based on Data from OECD iLibrary Statistical Database.
Note: We Report Only Coefficients Statistically Significant at the 5% (Bold) and 10% Level, Respectively.

4.6 Conclusion

The findings of this chapter shed light on the complex relationship between exchange rates and international trade in Czechia. The results suggest that the exchange rate has a significant impact on Czechia's foreign trade, with certain product categories and trading partners exhibiting variations in their long-term relationships. The analysis of long-term coefficients reveals that the majority of individual trade balances align with the expected negative effects of domestic GDP on the trade balance, although there are exceptions. Surprisingly, opposite effects are observed primarily in trade with Poland and Germany from a territorial perspective, as well as in the food and live animals and machinery and transport equipment sectors. On the other hand, the coefficients estimated for foreign partners' GDP indicate a consistently positive effect on the total bilateral trade balances. An increase in the GDP of trading partners is associated with increased purchasing power, higher demand for domestic goods and an overall increase in exported goods. Notably, the highest impact is observed for the GDP of Poland and the United Kingdom.

Regarding the impact of CZK depreciation, the results demonstrate a predominantly positive effect on the total bilateral trade balances, particularly with Germany, Hungary, Italy, the Netherlands, Poland and Slovakia. However, when examining disaggregated trade flows, the impact becomes less clear, with opposite effects observed in product categories such as manufactured goods, machinery and transport equipment and miscellaneous manufactured goods. These findings highlight the importance of analyzing industry-level data to understand the specific effects of exchange rate movements on different sectors of Czechia's foreign trade. From the J-curve perspective, only some short-term coefficients show statistical significance, supporting the J-curve pattern. The majority of cases do not exhibit the expected transition from negative short-run coefficients to positive long-run coefficients. These results are consistent with previous studies conducted on Czechia.

Overall, these findings contribute to the understanding of the effects of exchange rates on foreign trade in Czechia, offering valuable insights for various stakeholders. Companies operating in different sectors can benefit from these insights to make informed decisions and develop effective strategies in response to exchange rate fluctuations. Furthermore, central banks, in particular, can use these findings to evaluate the effectiveness of the exchange rate transmission mechanism within their monetary policy framework.

References

Bahmani-Oskooee, M. (1986). Determinants of international trade flows: The case of developing countries. *Journal of Development Economics*, *20*(1), 107–123. https://doi.org/10.1016/0304-3878(86)90007-6

Bahmani-Oskooee, M., & Brooks, T. (1999). Cointegration approach to estimating bilateral trade elasticities between U.S. and her trading partners. *International Economic Journal*, *13*, 119–128. https://doi.org/10.1080/10168739900000048

Bahmani-Oskooee, M., Harvey, H., & Hegerty, S. (2014). Brazil–US commodity trade and the J-curve. *Applied Economics*, *46*(1), 1–13. https://doi.org/10.1080/00036846.2013.824548

Bahmani-Oskooee, M., & Hegerty, S. (2011). The J-curve and NAFTA: Evidence from commodity trade between the U.S. and Mexico. *Applied Economics*, *43*(13), 1579–1593. https://doi.org/10.1080/00036840802360328

Bahmani-Oskooee, M., & Kutan, A. (2009). The J-curve in the emerging economies of Eastern Europe. *Applied Economics*, *41*(20), 2523–2532. https://doi.org/10.1080/00036840701235696

Bahmani-Oskooee, M., & Ratha, A. (2004). The J-curve: A literature review. *Applied Economics*, *36*(13), 1377–1398. https://doi.org/10.1080/0003684042000201794

Baxa, J., & Šestorád, T. (2019). *The Czech exchange rate floor: Depreciation without Inflation?* CNB Working Paper Series 1. Czech National Bank.

Caselli, F. G. (2017). *Did the exchange rate floor prevent deflation in the Czech Republic?* IMF Working Paper 17/206. International Monetary Fund.

Franta, M., Holub, T., & Saxa, B. (2018). *Balance sheet implications of the Czech National Bank's exchange rate commitment.* CNB Working Papers no 10/2018. Czech National Bank.

Gürtler, M. (2019). Dynamic analysis of trade balance behavior in a small open economy: The J-curve phenomenon and the Czech economy. *Empirical Economics*, *56*(2), 469–497. https://doi.org/10.1007/s00181-018-1445-4

Hacker, R., & Hatemi, J. A. (2004). The effect of exchange rate changes on trade balances in the short and long run. Evidence from German trade with transitional central European economies. *The Economics of Transition*, *12*(4), 777–799. https://doi.org/10.1111/j.0967-0750.2004.00202.x

Hájek, J., & Horváth, R. (2016). Exchange rate pass-through in an emerging market: The case of the Czech Republic. *Emerging Markets Finance and Trade*, *52*(11), 2624–2635. https://doi.org/10.1080/1540496X.2015.1090823

Hsing, Y. (2009). Test of the J-curve for six selected new EU countries. *International Journal of Economic Policy in Emerging Economies*, *2*(1), 76–85. https://doi.org/10.1504/IJEPEE.2009.022942

Johansen, S. (1997). *Likelihood-based interference in cointegrated vector autoregressive models*. Oxford University Press.

Lerner, A. (1944). *The economics of control.* Macmillan.

Machlup, F. (1939). The theory of foreign exchanges. *Economica*, *6*(24), 375–397. https://doi.org/10.2307/2548881

Magee, S. P. (1973). *Currency contracts, pass through and devaluation.* Brooking papers on economic activity.

Mahdavi, S., & Sohrabian, A. (1993). The exchange value of the dollar and the US trade balance: An empirical investigation based on cointegration and granger causality tests. *The Quarterly Review of Economics and Finance*, *33*(4), 343–358. https://doi.org/10.1016/1062-9769(93)90003-3

Marshall, A. (1923). *Money, credit, and commerce*. Macmillan.

Mehrotra, A., & Schanz, J. (2020). *Financial market development, monetary policy and financial stability in emerging market economies.* BIS Papers No 113. Bank for International Settlements.

Mishkin, F. S. (1996). *The channels of monetary transmission: Lessons for monetary policy*. NBER Working Paper Series. National Bureau of Economic Research. No. 5464.

Morales, R. A., & Raei, F. (2013). *The evolving role of interest rate and exchange rate channels in monetary policy transmission in eac countries*. IMF Working Paper No WP/13/X. International Monetary Fund.

Nusair, S. A. (2013). *The J-curve in transition economies: An application of the ARDL model*. Academic and Business Research Institute.

Opatrný, M. (2017). Quantifying the effects of the CNB's exchange rate commitment: A synthetic control method approach. *Czech Journal of Economics and Finance*, *67*(6), 539–577.

Robinson, J. (1937). *Essays in the theory of employment*. Basil Blackwell.

Rose, A. K., & Yellen, J. L. (1989). Is there a J-curve? *Journal of Monetary Economics*, *24*, 53–68. https://doi.org/10.1016/0304-3932(89)90016-0

Šimáková, J. (2016). Cointegration approach to the estimation of the long-run relations between exchange rates and trade balances in Visegrad countries. *Financial Assets and Investing*, *3*(7), 37–57. https://doi.org/10.5817/FAI2016-3-3

Šimáková, J. (2017). Assessing exchange rate sensitivity of bilateral agricultural trade for the Visegrad countries. *Outlook on Agriculture*, *46*(3), 195–202. https://doi.org/10.1177/0030727017726207

Šimáková, J. (2021). The exchange rate as a determinant of the development of foreign trade in the agri-food industry in the Visegrad region. *Forum Scientiae Oeconomia*, *9*(2), 5–21. https://doi.org/10.23762/FSO_VOL9_NO2_1

Šimáková, J., & Stavárek, D. (2015). The effect of the exchange rate on industry-level trade flows in Czechia. *E+M Ekonomie a Management*, *18*(4), 150–165. https://doi.org/10.15240/tul/001/2015-4-011

Chapter 5

Exchange Rate Commitment of the Czech National Bank

Jan Černohorský[a], *Liběna Černohorská*[a] *and Petr Teplý*[b]

[a]University of Pardubice, Czechia
[b]Prague University of Economics and Business, Czechia

Abstract

The aim of this chapter is to describe the purpose of the introduction of the exchange rate commitment by the Czech National Bank (CNB) in the period from November 2013 to April 2017 and its effects on the real economy. The main reason for introducing the exchange rate commitment was concern about the possibility of a prolonged deflationary period in Czechia. Given that the standard monetary policy instruments had already been exhausted on easing the monetary policy conditions, the CNB Bank Board opted for an exchange rate commitment. The secondary objective of the exchange rate commitment was to boost the economy through the positive effect of a weaker koruna on exports. Next, we focus in more detail on the effect of the exchange rate commitment in the economy and the course of the foreign exchange interventions. Overall, we can summarize that the CNB's foreign exchange interventions were an extraordinary monetary policy instrument – in a market economy with inflation targeting and a flexible exchange rate – used in extraordinary times.

Keywords: Exchange rate commitment; foreign exchange interventions; foreign exchange rate; Czech National Bank; inflation; deflation

5.1 Introduction

The aim of this chapter is to describe the purpose of the introduction of the exchange rate commitment by the Czech National Bank (CNB) in the period from November 2013 to April 2017 and its effects on the real economy. The motivation for writing this chapter is that this is a non-standard use of monetary

Modeling Economic Growth in Contemporary Czechia, 71–86

Published under exclusive licence by Emerald Publishing Limited
doi:10.1108/978-1-83753-840-920241005

policy instruments. We were therefore interested in how this use has been reflected in the real economy. We focus on explaining the context of the use of the exchange rate commitment.

The first problem and the main reason for introducing the exchange rate commitment were concerns about the possibility of a prolonged deflationary period in Czechia. This means that the CNB's main objective – price stability quantified as an inflation rate of 2% +/− 1% – was not being achieved. Given that the standard monetary policy instruments had already been exhausted on easing the monetary policy conditions – the main 2T repo rate was at 0.05% – and forward guidance was not working, the CNB Bank Board opted for an exchange rate commitment. The secondary objective of the exchange rate commitment was to boost the economy through the positive effect of a weaker koruna on exports.

The CNB decided to introduce the exchange rate commitment on 7 November 2013 and it lasted until 6 April 2017. The exchange rate commitment specifically meant that the CNB committed to keeping the exchange rate of the Czech koruna to a euro exchange rate above CZK 27 per euro. In real terms, the CNB carried out foreign exchange interventions which, in their first phase, included the purchase of about EUR 7.5 billion for about CZK 202 billion. This artificially depreciated the exchange rate to just above the CZK 27 per euro floor level.

In this chapter, we draw on reasoning for introducing the exchange rate commitment, the functioning of the exchange rate commitment, effects of the exchange rate commitment on the economy and its criticism and finally the impact of exchange rate commitment on the exchange rate system and the CNB's foreign exchange reserves.

5.2 Reasoning for Introducing the Exchange Rate Commitment

When looking for the reasons for introducing the exchange rate commitment, we should start from the CNB's objective, which is determined by law and the constitution of Czechia, that is, to ensure price stability. To be specific, the CNB sees a 2% inflation rate (+/− 1%) as price stability. This inflation target is essential for all monetary policy operations, not only those taking place in the context of the exchange rate commitment. Once price stability is achieved, the CNB's next objective is, by law, to support the government's general economic policy, leading to sustainable economic growth. We will not focus on the CNB's second main objective – ensuring financial stability – in this chapter as it is not closely related to the discussed topic.

It is important to understand the economic context that preceded the introduction of this major monetary policy intervention. After the financial crisis that began in 2007 and which affected the entire developed world, the Czech economy was on a growth trajectory starting from 2010. However, in 2012, it again fell into a moderate recession with GDP recording a 1–2.2% year-on-year decrease in each quarter. This entailed a slight increase in the unemployment rate (from 6.8% in 2011 to 8.2% in 2013), a decrease in household income and consequently in household consumption (by 1.1% in 2012 compared to 2011) (Czech Statistical Office, 2023). Businesses cut back on investment (a 3.3% decrease in 2012 compared to 2011 and a 2.2% decrease in 2013 compared to 2012) and profits dropped. Against the backdrop of a moderate recession and inflation heading from a 2% to a 1% growth (Czech Statistical Office, 2023), the CNB decided to bring down the base interest rate – 2T repo rate – from 0.75% to 0.05% in three steps (Czech National Bank, 2023a). This also reduced the other two interest rates announced by the CNB – the Lombard rate to 0.25% and the discount rate to 0.05%. In terms of the main monetary policy rate, 'technical zero', that is, an interest rate that is not exactly zero but just above zero, was reached, primarily because of the calculations of penalties and fines in accordance with law. This consequently resulted in an unprecedented easing of the monetary conditions with the main objective of preventing the Czech economy from falling into deflation. At the same time, the CNB announced that if the inflation rate did not return to its 2% inflation target, it was prepared to depreciate the exchange rate to avert any threat of deflation. In addition, the CNB's senior officials significantly increased their communication aimed at the professional and lay public and implemented 'forward guidance' leading to the depreciation of the koruna. This instrument's effect on the market lasted approximately one year and caused the koruna to depreciate by several tenths of a koruna. Starting from March 2013, forward guidance introduced by the CNB presented an early indication of the future direction of its monetary policy. By introducing it, it sought to influence the expectations of economic operators and thus accelerate economic recovery and inflation. However, the disinflationary trend in the economy was getting stronger, and the CNB's models expected a fall into deflation in 2014 (Czech National Bank, 2023a).

Deflation could, in the long term, create a deflationary–recessionary spiral because the long-term effects include but are not limited to a decrease in the prices of all goods in the economy, a decrease in wages and layoffs, an increase in the real costs of businesses and a decline in investment. This implies that the ultimate consequence of deflation is a deterioration of the economic situation, which is manifested by a decline in the economy's product and a rise in unemployment (Černohorský, 2020). Another issue brought about by deflation is ineffective monetary policy. As part of monetary policy, nominal interest rates can be reduced to zero to support economic growth (which the CNB already did in 2012), but real interest rates rise if deflation increases in the economy. At that point, monetary policy has no choice but to wait for the deflationary period to pass because there is no way to ease it by means of interest rates. Other negative effects of inflation are mentioned by, for example, Bagus (2020) and Koziol (2010). Eichengreen et al. (2017) discuss not only the negative aspects but also the possible positive aspects. Further historical context of deflation is represented by Bordo and Filardo (2005).

5.3 The Functioning of the Exchange Rate Commitment

Therefore, at its meeting held on 7 November 2013, the CNB Bank Board decided to introduce foreign exchange interventions, specifically to purchase bonds denominated in euro worth around EUR 7.5 billion for around CZK 202 billion (Czech National Bank, 2023a). This depreciated the exchange rate of the Czech koruna on the market and then, at a press conference, the CNB Governor announced an exchange rate commitment in the form of an exchange rate floor of CZK 27 per euro, which would last at least until the end of 2014. This threshold meant that the Czech koruna would depreciate by approximately 5.5%. The exchange rate commitment announced by the CNB was asymmetric because only the exchange rate minimum threshold was determined. The CNB declared that it would not intervene to strengthen the koruna towards 27 CZK/EUR if the koruna were significantly weaker. The specific CZK/EUR exchange rates are shown in the Fig. 5.1.

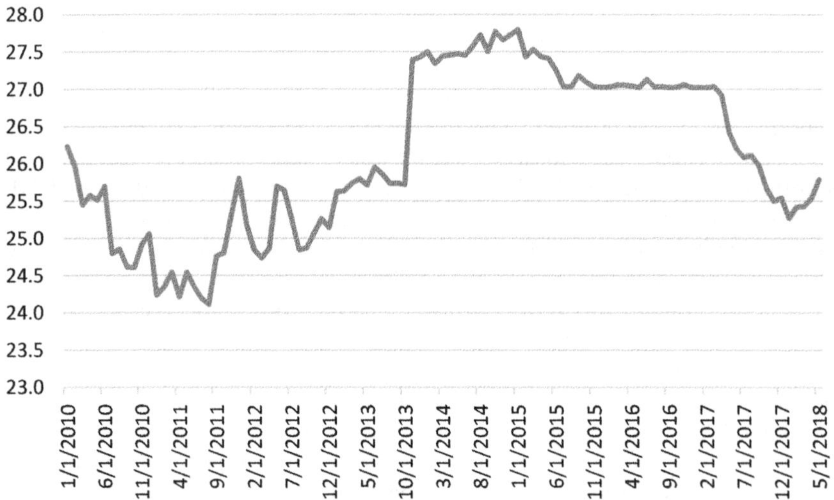

Fig. 5.1. CZK/EUR Exchange Rate Development. *Source:* CNB (2023b).

It should be noted that the CNB's objective did not change in any way as has sometimes been misinterpreted. The exchange rate commitment was used as an additional instrument to achieve the price stability objective.

The CNB's actions described above can be illustrated schematically as shown in Fig. 5.2.

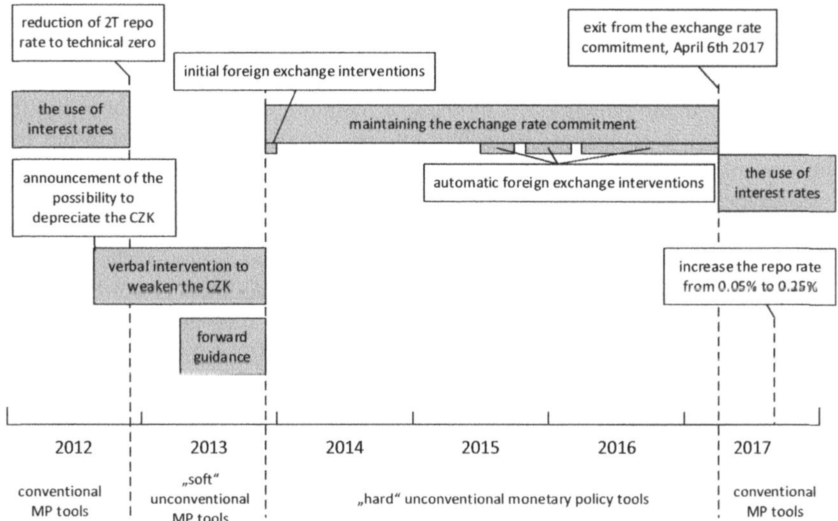

Fig. 5.2. Use of CNB Tools Between 2012 and 2017. *Source:* Authors' Illustration Based on Rusnok (2018).

Other unconventional monetary policy instruments used by some foreign central banks included quantitative easing and negative interest rates, for example, the European Central Bank (Černohorská & Teplý, 2019). The CNB did not opt for these two instruments for the reasons described below.

Quantitative easing was not chosen because surplus liquidity, that is, surplus of 'interbank money', existed in the Czech banking sector for a relatively long time. In other words, if a bank had needed financial resources to continue lending to its clients, there would certainly have been several banks in the Czech banking sector that had such free resources. It was therefore unnecessary to increase interbank liquidity and, consequently, the amount of money in circulation.

The CNB did not opt for setting negative interest rates because it had no experience with the instrument and central bankers were unable to predict how far the main interest rate would have to fall. In addition, the purpose of negative interest rates is to prevent commercial banks from holding their available liquidity with the central bank and lending it to clients, which was not a major problem in Czechia.

On the contrary, an exchange rate commitment in the form of depreciating the Czech koruna seemed the most appropriate because the Czech economy is a small open economy, that is, exports and imports account for a large share of its GDP. This effect works for economies with positive net exports, which was the case of Czechia at the time. Therefore, the use of the exchange rate channel of the monetary policy transmission mechanism was seen as the most effective and swiftest option. As mentioned above, a weaker koruna has a positive effect on exports and a negative effect on the price of imports, which makes this measure suitable for aiming at both increasing the inflation rate and boosting economic growth.

Two other central banks of countries with small and open economies decided to use the same unconventional instrument. This included the Swiss National Bank (SNB), which used foreign exchange interventions from 2008 to January 2015. In addition to the aforementioned motives of avoiding deflation and boosting the economy, the Swiss central bank had another important reason for using this instrument. It was the fact that in times of crisis, the Swiss franc (CHF) becomes a safe haven for investors. Whenever a crisis erupts, investors sell the currencies of small economies due to fears of such currencies depreciating and buy, among other things, the Swiss franc. This results in a significant appreciation of the currency, which is a major factor slowing down the growth of the Swiss economy (due to disadvantaged exports). After one-off interventions in 2008 and 2010, the SNB decided to enter the intervention regime in September 2011 with an exchange rate commitment of CHF 1.2 per euro. The SNB committed to not letting the franc fall below this threshold. The SNB ended this regime in January 2015. After this date, the franc appreciated significantly and settled around the CHF 1.05 per euro level. That means that the ultimate effect of the interventions was the opposite. The reason for discontinuing the intervention regime was the fear of quantitative easing by the ECB, which would have most likely led to further pressures on the appreciation of the franc. The other, rather specific reason was the SNB shareholders' (Swiss cantons') fear of significant losses for the SNB due to the abnormal exchange rate risk resulting from holding large amounts of assets in foreign currencies. The SNB then used negative interest rates to ease the monetary conditions.

The Bank of Israel (BoI) primarily decided to intervene because it wanted to increase its foreign exchange reserves. Other reasons included its fear of imminent deflation and a too strong shekel (Israel's currency). The BoI carried out foreign exchange interventions from 2008 to 2011. The BoI then intervened occasionally in 2013 and 2015. The BoI committed to keeping the shekel (NIS) at the NIS 3.8 per USD level. It achieved it by buying US dollars (USD) in the amount of USD 25 million per day (later USD 100 million per day). It then stopped applying this quantitative limit and bought USD without restrictions but only when needed (not daily).

5.4 Effects of the Exchange Rate Commitment on the Economy and Its Criticism

The effects of the exchange rate commitment on the real economy can be well illustrated using selected macroeconomic indicators presented in the following tables. Table 5.1 shows clear year-on-year changes in selected macroeconomic indicators after one year of the exchange rate commitment.

Table 5.2 shows year-on-year changes in selected macroeconomic indicators after 2 years of the exchange rate commitment. Both tables show positive developments in most indicators – GDP growth, including the household consumption and company investment segments, a decline in the unemployment rate, an increase in average nominal wages and the number of vacancies, a growth in gross profits of business and retail revenues. More significant changes can be observed in selected macroeconomic indicators after the 2 years of the exchange rate commitment. The only objective, which was not successfully achieved, was

Table 5.1. Changes in Selected Macroeconomic Indicators One Year After the Introduction of the Exchange Rate Commitment.

	Year-On-Year Changes in %			
	Data Available as of 07/11/2013		Data Available as of 07/11/2014	
GDP	11/2013	−1.3	11/2014	2.5
Household consumption	11/2013	0.0	11/2014	0.9
Company investments	11/2013	−5.2	11/2014	2.8
Consumer price index	9/2013	1.0	9/2014	0.7
General unemployment rate	9/2013	7.1	9/2014	5.9
Average nominal wage	11/2013	1.2	11/2014	2.3
Number of vacancies	9/2013	39,040	9/2014	56,600
Gross operating surplus of non-financial corporations	11/2013	1.3	11/2014	
Retail sales	9/2013	−0.1	9/2014	2.8

Source: CNB (2023c).

Table 5.2. Changes in Selected Macroeconomic Indicators 2 Years After the Introduction of the Exchange Rate Commitment.

	Year-On-Year Changes in %			
	Data Available as of 07/11/2013		Data Available as of 07/11/2015	
GDP	11/2013	−1.3	11/2015	4.4
Household consumption	11/2013	0.0	11/2015	3.1
Company investments	11/2013	−5.2	11/2015	5.9
Consumer price index	9/2013	1.0	9/2015	0.2
General unemployment rate	9/2013	7.1	9/2015	4.9
Average nominal wage	11/2013	1.2	11/2015	3.4
Number of vacancies	9/2013	39,040	9/2015	107,324
Gross operating surplus of non-financial corporations	11/2013	1.3	11/2015	9.2
Retail sales	9/2013	−0.1	9/2015	9.5

Source: Hampl (2015).

reaching the targeted 2% inflation rate measured using the consumer price index. Instead, the inflation rate dropped even closer to zero. This is also the reason why the exchange rate commitment lasted longer than originally anticipated. In this context, it should be noted that the CNB, as the central bank of a small and open economy, can only influence the inflation rate to a certain extent, while Czech exports and imports are largely dependent on global trade and price developments. Given that the prices of the main raw materials were decreasing in the analyzed period, this was also reflected in the prolonged disinflationary pressures in Czechia.

The primarily positive development of macroeconomic variables was, of course, not caused only by the CNB's exchange rate commitment but by the parallel effects of a number of other factors, including a positive effect from abroad. Nevertheless, it is undeniable that the CNB's exchange rate commitment contributed significantly to the positive development of the Czech economy in 2014–2015.

The CNB's initial foreign exchange intervention amounting to CZK 202 billion and the public announcement of the exchange rate commitment convinced the markets and the koruna remained above the threshold without any problems until the summer of 2015 without the need for further interventions. Starting in the summer of 2015, however, the CNB had to gradually carry out further interventions consisting of euro purchases. Finally, foreign exchange interventions reached their highest volume just before they ended in Q1 2017 – see Fig. 5.3.

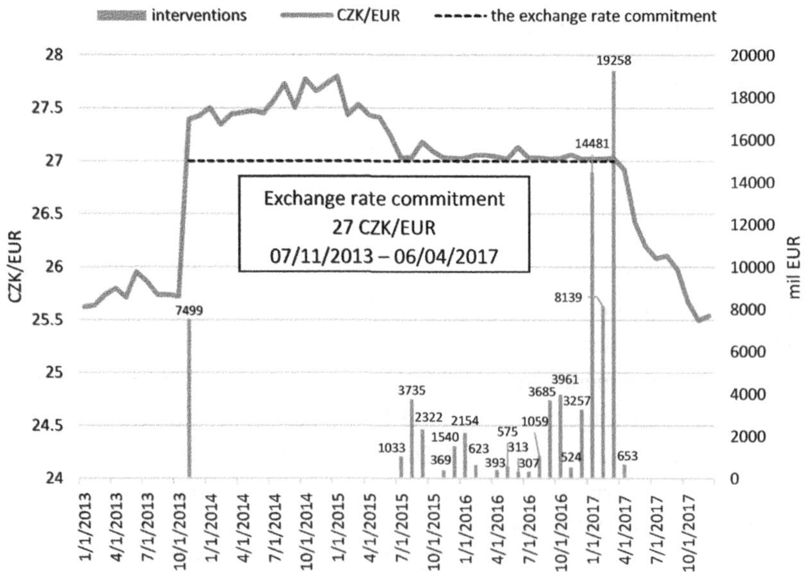

Fig. 5.3. The Course of the CNB's Foreign Exchange Interventions. *Source:* Rusnok (2018).

The figure also shows what was already stated above, that is, that only one intervention by the CNB depreciating the Czech koruna in November 2013 and the public and transparent announcement of the exchange rate commitment were all that was needed in the first year and a half of the exchange rate commitment. During this time, the CNB only verbally confirmed its commitment in official documents and communication. In reality, it did not have to buy euros on the financial markets at all. During the period in question, the exchange rate remained significantly above the 27 CZK per EUR commitment level and only started to approach this level in July 2015. Since then, the CNB intervened every month (except October 2015 and March 2016) in small volumes until the end of 2016 (mostly up to EUR 1 billion, twice it had to buy around EUR 2.3 billion and four times more than EUR 3.5 billion). The largest volume of foreign exchange interventions to maintain the exchange rate commitment was recorded in Q1 2017. The successive transactions included the purchases of EUR 14.5 billion in January 2017, EUR 8.1 billion in February 2017 and EUR 19.3 billion in March of the same year. The CNB's highest foreign exchange interventions were driven by the financial market speculation that the exchange rate commitment would be abandoned, creating pressure on the koruna to appreciate. In early April 2017, the CNB cancelled the exchange rate commitment, but before that it had to buy nearly EUR 0.7 billion.

The initial exchange rate commitment applied to a period of over 1 year, specifically until the end of 2014. In Q3 2014, the CNB extended the exchange rate commitment until Q3 2015 justifying it as follows: *By that time, domestic inflationary pressures should sufficiently recover as a result of the economic recovery and wage growth which should then allow a return to the standard monetary policy regime. This return should, however, not lead to an appreciation of the exchange rate to the level prior to the CNB's interventions because, in the meantime, the weaker exchange rate of the koruna will permeate through to the price level and other nominal variables* (CNB, 2014). The end date of the exchange rate commitment was then extended three more times, each time essentially accompanied by the above explanation and the addition that *the subsequent return to the standard monetary policy regime will not bring about an appreciation of the exchange rate to the level prior to the CNB interventions* (CNB, 2023a). This statement was very important because the 'exit from the exchange rate commitment' was a much discussed and feared step given the experience of the Swiss central bank. Fearing the effects of quantitative easing by the European Central Bank and under the pressure from its shareholders, the SNB exited the exchange rate commitment early and the resulting effect of its foreign exchange interventions was exactly the opposite of what was originally intended as the Swiss franc appreciated to a level higher than before the foreign exchange interventions.

The exit from the exchange rate commitment in Czechia was then further postponed three more times, specifically in November 2014, February 2015 and May 2016 when it was decided that the CNB would use the exchange rate as a monetary policy instrument until mid-2017. After this period, the CNB stated that a gradual increase in interest rates was in line with its forecast.

The characteristics of the exchange rate commitment, that is, its validity, changes, exit date and period of validity from its announcement or confirmation, are shown in the Table 5.3.

The CNB decided to end foreign exchange interventions in early April 2017 (i.e. right at the start of Q2 2017) because the inflation target had been reached. At the same time, the pressures on the koruna's appreciation were already increasing significantly as the end of the exchange rate commitment approached, which forced the CNB to continue to intervene significantly to keep its promise.

Foreign exchange interventions thus contributed to the recovery of economic growth and to a gradual rise in inflation towards its target. Ending the foreign exchange intervention regime was thus the first step towards the gradual normal implementation of monetary policy, mainly through interest rates. Since 2017, the CNB has raised interest rates in several steps (8 times in total) and, as one of only a few central banks, it succeeded to reach their normal equilibrium level before the coronavirus crisis erupted.

Table 5.3. Characteristics of the Foreign Exchange Rate Commitment.

Change in the Exit From the Exchange Rate Commitment	Month and Year of Establishment/ Confirmation of the Exchange Rate Commitment	Inflation Report Number	Date of Exit From the Exchange Rate Commitment (Quarters)	Duration of the Exchange Rate Commitment Since the Last Confirmation/ Change in Months
–	November 2013	IV/2013	*IV/2014*	13
No	February 2014	I/2014	IV/2014	10
No	April 2014	11/2014	IV/2014	8
Yes	August 2014	III/2014	*III/2015*	13
Yes	November 2014	IV/2014	*I/2016*	16
Yes	February 2015	I/2015	*IV/2016*	22
No	May 2015	II/2015	IV/2016	19
No	August 2015	III/2015	IV/2016	16
No	November 2015	IV/2015	IV/2016	13
No	February 2016	I/2016	IV/2016	10
Yes	May 2016	II/2016	*II/2017*	13
No	August 2016	III/2016	II/2017	10
No	November 2016	IV/2016	II/2017	7
No	February 2017	I/2017	II/2017	4

Source: Authors' Results Based on CNB (2023a).

Naturally, the CNB's foreign exchange interventions were criticized by some economists. One group of economists argues that the foreign exchange interventions should not have been implemented at all. Firstly, because foreign exchange interventions do not fit our type of economy as they are not a market instrument. They also claim that the economy was not facing any serious crisis, the trade balance was significantly positive and there was no threat of any significant currency appreciation. They emphasize that short-term moderate deflation is not harmful to the economy. It is difficult to assess this argument because the situation cannot be reversed and the development without foreign exchange interventions cannot be tested under real conditions. Furthermore, the CNB's backward-looking models show an even more pessimistic economic development (deeper and longer depression, longer recession) than at the time of the decision to use the exchange rate commitment (CNB, 2023a).

Another group of economists admit that the foreign exchange interventions were necessary, but they have some reservations. The most frequent argument is that the foreign exchange interventions should have started and ended earlier. However, this criticism was expressed several years after they were in place. Another argument is that the resulting foreign exchange reserves reached a level significantly higher than is appropriate for this type of economy. There were concerns about their subsequent sale, which would then again increase the pressure on the appreciation of the Czech koruna.

It was also criticized that the depreciation of the exchange rate had a minor effect on most companies because most export-oriented businesses incurred a significant part of their costs in euro. In other words, these businesses used natural hedging against exchange rate fluctuations.

The criticism of the exchange rate commitment being too short term, as it lasted for 10–13 months in most of the 41-month period, is certainly of significance. This period of roughly 1 year was too short in terms of business investment planning and therefore could not have had a major impact on investment formation and consequently on economic growth. Only from November 2014 to August 2015, this was a 15- to 22-month commitment. On the other hand, the primary objective of the CNB's exchange rate commitment was to avert impending deflation, not to support any economic operators.

The last major factor pointed out by critics of foreign exchange interventions was that they primarily helped businesses generating low added value. In addition, the critics argued that by artificially depreciating the Czech koruna, Czechia lost several years of convergence towards the West.

In defence of the central bankers in office at the time, it should be mentioned that it was obviously very difficult to make decisions under such extraordinary and uncertain circumstances. The truth is that the CNB Bank Board started talking about foreign exchange interventions as early as late 2012, and the CNB proceeded with foreign exchange interventions only after a year of discussions.

5.5 The Exchange Rate System and the CNB's Foreign Exchange Reserves

The CNB decided to use this unconventional instrument because its main instrument could no longer be used to ease monetary policy further to bring the inflation rate close to the inflation target of 2% +/− 1%. At the same time, the CNB did not want to abandon the exchange rate commitment until it was certain that the koruna would not appreciate to a level higher than before the foreign exchange interventions. Furthermore, the CNB wanted to start raising interest rates again as soon as possible to return to the standard implementation of monetary policy. To illustrate, Fig. 5.4 shows the interest rates announced by the CNB between 2006 and 2022, that is, before, during and after the exchange rate commitment.

The interest rate trajectory clearly shows the phases when the central bank pursued standard monetary policy and used interest rate setting. This period ends in October 2013. In the subsequent period from November 2013 to March 2017, it used the exchange rate as an additional instrument, that is, it pursued unconventional monetary policy. In April 2017, it started to use interest rates again, which is referred to as the 'normalization of monetary policy'. Specifically, the CNB first raised interest rates by quarter of a percentage point in August 2017 and half of a percentage point in November 2017. The subsequent rapid interest rate reduction in 2020 is already associated with the response to the coronavirus crisis and, conversely, the sharp increase in interest rates is a response to the significant increase in the inflation rate in Czechia. However, the target remains the same – price stability, that is, an inflation rate of 2% +/− 1%.

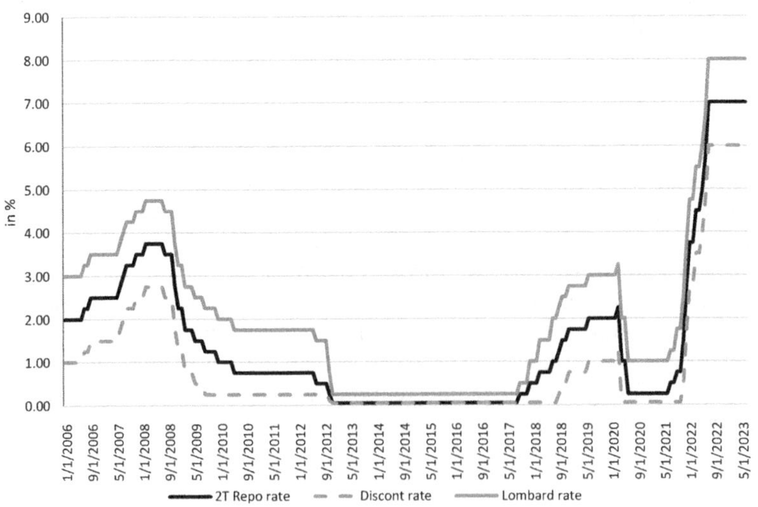

Fig. 5.4. CNB Interest Rate Development. *Source:* CNB (2023c).

In addition, we could classify the exchange rate systems used before, during and after the exchange rate commitment. For example, the International Monetary Fund (IMF) classified the Czech koruna exchange rate system as 'free floating' until November 2013. With this system, the IMF acknowledges that the central bank may, on an exceptional basis, carry out foreign exchange interventions to address adverse market conditions (specifically, a maximum of three interventions lasting no more than 3 days each, over a 6-month period). Monetary policy is thus independent and focuses only on achieving its objectives (IMF, 2019). The CNB has defined the Czech koruna exchange rate system as managed floating, which means that it evolves based on supply and demand and that the CNB can intervene in the event of significant fluctuations or changes that do not correspond to market pressures. In the more than 10 years before the exchange rate commitment, however, the CNB did not intervene at all and left the development of the Czech koruna exchange rate to market forces. At the time, the exchange rate commitment was implemented, the IMF changed the classification of the Czech koruna exchange rate system from 'free floating' to 'other managed arrangements' (IMF, 2014). This is a subset of soft peg exchange rates, that is, exchange rates that are managed by the central bank to a certain extent. Usually, this is used by the central bank of a given country to target the money supply. However, Czechia was the only country in this sub-category that targeted inflation. Essentially, this meant that this exchange rate system was difficult to fit into the categories used before. This classification continued in 2014. In 2015, the exchange rate classification changed to stabilized arrangements, which is characterized by IMF (2019) as follows: *Classification as a stabilized arrangement entails a spot market exchange rate that remains within a margin of 2% for six months or more (with the exception of a specified number of outliers or step adjustments) and is not floating*. This classification continued until 2017. In 2018, the IMF re-classified the Czech koruna as 'floating', which the IMF (2019) describes as follows: *Foreign exchange market intervention may be either direct or indirect, and such intervention serves to moderate the rate of change and prevent undue fluctuations in the exchange rate, but policies targeting a specific level of the exchange rate are incompatible with floating.* This means that it is still not free floating. In 2021, the Czech koruna was again reclassified by the IMF as 'free floating' (IMF, 2022).

Before the introduction of the exchange rate commitment, the CNB's foreign exchange reserves were EUR 34.8 billion, equivalent to 3.7 times the volume of monthly imports into Czechia. This is considered the standard level of foreign exchange reserves for developed countries without a fixed exchange rate. Immediately after the announcement of the exchange rate commitment and after the first purchases of EUR 7.5 billion, they increased to EUR 40.8 billion (17.5% increase), which was equivalent to 4.6 times the monthly imports.

The CNB did not intervene until the summer of 2015, yet its foreign exchange reserves increased to EUR 51.4 billion (5.4 times the monthly imports), thanks to the positive effect of foreign exchange interventions on exports. The following significant increase in foreign exchange reserves due to the interventions occurred in August 2015. This was an increase from EUR 51.4 billion to EUR 54.7 billion

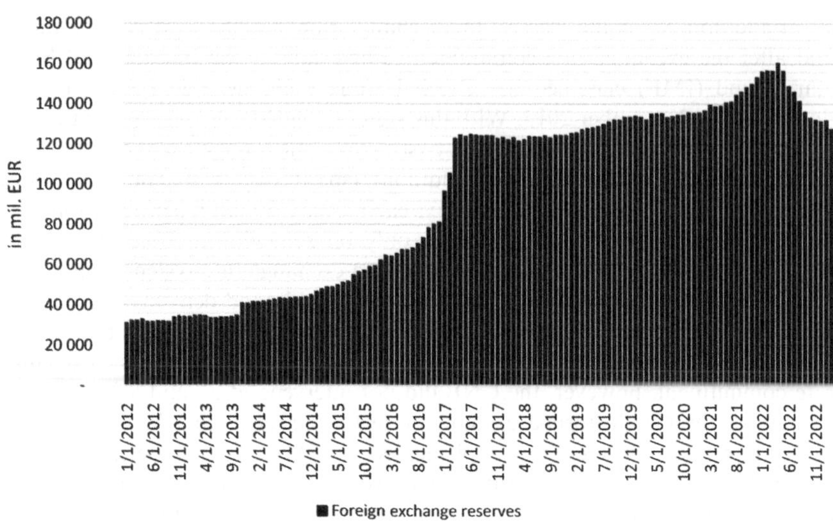

Fig. 5.5. Size of the CNB's Foreign Exchange Reserves. *Source:* CNB (2023c).

(i.e. 6.3%), equivalent to 6.7 times the monthly imports. From August 2015, the CNB intervened almost every month until its foreign exchange reserves rose to EUR 81.3 billion at the end of 2016, representing 8.9 times the monthly imports.

The most significant interventions took place in Q1 2017 when foreign exchange reserves gradually increased month-on-month by 18.8% in January, 9.3% in February and 16.5% in March to EUR 122.9 billion. This value was equivalent to 11.1 times the monthly imports.

Overall, the foreign exchange reserves increased more than 3.5 times over the exchange rate commitment period from November 2013 to April 2017. The trajectory of the CNB's foreign exchange reserves is shown in Fig. 5.5, clearly illustrating the increase in the foreign exchange reserves held during the exchange rate commitment.

For the sake of greater clarity, Table 5.4 shows selected significant month-on-month changes in the amount of the CNB's foreign exchange reserves.

5.6 Conclusion

The CNB's foreign exchange interventions were an extraordinary monetary policy instrument (in a market economy with inflation targeting and a flexible exchange rate) used in extraordinary times. From 2013, the Czech economy was at risk of deflation and at the same time the CNB's main inflation target of 2% +/− 1% was not being achieved. Given that the CNB had already exhausted its main monetary policy instrument a year earlier, that is, at the end of 2012 (it dropped the main interest rate

Table 5.4. Selected Values and Changes in Foreign Exchange Reserves.

Date	Mil EUR	M/M Growth	Foreign Exchange Reserves/Monthly Imports
31 October 2013	34,788		3.7
31 November 2013	40,864	17.5%	4.6
31 July 2015	51,447		5.4
31 August 2015	54,668	6.3%	6.7
31 December 2016	81,345		8.9
31 January 2017	96,604	18.8%	10.3
28 February 2017	105,552	9.3%	11.3
31 March 2017	122,946	16.5%	11.1

Source: CNB (2023c) and Authors' Calculations.

to 0.05%), and forward guidance aimed at depreciating the Czech koruna had not been working, the CNB decided to intervene and depreciate the Czech koruna. This depreciation represented an approximately 5.5% decline in the CZK/EUR exchange rate, but it was not a significant change in the longer term. Positive changes in the economy were already evident during the following year. The CNB's secondary objective and, at the same time, an objective pursued by the foreign exchange interventions, boosting the economy, was therefore met. The only objective that was not achieved was increasing inflation towards the 2% target. This state was prolonged during this period and it was caused by exogenous shocks in the form of decreasing commodity and food prices on world markets. However, the actual inflation rate gradually began to approach the target and the CNB was able to exit the exchange rate commitment in early April 2017 and return to standard monetary policy in the form of setting monetary policy rates. The CNB thus eventually and with a longer delay than originally expected achieved its statutory objective.

Acknowledgements

This chapter was supported by the Czech Science Foundation (Project No. GA 20-00178S), the Prague University of Economics and Business (Project No. VSE IP100040) and the University of Pardubice (Project No. SGS_2023_12).

References

Bagus, P. (2020). The anti-deflation bias. *Acta Oeconomica*, *70*(2), 147–161. https://doi.org/10.1556/032.2020.00008

Bordo, M., & Filardo, A. (2005). Deflation and monetary policy in a historical perspective: Remembering the past or being condemned to repeat it? *Economic Policy*, *20*(44), 799–844. https://doi.org/10.1111/j.1468-0327.2005.00151.x

Černohorská, L., & Teplý, P. (2019). Monetary policy after the 2007–2009 global financial crisis in the context of systemic risk. In R. F. Frait (Ed.), *Systematic risk in post-crisis financial markets* (pp. 48–58). University of Finance and Administration. https://doi.org/10.37355/03.2019/2

Černohorský, J. (2020). *Finance – od teorie k realitě*. Grada.

Czech National Bank. (2014, August 7). Inflation Report III/2014. https://www.cnb.cz/export/sites/cnb/cs/menova-politika/.galleries/zpravy_o_inflaci/2014/2014_III/download/zoi_III_2014.pdf

Czech National Bank. (2023a, March 17). Inflation Reports Archive. https://www.cnb.cz/cs/menova-politika/zpravy-o-inflaci/

Czech National Bank. (2023b, March 15). *Selected exchange rates*. https://www.cnb.cz/cs/financni-trhy/devizovy-trh/kurzy-devizoveho-trhu/kurzy-devizoveho-trhu/grafy_form.html

Czech National Bank. (2023c, March 17). *Time series database ARAD*. https://www.cnb.cz/docs/ARADY/HTML/index.htm

Czech Statistical Office. (2023, March 15). *National accounts databases*. https://apl.czso.cz/pll/rocenka/rocenkavyber.makroek_vydaj

Eichengreen, B., Park, D., & Shin, K. (2017). Should the dangers of deflation be dismissed? *Journal of Macroeconomics*, *52*, 287–307. https://doi.org/10.1016/j.jmacro.2017.04.003

Hampl, M. (2015, November 18). *The CNB's exchange rate commitment and the myths surrounding it*. Presentation for partners of the CNB branch in Hradec Králové.

International Monetary Fund. (2014, October). *Annual Report on Exchange Arrangements and Exchange Restrictions 2014*. https://www.imf.org/external/pubs/nft/2014/areaers/ar2014.pdf

International Monetary Fund. (2019, April 16). *Annual Report on Exchange Arrangements and Exchange Restrictions 2018*. https://www.imf.org/en/Publications/Annual-Report-on-Exchange-Arrangements-and-Exchange-Restrictions/Issues/2019/04/24/Annual-Report-on-Exchange-Arrangements-and-Exchange-Restrictions-2018-46162

International Monetary Fund. (2022, July 7). *Annual Report on Exchange Arrangements and Exchange Restrictions 2021*. https://www.imf.org/en/Publications/Annual-Report-on-Exchange-Arrangements-and-Exchange-Restrictions/Issues/2022/07/19/Annual-Report-on-Exchange-Arrangements-and-Exchange-Restrictions-2021-465689

Koziol, W. (2010). Deflation and investment activities of banks. The case of Japan in the years 1993–2008. *Equilibrium. Quarterly Journal of Economics and Economic Policy*, *4*(1), 191–201. https://doi.org/10.12775/EQUIL.2010.015

Rusnok, J. (2018, November 14). *Monetary policy of the CNB in times of economic crisis and boom*. Czech National Bank. https://www.cnb.cz/export/sites/cnb/cs/verejnost/.galleries/pro_media/konference_projevy/vystoupeni_projevy/download/rusnok_20181114_kosice.pdf

Chapter 6

Dilemma of the Czech National Bank: Factors of Adverse Macroeconomic Development in Czechia

Petr Rozmahel and Marek Litzman

Mendel University in Brno, Czechia

Abstract

This chapter elaborates on the main factors of the adverse macroeconomic development in Czechia and Europe. Currently, i.e. from 2022, Czechia mainly suffers from double-digit galloping inflation and GDP stagnation. The aim of this chapter is to identify and describe the influence of the main factors from the present and the more distant past on current inflation and approaching stagflation in Czechia. This chapter analyzes an unfavourable mix of demand and supply factors that leave the new banking board of the CNB facing a dilemma, that is, whether to pursue a disinflationary policy of increasing interest rates and thus push the Czech economy closer into recession or to rely on demand-driven economic growth, which will keep unemployment at a low level, but at the same time contribute to inflationary pressures. The new governor of the CNB completely changed the strategy of his predecessor and, despite strong criticism, did not raise interest rates even once. Based on the analysis of inflationary factors, this chapter tries to explain the motives for the Central Bank's new strategy in the fight against inflation, which is the systematic appreciation of the Czech koruna.

Keywords: CNB; Czech koruna; foreign exchange interventions; galloping inflation; monetary policy; stagflation

6.1 Introduction

During the previous 20 years, the Czech economy, like most European countries, went through all phases of the business cycle, including periods of mild deflation

Modeling Economic Growth in Contemporary Czechia, 87–101

Published under exclusive licence by Emerald Publishing Limited
doi:10.1108/978-1-83753-840-920241006

and high inflation. The factors that influenced the development of the economy during this period, including measures of stabilization and pro-growth macroeconomic policies, are reflected in today's development to varying degrees. Currently, from the beginning of 2022, Czechia is facing double-digit galloping inflation and GDP stagnation. Depending on the expected measures of the Czech National Bank (CNB) and the development of external factors, the fear of stagflation persists. Demand and above all negative external supply shocks contributed to the growth of inflation in Czechia. The inflation rate was 11% in February 2022, and in January 2023 it was already 17.5% in Czechia.

In July 2022, the governor of the CNB Jiří Rusnok, who set a clear policy of increasing interest rates, left his post. Rather surprisingly, he was replaced by a member of the bank board who had previous experience mainly in the commercial sphere, Aleš Michl. The new governor since the beginning of his term of office has faced growing criticism from economic experts, politicians and the interested public for having radically changed the current course of the CNB's monetary policy and not once during his tenure so far changing interest rates. However, in order to understand the reasons for the apparent hesitation and indecision of the CNB governor, it is important to take into account all the significant factors that contribute to the current inflation in Czechia and in Europe, and whose source of influence goes back to the deep past of the previous 20 years. It is also necessary to consider the significant slowdown of the Czech economy, which entered the recession phase at the beginning of 2023.

This chapter is devoted to a descriptive analysis of the factors that contribute to the current unfavourable development in the Czech economy and cause the dilemma of the CNB, that is, whether or not to raise interest rates. In particular, the aim of this chapter is to identify and describe the influence of the main factors from the present and the more distant past on current inflation and approaching stagflation in Czechia. The new governor of the CNB completely changed the strategy of the previous governor and, despite strong criticism, did not raise interest rates even once for more than a year. Accordingly, based on the analysis of inflationary factors, this chapter tries to explain the motives for the Central Bank's new strategy in the fight against inflation, which is the systematic appreciation of the Czech koruna.

6.2 Two Decades of Macroeconomic Turbulence in Europe and Worldwide

The new millennium started promisingly in the European Union (EU), especially for the countries of Central and Eastern Europe. In addition to the fact that 2004 marked the moment of their entry into the EU, it was also a period of continuous growth. The economic growth of these countries culminated in 2007, when, for example, Slovakia achieved GDP growth of 11%, Slovenia 7%, Poland 7% and Czechia 6%. The growth of the countries of Central and Eastern Europe contrasted with the slower growth of the original member countries and the rest of the EU.

The fall of the American bank Lehman Brothers in 2008 started a global economic crisis that affected all developed countries, including the economies of the EU. In the following year, the US economy and almost all EU member states experienced a decline in real GDP, with the average decline in GDP in the EU as a whole amounting to −4.3%. The period after the crisis year of 2008 can be described as a long-lasting stagnation, which was noticeable especially in Europe. In the period 2010–2019, the economic growth of GDP in Europe ranged from −0.7% (2012) to 2.8% (2017). Despite the European Central Bank's (ECB) active policy of quantitative easing, the expected recovery did not occur. Compared to the cautious ECB, the Federal Reserve System (FED) chose a policy of massive quantitative easing. However, this monetary expansion also did not lead to significant effects, as in the following almost 10-year period, the American economy grew at low GDP growth rates in the range of 1.5% (2011)–2.9% (2018).

However, this period of long-lasting stagnation was also characterized by a low-inflationary environment, when inflation reached very low and often zero values. Back in the crisis year of 2008, the average annual inflation rate in the EU reached 4.2%. The economies of Central and Eastern Europe recorded comparable or slightly higher price level growth, e.g. Poland 4.2%, Slovakia 4.6%, Slovenia 5.6%, Hungary 6% and Czechia 6.4%. In the very following year, 2009, in accordance with the fall in aggregate demand, inflation decreased to values approaching zero. Average inflation in 2009 was 0.8% in the EU as a whole.

For the next 10 years, inflation in the EU and the United States oscillated between 0% and 3%, while the years 2014–2016 were exceptional in this sense, when inflation reached values of 0.2 in the EU; −0.1 and 0.2%. In 2015, the EU thus recorded a slight deflation. In 2014, the price level fell in 16 countries out of a total of 28. The deepest deflation was recorded in Greece, where the price level decreased by −2.5%. Among the countries of Central and Eastern Europe, for example, Poland −0.9% (2015), Slovenia −0.5% (2015) and Slovakia −0.5% (2016) recorded deflation. Even deeper deflation in Europe during this period was reported by, for example, Bulgaria in the amount of −1.4% (2014), Romania −1.5% (2016) or Croatia −1.1% (2016), which joined the EU later in 2007 or 2013. This period was an unprecedented experience for Europe, when it aimed its monetary policy not only at supporting economic growth but also at increasing inflation. This period was characterized by European states' fears of deflation. In 2014, the ECB responded by significantly reducing interest rates, when in June 2014, for the first time, a decision was made to introduce a negative interest rate on the deposit facility to −0.1%. Contrary to expectations, the policy of negative interest rates due to fears of deflation and economic stagnation persisted in Europe until 2022, when, on the contrary, significant inflationary pressures began to manifest themselves in most European economies. Malovaná et al. (2020) examine the adverse effects of a prolonged period of low interest rates from different perspectives.

In the period of price level stagnation associated with fears of deflation, especially between 2014 and 2016, central banks tried to prevent deflation and start inflation in various ways. While the ECB followed the path of quantitative easing of monetary policy and negative interest rates, the CNB chose the path of targeted depreciation of the exchange rate of the Czech koruna. In November

2013, the CNB announced an exchange rate commitment to depreciate the exchange rate of the Czech koruna by means of foreign exchange interventions. The CNB considered this instrument to be the most appropriate in the conditions of a small open economy with a long-term surplus of liquidity in the banking sector. The CNB used this tool after it lowered the key interest rate to 0.05%, i.e. to the so-called technical zero. In an effort to prevent deflation, the central bank maintained this exchange rate commitment until April 2017.

The efforts to achieve higher economic growth were interrupted by the COVID-19 pandemic. This hit hard in Europe in 2020. The impact of the COVID-19 Pandemic on the world economy describes Motl (2020). Measures against the spread of the COVID-19 pandemic brought with it a noticeable reduction in household consumption and firms' investment. The business cycle of the vast majority of the world and European economies then moved into a recession phase. In 2020, Czechia achieved an average annual decrease in GDP of −5.6%, while in the second quarter of 2020 it was even a year-on-year decrease of −11%. The EU as a whole decreased by −5.7% in 2020, the American economy by −2.8%.

After the end of the restrictive measures against the spread of the COVID-19 the macroeconomic development worldwide was significantly influenced by the Russian Federation's invasion of Ukraine in February 2022. For European countries, from a macroeconomic point of view, this event primarily meant a significant negative supply shock, caused by the increase in the price of imported raw materials, especially oil and natural gas. Another impact on European economies was the influx of Ukrainian refugees, representing in the host countries a contribution to domestic aggregate demand, labour supply and, last but not least, increased demands for expenses from state budgets. This period is characterized in Europe by a significant increase in inflation, when many European countries are facing double-digit, i.e. so-called galloping inflation, which was previously more characteristic of developing and less developed countries.

6.3 Adverse Macroeconomic Situation in the Early Twenties in Czechia: Galloping Inflation and Recession

After getting through the pandemic period, general optimism manifested itself in an increase in aggregate demand, fuelled primarily by deferred consumption by households and investment activity by companies. Together with the excess of financial liquidity in the banking systems, which arose mainly during the period of central banks' efforts to revive economic growth and prevent deflation between the outbreak of the global crisis and the mild recovery before the pandemic, i.e. in the years 2008–2019, the increase in demand manifested itself in a rapidly increasing rate of inflation mainly in Europe and specifically in Central and Eastern Europe. Babická Kucharčuková et al. (2022) suggest that the COVID-19 pandemic was primarily a negative supply shock that combined with accommodative monetary policy and fiscal stimuli worldwide leading to global inflationary overheating. Having analyzed the inflationary factors in 2021–2022, Baba et al. (2023) find that inflation is more sensitive to external price pressures in emerging European economies compared to the advanced ones.

The Czech National Bank (CNB) increased the interest rate 10 times from May 2020 to June 2022 from 0.25% to the current 7% (2023). However, in the spring of 2022, another shock came in the form of the invasion of Russian troops into Ukraine. From a macroeconomic point of view, this fact meant a significant negative supply shock due to the sharp increase in the price of all key input raw materials. This supply shock again contributed to the already quite high inflation in Czechia and the rest of Europe.

Czechia is among the states in which the largest increase in inflation occurred during the years 2021 and 2022 within the EU. The current situation in Czechia is unique in its own way from a macroeconomic point of view. The record low unemployment rate, the pressure on the growth of nominal wages and the high rate of inflation indicate that the Czech economy is close to the level of potential output and is in danger of overheating. On the other hand, during 2022, there was a significant slowdown in economic growth in Czechia, while in the first quarter of 2023 there is a year-on-year decline in GDP, and the Czech economy is thus entering a recession.

The unfavourable economic situation, which was fully manifested in Czechia in 2022 primarily by dynamically increasing inflation, continues in the following year 2023 (Fig. 6.1). At the same time as double-digit inflation, which at the turn of 2022 and 2023 reached over 19% year-on-year growth of the HICP index, there is a significant slowdown in economic growth, when GDP in the individual quarters of 2022 grew successively at rates of 4.8%, 3.7%, 1.5% and finally in the fourth quarter even only at a rate of 0.2%. At the beginning of 2023, GDP even

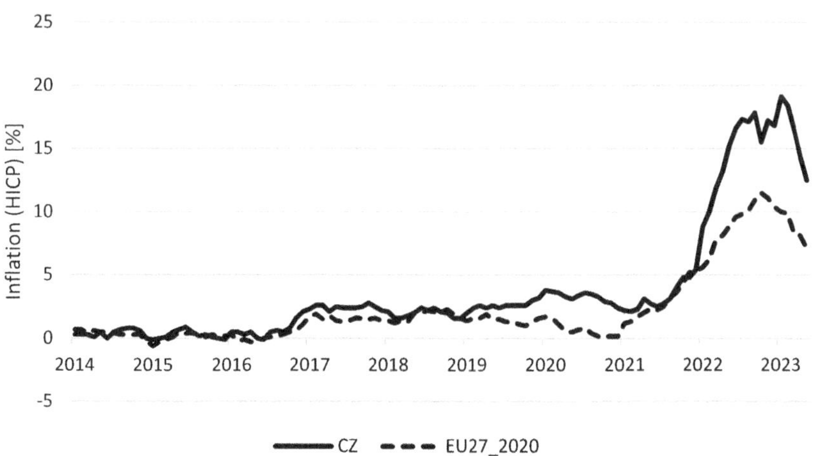

Fig. 6.1. Inflation Rate in Czechia and the EU27. *Source:* Eurostat (2023).

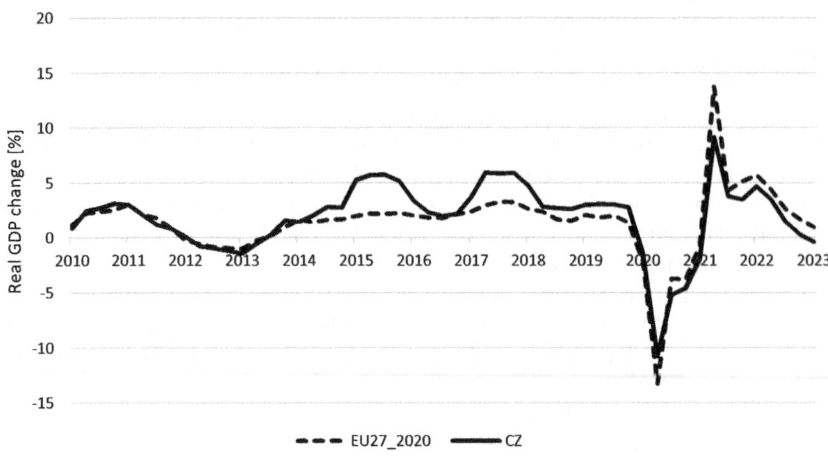

Fig. 6.2. GDP Growth in Czechia and the EU27. *Source:* Eurostat (2023).

decreased by −0.4% (Fig. 6.2). The Czech economy is thus slowly transitioning from stagflation to slumpflation. The labour market shows surprisingly favourable results. In recent years, Czechia has been among the countries with the lowest unemployment rate in the EU. During the past five years, i.e. since 2018, the unemployment rate has fluctuated between 2.6% and 4.3%. The development of real wages contributes to high employment. Over the past 4 years, the real wage index has been gradually falling, with a drop of just under 9% in 2022. This development of real wages has a favourable effect on the high demand for labour in Czechia, which is thus able to absorb, in addition to domestic labour, a considerable amount of labour from abroad, most recently from Ukraine.

From the point of view of the situation on the labour market, when the current unemployment rate from the turn of 2022 and 2023 fluctuates around the value of 3%, it can be concluded that the Czech economy is close to the limit of potential output, while until the first half of 2022, when GDP grew for six quarters consecutively at a stable pace with rising inflation, the situation may indicate a state of overheating. However, this is no longer matched by the continued development of GDP, when towards the end of 2022 there is a significant slowdown in the growth rate of GDP, indicating the risk of an approaching recession. The expected drop in GDP actually occurred in the following quarter, i.e. the first quarter of 2023. The Czech economy is thus entering a phase of recession accompanied by galloping inflation. At the same time, the CNB is coming under pressure, and despite this unfavourable development, it has not changed interest rates for almost a year.

6.4 Dilemma of the Governor of the CNB: Factors of Adverse Macroeconomic Development in Czechia

As can be seen from the previous text, European economies have gone through a very turbulent development in the past 20 years, when periods of business cycle expansion alternated with periods of recession and periods of inflation alternated with periods of several years of price stagnation or deflation followed by double-digit inflation. All these changes happened in relatively quick succession in an overall short period of time. The current galloping inflation in Czechia is the result of the accumulation of many factors from the present and past. Some of these factors are of a global nature and result from current macroeconomic developments in Europe and the world, and some are more country-specific and related to events and macroeconomic policy measures in Czechia. From the point of view of deciding on the appropriate setting of the macroeconomic policy mix, it is useful to divide the factors of aggregate supply and demand. In the same way, it is useful to analyze the potential contribution of selected factors to the current inflationary development. While demand factors can be influenced to some extent by changes in central bank interest rates, supply factors stemming mostly from the external environment are difficult to influence with monetary policy as explained in influential papers by Phelps (1978) and Gordon (1984).

Among the supply factors of inflation in Czechia and in Europe, there is no doubt an increase in the prices of key raw materials, including oil and gas, on the import of which the Czech economy depends. The COVID-19 pandemic also contributes to the current inflation in terms of aggregate supply. Preventive national lockdowns significantly disrupted global logistics networks and caused shortages of raw materials, spare parts and other production components. At a time when modern manufacturing companies minimize costs with 'just-in-time' logistics strategies and do not build significant stocks of raw materials and production parts, a disruption in the global logistics network means a temporary halt in production. This resulted in shortages of goods and increased prices on a global scale. An often-mentioned example of such an affected sector is the automotive industry. The experience of the lockdowns also revealed the real dependence of Czechia and Europe on sub-supplies of production components from China. The impact of national lockdowns on aggregate supply distortions in Europe is obvious, but difficult to quantify.

As for the energy and oil crisis caused by the invasion of the Russian troops into Ukraine, it was mainly manifested by a sharp increase in the input prices of raw materials, including oil and natural gas. From today's point of view, i.e. the beginning of 2023, the oil and natural gas market can already be considered relatively balanced. In the period 1/2020, the price was 65.251 USD/barrel, 3 years later, i.e. 1/2023, a year after the invasion of the Russian troops in Ukraine, the price is 80.086 USD/barrel. However, within this period there was a dynamic jump, when in April 2020 oil was traded at USD 20.407/barrel and in June 2022 it reached its maximum of USD 117.214/barrel. The increase in oil prices in Czechia resulted in a corresponding increase in the prices of motor gasoline and diesel, which the government of Czechia decided not to cap, unlike, for example,

Hungary. With hindsight, this decision appears to be rational, as the Hungarian capping of fuel prices did not have the desired effect. In Hungary, the negative manifestations of capping prevailed, such as the flourishing of the black market, pre-stocking and shortage of fuel and, last but not least, the increase in expenses from the state budget for compensation to fuel distributors. The natural gas market went through a similar turbulent development. During the last 3 years, the price minimum was 3.509 EUR/MWh in April 2020, while in August 2022 the price of gas on the TTF Exchange in the Netherlands reached 339.196 EUR/MWh. These price shocks were manifested in many cases in a significant increase in energy prices for end customers, i.e. Czech households, which did not have long-term contractually fixed prices. With a gap of one year, the situation seems relatively stabilized again, when the price of gas in May 2023 was 24.15 EUR/MWh. The development of oil and natural gas prices is shown in Fig. 6.3.

Eurostat also attributes the largest share of current inflation in Czechia to energy and housing. Energy and housing prices increased by 54% from the beginning of 2020–2023. In comparison, food prices rose by 32.5% over the same period, and the prices of telecommunications and postal services by just under 3%.

Among the demand factors of the current high inflation in Czechia, the excess liquidity in the banking systems, deferred consumption from the time of COVID-19, the fiscal stimulus of the Czech government from the time of lockdowns during the COVID-19 pandemic and also during the current period of high inflation are cited as part of the current expert discussion in Czechia. Higher purchasing power represented by refugees from Ukraine also contributed to the increase in demand. Last but not least, the impact of compliance with the

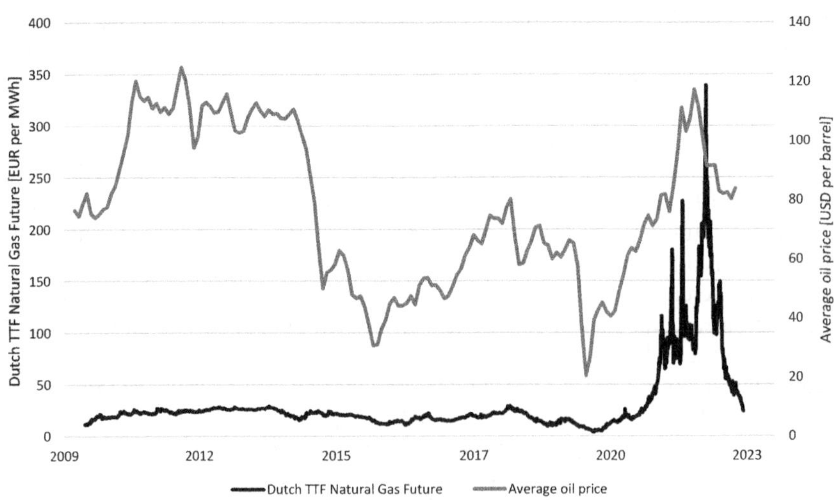

Fig. 6.3. Development of Oil and Gas Prices. *Source:* Eurostat (2023) and Investing (2023).

exchange rate commitment of the targeted depreciating of the Czech koruna exchange rate by the CNB from 2013 to 2017 is also ranked among the demand factors.

The impact of deferred consumption from the COVID-19 era on current inflation is debatable upon closer analysis. As can be seen from Fig. 6.4, since 2015 the consumption of goods and services by Czech households has been continuously growing. After 2019, in connection with the COVID-19 pandemic, there was a significant decrease in the consumption of goods and services in Czechia. This decrease is particularly noticeable in the area of services. After the end of the COVID-19 measures and economic lockdowns, there was a renewed increase in consumption. However, this increase did not reach the values from the period before 2019, and in the following period the consumption of goods and services is consistently decreasing. As shown in Fig. 6.5, households created a huge amount of savings, which, surprisingly, they do not dissolve even after the end of the COVID-19 pandemic. The behaviour of households leading to the accumulation of savings during the pandemic is described by Lydon and McIndoe-Calder (2021). Rather than consumption, investments grew, which caused asset prices, including real estate, to rise. While between 2000 and 2019, the average propensity to consume in Czechia was in the range of 73%–75%. In 2020–2021, the average propensity to consume was 66%, 65% and 68%, respectively. In this context, the question arises as to why consumer prices in Czechia reacted much more sensitively to the renewed increase in demand than in other countries, where consumer inflation is significantly lower. Among other things, the explanation may be the efforts of producers and distributors to catch up with profits and harvests from the time before COVID-19, which was reflected in increased trade margins and therefore higher end market prices. This effect is

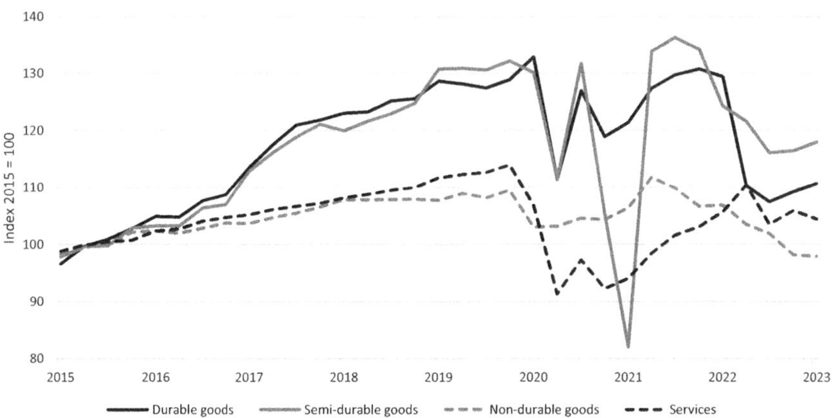

Fig. 6.4. Development of Consumption of Czech Households.
Source: Eurostat (2023).

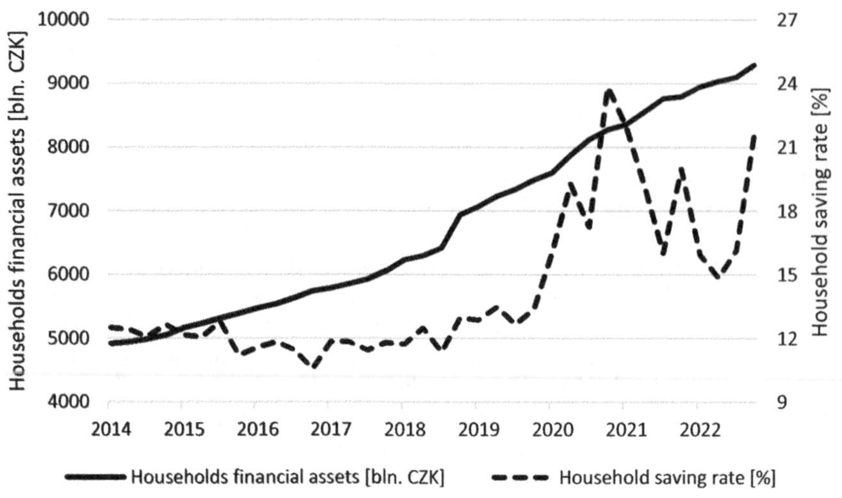

Fig. 6.5. Development of Savings of Czech Households and Average Propensity to Save. *Source:* Eurostat (2023).

reinforced by strong oligopoly structures, especially in the food industry and retail in Czechia. Imperfectly competitive market structures present less competitive pressure on producers, traders and distributors of goods and services and allow trade markups to persist.

In connection with the fight against high inflation, there is a discussion in Czechia about the effect of the government's fiscal expansionary measures during the lockdown period due to the COVID-19 pandemic. With its measures, the government of Czechia tried to mitigate the negative economic effects of lockdown on households and businesses as well as self-employed people. In this sense, however, it should be noted that although this was a significant amount of funds, a significant part was made up of government guarantees, which were ultimately not paid out. The fight against so-called inflationary poverty was also necessary in Czechia to increase spending from the state budget, when the government tried to provide financial assistance to households threatened by high inflation and, above all, rising energy prices. Other expenses were associated with the support of war refugees from Ukraine. According to UN data, Czechia registers approximately 520,000 refugees from Ukraine registered for temporary protection or similar protection schemes. This is therefore 5% of the population of Czechia, which represents a non-negligible increase in consumer demand in Czechia and thus another inflationary demand factor. As can be seen from Fig. 6.6, the development of the state budget deficit in Czechia in the analyzed period copied the development of other selected countries, for example Slovakia, Poland, Germany and the EU27 average. Czechia reaches roughly the average of the EU during this period, when the deficit amounts to approximately 6% of GDP. Czechia will copy

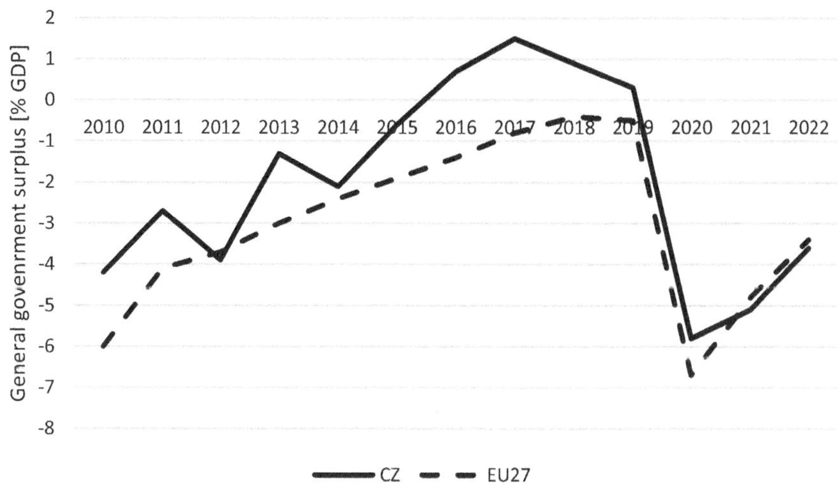

Fig. 6.6. Development of State Budget Deficits in Czechia and EU27. *Source:* Eurostat (2023).

this development in the following period as well. In this sense, similar to the deferred consumption factor, the question arises as to how much fiscal stimulus in Czechia is a country-specific factor and how much they contribute to the high rate of inflation, which is remarkably higher in Czechia than in most countries of the EU.

A special chapter is devoted to the exchange rate commitment of the CNB from the period 2013 to 2017 in this book. Therefore, let us just briefly recall that in the mentioned period, the CNB intervened in the foreign exchange markets with the aim of depreciating the Czech koruna due to the fears of deflation. The CNB publicly declared an exchange rate commitment to weaken the Czech koruna with an exchange rate day of 27 CZK/EUR (Fig. 6.7).

The initial volume of foreign exchange reserves of USD 47 billion, which the central bank owned before the start of the interventions, grew to USD 61 billion at the end of 2015 and USD 83 billion at the end of 2016. However, macroeconomic pressures intensified and the CNB continued its interventions until April 2017, when the total volume of foreign exchange reserves grew to USD 140 billion, more than three times higher than before the start of the interventions.

In addition to short-term effects, the targeted depreciating of the Czech koruna exchange rate also had long-term effects. These include an increase in the money supply and a contribution to excess bank liquidity, which the Czech Central Bank is trying to withdraw in a targeted manner using repurchase agreement operations. Another effect is also a significant increase in foreign exchange reserves, which now, six years later, the CNB is using for exactly the opposite purpose. The CNB is currently purposefully appreciating the exchange rate of the Czech koruna

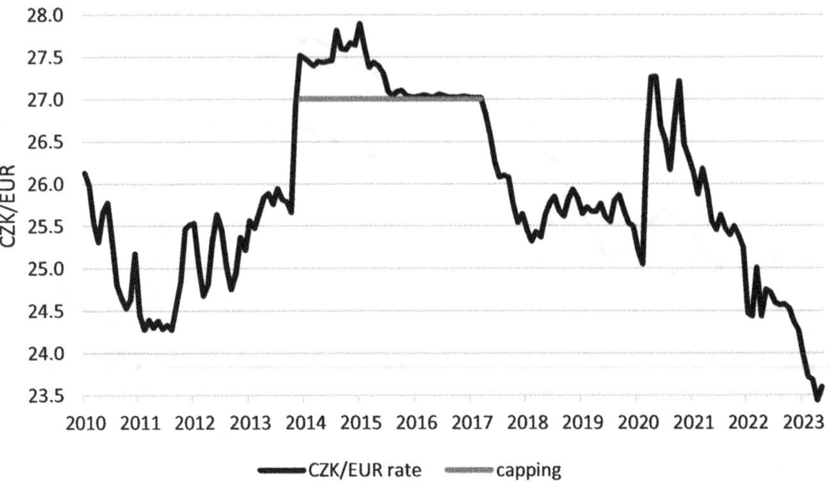

Fig. 6.7. Exchange Rate Commitment of CNB 2013–2017. *Source:* Eurostat (2023).

and reducing foreign exchange reserves. This strategy now appears to be the main monetary policy strategy of the CNB to stabilize the price level and reduce the rate of inflation in Czechia.

6.5 The Current Strategy of the CNB in the Fight Against Inflation: A Lesson to Be Learnt?

With the new governor of the CNB, the strategy to fight galloping inflation has changed. As mentioned in the introduction, the previous board of the Czech Central Bank increased interest rates 10 times in the last year of its operation (6/2021–6/2022) up to a value of 7%. The new board of the CNB has not changed rates since then, i.e. for a year (6/2022–6/2023). During the same period, the ECB raised rates seven times to the current 3.75% (5/2023). Since April 2022, the FED has raised interest rates 10 times in a row to the current 5.25%. The US and EU economies have thus far faced only single-digit inflation. A comparison of the development of the key interest rates of the CNB, the ECB and the FED is shown in Fig. 6.8.

The apparent inactivity of the CNB, which decided not to raise interest rates even in times of the highest inflation, can be justified by several main arguments. The first argument is the growing threat of an impending recession of the Czech economy, which is signalled by the stagnation of GDP in 2022 and the subsequent decline in GDP at the beginning of 2023. The increase in interest rates could thus contribute to dampening aggregate demand and increasing the threat of economic recession. The uncertain effects of monetary restriction in the fight against high

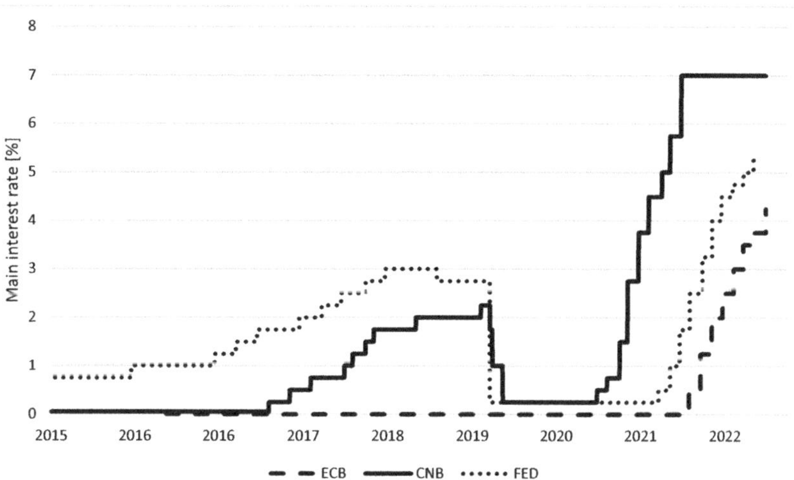

Fig. 6.8. Development of Key Interest Rates of CNB, ECB and FED. *Source:* CNB (2023), The Federal Reserve (2023), and ECB (2023).

inflation and its negative effects on real economic activity are clearly described by Gern et al. (2023). The second factor is the possibility of using an above-average amount of foreign exchange reserves, originating from the exchange rate commitment period from 2013 to 2017 described above. Targeted appreciating of the exchange rate of the Czech koruna through foreign exchange interventions now appears to be the CNB's main strategy in the fight against galloping inflation. As follows from the descriptive analysis of inflation factors in Czechia described in the previous text, another argument for not raising rates can be the fact that the CNB attributes a greater influence on external supply factors. Increasing interest rates does not have a major impact on these factors.

In February 2022, after the unexpected invasion of Russian troops into Ukraine, there was a temporary panic in the foreign exchange markets. Economic agents began to get rid of small currencies, including the Czech koruna, which within a few days depreciated from 24.30 CZK/EUR to 25.80 CZK/EUR. On March 4, the CNB issued an official press statement containing two main messages to the public. The first was the announcement that the Czech Central Bank is active on the foreign exchange market and is conducting operations to dampen excessive exchange rate fluctuations and the depreciating of the Czech koruna. The second key message in the aforementioned press statement, which is no less important, is the information that the CNB has high foreign exchange reserves in international comparison, the use of which is fully justified in the current situation. In other words, the CNB says that it intends to strengthen the Czech koruna and has enough foreign exchange reserves to do so, so the public need not fear further fluctuations in the exchange rate. The fact is that the situation stabilized again within a few weeks and similar rate fluctuations did not occur any further. With this step, the CNB confirmed the implicitly initiated policy of a strong Czech koruna. The CNB intervenes in a targeted manner in favour of a strong Czech koruna, while using foreign exchange reserves accumulated mainly during the exchange rate commitment period from 2013 to 2017, when the central bank, on the contrary, purposefully weakened the koruna. It can therefore be said that, from 2022, the central bank holds an implicit, but exactly the opposite, exchange rate commitment with the aim of strengthening the koruna. This situation is unique in its own way and points to the growing dynamics of changes and turbulence in the global economy, when the governments and central banks of developed countries, including Czechia, are facing completely different situations in less than 10 years. While in the period 2013–2017 we faced the threat of deflation and economic stagflation, which the central banks dealt with by monetary expansionary policy or by depreciating the exchange rates of national currencies, from 2021 we face the threat of high double-digit inflation, which we are trying to prevent by monetary restrictions or appreciating of exchange rates.

6.6 Conclusion

This chapter identified and described the demand and supply factors that contribute to the current double-digit inflation in Czechia. In addition, the macroeconomic development in Czechia, which was influenced by the activist policy of the CNB during the previous 20 years, was described. The combination of all the identified factors led to the decision of the current CNB board not to raise interest rates, but to conduct a policy of a strong exchange rate of the Czech koruna by means of foreign exchange interventions.

From the point of view of economic theory, recent macroeconomic development, and above all the reaction of central banks, contradicts the monetarist doctrine and the golden rule of monetary growth formulated by the winner of the Nobel Prize for economics, Milton Friedman (Friedman, 1959). He also warned against activist monetary policy in the sense of 'stop and go policy', which, however, we seem to be witnessing on a global scale in recent years. In the light of events and experiences with macroeconomic developments in Europe and the world, in connection with the activity of central banks from the last 20 or even only the last 10 years, the historical question again arises to what extent these processes are endogenous. In other words, one can ask to what extent monetary policy contributes to the emergence of macroeconomic turbulence and to what extent it dampens it. When looking for arguments to answer this question, it is also necessary to consider whether we are judging from the position of a small open economy or a large and relatively closed economy. Czechia is undoubtedly a small open economy with a significant share of exports and imports, while it is significantly dependent on the import of key raw materials. This makes it highly dependent on external factors. From this point of view, the reaction of the CNB, which does not retreat from its position of fixed interest rates even in times of high public pressure arising from unclear prospects for future inflation, appears to be a rational and moderate approach. However, we will only be able to responsibly judge the correctness and appropriateness of the chosen strategy of the CNB under the given conditions only after some time has passed. However, the most important thing will be whether we will be able to learn from this interesting historical episode and draw appropriate implications for economic policy and the development of international relations.

References

Baba, C., Duval, R., Lan, T., & Topalova, P. B. (2023). The 2020–2022 inflation surge across Europe: A phillips-curve-based dissection. IMF Working Paper No. 2023/30. https://doi.org/10.5089/9798400234385.001

CNB. (2023). Jak se vyvíjela dvoutýdenní repo sazba ČNB? https://www.cnb.cz/cs/casto-kladene-dotazy/Jak-se-vyvijela-dvoutydenni-repo-sazba-CNB/

ECB. (2023). *Key ECB interest rates.* https://www.ecb.europa.eu/stats/policy_and_exchange_rates/key_ecb_interest_rates/html/index.en.html

Eurostat. (2023). *Eurostat database.* https://ec.europa.eu/eurostat/web/main/data/database

Friedman, M. (1959). *A program for monetary stability.* Fordham University Press.

Gern, K., Jannsen, N., Sonnenberg, N., Gros, D., Shamsfakhr, F., Wyplosz, C., & Hartwell, C. A. (2023). The effects of high inflation and monetary tightening on the real economy-compilation of papers. EPRS: European Parliamentary Research Service. Monetary Dialogue Papers.

Gordon, R. J. (1984). Supply shocks and monetary policy revisited. *National Bureau of Economic Research Working Paper Series*, (w1301).

Investing. (2023). *Dutch TTF natural gas futures.* https://www.investing.com/commodities/dutch-ttf-gas-c1-futures

Kucharčuková, O. B., Brůha, J., Král, P., Motl, M., & Tonner, J. (2022). Assessment of the nature of the pandemic shock: Implications for monetary policy. *Czech National Bank: Research and Policy Notes 1/2022.*

Lydon, R., & McIndoe-Calder, T. (2021). Saving during the pandemic: Waiting out the storm. *Central Bank of Ireland Economic Letter Series, 4.*

Malovaná, S., Bajzík, J., Ehrenbergerová, D., & Janků, J. (2020). A prolonged period of low interest rates: Unintended consequences. *Czech National Bank: Research and Policy Notes 2/2020.*

Motl, M. (2020). Impacts of the COVID-19 pandemic on the world economy. Occasional publications-chapters in edited volumes, 12–24.

Phelps, E. S. (1978). Commodity-supply shock and full-employment monetary policy. *Journal of Money, Credit and Banking*, *10*(2), 206–221. https://doi.org/10.2307/1991872

The Federal Reserve. (2023). *Historical discount rates.* https://www.frbdiscountwindow.org/Pages/Discount-Rates/Historical-Discount-Rates

Chapter 7

Corporate Taxation in Czechia: A Proper Tax Mix Stimulating Economic Growth

Jana Janoušková and Šárka Sobotovičová

Silesian University in Opava, Czehia

Abstract

It is important to consider economic and political factors when designing the tax mix and setting the level of corporate taxation. Increasing corporate taxation can be seen as an inefficient way to raise revenue for the state, as it can have a negative impact on investment and the competitiveness of firms. However, lowering corporate taxation can encourage investment and job creation, but it can also be perceived as supporting large corporations. The aim of this chapter is to evaluate corporate taxation, its position in the tax mix and its potential impact on economic growth. The revenues of corporate income tax (CIT) have an increasing tendency even though the tax rate was reduced from 41% to 19%. Revenues are influenced by both legislative changes and economic cycles. The level of taxation is also influenced by deductions, which include asset depreciations, research and development expenses, or loss deductions. The Pearson Correlation Coefficient was used to examine the correlation between the selected factors. A moderately strong positive correlation was found between GDP growth and CIT as a percentage of total taxes, as well as between GDP growth and CIT as a percentage of GDP.

Keywords: Corporate income tax; tax rate; tax deduction; tax revenue; gross domestic product; tax mix

7.1 Introduction

Corporate taxation is one of the newest types of taxation in tax systems. Theoretical approaches to the existence of a corporate income tax (hereafter CIT) are different (Mirrlees et al., 2011; Široký, 2018). Some views even criticise the

Modeling Economic Growth in Contemporary Czechia, 103–120

doi:10.1108/978-1-83753-840-920241007

rationale of CIT because ultimately corporate profits become an individual's personal income anyway. It is also pointed out that the tax on profits has the negative effect of making production more expensive. Multinational companies are more able to manipulate their tax base due to the complexity of tax legislation in different countries, and the tax loses its neutral character. Legislation in many countries defines accounting and tax expenses, accounting and tax depreciation or the inclusion of losses, donations or parts of investments in items reducing the tax base differently. Unlike the personal income tax (PIT), the primary objective of the CIT is not to ensure that the principle of equity is fulfiled. For this reason, CIT rates are linear and are usually determined by a percentage of taxable profits.

However, corporate taxation is maintained and has its supporters (Straub & Werning, 2020). Corporations are a legal entity with their own decision-making power, they have their own taxation capacity, and they influence economic processes. CIT can also be seen as compensation for the limited liability of the owners of the corporation for their liabilities, which contradicts the requirement of neutrality of taxation. In the context of the benefit principle, the tax is seen as a 'payment' for the use of public services and infrastructure on the territory where entities do business (James & Nobes, 2018; Kubátová, 2018).

Governments can influence both the tax rate and the tax base, and can encourage companies to export more products abroad, to adopt new technologies more quickly, or to promote certain sectors, thereby affecting economic growth (Neicu et al., 2016). Tax measures in the form of exemptions, deductions and tax credits can attract foreign investors.

CIT in Czechia is a significant tax in terms of tax revenues to public budgets. The motivation for this research is finding solutions for CIT modification in Czechia. The aim of this chapter is to evaluate CIT, its position in the tax mix and its potential impact on economic growth.

7.2 Corporation Taxation

CIT exists in all developed countries, but its yields are usually relatively low compared to those of PIT (with the exception of Cyprus). In Czechia this trend was reversed, and in 1995 the share of PIT was only 13.3% of total tax revenues and the share of CIT was 12.7%. This trend has gradually changed, and CIT as a percentage of total tax revenues has been declining. However, CIT as a percentage of total tax revenues in 2020 in Czechia (8.6%) is above the EU average (6%) (see Fig. 7.1).

Tax theory and practise are facing the problem of the possible link between personal and corporate income taxes and the possibility of neutrally affecting both distributed and retained earnings at the firm level. Tax systems use different methods to tax profits and avoid double taxation. According to Široký (2018), this is the case for the so-called zero integration (classical double taxation system), and it means that there is full economic double taxation. Profits are taxed at the level of the company and also at the level of the shareholder, and no tax relief or discount is provided when dividends or profits are taxed. Both income taxes are

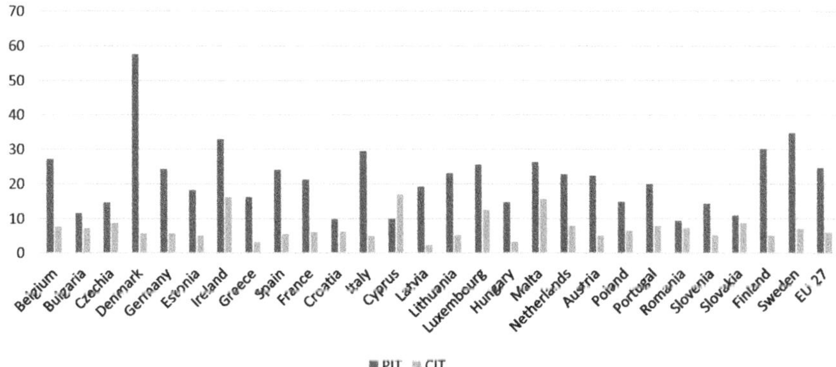

Fig. 7.1. PIT and CIT as a Ratio of Total Tax Revenue in EU Countries (2020, in %). *Source:* European Commission (2023), Authors' Calculations.

viewed as completely separate taxes. The advantage is simplicity and the disadvantage is the complete double taxation of dividends. This system is mainly applied in small economies and also in Czechia at present.

Some modification is reflected in the integration of systems that reduce, mitigate, or eliminate double taxation for one of the taxes at least (i.e. either at the company or shareholder level). The instruments of partial integration may be a deduction of tax paid on distributed profits from the corporation's tax base (dividend deduction system), a different tax rate on distributed and undistributed profits to be reinvested (split-rate system), a special tax on dividends received, a dividend tax credit, a refund or an exemption. In Czechia, the dividend deduction system was applied until 2004. A corporation that paid out profit shares (dividends) had the option to offset half of the tax it withheld on these shares as a corporate tax credit for the tax year in which it withheld the withholding tax (15%). This measure reduces the taxation of profit shares to 7.5%. This deduction was abolished in Czechia in connection with the decrease in the statutory CIT rate.

However, the whole system of integrating the two income taxes is constantly evolving and is complicated by the fact that many countries apply different rules for domestic and foreign dividends.

7.3 Corporation Taxation in Czechia

The year 1989 marked the transition to a market economy for the Czech economy, and the tax reform concept also aimed to reduce the tax quota and change the distribution of the tax mix and promote economic growth. The biggest change in the tax system introduced in Czechia was undoubtedly the introduction of the value added tax on the one hand and two universal income taxes on the other hand. An important aspect was the reintroduction of social security contributions as separate revenue for public budgets. There was a call for a gradual reduction in the taxation of incomes (especially CIT) and an increase in the share of indirect taxes.

Corporate income tax was introduced in 1993 in connection with the introduction of a new tax system in Czechia. The tax rate has been linear from the beginning and was set at 45% in the year of introduction. Similarly, in other transition economies, Czechia has gradually reduced the statutory tax rate to the current 19% (see Table 7.1). CIT is an important revenue item for public budgets in most countries, but the mobility of its tax base has made it subject to tax competition between EU countries. Czechia has been exposed even more to this competition in the context of its planned accession to the EU. Although the pressure on CIT is not directly due to the harmonisation of this tax by the EU, it has been in the interest of small economies (such as Czechia) in particular that an unfavourable tax system should not discourage foreign capital entry. In this respect, measures were taken (e.g. tax holidays for foreign entities) to stimulate foreign entrepreneurs to invest in Czechia.

Table 7.1 shows the development of CIT revenues and growth rates in Czechia. In most years, a gradual increase in CIT revenues can be observed, with only eight years showing a decrease compared to the previous year. Despite the decrease in the statutory CIT rate, CIT revenue in 2021 is 3.4 times that of 1995.

During the period under review, the impact of economic cycles can be seen in CIT revenues. The beginning of the global economic crisis in 2008 led to a year-on-year decline in national aggregate accounting results compared to 2007. This impacted tax collections through the deduction of tax losses from 2009 onwards. The decline in the performance of the Czech economy could not be significantly eliminated by legislative changes aimed at broadening the tax base. In addition, the impact of the gradual reduction of the tax rate between 2008 and 2010 has been felt.

The year-over-year decline in total CIT revenue in 2020 was related to the economic downturn accompanied by other negative phenomena (decline in employment, wage volume, and other measures resulting from measures triggered by the need to prevent the spread of the COVID-19 pandemic). Furthermore, this is a comparison with the economically successful year of 2019. In 2021, there was an improvement in the performance of corporations and a reduction in the number of corporations reporting a zero or negative trading result.

The European Commission recommended EU member states to introduce temporarily some form of extraordinary taxation on profits as early as March 2022, in the context of a sharp rise in energy prices. The concept of windfall taxes has been used in the past (e.g. in the US or the UK in 1981). The purpose of windfall taxes was to share the burden of an external shock and to maintain social harmony in society by reallocating excessive profits. Czechia implemented windfall taxes with effect from January 2023 with a duration of three years in order to raise temporary additional revenue for the state budget and to compensate companies and citizens for high energy prices (MFCR, 2022).

Table 7.1. Evolution of CIT Revenues and Statutory CIT Rates in Czechia.

Year	Revenue (Billion CZK)	Growth Rate	Statutory CIT Rates (%)
1995	67		41
1996	57	0.84	39
1997	69	1.23	39
1998	67	0.97	35
1999	79	1.18	35
2000	75	0.95	31
2001	94	1.26	31
2002	107	1.13	31
2003	119	1.11	31
2004	129	1.08	28
2005	135	1.05	26
2006	154	1.14	24
2007	171	1.11	24
2008	162	0.95	21
2009	132	0.82	20
2010	127	0.96	19
2011	129	1.01	19
2012	127	0.99	19
2013	133	1.04	19
2014	144	1.09	19
2015	157	1.09	19
2016	167	1.07	19
2017	176	1.05	19
2018	187	1.06	19
2019	192	1.03	19
2020	177	0.92	19
2021	228	1.29	19

Source: MFCR (2023), Act No. 586/91 Coll. on Income Taxes as Amended, Authors' Calculations.

7.3.1 Tax Instruments and Tax Base Construction

It is clear that each country's tax policy is part of its broader economic policy. The tax instruments are then aimed at promoting economic growth within the framework of political compromises. Thus, not only the level of the tax rate that can be compared to determine the tax burden but the setting of the breadth of the tax base is important. But differences arise from inequalities in taxation and financing with domestic and foreign capital, tax base design, stock valuation, inflation rates, etc., which induce distortions in taxation and negatively affect the effective tax rate. The issue of depreciation policy and support for research and development is very often discussed.

CIT in Czechia is calculated from the tax base, which is derived from the pre-tax trading result. The tax base can be reduced by deductible items and tax credits can be deducted from the calculated tax. Deductible items are losses recognised in previous accounting periods, the research and development deduction, and the vocational training deduction. The value of gratuitous transactions provided for statutory purposes may also be deducted from the tax base (Table 7.2).

The tax deductions include deductions for the employment of disabled persons and a deduction for corporate taxpayers who have been granted an investment incentive promise.

In connection with the support of economic growth, one of the tax measures was the reduction of the effective taxation of profits. This was done by accelerating depreciation (i.e. reducing the depreciation period in the first three depreciation groups, e.g. for computers, selected means of transport, machinery, and equipment) and introducing a deductible item in connection with expenditure to support science and research. Although the reduction in the statutory CIT rate increased the rate of return on capital and increased the attractiveness of business in general, the acceleration of depreciation mainly stimulated investment activity, and thus strengthened the supply side of the economy.

7.3.2 Depreciation of Tangible Assets in Czechia

Depreciation of assets plays a significant economic role and, therefore, depreciation for tax purposes is regulated by legislation. All developed countries have the tax treatment of fix asset depreciation (Furno, 2021), and the amount of tax depreciation and the timing of depreciation affect the size of the tax liability (Gravelle, 2011). At the same time, an appropriate investment policy motivates the investment activity of companies. Czech companies have a choice between straight-line and accelerated depreciation.

The depreciation period is also significant, and the reduction in the depreciation period will result in a one-time decrease in the tax revenue in the years following the change. The tax law does not have the ambition to model reliably the performance of companies because tax depreciations are more indicative of the fiscal policy or investment priorities of the state. An appropriate depreciation policy can dampen or encourage investment activity by companies, and different depreciation rules are applied in different countries. Faster depreciation means that companies are partly freed up to invest further. However, there is also a government concern that, if the acquisition of assets were a tax cost, not enough taxes would be collected from business in the economic expansion years because

Table 7.2. Depreciation of Tangible Assets, Deductions and Tax Credits in Years 2011–2021 (in CZK Billion).

	2011	2012	2013	2014	2015	2016	2017	2018	2019	2020	2021
Depreciations of assets	385.1	383.9	379.9	395.7	426.1	443.1	458.1	469.9	505.7	525.2	501.2
Tax loss deduction	94.5	64.6	79.0	62.9	65.4	63.7	64.0	54.5	73.0	54.1	66.6
Gratuitous transactions	2.7	2.7	2.6	3.6	3.7	3.9	3.4	3.8	4.1	5.3	5.7
Research and development	9.7	10.4	12.1	11.9	13.3	12.5	13.2	13.6	14.4	11.1	12.8
Tax reliefs	5.6	6.5	5.9	6.2	7.0	6.7	5.1	4.2	3.6	3.0	3.4

Source: Financial Administration CR (2023a) and CSO (2022a).

taxpayers would incur high investment costs. Czechia is still one of the countries with slower depreciation and still suffers from overregulation.

The negative effects of inflation on the corporate reproduction process are directly related to the difference between the accumulated own resources (depreciation derived from historical cost) and the current market price of the asset, depending on the magnitude of inflation and the economic life of the asset. In practise, inflation depreciates the fair value of depreciation, leaving the firm with less realistic funds for asset replacement. The historical cost depreciation system leads to an underestimation of depreciation when prices rise in line with inflation. The problem of taking inflation into account in depreciation has not yet been reasonably resolved. The so-called reinvestment (it was also used in Czech tax law until 2004), which was an off-accounting benefit for newly acquired property, can also be considered a solution. Reinvestment as an item reducing the tax base is a tax support for the acquisition of new tangible fixed assets if specified conditions are met. Reinvestment can also be seen as a means of reducing the adverse impact of the current depreciation system on income tax.

Reinvestment in Czechia was a targeted form of business support that favoured companies investing in new equipment or technology. Reinvestments were applied as a share of the entry price of the assets in a differentiated manner. Higher percentage rates favoured investment in equipment used to protect the environment and help primary agricultural production. The deductions were 10%, 15% and 20%.

In connection with the reform of public finances and the requirement to simplify the legal regulation, since 2005, the projection of this form of business support into the possible increase of depreciation in the first year of depreciation has been shifted. However, by abolishing the reinvestment deduction and replacing it with the possibility of increased depreciation of assets in the year of acquisition, only 100% of the value of the investment is deducted from the tax base. Under the legislation in force until the end of 2004, 110%–120% of the value of investments could be deducted in connection with reinvestment.

The authorities have introduced a broad and generous package of fiscal measures to support taxpayers as they deal with the consequences of the COVID-19 pandemic. In the context of support for investment activities and the modernisation of Czech industry, the threshold for compulsory depreciation has been increased (from CZK 40 000 to CZK 80 000), the obligation to tax depreciation of intangible assets has been abolished, and the so-called extraordinary depreciation has been introduced, which will enable faster amortisation of investment expenditure.

7.3.3 Support for Research and Development

Tax support for research and development (hereinafter referred to as R&D) is in the Czech system of public support a secondary instrument. This support is based on the tax deduction of deductible costs (expenses) for R&D from the income tax base. This instrument was introduced in 2005 in Czechia.

Mainly large companies because of complex legislation and practical feasibility use the deduction for R&D. They can afford to spend money on specialised consultants, and thus find it easier to obtain the tax deduction. A negative phenomenon is that most of the investments are made by foreign companies through their subsidiaries (OECD, 2020). Therefore, it would be beneficial to promote more the use of R&D by small and medium enterprises, as they have an impact on economic growth. In 2020, approximately 30% of private companies in Czechia used R&D tax support. In the case of foreign-controlled companies, this figure was almost 40% (CSO, 2022a). As part of the increase in the tax incentive, the R&D deduction was amended in April 2019. This strengthened the legal certainty of companies regarding the procedure to claim the deduction.

7.3.4 Tax Loss Deduction

The possibility of recovering losses from a business assessed in previous years is related to the risk inherent in any investment. The possibility of including the loss in tax deductions in subsequent tax periods entails the problem of discounting the value of the loss in future years. Until 2003, the tax loss could be deducted in the seven tax years immediately following the period for which the tax loss is assessed. Since 2004, this loss claim period has been reduced to five tax years. The taxpayer may claim the loss in full or in stages according to its tax optimization plan.

In connection with the COVID-19 pandemic, a measure was adopted (for the first time in Czech tax law) that allowed the tax loss to be claimed retroactively. The purpose of the measure is to support domestic companies in maintaining employment and mitigate the adverse economic impact of the pandemic. Unlike direct support schemes, their current cost to public budgets is relatively low and, de facto, none in the medium term (MFCR, 2020). Loss recapture is limited to the two previous tax years and is limited to the amount of tax loss that can be recaptured (maximum CZK 30 million). This is a positive change in favour of taxpayers. The intention of the government was to provide tax entities with a quick tool to improve cash flow.

7.4 Tax Mix in Czechia

Tax mix optimization depends on political and economic objectives and can be modified to achieve the best balance between raising the necessary revenue to finance public expenditure and minimising the negative impact on economic growth. Thus, changes in the CIT cannot be considered in isolation, but always in the context of changes in the tax mix or changes in government measures. In Czechia, as in other developed countries, the tax system consists of several different taxes, as each tax behaves differently and affects taxpayers in a different way. Fig. 7.2 shows the tax system (in force in 2023).

Until the end of 2013, inheritance and gift taxes were also applied separately in Czechia, however their revenues for the public budget were negligible. The inheritance tax was abolished completely and the gift tax was implemented in the

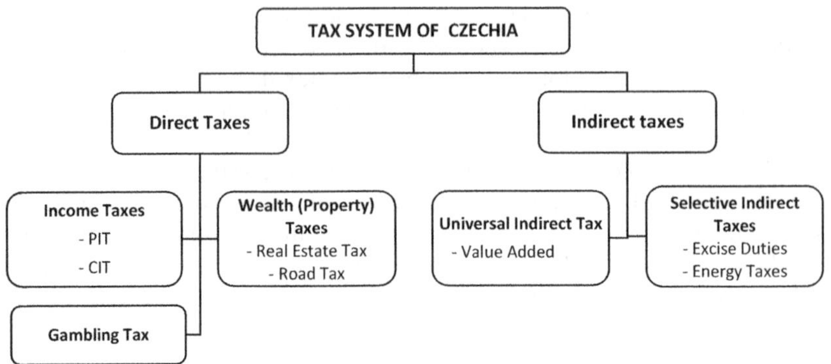

Fig. 7.2. Tax System of Czechia. *Source:* Financial Administration CR (2023b).

income tax. The tax on the acquisition of immovable property was abolished on 1 December 2019.

In addition to taxes, social security contributions are an important source of revenue for public budgets. The Czech tax system relies heavily on labour taxation (PIT and social security contributions), which increases costs for employers and slows economic growth. PIT revenues are relatively low with little progressivity. On the other hand, social security contributions are significantly higher than the EU average.

VAT revenues are on an upward trend, more than doubling in 2021 compared to 2004 (Czechia's accession to the EU). The growth in VAT revenue before the COVID-19 crisis was mainly driven by efforts to reduce tax evasion, including the introduction of the control statement (2016) and the electronic sales registration. The electronic sales registration was suspended due to the COVID-19 crisis and cancelled as of 2023. The OECD (2020) recommends Czechia to strengthen VAT collection and to abolish VAT exemptions granted in recent years in the context of the COVID-19 pandemic.

Within excise duties, the highest revenues are generated by the mineral oil tax, followed by the tax on tobacco products and the tax on alcohol. The lowest revenues are for the tax on wine and intermediate products, and this is due to the zero-tax rate on still wine. In 2019, a new tax on heated tobacco products was introduced. In 2008, energy taxes were introduced in Czechia (a tax on electricity, a tax on solid fuels, and a tax on natural gas and other gases). The main reason for introducing energy taxes was to shift the taxation of labour towards the taxation of consumption.

Property taxes are of limited importance, but they are a stable revenue source for public budgets in most countries (Birch & Sunderman, 2013). They do not have a distortionary effect on labour, nor do they inhibit economic activity. Property taxes in Czechia include the immovable property tax. Czechia is below

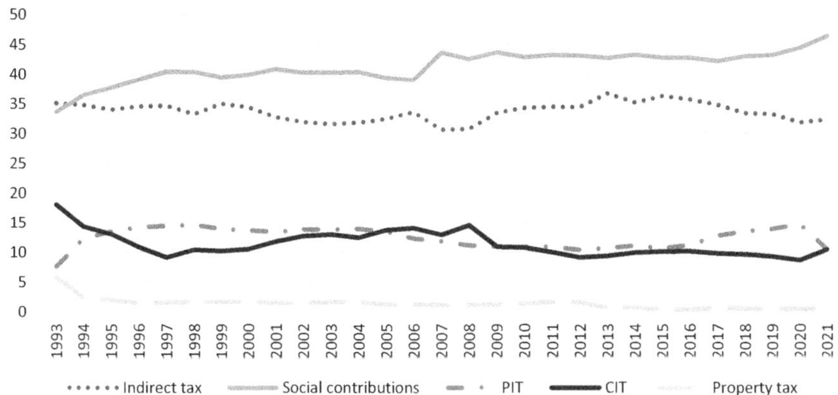

Fig. 7.3. Evolution of the Share of Individual Taxes in Total Tax Revenue 1993–2021 (in %). *Source:* MFCR (2023).

the OECD average and this fact is repeatedly criticised by the OECD (2020), which recommends increasing the share of property taxes in total tax revenue.

Based on the above, it is clear that the tax mix in Czechia is in some respects out of line with EU countries. These include, for example, high social security contributions or relatively low property taxes and PIT (Fig. 7.3). The tax mix is still tilted towards high taxation of labour (especially social security contributions), which slows down economic growth. The share of CIT is mostly on a downward trend from 18% (in 1993) to 10.4% (in 2021).

Recommendations (Government of Czechia, 2022; OECD, 2020) have long been directed at changing the tax mix in a revenue-neutral manner to reduce tax distortions and promote economic growth, which in turn would help restore fiscal sustainability. Taxes on factors of production are the most damaging to economic growth. It is recommended to shift the tax burden away from labour (reducing high social security contributions) and to increase the progressivity of the PIT. Increasing property taxation (which is the least growth distortion) and raising revenues from excise and environmental taxes could generate more revenue.

The following chart shows a comparison of GDP growth rates and CIT revenue growth rates. The chart shows that in the years 2009 and 2020, when the largest GDP declines occur (−4.66%, respectively, −5.5%), the lowest revenues from the CIT were also recorded (Fig. 7.4).

In relation to the above, the correlation between the selected variables was verified using Pearson's coefficient. The selected variables were GDP growth, CIT revenue growth, CIT rate, CIT as a percentage of total taxes, CIT as a percentage of GDP, simple tax quota (taxes to GDP), and compound tax quota (taxes and social insurance to GDP).

Based on Pearson's Correlation Coefficient (Table 7.3), a moderately strong positive correlation was found between GDP growth and CIT as a percentage of

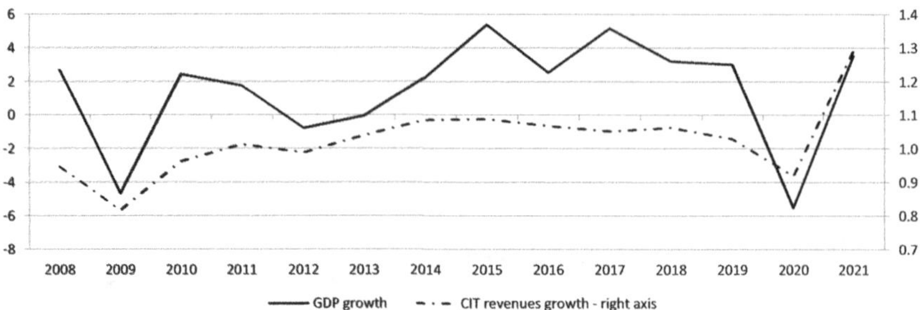

Fig. 7.4. Evolution of GDP and CIT Revenues. *Source:* MFCR (2023), CSO (2022b), Authors' Calculations.

total taxes and between GDP growth and CIT as a percentage of GDP at the significance level of 0.05 (respectively 0.01). A statistically significant positive effect of CIT on long-term economic growth has already been found by Kotlán et al. (2011). Their findings suggest that reducing the CIT burden in OECD countries does not help growth but can even undermine it. They further argue that a reduction in the effective tax burden on corporations can lead to a de facto increase in the tax quota in the sense of the Laffer curve and thus to increase economic growth. This has also been confirmed in Czechia, where a moderately strong negative correlation has been found between the CIT rate and the tax quota (both simple and compound), which is the basic indicator used to measure the tax burden.

However, other authors, such as Arnold et al. (2011), conclude that an increase in CIT has a stronger negative impact on economic growth than a comparable increase in PIT. The empirical literature points out that changes in the CIT cannot be considered in isolation but need to be viewed in light of changes in other tax components. Other authors, such as Lee and Gordon (2005), have found differences in the impact of the CIT on growth, but these differences are not robustly significant. As Gechert and Heimberger (2022) note, the existing empirical literature provides inconclusive evidence on the impact of CIT on economic growth. However, the heterogeneity of the results may be driven by different data and methods. The underlying sample of countries, the choice of measurement of the CIT variable, as well as different approaches to dealing with potential endogeneity or reverse causality problems may have important implications for the reported results.

7.5 Corporate Taxation in the EU

The statutory tax rate is set by law, the effective tax rate is the actual tax rate paid by the entity. It may differ from the statutory tax rate if the taxpayer can take advantage of any tax credits that reduce the calculated tax. Since 2006, the

Table 7.3. Pearson's Correlation of Selected Factors.

Factors	GDP Growth	CIT Revenues Growth	CIT Rate	CIT on Total Tax	CIT on GDP	Tax on GDP With SSC	Tax on GDP Without SSC
GDP growth	1	0.358	0.068	0.492[a]	0.547[b]	0.111	0.162
CIT revenues growth	0.358	1	0.153	0.414[a]	0.474[a]	0.179	0.071
CIT rate	0.068	0.153	1	0.288	0.123	−0.615[b]	−0.583[b]
CIT on total tax	0.492[a]	0.414[a]	0.288	1	0.959[b]	−0.193	−0.266
CIT on GDP	0.547[b]	0.474[a]	0.123	0.959[b]	1	0.080	−0.009
Tax on GDP with SSC	0.111	0.179	−0.615[b]	−0.198	0.080	1	0.908[b]
Tax on GDP without SSC	0.162	0.071	−0.583[b]	−0.266	−0.009	0.908[b]	1

Source: Authors' Calculations.

[a]Correlation is Significant at the 0.05 Level (2-Tailed).
[b]Correlation is Significant at the 0.01 Level (2-Tailed).

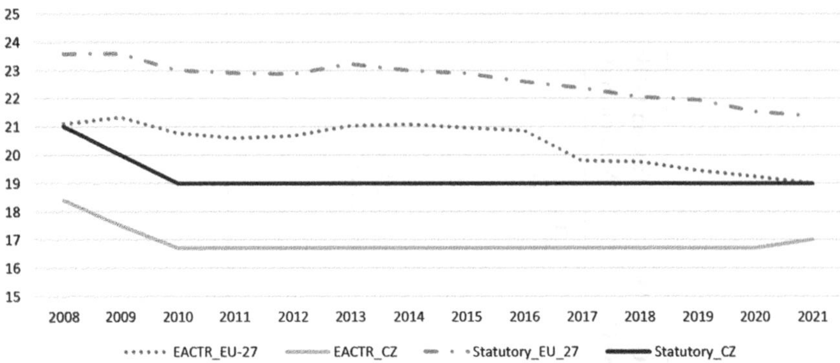

Fig. 7.5. Evolution of Statutory and Effective CIT Rates in Czechia and Average EU-27 (in %). *Source:* European Commission (2023).

statutory CIT rate in Czechia has been below the average of EU countries, which was 21.22% in 2022. Similarly, to the statutory CIT rate, Fig. 7.5 shows that the effective CIT rate in Czechia has been below the average of EU countries in all years since 2008. The statutory CIT rate in Czechia has been 19% since 2010, and this corresponds to an effective CIT rate of 16.7%. The effective CIT rate only increased to 17% in 2021, when there was also a significant increase in CIT revenues.

The following chart (Fig. 7.6) shows the evolution of the share of CIT revenues as a percentage of total tax revenues in Czechia compared to the average of the EU-27. The share of CIT as a percentage of total taxes in Czechia is above the EU-27 throughout the period under review.

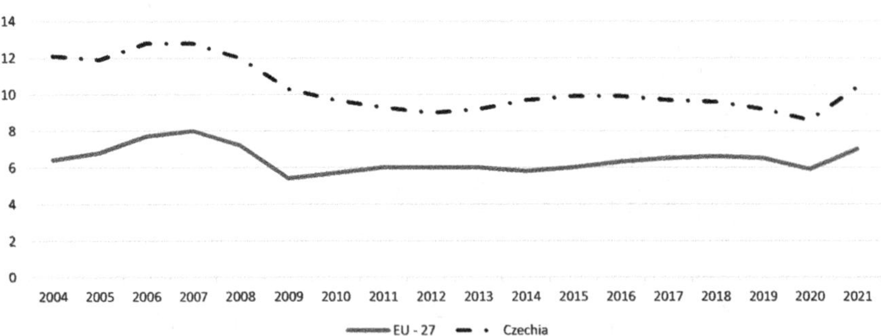

Fig. 7.6. Evolution of Taxes on the Income and Profits of Corporations Including Holding Gains as Percentage of Total Taxation in Czechia and EU27 Average (in %). *Source:* European Commission (2023).

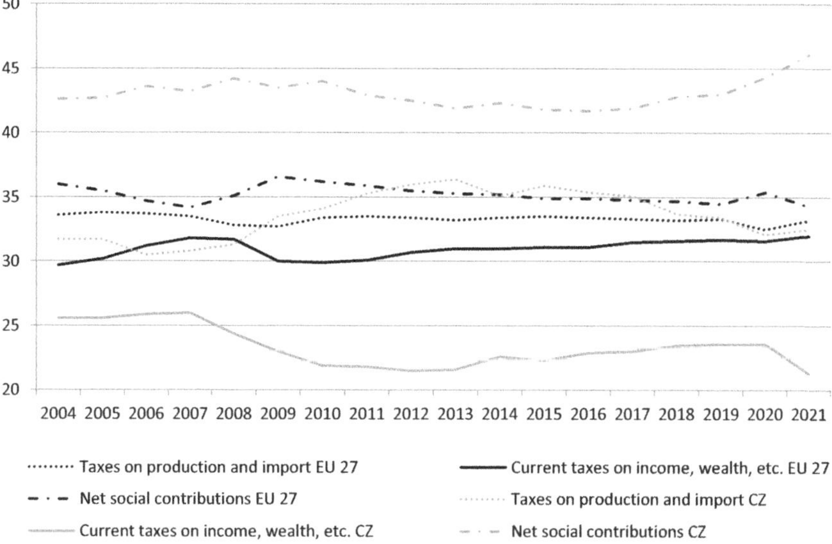

Fig. 7.7. Evolution of the Main Components of Tax Revenue in Czechia and in the EU27 in 2004–2021 (% of GDP). *Source:* Eurostat (2023).

For the purpose of comparison, tax and social contribution revenues have been divided into three main categories or types, namely indirect taxes, defined as taxes related to production and imports (value added tax, excise duties, etc.), direct taxes consisting of current taxes on income and wealth, and net social contributions. The following Fig. 7.7 compares their evolution in Czechia with the EU-27 average between 2004 and 2021.

The share of indirect taxes in Czechia was below the EU-27 average when the country joined the EU (2004). When comparing direct taxes, it can be seen that their share in Czechia has been below the EU-27 average throughout the years, and in 2021 the share of direct taxes in Czechia was even 10.7 percentage points below the EU-27 average. The situation is completely opposite for net social contributions. Here we can clearly see the high share of these contributions, which exceeds the EU-27 average throughout the period, ranging from 6.6 pp (in 2013) to 11.8 pp (in 2021), which increases labour costs and may have a negative impact on economic growth.

7.6 Conclusion

The CIT is a significant tax in terms of tax revenues to public budgets in Czechia and the share of CIT revenues in total taxes is above the EU-27 average. CIT revenues are affected by economic cycles and legislative changes. Both the statutory tax rate and the effective tax rate have been below the EU27 average since

2008. In this context, the CIT rate could be increased. However, it would be advisable to introduce uniform rules for corporate taxation in the EU. An increase in corporate tax means less money for investment and a shift of part of the burden to companies, which are currently facing a number of other problems (rising input prices, upward pressure on wages).

Simplifying the CIT by limiting exemptions, deductions and tax deductibility of certain costs could also be a good step. Simple and clearly structured legislation with a minimum of interpretative ambiguities, which reduce the costs for companies in meeting their tax obligations, is a great support for the business environment.

A moderately strong positive correlation was found between GDP growth and the share of CIT in total taxes as well as between GDP growth and the share of CIT in GDP. The positive effect of the CIT on long-term economic growth is a significant finding. Economic growth can have a number of positive effects, such as increased employment, higher wages and higher overall living standards. It can also contribute to the development of infrastructure and improve the quality of life of a country's inhabitants. However, as mentioned, some empirical studies have confirmed the negative impact of CIT on economic growth. Hence, the impact of CIT on economic growth is not conclusive.

Changes in the CIT cannot be considered in isolation but always in the context of changes in the tax mix. In some respects, the tax mix in Czechia is out of line with EU countries. It still tends towards high taxation of labour (especially social security contributions), which increases costs for employers and slows down economic growth. Taxes on factors of production are the most damaging to growth. Increasing the progressivity of the PIT, raising immovable property taxes (the least distortive to economic growth) and increasing revenues from excise duties and environmental taxes could raise more revenue.

References

Act No.586/1992 Coll. on Income Taxes, as amended.

Arnold, J. M., Brys, B., Heady, C., Johansson, L., Schwellnus, C., & Vartia, L. (2011). Tax policy for economic recovery and growth. *The Economic Journal*, *121*(550), 59–80. https://doi.org/10.1111/j.1468-0297.2010.02415.x

Birch, J., & Sunderman, M. (2013). Regression modelling for vertical and horizontal property tax inequity. *Journal of Housing Research*, *23*(1), 89–104. https://doi.org/10.1080/10835547.2013.12092083

Czech Statistical Office (CSO). (2022a, April 15). *Nepřímá veřejná podpora výzkumu a vývoje v České republice*. https://www.czso.cz/documents/10180/164606760/21100322.pdf/386c4967-1af6-44a4-9fe7-bb4abe8e73a9?version=1.1

Czech Statistical Office (CSO). (2022b, April 15). *Statistical yearbook of the Czech Republic – 2022*. https://www.czso.cz/documents/10180/171419384/32019822.pdf/8ac5e2b3-d4f3-44c5-aa3f-35909556d663?version=1.1

European Commission. (2023, March 15). *Data on taxation trends*. https://taxation-customs.ec.europa.eu/taxation-1/economic-analysis-taxation/data-taxation-trends_en

Eurostat. (2023, March 15). *Annual government finance statistics*. https://ec.europa.eu/eurostat/databrowser/view/GOV_10A_TAXAG__custom_4397404/default/table?lang=en

Financial Administration CR. (2023a, March 15). *Analysis and statistics*. https://www.financnisprava.cz/cs/dane/analyzy-a-statistiky/udaje-z-danovych-priznani

Financial Administration CR. (2023b, March 15). *Tax system of the Czech Republic*. https://www.financnisprava.cz/cs/dane/danovy-system-cr/popis-systemu

Furno, F. (2021). *The macroeconomic effects of corporate tax reforms*. Cornell University. arXiv preprint arXiv:2111.12799. https://doi.org/10.48550/arXiv.2111.12799

Gechert, S., & Heimberger, P. (2022). Do corporate tax cuts boost economic growth? *European Economic Review*, *147*(2022), 104157. https://doi.org/10.1016/j.euroecorev.2022.104157

Government of the Czech Republic. (2022, April 10). *Návrhy NERV na snížení výdajů a zvýšení příjmů veřejných rozpočtů v ČR*. https://www.vlada.cz/cz/ppov/nerv/aktuality/nerv-prezentoval-vlade-namety-z-oblasti-rozpoctu-a-energeticke-krize-200401/

Gravelle, J. G. (2011). Reducing depreciation allowances to finance a lower corporate tax rate. *National Tax Journal*, *64*(4), 1039–1053. https://doi.org/10.17310/ntj.2011.4.07

James, S. R., & Nobes, C. II (2018). *The economics of taxation: Principles, policy and practice* (18th ed.). Fiscal Publications.

Kotlán, I., Machová, Z., & Janíčková, L. (2011). Vliv zdanění na dlouhodobý ekonomický růst. *Politicka Ekonomie*, *2011*(5), 638–658.

Kubátová, K. (2018). *Daňová teorie a politika*. Wolters Kluwer.

Lee, Y., & Gordon, R. H. (2005). Tax structure and economic growth. *Journal of Public Economics*, *89*(5–6), 1027–1043. https://doi.org/10.1016/j.jpubeco.2004.07.002

Ministry of Finance of the Czech Republic (MFCR). (2020, March 20). *Loss carry-back je levná a rychlá pomoc pro malé i velké firmy*. https://www.mfcr.cz/cs/aktualne/v-mediich/2020/loss-carryback-je-levna-a-rychla-pomoc-p-38611/

Ministry of Finance of the Czech Republic (MFCR). (2022, March 20). *Mimořádná daň z neočekávaných zisků bude platit od 1.* ledna 2023. https://www.mfcr.cz/cs/aktualne/tiskove-zpravy/2022/mimoradna-dan-z-neocekavanych-zisku-bude-48951/

Ministry of Finance of the Czech Republic (MFCR). (2023, February 25). *Fiscal outlook of the Czech Republic*. https://www.mfcr.cz/cs/verejny-sektor/makroekonomika/fiskalni-vyhled/2022/fiskalni-vyhled-cr-listopad-2022-49281

Mirrlees, J., Adam, S., Besley, T., Blundell, R., Bond, S., Chote, R., Gammie, M., Johnson, P., Myles, G., & Poterba, J. (2011). *Tax by design: The Mirrlees review*. Oxford University Press.

Neicu, D., Teirlinck, P., & Kelchtermans, S. (2016). Dipping in the policy mix: Do R&D subsidies foster behavioral additionality effects of R&D tax credits? *Economics of Innovation and New Technology*, *25*(3), 218–239. https://doi.org/10.1080/10438599.2015.1076192

OECD. (2020, March 30). *OECD economic surveys: Czech Republic 2020*. OECD Publishing. https://doi.org/10.1787/1b180a5a-en

Široký, J. (2018). *Daně v Evropské unii*. Leges, s.r.o.

Straub, L., & Werning, I. (2020). Positive long-run capital taxation: Chamley-Judd revisited. *The American Economic Review*, *110*(1), 86–119. https://doi.org/10.1257/aer.20150210

Chapter 8

Tax Policy to Internalize Road Transport Externalities

Petr David

Mendel University in Brno, Czechia

Abstract

Road transport is an important sector of the economy, however, its negative impacts on the environment, human health and sustainability of potential economic growth are significant. Transport externalities tend to be neglected within the market process. The damage generated through significant externalities of road transport in Czechia was identified, based on unique data processing, to reach almost 3.5 billion € annually. This chapter presents an overview of internalization taxes and fees, their current rates and generated receipts. If excise duty is disregarded as fundamentally unsuitable for the internalization of externalities, then the receipts from other applied taxes and fees, particularly the road tax, seem to be insufficient. Although economic growth is encouraged, its form is not sustainable in view of the rising phase of the Kuznets curve and the related irreversible environmental impacts.

Keywords: Fiscal policy; road transport; externality; emission; sustainable economic growth; internal taxes and fees

8.1 Introduction

The transport sector is one of the important parts of economy and one of the determinants of its development. However, its impacts on the environment and directly or indirectly on human health are negative. The contribution of transport to economic development must be viewed in the context of sustainability. Transport externalities tend to be neglected within the market process. It is necessary to identify social costs to be able to consider internalization of externalities generated. Against this background, it is possible to identify potential

Modeling Economic Growth in Contemporary Czechia, 121–136

Published under exclusive licence by Emerald Publishing Limited
doi:10.1108/978-1-83753-840-920241008

public sector instruments appropriate for this purpose and to compare them with the current state of public policies in the given area.

The sources of emission externalities are logically all modes of transport of goods and passengers, i.e. road, air, railway and water transport. Statistics from the Ministry of Transport of Czechia (MTCR, 2022) show that almost 55 terajoules (TJ) of energy were consumed in the transport sector in Czechia in 2021, with more than 80% of this value coming from diesel fuel. Road transport accounts for 92% of energy from diesel fuel consumed by the transport sector in Czechia. Road transport is also the greatest source of emissions with 97% of CO_2 emissions, 89% NO_X emissions and 96% PM generated. Therefore, it has great potential to reduce the absolute quantity of emissions. Moreover, emissions from this type of transport are concentrated in areas with the highest population density per square unit and fundamentally affect human health. Due to the above reasons, this chapter will focus on road transport.

The aim of this chapter is to quantify the production of emissions and determine the external costs of high-impact emissions generated by road transport and its segments in Czechia by processing of unique data. These social costs may be confronted with fiscal instruments with the internalisation potential, and the implications on public policy aimed at the support for sustainable economic growth may be formulated.

8.2 The Theory of Externalities and the Need for Their Economic Internalisation

Road transport accounts for the emission of many air pollutants with negative impacts on human health, yields from agriculture and forestry or defects of structures. These substances include particulate matter (PM), nitrogen oxides (NO_X), sulphur dioxide (SO_2) and volatile organic compounds (VOCs) (van Essen et al., 2019). Road transport is also a source of substances that cause the greenhouse effect (GHG), global warming and climate change on Earth with significant irreversible negative impacts on the environment and human society, especially carbon dioxide CO_2, methane CH_4 and nitrous oxide N_2O. These externalities must be included in the market process through fiscal policy instruments taking into account traditionally accepted paradigms of internalisation of externalities in accordance with Pigou (1920) or Hay and Trinder (1991).

The issue of emissions and their environmental impact is closely related to economic growth and its sustainability. The natural development of emissions in a society is explained by the environmental Kuznets curve (EKC) (Grossman & Krueger, 1995) that has been accepted in the field of social sciences (Yandle et al., 2002). The EKC suggests that initially, economic growth brings about increased deterioration of the environment and larger production of emissions. After a certain level of economic growth, the emissions start to decrease naturally. This level is determined by the feeling of economic security of the population, who then have the potential to think about environmental issues (Stern, 2004). Prieur (2009) defines this level as the level of income per capita. The validity of EKC's implications has been investigated many times over the years, and although it is the subject of some criticism, it has not been contested for CO_2 and NO_X emissions (Mills & Waite, 2009). Other contexts of economic growth and emissions have been researched by Zhang and Nian (2013).

In practice, however, society cannot wait for a natural decline in emissions or for the subsequent gradual decrease of environmental impacts. Natural development in this area need not be and most probably is not sufficient to ensure sustainable development and growth of human society. The impacts of the natural development of emission production seem to be irreversible and fatal unless internalisation measures are taken. Economic growth being desirable, the population directly determines the growth of the generated pollution. The spontaneously occurring turning point of production of polluting emissions cannot be predicted with certainty and relied on; therefore, fiscal instruments must be applied to control and reduce emissions. This requirement is expressed by Santos (2017), who also emphasises that taxes and subsidies may resolve the problem of the high cost of renewable energy in comparison with non-renewable energy. The effectiveness of environmental taxes imposed on vehicles using fossil fuels as a means to reduce emissions is supported, inter alia, by Rasool et al. (2019). The effectiveness of fiscal instruments for the determination of the transportation sectors manufacturers' and consumers' behaviour has been proven in literature (Marriott & Mortimore, 2017). Parry et al. (2014) assert that an equilibrium must be reached between the tax benefits for the environment on the one hand and economic costs on the other, whereby ensuring the optimal level of green growth. Pui and Othman (2017) confirm that tax policy is able to contribute to a better environmental quality. When designing regulatory instruments, it is advisable to base them not only on theoretical assumptions but also on their practical application to date. Cnossen (2005) maintains that significant externalities should be quantified, and the less significant consequences may be disregarded.

In order to implement an appropriate setting of national fiscal policy instruments to determine the environmental impacts of road transport, the knowledge of the existing regulatory framework, its development, direction and impacts is crucial. It is also apparent that national regulations of fiscal instruments in the EU member states, including Czechia, are in place in various forms. The relevant policies in Czechia should therefore be based on the valuable experience of other countries while keeping in mind that the design of such instruments cannot start at the zero baseline.

8.3 Data and Methods

The input data are consistent with the requirement to quantify emissions generated by road transport and to subsequently appraise them. The calculations of the respective emitted pollutant values are based on the processing of real data from the Register of Motor Vehicles (RMV, 2022) in 2018. The processed data include information from the RMV in 2018 and mileages as recorded by Vehicle Testing

Stations (VTS) over a period of four years so that the data may be considered as complete. The results of activity data are completed always only four years before the current year of calculation. This is why data from 2018 had to be used. The source of such non-public and completely unique data is the national organization called the Transport Research Centre (TRC, 2022). The information about mileage recorded by VTS is used to determine the values of average distances travelled. These data are currently not comparable in time due to their non-publicity and the considerable cost of their generation and optimization for the possibility of computer processing. The last similar research in the area was carried out in Czechia in 2013 (David, 2013), when data on mileage was unavailable. Moreover, the analysis only concerned the CO_2 emissions and adequately recorded 4,067,039 passenger vehicles. Therefore, these calculations were based on unit emissions per one kilometre amounting to 773.79 tonnes of CO_2 and related unit emission costs.

The data from the RMV and VTS are interconnected by means of unique identifiers of technical characteristics of the vehicle in each category. Emissions are calculated on the basis of distances travelled. Because of a poorer quality of records in the RMV, the activity data only amount to 60.30%. The problem was resolved by supplementing the real mileages of vehicles lacking records with average mileages of vehicles with the record in the corresponding category.

In 2018, the Czech RMV registered in total 7,423,824 passenger vehicles (PV), light utility vehicles (LUV), heavy goods vehicles (HGV), tractors (T), buses (B) and L-category vehicles (L). The Czech fleet accounts for 2.41% of the vehicle fleet in the EU (WHO, 2020).

A practical application of the Copert programme for emission inventories in Czechia is used for the quantification of aggregate emissions in road transport (Pelikán et al., 2018). Copert is a software tool for the calculation of air pollutants and greenhouse gas emissions from road transport on a regional or country scale and a technologically advanced and transparent model including all main pollutants, used by many European countries for reporting official emission data (Emisia, 2022). The resulting emission inventory provided by the TRC (2022) contains emission values based on the real data of the fleet, divided into nearly 400 vehicle groups depending on their objective technical parameters.

The input appraisal values of emitted pollutants are based on the data of van Essen et al. (2019). The basis for air pollution costs is an average damage cost in €/kg for transport emissions in Czechia, used by David (2022) in the past. Nominal amounts per unit of NO_X, $PM_{2.5}$ and CO_2 emissions include national average emission damage cost for transport emissions, which includes health effects, crop loss, biodiversity loss and material damage for NO_X and $PM_{2.5}$. The value for CO_2 takes into account climate change avoidance costs using CO_2 equivalent. The values are further adjusted through the annual average rate of change of harmonised indices of consumer prices HICP (Eurostat, 2023) in accordance with Schwermer et al. (2014) to ensure consistency with the input data of the Czech fleet. A specifying parameter for the determination of the nominal emission damage cost in Czechia is the appraisal of an emitted pollutant unit depending on the locality where people are exposed to pollution. It is apparent that the nominal emission factor costs increase with the growing concentration of inhabitants. The differentiation of NO_X values for urban areas is 25.9031 $€_{2018}$/kg and for rural areas 15.4583 $€_{2018}$/kg. $PM_{2.5}$ appraisal for urban areas is 121.1597 $€_{2018}$/kg and for rural areas 75.2026 $€_{2018}$/kg. We also include metropolitan areas, which means cities with more than 0.5 million inhabitants, where the value is 377.0573$€_{2018}$/kg. CO_2 emissions are not differentiated in this way due to their global impact. The central estimate for short-and-medium-run up to 2030 is used to appraise CO_2 emissions at a conservative value of 0.1044 $€_{2018}$/kg.

The appraisals are based on the data concerning production of emitted pollutants in Czechia. NO_X emissions are differentiated by urban and rural areas in a ratio of 30:70 in accordance with the assumption of Schwermer et al. (2014). For the purposes of $PM_{2.5}$ emissions, the only metropolitan area in Czechia is the city of Prague under CSO (2023), whose population was 1,294,513 in the given year. The population of Czechia was 10,610,055 in that year. The percentage of inhabitants exposed to emissions in the metropolitan area was 12.20%. This share will be deducted from the percentage of emissions generated in urban areas. The resulting ratio for the application of individual appraisal values of unit emissions is 70:17.80:12.20 for $PM_{2.5}$. Given the global nature of CO_2 emissions, it is not meaningful to distinguish between areas in this case.

8.4 Results of Emission Parameter Calculations and Road Transport Damage Cost Appraisal

On the basis of processing the input data from the RMV, VTS, emission inventory and of the appraisal procedure for CO_2, NO_X and $PM_{2.5}$ emission units, it is possible to calculate the quantity of emissions and emission damage cost for the respective vehicle categories, which appears to be expedient in particular for the regulation regarding road tax in Czechia and its recent amendments.

Table 8.1 shows that vehicles subject to road tax in Czechia generate substantial quantities of all three pollutants examined. These are vehicles in the N and O categories (acc. to Czech classification) used for business purposes. Heavy goods vehicles account for the largest part of these quantities. This proportion also corresponds to the values calculated through the appraisal of an emission unit. The total annual damage cost generated by vehicles taxed in Czechia amounts to 820.25 mil €, where the average damage cost per vehicle is 6,292.34 €.

Vehicle categories of A, LUV, L and PV are not subject to road tax, although they may be used for business. The quantities of emissions generated by these vehicles (Table 8.2) are clearly higher than emissions of vehicles subject to road tax (T and HGV). The total emission damage costs of included externalities amount to 999.12 mil €, which means an average amount of 655.94 € per vehicle per year. An average damage cost is thus much lower than the case with vehicles subject to road tax. The total amount of costs is attributed to the significantly larger frequency of vehicles used for business that are not subject to tax.

Table 8.1. Emissions and Damage Costs of T and HGV Types.

Vehicle Type	NO_X Quantity (kt)	NO_X Appraisal (mil €)	CO_2 Quantity (kt)	CO_2 Appraisal (mil €)	$PM_{2.5}$ Quantity (kt)	$PM_{2.5}$ Appraisal (mil €)	No. of Vehicles
T	1.18	21.88	223.93	23.39	0.04	4.57	6,285
HGV	12.56	233.47	4,514.50	471.53	0.54	65.40	124,072
Total	13.73	255.35	4,738.43	494.92	0.58	69.98	130,357

Source: Author's Calculations.

Table 8.2. Non-Taxed Emissions and Damage Costs According to Vehicle Types.

Vehicle Type	NO_X Quantity (kt)	NO_X Appraisal (mil €)	CO_2 Quantity (kt)	CO_2 Appraisal (mil €)	$PM_{2.5}$ Quantity (kt)	$PM_{2.5}$ Appraisal (mil €)	No. of Vehicles
A	3.83	71.18	850.27	88.81	0.10	12.34	18,497
LUV	6.24	116.00	1,500.54	156.73	0.25	30.45	310,651
L	0.01	0.26	13.09	1.37	0.00	0.25	54,370
PV	6.41	119.13	3,445.00	359.82	0.36	42.78	113,9662
Total	16.49	306.57	5,808.90	606.73	0.71	85.82	152,3180

Source: Author's Calculations.

Table 8.3 shows the quantified emission values and damage costs of vehicles that are not subject to road tax because they are not used for commercial purposes. The table includes all categories of road motor vehicles owned by private persons as well as foreign persons (as defined by the RMV). Emissions generated by the PV category markedly prevail due to their large frequency. The emissions from these vehicles are almost twice as high as the emissions of vehicles subject to tax, $PM_{2.5}$ even more than double. The damage costs attributable to PVs amount to 1,639.16 mil € per year with an average cost of 296.15 mil € per vehicle.

Table 8.4 shows total emissions of vehicles that are not subject to road tax, including their appraisal. In terms of emission quantities and damage costs, PV vehicles clearly dominate due to their high frequency. The quantities of emissions are approximately threefold compared to the values of the fleet subject to road tax. The total damage costs attributable to vehicles not subject to road tax are 2,638.28 mil € per year. Although these vehicles generate lesser average damage costs (373.80 €), their total value is four times higher than the case with vehicles subject to tax.

Table 8.5 demonstrates the potential for the internalisation of externalities and identifies the total emissions of three essential pollutants generated by road transport including the classification by categories and frequency of vehicles. CO_2 emissions are the most costly, NO_X emissions are about half as high and $PM_{2.5}$ emissions are significantly lower. The total damage costs amount to 3,459.74 mil €, the average damage cost per vehicle operated in Czechia is 466.03 € per year.

8.5 Policy Implications

Czechia, as well as other European Union countries have to adjust their national legislation to regulatory measures adopted at the EU level, currently the "Fit for 55" (European Council, 2023) package, the REPowerEU plan (European Commission, 2023), many directives, regulations and other documents.

Of all the potential instruments for the regulation of road transport emissions, Czechia uses road tax, registration fee, time-based charges, tolls and excise tax. Other instruments for the internalisation of emission externalities, such as registration tax, carbon tax, bonus-malus system and others are not used in this country.

8.5.1 Road Tax

Taxes on ownership and operation of road motor vehicles are levied in 21 EU countries including Czechia, whereas 15 countries take into account CO_2 emissions. The tax rate decreases with vehicle age in three countries; it increases with age only in Czechia and Slovakia. From 2024 onwards, this provision will not apply in Czechia. All EU countries except for four apply road tax on passenger cars and all the countries applying road tax levy the tax on commercial cars. Czech regulation of the tax seems rather exceptional within the EU.

Table 8.3. Non-Taxed Emissions and Damage Costs According to Purpose of Use.

Vehicle Type	NO_X Quantity (kt)	NO_X Appraisal (mil €)	CO_2 Quantity (kt)	CO_2 Appraisal (mil €)	$PM_{2.5}$ Quantity (kt)	$PM_{2.5}$ Appraisal (mil €)	No. of Vehicles
A	0.28	5.21	28.14	2.94	0.01	1.06	2,218
LUV	2.66	49.45	741.79	77.48	0.21	25.66	233,423
L	0.37	6.94	147.49	15.41	0.04	4.58	933,872
PV	19.68	365.91	8,187.71	855.19	1.33	159.56	4,348,885
T	0.16	2.89	23.45	2.45	0.01	0.65	410
HGV	1.54	28.69	259.85	27.14	0.07	7.96	16,061
Total	24.69	459.09	9,388.43	980.60	1.66	199.47	5,534,869

Source: Author's Calculations.

Table 8.4. Total Non-Taxed Emissions and Societal Damage.

Vehicle Type	NO_X Quantity (kt)	NO_X Appraisal (mil €)	CO_2 Quantity (kt)	CO_2 Appraisal (mil €)	$PM_{2.5}$ Quantity (kt)	$PM_{2.5}$ Appraisal (mil €)	No. of Vehicles
A	4.11	76.39	878.41	91.75	0.11	13.39	20,715
LUV	8.90	165.45	2,242.33	234.21	0.47	56.12	544,074
L	0.39	7.21	160.59	16.77	0.04	4.83	988,242
PV	26.09	485.04	11,632.70	1,215.01	1.68	202.34	5,488,547
T	0.16	2.89	23.45	2.45	0.01	0.65	410
HGV	1.54	28.69	259.85	27.14	0.07	7.96	16,061
Total	41.18	765.67	15,197.33	1,587.33	2.37	285.28	7,058,049

Source: Author's Calculations.

Table 8.5. Potential for the Taxation of Emissions and Societal Damage Caused.

Vehicle Type	NO_X Quantity (kt)	NO_X Appraisal (mil €)	CO_2 Quantity (kt)	CO_2 Appraisal (mil €)	$PM_{2.5}$ Quantity (kt)	$PM_{2.5}$ Appraisal (mil €)	No. of Vehicles
A	4.11	76.40	878.45	91.75	0.11	13.40	21,722
LUV	8.90	165.47	2,242.53	234.23	0.47	56.12	548,419
L	0.39	7.25	161.22	16.84	0.04	4.86	1,124,058
PV	26.11	485.48	11,636.11	1,215.37	1.68	202.40	5,576,583
T	1.33	24.77	247.39	25.84	0.04	5.22	7,420
HGV	14.10	262.21	4,774.96	498.74	0.61	73.38	145,622
Total	54.95	1021.59	19,940.66	2,082.76	2.96	355.39	7,423,824

Source: Author's Calculations.

Under Czech Act No. 16/1993 Coll. (Czechia, 2023d), the subject of road tax is a road motor vehicle in N2 and N3 categories and its trailer in O3 and O4 categories, kept in the RMV of Czechia. These are specific vehicles designed and constructed for the transport of loads with a maximum weight exceeding 3.5 tonnes but not exceeding 12 tonnes, vehicles designed and constructed for the transport of loads with a maximum weight exceeding 12 tonnes and trailers for these vehicles. Regardless of the date of first registration, the tax rate is reduced by 100% for trucks and trailers with a maximum permissible weight of more than 3.5 tonnes and less than 12 tonnes if these vehicles are used by a natural person only for activities not related to business. In reality, road tax in Czechia is levied on a very small share of vehicles operated in the country.

Before the effectiveness of amendment No. 142/2022 to the Road Tax Act (Czechia, 2023c), all vehicles used for commercial purposes, regardless of their category, were subject to road tax. An exception was trucks with the maximum permitted weight over 3.5 tonnes, whose owners paid road tax regardless of the purpose of use. The primary insufficiency of tax revenues may be attributed to the significant restriction of the subjects of the tax, which was brought about by the amendment.

In general, the purpose of Czech road tax is to levy charges on the use of roads and motorways by motor vehicles in the territory of Czechia. In fact, this purpose is not realized in that the subjects of the tax are limited to certain vehicle categories. Similarly, the primary purpose of road tax is not to take into account road transport externalities.

Fiscal revenues collected through road tax in 2021 amounted to 217.20 mil € by the Ministry of Finance of Czechia (MFCR, 2022). At the same time, the 2022 amendment to the Road Tax Act accounted for a significant decrease in the road tax revenues, which has not been quantified yet. The total road tax revenues belong to the budget of the State Fund for Transport Infrastructure, which is expended on the construction, repairs and modernisation of roads and motorways in accordance with Act No. 104/2000 Coll. (Czechia, 2023a).

Given the concept of road tax, which is determined according to the weight of the vehicle and the number of axles, it is clear that the load and wear of the road, and not primarily the volume of emissions, are taken into account. The truth is that there is a direct proportion between weight and number of axles on the one hand and fuel consumption, tyre, brake and road wear on the other. It may be said that these facts are also related to CO_2, NO_X and $PM_{2.5}$ emissions, and they may be considered as proxies for real emission parameters of the vehicles.

8.5.2 Other Taxes and Fees Related to Road Transport

A registration tax or fee is applied in 17 countries of the European Union; 14 countries factor CO_2 emissions (Ireland also considers NO emissions), and four countries take into account the Euro standard (ACEA, 2022). Inspiring features may be found in the bonus-malus system of this tax, applied, e.g. in France, Italy and Sweden. The Czech emission fee imposed on the first re-registration of a vehicle under Act No. 542/2020 Coll. (Czechia, 2023e). may be considered a registration fee to an extent. The amount of the emission fee is 120.00 € if the vehicle meets the Euro 2 standard, 200.00 € for Euro 1 and 400.00 € for Euro 0. Extension of this fee to vehicles of higher Euro standards or adjustment of the mentioned amounts have been considered for a long time, yet these plans have not been put into practice. Moreover, this taxation method, which corresponds to emission indicators, is not very popular in the European Union and may pose issues of discrimination of cross-border trade within the Community. The data on the collection of the environmental fee are not available and the Czech Ministry of Finance has no statistics in this respect. We have calculated theoretical receipts based on a simulation using the data from the RMV, which amount to 6.72 mil. € (David & Andrlík, 2020). Czechia does not apply the traditional registration tax. An administrative registration fee is stipulated by Czech Act No. 56/2001 Coll. (Czechia, 2023f). The amount of the administrative fee, paid on the registration in the Register of Motor Vehicles, is determined by Act No. 634/2004 Coll. (Czechia, 2023g), depends on the vehicle category and amounts to 30 € at the maximum. The fees are collected and administered by local authorities. The data regarding the collection of the registration fees are not available and no relevant statistics exist according to the Ministry of Finance.

EU countries currently tend to abandon time-based charges. Similar charges are valid in more than a half of the EU member states. Charges for vehicles below 3.5 tonnes are virtually unregulated at the European level. The individual member states are entitled to introduce any system of charges that respects the principle of non-discrimination and proportionality in connection with nationality. Time-based charges are regulated by Act No. 13/1997 Coll. (Czechia, 2023b). Current amounts in Czechia are 60.00 € for an annual vignette, 17.06 € for a 30-day vignette and 12.40 € for a 10-day vignette for vehicles up to 3.5 tonnes. An increase in the prices and introduction of a one-day vignette may be expected soon. According to the State Fund for Transport Infrastructure, SFTI (2022), the receipts from this charge in 2018–2021 were 169.60 mil. € to 216.80 mil. €.

An effort to extend tolls to all types of road motor transport is apparent in the EU. Most EU countries apply pricing through a system of tolls. Each country is entitled to determine the categories of vehicles that shall be subject to toll, and the differences among European countries are significant. In the EU, these charges are levied on freight vehicles with the maximum permissible weight exceeding 3.5 tonnes. The criteria for paying tolls differ by country. The tendency is to extend tolls to all types of road motor transport. Tolls are not charged in 10 countries of the EU (ACEA, 2022). Ten EU countries including Czechia use Euro standards for the determination of tolls. In Czechia, tolls are regulated by Act No. 13/1997 Coll. (Czechia, 2023b). The amount of toll for vehicles over 3.5 tonnes depends on the number of axles, vehicle weight, emission standard, road type and time of day in connection with noise. Toll rates increase with the growing number of axles, vehicle weight, and a lower emission standard. Toll rates are equal for vehicles under Euro 0 to Euro IV. Some vehicles are exempt from tolls due to their low emission parameters. According to SFTI (2022), the receipts were 429.2 mil. € to 543.6 mil. € in 2018–2021.

Excise tax rates in the EU are regulated through the setting of minimum rates for unleaded petrol, amounting to 359 €, and for gas oil, amounting to 330 € per 1,000 litres. Excise tax on mineral oils is regulated by Act No. 353/2004 Coll. in Czechia. Current rates are 523.5047 CZK/1,000 litres of unleaded petrol and 344.5183 CZK/1,000 litres of gas oil, whereas the rate for gas oil dropped from 425.4097 CZK/1,000 litres valid in 2020. According to MFCR (2022), the receipts from mineral oil excise tax were 3,292.00 mil. € to 3,600.00 mil. € in 2018–2021.

8.6 Conclusion

Czechia imposes road tax, registration fee, time-based charges, tolls and excise tax, which are some of the potential instruments for the regulation of emissions from transport, and thus its externalities. The position of Czechia is that of a recipient of EU policies rather than a leader in the area of internalisation of road transport externalities. The regulation and introduction of fiscal policy instruments to internalise emission externalities are rigid and fail to utilise the potential of existing instruments. Some of them are not used at all, such as carbon tax on conventional fuels that is becoming more widely applied in the European, registration tax or the bonus-malus system. Only a part of the instruments applied in this country is conceived to relate to road transport externalities, and most of them clearly have a different purpose than to internalise emission externalities. The rigid approach and incorrect tendencies in the changes to fiscal instruments in Czechia together with regulatory trends of the European Union bring about serious social impacts as well as possible aggravation of the emission burden and the related environmental and health impacts.

A crucial instrument with the potential to internalise emission externalities at least through the taxation of proxies for vehicle emission parameters is road tax. However, its scope is limited in Czechia, and it does not include vehicle types with substantial emissions and various purposes of vehicle use. This in particular includes passenger cars used for business purposes as well as those privately owned. The introduction of a general taxation of road motor vehicles would lead to an increase in public budget revenues so that these receipts would at least come close to the social cost of 3,459.74 mil. € generated by the production of emissions in road transport.

The road tax must be made universally applicable, and fiscal policy instruments to internalize the externalities must be defined. Because energy tax or excise tax on mineral oils is generally not recommended to be levied for the purpose of internalization of externalities, other payments in Czech road transport in the aggregate amount of 800 mil. € are totally insufficient as well as road tax itself.

References

ACEA. (2022). *ACEA tax guide 2022*. https://www.acea.auto/files/ACEA_Tax_Guide_2022.pdf

Cnossen, S. (2005). *Theory and practice of excise taxation: Smoking, drinking, gambling, polluting, and driving*. Oxford University Press.

CSO. (2023). *Population of municipalities*. https://www.czso.cz/csu/czso/population-of-municipalities-mg2kmr7h39

Czechia. (2023a). *Act No. 104/2000*.

Czechia. (2023b). *Act No. 13/1997*.

Czechia. (2023c). *Act No. 142/2022*.

Czechia. (2023d). *Act No. 16/1993*.

Czechia. (2023e). *Act No. 542/2020*.

Czechia. (2023f). *Act No. 56/2001*.

Czechia. (2023g). *Act No. 634/2004*.

David, P. (2013). Construction of environmental road tax in the Czech Republic. *Trends economics and management*, *7*(15), 27–36.

David, P. (2022). The right time for general road tax: Evidence from the Czechia. *Scientific Papers of the University of Pardubice*, *30*(2), 1598. https://doi.org/10.46585/sp30021598

David, P., & Andrlík, B. (2020). *Analysis of charging and taxation of vehicles*. Transportation Research Centre. Final Project Report 22 202.

Emisia. (2022). *Copert*. https://www.emisia.com/utilities/Copert/

European Commission. (2023). *REPowerEU*. https://commission.europa.eu/strategy-and-policy/priorities-2019-2024/european-green-deal/repowereu-affordable-secure-and-sustainable-energy-europe_en

European Council. (2023). *Fit for 55*. https://www.consilium.europa.eu/en/policies/green-deal/fit-for-55-the-eu-plan-for-a-green-transition/

Eurostat. (2023). *HICP – Inflation rate – Annual average rate of change (%)*. https://ec.europa.eu/eurostat/databrowser/view/tec00118/default/table?lang=en

Grossman, M. G., & Krueger, A. B. (1995). Economic growth and the environment. *Quarterly Journal of Economics*, *110*(2), 353–377.

Hay, A., & Trinder, L. (1991). Concepts of equity, fairness, and justice expressed by local transport policy-makers. *Environment and Planning C: Government and Policy*, *9*(4), 453–465. https://doi.org/10.1068/c090453

Marriott, L., & Mortimore, A. (2017). Emissions, road transport, regulation and tax incentives in Australia and New Zealand. *Journal of the Australasian Tax Teachers Association*, *12*(1), 23–52.

MFCR. (2022). *Reports on the activities of the financial and customs administration*. https://www.mfcr.cz/cs/verejny-sektor/dane/danove-a-celni-statistiky/zpravy-o-cinnosti-financni-a-celni-sprav

Mills, J. H., & Waite, T. A. (2009). Economic prosperity, biodiversity conservation, and the environmental Kuznets curve. *Ecological Economics*, *68*(7), 2087–2095.

MTCR. (2022). *Transportation yearbook 2021*. https://www.sydos.cz/cs/rocenka-2021/rocenka/htm_cz/obsah7.html

Parry, I., Heine, D., Li, S., & Lis, E. (2014). How should different countries tax fuels to correct environmental externalities? *Economics of Energy & Environmental Policy*, *3*(2), 61–77.

Pelikán, L., Brich, M., & Ličbinský, R. (2018). *Introduction of the Copert 5 program for calculation of road transport emissions in Czechia.* Final Project Report. Transportation Research Centre.

Pigou, A. C. (1920). *The economics of welfare.* McMillan & Co.

Prieur, F. (2009). The environmental Kuznets curve in a world of irreversibility. *Economic Theory*, *40*(1), 57–90. https://doi.org/10.1007/s00199-008-0351-y

Pui, K. L., & Othman, J. (2017). Economics and environmental implications of fuel efficiency improvement in Malaysia: A computable general equilibrium approach. *Journal of Cleaner Production*, *156*, 459–469.

Rasool, Y., Zaidi, S. A. H., & Zafar, M. W. (2019). Determinants of carbon emissions in Pakistan's transport sector. *Environmental Science and Pollution Research*, *26*(22), 22907–22921. https://doi.org/10.1007/s11356-019-05504-4

RMV. (2022). *Data from the Czech vehicle register.* Internal Data.

Santos, G. (2017). Road transport and CO_2 emissions: What are the challenges? *Transport Policy*, *59*, 71–74. https://doi.org/10.1016/j.tranpol.2017.06.007

Schwermer, S., Preiss, P., & Müller, W. (2014). *Best-practice cost rates for air pollutants, transport, power generation and heat generation.* https://www.umweltbundesamt.de/sites/default/files/medien/378/publikationen/economic_valuation_methods_-_annex_b.pdf

SFTI. (2022). *Annual reports and financial statements.* https://www.sfdi.cz/rozpocet/vyrocni-zpravy-a-ucetni-zaverky/

Stern, D. (2004). The rise and fall of the environmental Kuznets curve. *World Development*, *32*(8), 1419–1439. https://doi.org/10.1016/j.worlddev.2004.03.004

TRC. (2022). *Czechia fleet activity data.* Internal Data.

Van Essen, H., van Wijngaarden, L., Schroten, A., Sutter, D., Bieler, C., Maffii, S., Brambilla, M., Fiorello, D., Fermi, F., Parolin, R., & KBeyrouty, K. E. (2019). *Handbook on the external costs of transport.* https://www.cedelft.eu/assets/upload/file/Rapporten/2019/CE_Delft_4K83_Handbook_on_the_external_costs_of_transport_Final.pdf

WHO. (2020). *Registered cehicles.* Data by Country. https://apps.who.int/gho/data/node.main.A995

Yandle, B., Vijayaraghavan, M., & Bhattarai, M. (2002). *The environmental Kuznets curve: A primer.* https://www.perc.org/wp-content/uploads/2018/05/environmental-kuznets-curve-primer.pdf

Zhang, C. H., & Nian, J. (2013). Panel estimation for transport sector CO_2 emissions and its affecting factors: A regional analysis in China. *Energy Policy*, *63*, 918–926. https://doi.org/10.1016/j.enpol.2013.07.142

Chapter 9

Relationship Between General Government Expenditure and Economic Growth in Czechia*

Irena Szarowská

Silesian University in Opava, Czechia

Abstract

Government spending plays a crucial role in fiscal policy in any country, both as a tool for implementing individual government policies and as a possible instrument for mitigating uneven economic developments and economic shocks. This chapter provides direct empirical evidence on the development and structure of general government expenditure and its relationship with real economic growth in Czechia and the European Union countries. Compared to theoretical recommendations, general government expenditure has not been used as a stabiliser in Czechia and EU countries and has been observed to be pro-cyclical in the period under review. Granger causality analysis identified the direction of causality between the macroeconomic variables analysed and found that in most cases economic growth came first, followed by government spending.

Keywords: Government expenditure; economic growth; COFOG classification; granger causality; cyclicality; stabiliser

9.1 Introduction

Nowadays, the growing concerns of many governments are focused on the problem of how to ensure economic growth. The growth of government spending

---

*This article contains sections previously published in: Szarowska, I. (2022). Relationship between government expenditure and economic growth in Visegrad Group. *Financial Internet Quarterly*, 18(4), 12–22. https://doi.org/10.2478/fiqf-2022-0024

Modeling Economic Growth in Contemporary Czechia, 137–151

Published under exclusive licence by Emerald Publishing Limited
doi:10.1108/978-1-83753-840-920241009

and the factors contributing to it pose a significant challenge for many countries, especially in light of depleted public budgets following the COVID-19 pandemic and other external shocks (energy crisis, war in Ukraine and related spending).

Government spending plays a pivotal role in the fiscal policy of a country, functioning as both a potential stabiliser and a tool for the implementation of individual government policies, as well as the provision of public goods and services. Therefore, general government expenditure (hereinafter GGE) is an important and relevant indicator of the size and role of the public sector in the economy. It also reflects the fiscal policy settings and the fiscal space available to the government to respond to shocks and pursue its development objectives. Economic growth is influenced by many factors such as physical and human capital, technology, institutions, trade and natural resources. However, one of the key determinants of economic growth is GGE.

The effect of GGE on economic growth depends on several factors such as the level, composition, efficiency, quality and sustainability of public spending, the state of the economic cycle, the structure of the economy, the institutional framework and the current economic situation in the form of external shocks or spillovers. Therefore, there is no simple or universal answer to the question of how much or what kind of GGE is optimal or desirable for economic growth. Different countries may have different preferences or constraints on the choice of GGE and these choices may change over time depending on circumstances and objectives. Moreover, while a number of studies have focused on the relationship between GGE and economic growth, the nature of this relationship remains inconclusive and it cannot be conclusively argued that increasing GGE has a positive effect on economic growth (see Nyasha & Odhiambo, 2019 for a more detailed discussion).

The aim of this chapter is to provide direct empirical evidence on the development and structure of general government expenditure (hereinafter GGE) and its relationship with real economic growth in Czechia and the European Union countries in the period 2000–2021. The intention is also to determine whether government spending has been used as a stabiliser in the period under review.

9.2 Methodology and Data

The dataset consists of annual GDP and GGE data in accordance with the international COFOG standard for the period 2000–2021 (latest available data). All data for Czechia and the EU were obtained from the Eurostat database. The time series of GDP, total GGE and its sub-components are adjusted in constant prices.

Many studies point out that the use of a non-stationary macroeconomic variable in time series analysis causes problems with regression superiority. Therefore, any empirical study using such variables should be preceded by a unit root test. The decision on the existence of a unit root is based on the Augmented Dickey-Fuller test (ADF test). To test for stationarity, Eq. (9.1) is formulated.

$$\Delta y_t = \alpha + \beta t + \gamma y_{t-1} + \sum_{j-1}^{p} (\delta_j \Delta Y_{t-j}) + \varepsilon_t \tag{9.1}$$

where

t is the time index
α is an intercept constant
β is the coefficient on a time trend
γ is the coefficient presenting process root, i.e. the focus of testing
p is the lag order of the first-differences autoregressive process
ε_t is an independent identically distributed residual term.

An ADF test is used to determine a unit root y_t at all variables in the time t. Variable Δy_{t-i} expresses the lagged first difference and ε_t estimate autocorrelation error. Coefficients δ_0, δ_1, δ_2 are estimated. Zero and the alternative hypothesis for the existence of a unit root in the y_t variable are specified in Eq. (9.2). The result of the ADF test confirmed the stationarity of all-time series.

$$H_0: \delta_2 = 0, \; H_\varepsilon: \delta_2 < 0 \tag{9.2}$$

The Hodrick Prescott filter (HP) estimates an unobservable time trend for time series variables. Let y_t denote an observable macroeconomic time series. The HP filter decomposes y_t into a nonstationary trend g_t and a stationary residual component c_t, i.e. Eq. (9.3):

$$y_t = g_t + c_t \tag{9.3}$$

Note that g_t and c_t are unobservables. For a suitably chosen positive value of λ, there is a trend component that will be minimised Eq. (9.4):

$$\sum_{t=1}^{T} (y_t - g_t)^2 + \lambda \sum_{t=2}^{T-1} ((g_{t+1} - g_t) - (g_t - g_{t-1}))^2 \tag{9.4}$$

The first term of the equation is the sum of the squared deviations, which penalises the cyclic component. The second term is λ times the sum of the squares of the squared deviations of the trend component. This second term penalises deviations in the growth rate of the trend component. The larger the value of λ, the higher the penalty. Hodrick and Prescott recommend a smoothing parameter value of $\lambda = 100$ for annual data.

Next, a cross-correlation is applied to all combinations of GDP–GGE Eq. (9.5). The cross-correlation assesses how one reference time series correlates with another time series or several other series depending on the time lag. The cross-correlation does not provide a single correlation coefficient but a range of correlation values. Like all correlations, cross-correlation shows only statistical associations, not causation. Consider two financial series and, then the cross-correlation with lag (lead) k is defined as follows:

$$\rho(y_{t+k}, x_t) = \frac{T \sum_{t=k-1}^{T} (y_{t+k} - m_y)(x_t - m_x)}{(T+k)\sqrt{\sum_{t=k}^{T} (y_{t+k} - m_y)^2}\sqrt{\sum_{t=k}^{T} (x_t - m_x)^2}} \tag{9.5}$$

where

ρ – correlation coefficient,
m_x, m_y – the means of corresponding series.

The correlation coefficient can vary from -1 to $+1$. The coefficient -1 indicates perfect negative correlation, and $+1$ indicates perfect positive correlation. Its value smaller than 0.1 means zero correlation, from 0.1 to 0.35 weak correlation, from 0.35 to 0.7 moderate correlation and higher than 0.7 express strong correlation. A positive correlation coefficient indicates the pro-cyclicality of government expenditure, a negative value means that variables are counter-cyclical and a value close to zero expresses acyclicality.

The standard Granger causality test developed by Granger (1980) is commonly used to test whether past changes in one variable help explain current changes in other variables, and is also used in most empirical studies to test the relationship between economic growth and government spending (Ahuja & Pandit, 2020; Dudzevičiūtė et al., 2018; Lupu et al., 2018; Nyasha & Odhiambo, 2019; Pula & Elshani, 2018; Roşoiu, 2015; Zamanian et al., 2012). Therefore, the Granger causality test is used to model the relationship and estimate the causality between all the COFOG government expenditure sub-components and economic growth. The Granger causality test assumes that only time series data can interpret the information needed for the relationship between variables. The methodology is described in detail in Szarowská (2011).

9.3 Literature Review

The relationship between GGE and economic growth has long been debated in theoretical and empirical literature. Different schools of thought have proposed different mechanisms and implications for how government spending affects output growth. As Szarowská (2022) argues, there are two basic opposing views in terms of the endo and exogeneity of the impact of government spending and economic growth. The Keynesian view argues that government spending is an exogenous factor that affects economic growth and can be used as a policy tool. On the other hand, the Wagnerian view argues that government spending is an endogenous factor or a consequence (not a cause) of economic growth. In contrast, from the Keynesian view, government spending should act as a stabiliser and move countercyclically. Pro-cyclical fiscal policy, on the other hand, is a policy that is expansionary in times of boom and contractionary in times of recession.

Nyasha and Odhiambo (2019) and Alqadi and Ismail (2019) provide a comprehensive review of empirical evidence and theoretical and empirical literature on the relationship between government spending and economic growth. The papers conclude that neither the theoretical literature nor the empirical literature provides convincing evidence on the nature of this relationship.

The empirical literature on this topic is vast and inconclusive, as different studies use different methodologies, datasets, time periods, country samples and control variables to test the relationship between GGE and economic growth. The first studies can be found in the 1980s when Romer (1986) confirms the positive effect of higher GGE generating higher economic growth due to expansionary fiscal policy. Alexiou (2009) empirically estimates this relationship in Central and Eastern European (CEE) countries using a panel data model and finds a strong positive effect of GGE on economic growth. Afonso and Alves (2017) focus on 14 EU countries and find some GGE categories that support the approach that GDP growth causes higher government spending. Sáez et al. (2017) also tested this relationship using regression and panel data analysis, but revealed mixed results. Shkodra et al. (2022) found a positive effect of GGE on economic growth for a panel of six SEE countries, supporting the Keynesian school. In contrast, a negative effect can be found in Lupu et al. (2018), who examined the effects in 10 selected Central and Eastern European countries and found that GGE on defence, economic affairs, general public services and social security have a negative impact on economic growth.

Contrary to theoretical assumptions, empirical observations and a number of studies show a procyclical tendency of GGE and economic growth (Alesina et al., 2008; Devarajanet et al., 1996; Fiorito & Kollintzas, 1994; Hercowitz & Strawczynski, 2004; Lane, 2003; Rajkumar & Swaroop, 2008). Lane (2003) and later the analysis of Talvi and Vegh (2005) summarise that fiscal procyclicality is evident in a much larger sample of countries. Using a sample of 20 OECD countries, Abbott and Jones (2011) suggest that the degree of procyclicality varies not only across countries but also across spending categories (procyclicality is more likely for smaller functional budgets, while procyclicality is more likely for larger capital expenditures). Alesina et al. (2008) present the conclusion that fiscal policy procyclicality is more pronounced in more corrupt democracies.

Not only the relationship but also the direction of action of the two variables is examined. Pula and Elshani (2018) used Granger causality test to identify the direction of flow between variables in Kosovo (2002–2015) and found unidirectional causality. Similarly, Dudzeviciute et al. (2018) offer similarly mixed conclusions, using correlation analysis and the Granger causality test to suggest that eight EU countries had a significant relationship between 1995 and 2015. Specifically, a unidirectional causal relationship from economic growth to GGE was found in France, Belgium, Germany, Portugal and Cyprus, a unidirectional causal relationship from GGE to economic growth was found in Sweden and Slovakia, and no causal relationship was found in Poland. Different results can be observed in the study of Roşoiu (2015), who found bidirectional causality in Romania (1998–2014).

In addition, some studies have found that the relationship between GGE and economic growth is non-linear and depends on various factors such as the type, composition, financing and level of GGE, as well as the institutional and macroeconomic environment of the country (Karagianni et al., 2019). For example, Arawatari et al. (2023) show that government investment spending has a positive effect on economic growth in a model with heterogeneous agents and endogenous growth. On the other hand, Parui (2020) analyses the implications of different types of VGE on aggregate demand and economic growth in a post-Keynesian model. He finds that shifting government spending from consumption to investment leads to a clear increase in aggregate demand and economic growth in the profit-led demand regime, but the result is ambiguous in the wage-led demand regime.

9.4 Development of Government Expenditure

GGE is one of the key components of aggregate demand in an economy, and it can have significant effects on economic growth, both in the short and long term. Government expenditure can be classified by its main socio-economic function, according to the Classification of the Functions of Government (COFOG). The GGE (CF) can be divided into 10 groups:

(1) CF10: General public services
(2) CF20: Defence
(3) CF30: Public order and safety
(4) CF40: Economic affairs
(5) CF50: Environment protection
(6) CF60: Housing and community amenities
(7) CF70: Health
(8) CF80: Recreation, culture and religion
(9) CF90: Education
(10) CF100: Social protection

Fig. 9.1 focuses on the average GGE in each country over the period 2000–2021 and in 2021. The shares of percentage GDP show the existing differences and perceptions of the role of the state across countries. From this perspective, France is the country with the highest role of the state and its redistribution, although its role has also decreased (except during the pandemic

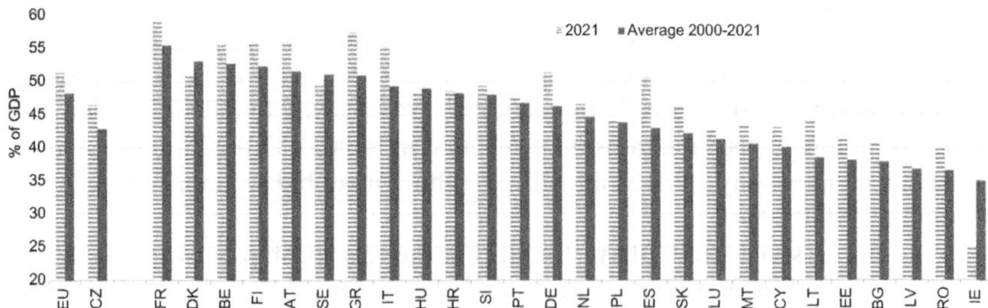

Fig. 9.1. GGE Average (2000–2001) and in 2021 (in % GDP). *Source:* Author's comparison based on Eurostat data.

period). On the other hand, Ireland is the country with the lowest share of GGE in GDP (average value is 35% GDP), which means the smallest size of the public sector. According to Eurostat data, the EU average is 48.2% of GDP, with a difference of more than 20 percentage points between the highest and the lowest GGE. This is due not only to differences in the structure of the economy, the demographic structure of the population, historical habits, but above all to the type of social and fiscal policy (social democratic or conservative) and the role of the state and the responsibilities of the citizen. In 2021, the average total GGE was 46.5% GDP in Czechia and 51.5% GDP in the EU, which is still affected by the COVID-19 pandemic and government measures to mitigate its impact. The decrease in the ratio from the previous year (53.1%) was mainly due to the increase in GDP, while growth in total expenditure was still observed. The Czech average GGE is 42.9% (5.5 percentage points below EU) for the whole period.

According to Eurostat data, Fig. 9.2 shows that social protection is the largest category of GGE in the EU, accounting for 20.5% GDP in 2021, up from 18% in 2000. Social protection includes spending on pensions, unemployment benefits, family and child allowances, social assistance and other social programmes. The increase in social protection GGE reflects the ageing population, the economic crisis and the social impact of the pandemic in the EU.

The second most important category of GGE is health care, which accounted for 8.1% GDP in 2021 compared to 6.1% in 2000. Health GGE includes medical services, hospital services, public health services and health administration. The increase in health GGE is partly due to an ageing population, technological advances and higher demand for health services during pandemics.

The third largest category of GGE is education, which accounted for 4.8% of GDP in 2021, the same as in 2000. Education GGE includes spending on pre-primary, primary, secondary, tertiary and post-secondary non-tertiary education, as well as education administration and student subsidies. The decline in education GGE is partly due to demographic changes, efficiency gains and budget constraints in some countries.

General public services GGE (which include spending on the executive and legislature, financial and fiscal affairs, foreign affairs, public debt transactions,

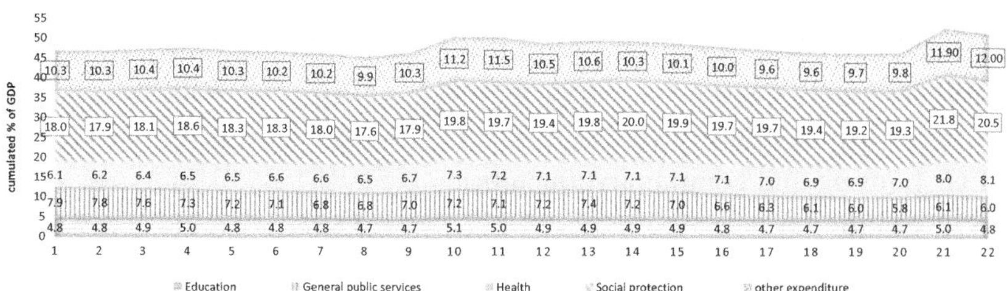

Fig. 9.2. Development of Main Categories of GGE (EU Average, in % GDP). The individual categories of GGE from the legend are shown in order from bottom to top. *Source:* Eurostat data.

etc.) have declined from 7.4% of GDP in 2000 to 6.4% of GDP in 2021. Other categories of GGE have a smaller share of GDP and show different trends over time. For example, defence GGE has also decreased from 1.9% of GDP in 2000 to 1.5% of GDP in 2021. The common trend is that the five main expenditure functions cover on average more than 85% of total GGE and their share is slightly increasing.

Table 9.1 reports the average structure of GGE by function in percentage GDP and differences between Czechia and the EU. Among the main functions of GGE, Social protection (CF100) remained the most important in the analysed period, equivalent to 12.9% GDP in Czechia and 19.1% GDP in the EU, followed by Health (CF70) with 7.5% GDP, resp. 7% GDP, Economic affairs (CF40) with 7% GDP, resp. 4.8% GDP and General public services (CF10) with 4.7% GDP and 6.9% GDP. The functions Education CF90 (4.6% GDP vs. 4.8% GDP), Public order and safety (CF30), Environmental protection (CF50) and Housing and community amenities (CF60) had more limited weights. The categories that showed notable differences between Czechia and the EU were education, defence, economic affairs, environmental protection, housing and community affairs, and education. Czechia spent less on defence than the EU average (1.1% GDP vs. 1.3% GDP in 2021), while spending more on Economic affairs, Environmental protection, Housing and community affairs and Education (5.4% GDP vs. 4.9% GDP in 2021).

Fig. 9.3 briefly compares the structure of GGE over the period under review. The structure of GGE has changed significantly from 2000 to 2021, reflecting the impact of the COVID-19 pandemic and the policy response to it. Fig. 9.3 shows that in both years, social protection and health were the largest categories for Czechia and the EU, accounting for more than half of GGE. These functions are

Table 9.1. Average GGE by Functions (2000–2021, in % GDP).

	Czechia	**EU**	**Difference**
CF_total	42.85	48.20	−5.35
CF10_general public services	4.66	6.89	−2.23
CF20_defence	1.11	1.29	−0.18
CF30_public order and safety	1.89	1.70	0.20
CF40_economic affairs	6.96	4.77	2.20
CF50_environmental protection	0.97	0.79	0.18
CF60_housing and community amenities	0.91	0.74	0.17
CF70_health	7.53	6.91	0.62
CF80_recreation, culture and religion	1.39	1.19	0.20
CF90_education	4.61	4.84	−0.23
CF100_social protection	12.85	19.14	−6.29

Source: Author's calculation based on Eurostat, 2023.

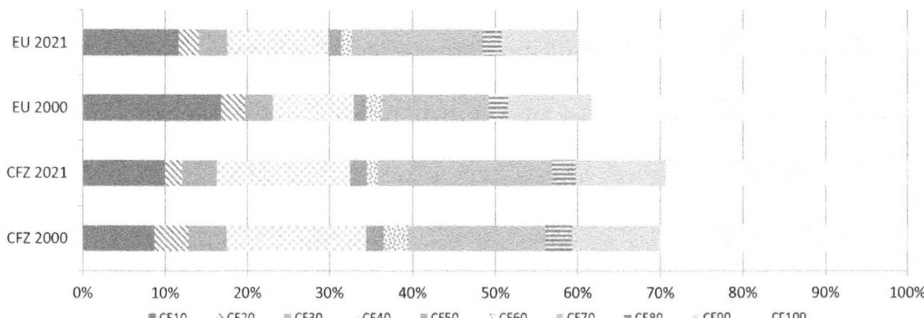

Fig. 9.3. Changes in Structure of COFOG Expenditure. *Source:* Author's comparison based on Eurostat data.

key to providing social security and health services to the population, especially in times of crisis. Social protection is one of the main functions of GGE as it includes various benefits and services aimed at reducing social risks and needs such as old age, sickness, disability, unemployment, family, housing and social exclusion. Czechia spends more on social protection than the EU average (24.7% compared to 20.5% in 2021), while it spends less on health (13.4% compared to 15.8% in 2021). The share of GGE devoted to social protection has increased in the EU from 38.8% in 2000 to 39.9%, reaching 20.5% GDP in the last year. In Czechia, the same category has slightly decreased from 30% to 29.3%. It can be seen that both in Czechia and in the EU, the share of health expenditure in GDP and in GGE has increased over the last two decades. However, Czechia has seen a more significant increase than the EU average. In 2021, Czechia had the second highest share of health GGE in GDP among EU Member States. This suggests that Czechia has allocated more resources to healthcare than most other EU countries, where the share of healthcare spending increased from 12.9% in 2000 to 15.8% in 2021 (EU), representing 8.1% of GDP, or from 16.6% to 21.1% of GDP in Czechia. Health is one of the most important functions of the GGE as it reflects the public provision of health services and goods to the population. According to COFOG, health GGE can be further divided into four sub-functions: hospital services, outpatient services, medical products, devices and equipment and public health services.

Another important functional category of GGE is Economic affairs, which includes spending on transport, communication, energy, agriculture, industry, trade, tourism, research and development (R&D), and General economic services. In 2021, Economic affairs in the EU represented 12.3% GGE (resp. 6.1% GDP), a significant increase from 9.8% GGE in 2000. In Czechia, this share was still 4 percentage points higher despite a slight decline from 16.9% to 16.2%. Government spending on economic affairs can have positive effects on economic growth by enhancing the productive capacity of the economy, improving infrastructure and connectivity, supporting innovation and competitiveness, creating jobs and income opportunities, and stimulating private sector activity.

However, not all types of GGE on economic affairs have the same impact on economic growth. Some studies suggest that spending on R&D, education, and infrastructure has a higher growth-enhancing effect than spending on subsidies or consumption. Moreover, the efficiency and effectiveness of government spending depends on several factors, such as the quality of governance and institutions, the level of public debt and fiscal sustainability, the degree of crowding-out or crowding-in of private investment and the complementarity with other policies.

The categories that showed significant changes over time for both Czechia and the EU were general public services, economic affairs, health, recreation, culture and religion, and social protection. General public services decreased from 7.6% to 5.9% for Czechia and from 7.2% to 6.3% for the EU between 2000 and 2021, mainly due to lower interest payments on public debt. Economic affairs increased from 6.8% to 9.6% for Czechia and from 5.2% to 7.8% for the EU between 2000 and 2021, mainly due to higher spending on transport infrastructure. The shares of other categories remained relatively stable over time. The changes in the structure of GEE reflect the different priorities and challenges faced by governments over the past two decades, especially during the COVID-19 crisis, which required increased spending on social protection and health to support households and businesses affected by the pandemic and to contain the spread of the virus.

9.5 The Relationship Between GGE and Economic Growth

As mentioned above, GGE can affect economic growth in several ways. Therefore, the relationship between economic growth and GGE is further examined.

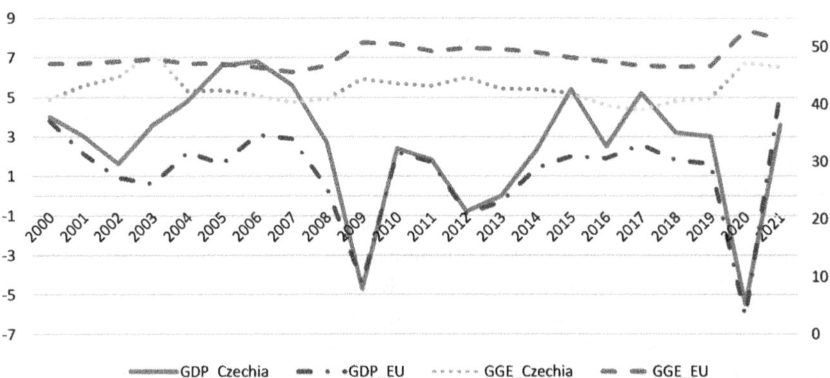

Fig. 9.4. Real GDP Growth and GGE (in % GDP). *Source:* Author's comparison based on Eurostat data.

The trend in GGE can be found above, while Fig. 9.4 completes the information on real GDP growth. Czechia's real GDP growth averaged 2.4% per year from 2000 to 2021, while the EU's real GDP growth averaged 1.0% per year over the same period. This means that Czechia's economy grew faster than the EU's economy by 1.4% points per year on average. The following Fig. 9.4 summarises the real GDP growth rates and GGE for both regions from 2000 to 2021, based on the Eurostat data.

The data shows that Czechia's real GDP growth was higher than the EU's real GDP growth in every year from 2004 to 2021, except for 2008 and 2020, when both regions experienced negative growth due to the global financial crisis and the COVID-19 pandemic. Czechia has achieved more volatile but higher real growth than the EU over the past two decades, despite being a small open economy that is highly integrated with the EU single market.

As already mentioned, GGE is a possible stabiliser. From this perspective, government spending should move in a countercyclical direction. Cyclicality can be tested by correlation analysis using cyclically adjusted time series. First, the logarithms of the variables are calculated and then the cycle components are extracted using the Hodrick-Prescott filter. Fig. 9.5 shows cyclically adjusted GGE and real GDP growth in Czechia and the EU (average).

The results suggest that both in Czechia and in the EU the correlation coefficients are positive and reflect pro-cyclical developments. Differences are evident in the value of the correlation coefficients – a weak positive correlation is found in Czechia (0.34), while a moderate pro-cyclical trend is observed in the EU (0.63).

It can be concluded that, contrary to the expectations and recommendations of the theoretical literature, countries did not use GGE as a stabiliser in the period under review. The results of the empirical evidence are consistent with the findings of other empirical studies that have confirmed that government spending is

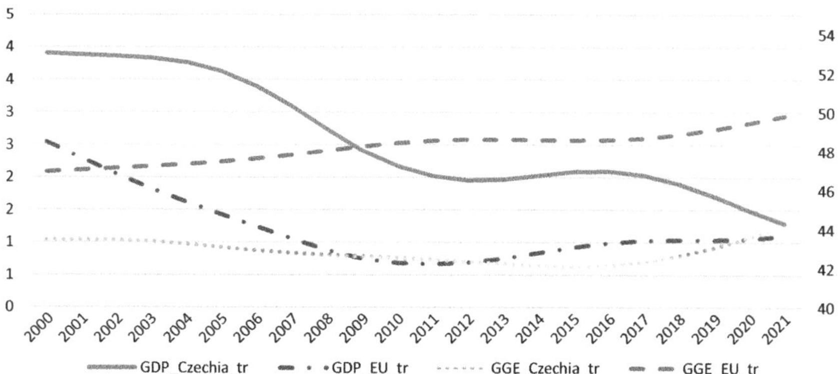

Fig. 9.5. Cyclically Adjusted GGE and Real GDP Growth. *Source:* Author's comparison based on Eurostat data.

pro-cyclical (e.g. Abbott & Jones, 2011; Alesina et al., 2008; Fiorito & Kollintzas, 1994; Hercowitz & Strawczynski, 2004; Lane, 2003; Rajkumar & Swaroop, 2008; Szarowská, 2022). The results for Czechia and the EU confirm the claim of Talvi and Vegh (2005) that fiscal procyclicality is evident in a broader sample of countries.

Moreover, the relationship between GGE and economic growth is not necessarily unidirectional. Public spending affects economic growth, but at the same time, economic growth can lead to changes in either GGE (e.g. in line with Wagner's Law) or in some of its components (e.g. through changes in the demand for certain public services). The main obstacles encountered in the studies include the difficulties associated with (1) valuing public sector outputs, (2) estimating separately the impact of how public spending is financed (including the possible crowding out of private investment), and (3) measuring the impact of other factors on economic growth. In addition, using current cross-country data to link GGE to economic growth may not yield the right results, as many public spending projects (e.g. basic education and physical infrastructure projects) have a long-time horizon.

As noted above, Granger causality refers to a specific notion of causality in time series analysis. The Granger causality test is applied to time series data to determine the causality between aggregate and individual GGE (CF10...CF100) and economic growth (GDP). It is important to note that, for example, the statement 'CF10 Granger causes GDP' does not imply that GDP is a consequence or result of GGE (CF10). Granger causality measures precedence and information content but does not itself indicate causality in the more common use of the term. The null hypothesis should be rejected if the probability is less than 0.05. Table 9.2 summarises the results only for the COFOG categories with identified causes (the total number of observations for each country is 21 and 20, respectively). GC indicates Granger causality and bold values identify the hypothesis that should be rejected.

The results presented in Table 9.2 show causality and its direction between the macroeconomic variables analysed. Only one example of unidirectional GC from GGE to GDP growth can be found, namely from public order and security (CF30) to GDP growth, reported with a two-year lag in Czechia, thus providing support for the validity of the Keynesian view. Hence, it can be concluded that this expenditure function was a very important factor for economic growth in Czechia during the period under review. The results of the evidence parallel the findings of Alexiou (2009), Afonso and Alves (2017), Dudzevičiūtė et al. (2018) and Korkmaz and Güvenoğlu (2021).

On the other hand, there are more cases of unidirectional GC from GDP growth to GGE and its divisions, namely four in Czechia and three in the EU. The results show that economic growth comes first, followed by government spending. A deeper analysis focussing on the direct effect of the variables will follow in the future. The same direction of causality leading from economic growth to GGE is also reported in Afonso and Alves (2016), Sáez et al. (2017) and Dudzevičiūtė et al. (2018). Bidirectional GC is only reported between economic affairs (CF40) and GDP growth in Czechia with a lag of 2 years. This result is

Table 9.2. Results of Granger Causality.

	Czechia (Lag 2 Years)		EU (Lag 2 Years)	
Null Hypothesis	**F-Stat**	**Prob.**	**F-Stat**	**Prob.**
GDP does not GC CF10	3.512	0.048	4.351	0.034
CF10 does not GC GDP	0.710	0.689	0.836	0.454
GDP does not GC CF30	3.724	0.069	4.310	0.644
CF30 does not GC GDP	0.805	0.391	1.458	0.042
GDP does not GC CF40	4.513	0.041	3.690	0.128
CF40 does not GC GDP	1.221	0.028	3.758	0.113
GDP does not GC CF70	3.096	0.040	5.423	0.018
CF70 does not GC GDP	0.402	0.676	0.147	0.865
GDP does not GC CF90	5.474	0.012	6.643	0.009
CF90 does not GC GDP	0.587	0.059	0.304	0.743
GDP does not GC CF100	4.301	0.022	2.289	0.138
CF100 does not GC GDP	0.235	0.681	0.802	0.468

Source: Author's calculation based on Eurostat data.

similar to the earlier findings of Roşoiu (2015) who found a bidirectional causal relationship between GGE and economic growth in Romania.

Generally, the empirical evidence provides a mixed conclusion on the relationship between GGE and economic growth, which is consistent with Nyasha and Odhiambo (2019) and like Alqadi and Ismail (2019) who reviewed the theoretical and empirical literature. This heterogeneity arises due to differences in the econometric models used, country samples, observation periods and variables considered.

9.6 Conclusion

The aim of this chapter was to examine the relationship between general government expenditure and economic growth, including the direction of influence between the variables. The descriptive analysis showed major differences across the EU countries and Czechia over the period 2000–2021. The data suggest a volatile and cyclical development of total GGE as a share of GDP in all countries. Empirical evidence confirms differences in the size of the public sector. Although Czech GGE is 5.4% points of GDP lower than the EU average, GGE is higher in the following functional areas: economic affairs, health, public order and security. On the other hand, Czechia spends 6.3% points less than the EU on social protection and 2.2% points less on general public services. Anyway, spending on social protection and health accounts for the largest part of the GGE (more than a half of the total). The share of other functions is similar to other EU countries.

The correlation analysis confirmed the pro-cyclical development of GGE. It can be concluded that, compared to the expectations and theoretical recommendations, neither Czechia nor other EU countries used GGE as a stabiliser in the period under review. Paired Granger causality tests were used to examine the relationship and the direction of causality between GDP growth and GGE. The empirical evidence provides a mixed conclusion on the relationship between GGE functions and economic growth. Only one case of unidirectional Granger causality from GGE to GDP growth can be found, namely from public order and security to GDP growth, reported in Czechia, which suggests that this expenditure function was a very important factor in economic growth in Czechia. Furthermore, many cases of unidirectional Granger causality from GDP growth to GGE and its division were observed, implying that economic growth comes first followed by government spending.

References

Abbott, A., & Jones, P. (2011). Procyclical government expenditure: Patterns of pressure and prudence in the OECD. *Economics Letters*, *111*, 230–232.

Afonso, A., & Alves, J. (2017). Reconsidering Wagner's law: Evidence from the functions of the government. *Applied Economics Letters*, *24*(5), 346–350.

Ahuja, D., & Pandit, D. (2020). Public expenditure and economic growth: Evidence from the developing countries. *FIIB Business Review*, *9*(1). https://doi.org/10.1177/2319714520938901

Alesina, A., Tabellini, G., & Campante, F. R. (2008). Why is fiscal policy often procyclical? *Journal of the European Economic Association*, *6*(5), 1006–1030.

Alexiou, C. (2009). Government expenditure and economic growth: Econometric evidence from the South Eastern Europe (SEE). *Journal of Economic and Social Research*, *11*(1), 1–16.

Alqadi, M., & Ismail, S. (2019). Government expenditure and economic growth: Contemporary literature review. *Journal of Global economics*, *7*(4), 1–4.

Arawatari, R., Hori, T., & Mino, K. (2023). Government expenditure and economic growth: A Heterogeneous-agents approach. *Journal of Macroeconomics*, *75*. https://doi.org/10.1016/j.jmacro.2022.103486

Devarajan, S., Swaroop, V., & Zou, H. (1996). The composition of public expenditure and economic growth. *Journal of Monetary Economics*, *37*(2), 313–344. https://doi.org/10.1016/S0304-3932(96)90039-2

Dudzevičiūtė, G., Šimelytė, A., & Liučvaitienė, A. (2018). Government expenditure and economic growth in the European Union countries. *International Journal of Social Economics*, *45*(2), 372–386.

Eurostat. (2023). *General government expenditure by function (COFOG)*. gov_10a_exp. https://appsso.eurostat.ec.europa.eu/nui/show.do?dataset=gov_10a_exp&lang=en

Fiorito, R., & Kollintzas, T. (1994). Stylized facts of business cycles in the G7 from a real business cycles perspective. *European Economic Review*, *38*, 235–269.

Granger, C. W. J. (1980). Testing for causality. *Journal of Economic Dynamics and Control*, *4*, 229–252.

Hercowitz, Z., & Strawczynski, M. (2004). Cyclical ratcheting in government expenditure: Evidence from the OECD. *The Review of Economics and Statistics*, *86*(1), 353–361.

Karagianni, S., Pempetzoglou, M., & Saraidaris, A. (2019). Government expenditures and economic growth: A nonlinear causality investigation for the UK. *European Journal of Marketing and Economics*, *2*(2), 52. https://doi.org/10.26417/ejme-2019.v2i2-70

Korkmaz, S., & Güvenoğlu, H. (2021). The relationship between government expenditures. Economic growth and inflation in OECD countries. *Research of Financial Economic and Social Studies*, *6*(3), 490–498.

Lane, P. R. (2003). The cyclical behaviour of fiscal policy: Evidence from the OECD. *Journal of Public Economics*, *87*(12), 2661–2675.

Lupu, D., Petrisor, M. B., Bercu, A., & Tofan, M. (2018). The impact of public expenditures on economic growth: A case study of central and Eastern European Countries. *Emerging Markets Finance and Trade*, *54*(3), 552–570.

Nyasha, S., & Odhiambo, N. M. (2019). The impact of public expenditure on economic growth: A review of international literature. *Folia Oeconomica Stetinensia*, *19*(2), 81–101.

Parui, P. (2020). Government expenditure and economic growth: A post-Keynesian analysis. *International Review of Applied Economics*, *35*. https://doi.org/10.1080/02692171.2020.1837744

Pula, L., & Elshani, A. (2018). The relationship between public expenditure and economic growth in Kosovo: Findings from a Johansen co-integrated test and a granger causality test. *Ekonom*, *97*(1), 47–62.

Rajkumar, A. S., & Swaroop, V. (2008). Public expenditure and outcomes: Does governance matter? *Journal of Development Economics*, *86*(1), 96–111.

Romer, P. M. (1986). Increasing returns and long-run growth. *Journal of Political Economy*, *94*(5), 1002–1037.

Roşoiu, I. (2015). The impact of the government revenues and expenditures on the economic growth. *Procedia Economics and Finance*, *32*, 526–533.

Sáez, M. P., Álvarez-García, S., & Rodríguez, D. C. (2017). Government expenditure and economic growth in the European Union Countries: New evidence. *Bulletin de Geographie. Socio Economic Series*, *36*, 127–133.

Shkodra, J., Krasniqi, A., & Ahmeti, N. (2022). The impact of government expenditure on economic growth in Southeast European countries. *Journal of Management Information and Decision Sciences*, *25*(S1), 1–7.

Szarowská, I. (2011). Relationship between government expenditure and economic growth in the Czech Republic. *Acta Universitatis Agriculturae et Silviculturae Mendelianae Brunensis*, *59*(7), 415–422.

Szarowská, I. (2022). Relationship between government expenditure and economic growth in Visegrad group. *Financial Internet Quarterly*, *18*(4), 12–22. https://doi.org/10.2478/fiqf-2022-0024

Talvi, E., & Vegh, C. A. (2005). Tax base variability and procyclical fiscal policy in developing countries. *Journal of Development Economics*, *78*, 156–190.

Zamanian, G., Mahmoodi, M., & Mahmoodi, E. (2012). Government expenditure and GDP: The case of 12 Asian developing countries. *Journal of American Science*, *8*(9), 66–69.

Chapter 10

Inflation Expectations in Czechia: Measurement and Determinants

Vojtěch Koňařík, Zuzana Kučerová and Daniel Pakši

VSB-Technical University of Ostrava, Czechia

Abstract

Inflation expectations are an important part of the transmission mechanism of the inflation targeting regime. As such, central bankers must study the inflation expectations of economic agents to anchor them close to the level of the inflation target. However, economic agents are affected by the past and current macroeconomic situation when they form their expectations concerning future inflation. Using survey data on inflation expectations in Czechia, we investigate the macroeconomic determinants of Czech analysts' and managers' inflation expectations. We find that both actual and past inflation have a substantial impact on inflation expectations of the agents surveyed. We also identify backward-looking behaviour among these agents: persistence in inflation expectations of up to two quarters was detected. Moreover, financial analysts formed inflation expectations more in line with economic theory, while company managers evinced expectations similar to those of consumers.

Keywords: Inflation expectations; central bank; monetary policy; inflation targeting; inflation persistence; macroeconomics

10.1 Introduction

Recently, central bankers have been focused on the problem of strong inflation pressures and have been trying to find a way to tame inflation. As an important part of the transmission mechanism of the inflation targeting regime, central bankers have to anchor the inflation expectations of economic agents (Reid et al., 2021) as they directly influence the setting of monetary policy in the country. Central bankers should ideally use open communication channels (Scharnagl &

Modeling Economic Growth in Contemporary Czechia, 153–170

doi:10.1108/978-1-83753-840-920241010

Stapf, 2015) targeted towards different groups of economic agents such as policymakers, professional forecasters, households and firms (Binder, 2017; Cornand & Hubert, 2022). Central bank communication has proved to be an important factor affecting expectations of economic agents (Blinder et al., 2008; Brouwer & De Haan, 2022).

However, due to central banks' lack of success in reducing inflation, their credibility is falling, and as a result, inflation expectations adjust to actual and past inflation and not to the predictions produced by central bank models. Therefore, it is of high importance to identify factors that potentially determine inflation expectations, as these may strongly affect the inflation dynamics in future months. Empirical studies show that inflation expectations are determined by macroeconomic fundamentals (see, e.g. Cerisola & Gelos, 2009; Coibion & Gorodnichenko, 2015; Feldkircher & Siklos, 2019; Łyziak & Mackiewicz-Łyziak, 2020; Ueda, 2010). Furthermore, monetary policy regimes, such as inflation targeting, also affect the formation of inflation expectations (Castelnuovo et al., 2003; Ehrmann, 2021).

Using quarterly data from 1999:Q2 to 2022:Q4, we aim to identify what influences the inflation expectations of financial analysts and company managers in Czechia. We study the impact of actual and past inflation, real gross domestic product, nominal wages and the central bank repo rate on their inflation expectations. We find that actual inflation has a substantial impact on inflation expectations of the economic agents surveyed. Second, we find persistence in inflation expectations, i.e. that agents are backward-looking, as stated by Galí and Gertler (1999), and are affected by past inflation values. Third, financial analysts form inflation expectations more in line with economic theory compared to company managers, whom we assume to be less well informed or financially educated, not unlike consumers.

10.2 Inflation Expectations Measurement in Czechia

Usually, central banks or national statistical offices estimate inflation expectations using data obtained from surveys of professional forecasters, firms or households. The drawback of survey data is that the results can be sensitive to the behaviour of survey researchers and questionnaire design, and thus influenced by the information gathering process, which is particularly the case with consumer surveys (Reid et al., 2021).

Since 1999, the Czech National Bank (CNB) has been providing (1) monthly surveys of financial market expectations (represented by analysts in major banks and brokerage companies, i.e. traders on both the money and capital markets) and (2) quarterly surveys of expectations of non-financial company managers. Using standardized questionnaires, both analysts and managers are regularly asked to express their views on inflation expectations (consumer price index) and selected macroeconomic indicators (interest rates, exchange rate, GDP growth, nominal wage growth) at the one- and three-year horizons. Then, these expectations are compared with those of the CNB to examine their future development and find whether they are similar or not (CNB, 2023a). Results of these surveys are publicly available in the time series database of the CNB ARAD (CNB, 2023b).

Moreover, the CNB conducted quarterly household surveys between 1999 and 2004. These surveys were based on a sample of 600 households. In order to estimate inflation expectations of Czech consumers, the CNB asked about their inflation expectations at the one- and three-year horizons. Only the three-year horizon data was included starting in 2003. In 2007, the CNB abandoned this approach and started using the results of the European Commission's Business and Consumer Survey (EC, 2023). This survey provides information about inflation expected in the next 12 months by consumers in the European Union, including approximately 1000 Czech consumers.

This data enables researchers to use a proxy for future inflation expected by financial analysts and company managers. It is expected that both analysts and managers are better informed than consumers about the general financial and economic situation in the country. The CNB also estimates inflation expectations indirectly from yield curves.

10.3 Inflation Expectations Data in Czechia

Fig. 10.1 presents the inflation expectations of financial analysts and company managers for the time period from 2000:Q1 to 2022:Q4, with values sampled at the end of the given time period (thus, March 31 = Q1 and September 30 = Q3).

We use quarterly data on the inflation expectations of financial analysts (InfExp_Fin) and company managers (InfExp_Comp) at the one-year (Y1) and three-year (Y3) horizons. Inflation expectations are not formed in a vacuum, but arise as a result of the interaction between economic agents and important economic and political events. Thus, we include a list of various events that occurred during the time period observed. Both central bank monetary policy actions and events affecting both the global and domestic economy can be responsible for increasing the variability in expectations.

At the beginning of the surveyed time period, there is a decline in expectations reaching a local minimum after the revision of the inflation target that was officially valid from January 2002. This revision, in the form of a linearly decreasing inflation band (from a target band of 3%–5% in 2002 to a band of 2%–4% in 2005) seems to be followed by agent expectations until Czechia's EU accession in 2004. In January 2006, the band was replaced by a target of 3% with a tolerance band of ±1 percentage points to manage the agent expectations more precisely.

However, inflation expectations rose before the 2008 tax reform, reaching a maximum at the end of 2007. During this period, the economy experienced the impact of a tax reform that harmonised and changed indirect taxes (including new ecological taxes, increased consumption taxes and reduction of the VAT rate), accompanied by growth of state-regulated energy prices. All these changes were reflected in the behaviour of market prices, which probably caused the sharp jump

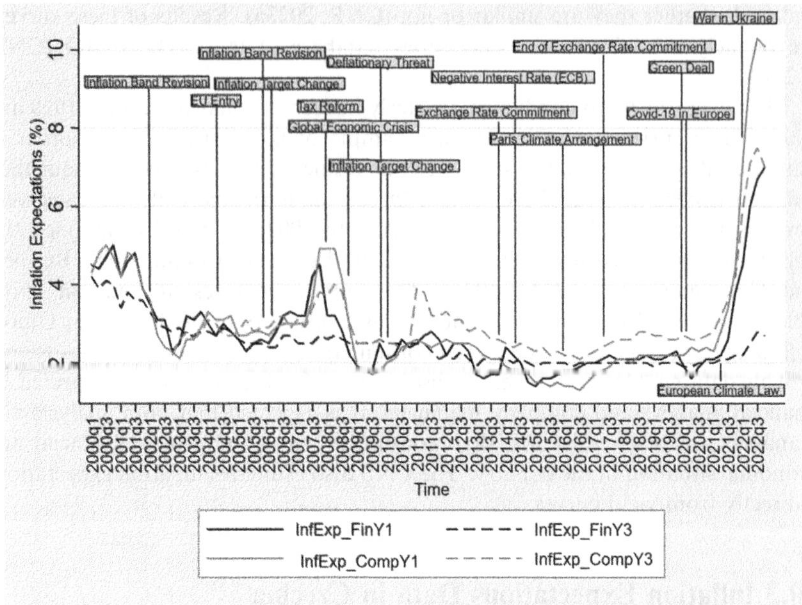

Fig. 10.1. Inflation Expectations of Financial Analysts and Company Managers in Czechia (2000/Q1–2022/Q4, in %).

Notes: InfExp_FinY1 and InfExp_FinY3 represent inflation expectations of financial analysts estimating inflation for 1 and 3 years ahead. InfExp_CompY1 and InfExp_CompY3 are inflation expectations of company managers for 1 and 3 years. *Source:* CNB (2023a, 2023b).

seen in inflation expectations. Then, a steep fall in inflation expectations occurred in 2008 on expectations of energy price stabilisation. The two-week repo rate during 2007 and 2008 exceeded the 3% mark; this CNB policy action helped push inflation expectations back to the vicinity of the inflation target.

With the global economic crisis that followed the financial crisis, there was a steep global fall in prices accompanied by a slowdown in aggregate demand. In October 2009, deflationary pressures occurred in the Czech economy. Nevertheless, inflation expectations were still above zero. In early 2010, the inflation target was changed to 2% with a tolerance band ±1 percentage points. This was accompanied by changes in the CNB's public communication strategy aimed at increasing the transparency of inflation forecasts and central bank policy decisions. In an ongoing convergence process, Czech economic growth reached its highest level since the beginning of the post-communist transformation process. The decline in Czech economic performance in the crisis year of 2009 was followed by a short recovery lasting until 2012, when post-crisis problems returned, leading to W-shaped growth curve. Restrictive fiscal policy related to budget consolidation efforts most likely contributed to this slowdown. However, expectations generally remained at a relatively stable level, oscillating around the 2% target.

While expectations evolved calmly in the following years, the development of real indicators was different. By the end of 2012, CNB interest rates were extremely low, reaching the 'technical zero' level of 0.05%. Still, this proved insufficient to stimulate the Czech economy, opening the way for unconventional monetary policy tools.

With deflationary trends in other European economies, weak aggregate demand and the suspected existence of a liquidity trap in the Czech economy, the CNB decided to intervene in the foreign exchange markets. In November 2013, the asymmetric exchange rate commitment was announced. The depreciation of the Czech currency was supposed to increase the inflation rate by raising import costs and stimulating aggregate demand with higher exports. This affected inflation expectations, as seen in Fig. 10.1. However, inflation expectations seemed to remain on a downward trend, suggesting low confidence among economic agents in the CNB achieving its goal. Expectations stabilised in late 2014 and early 2015. This may have been due to rising economic performance indicators, as well as a slowly changing situation in the world economy. Expectations hovered around the 2% inflation target through most of 2015 and 2016.

In 2016, the macroeconomic fundamentals of the Czech economy significantly improved, particularly due to a foreign trade surplus and rising domestic consumption. It remains unclear to what extent the recovery was due to forex interventions, as opposed to global economic development. Inflation expectations then remained stable around the 2% target from 2016 to early 2020. Surprisingly, we observe a modest rise in expectations after the exchange rate commitment was abandoned in April 2017. Inflation expectations remained stable until an unexpected shock rocked the economy in 2020.

Soon after the Green Deal for Europe was approved in December 2019, COVID-19 started spreading around the European Union. In March 2020, the Czech government declared a nationwide state of emergency, and the WHO declared COVID-19 a pandemic shortly after. Throughout the pandemic, the Czech government and EU institutions engaged in enormous fiscal transfers to the general population. Despite fairly generous government support, the pandemic took a toll on society. Three facts are worth mentioning in connection with inflation in this unusual period. First, we observe a slight shift into the inflationary gap within the economic cycle. Second, the average annual inflation rate reached 2.1% in 2018 and 2.8% in 2019 (i.e. a 0.7% point growth). Third, intertemporal substitution in household consumption sharply increased aggregate demand in the Czech economy in the months following the relaxation of COVID-19 restrictions, with a corresponding rise in the level of inflation expectations.

Unfortunately, the chain of disruptive economic developments did not end there. First, the European Climate Act stirred up heated discussion across the EU in June 2021, driving up uncertainty in related market segments. Second, the Russian invasion of Ukraine caused a severe supply shock, leading to massive increases in energy prices and inflation expectations. Inflation expectations reached a peak of around 18% in June 2022. However, they had begun growing as early as 2021, well before war broke out in Ukraine. Given the long list of major disruptive events, any number of factors may have significantly contributed to the observed development in inflation expectations.

Nevertheless, expectations differ by time period and by economic entity type. To demonstrate this, Fig. 10.2 illustrates the difference between inflation expectations and the actual inflation rate, while Fig. 10.3 shows the difference between inflation expectations and the inflation target. In modelling the inflation expectations gap, we work with a time differential (InfExpGAP), defined as inflation expectations in time t measured in time $t - i$ minus inflation in time t measured as change of a price index. A positive gap means inflation expectations for the time period in question are higher than actual inflation. For inflation expectations and inflation target difference, we work with differential in time t (InfExpGAPT), defined as the difference between inflation expectations in time t for time $t + 1$ or

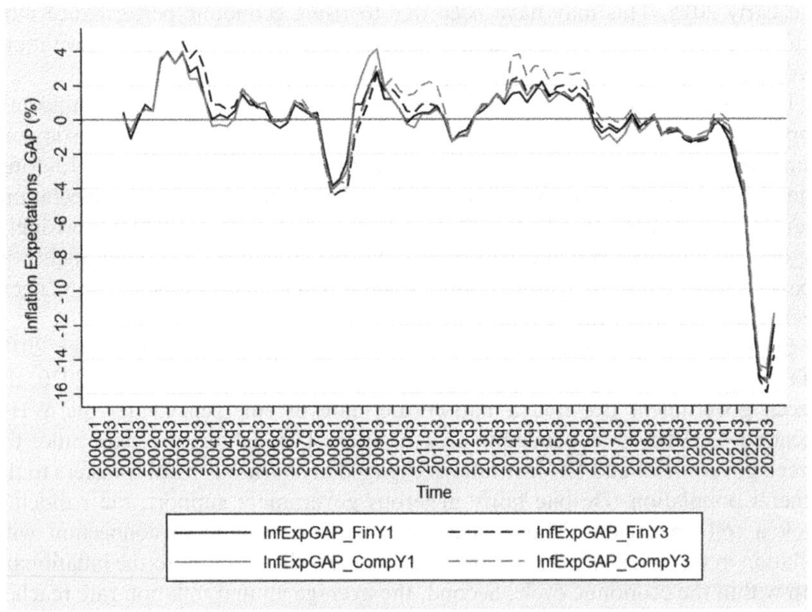

Fig. 10.2. Inflation Expectations Gap by Economic Entity Type. *Notes:* InfExpGAP_FinY1 and InfExpGAP_FinY3 represent the inflation expectations gap of financial analysts (difference between expected and actual inflation) for 1 and 3 years ahead. InfExpGAP_CompY1 and InfExpGAP_CompY3 represent the inflation expectations gap of company managers for 1 and 3 years ahead. *Source:* CNB (2023a, 2023b).

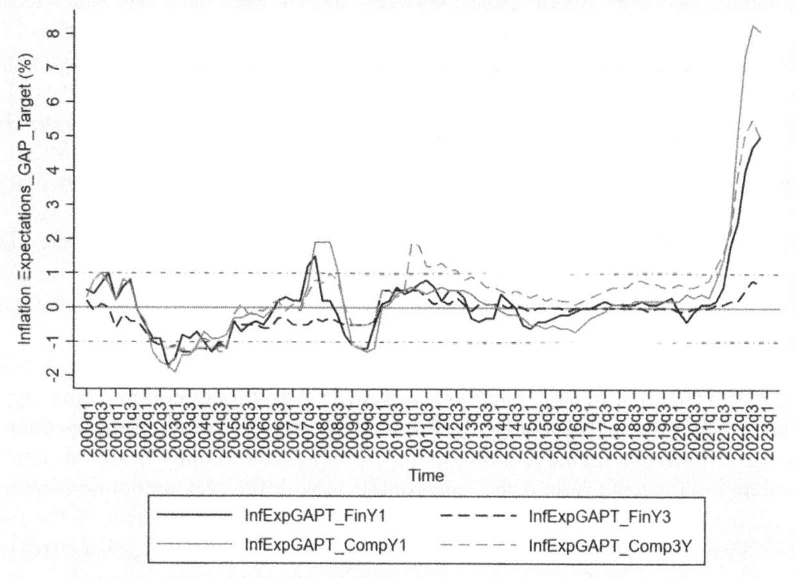

Fig. 10.3. Inflation Expectations Target Gap by Economic Entity Type. *Notes:* InfExpGAPT_FinY1 and InfExpGAPT_FinY3 represent the inflation expectations target gap (difference between inflation expectations and the inflation target) of financial analysts for 1 and 3 years ahead. InfExpGAPT_CompY1 and InfExpGAPT_CompY3 represent the inflation expectations target gap of company managers for 1 and 3 years ahead. *Source:* CNB (2023a, 2023b).

$t+3$, and the inflation target (anchor) in a given year t $(\pi_{a,t})$. Positive values mean that inflation expectations exceed the set inflation target, and vice versa.

Fig. 10.2 shows inflation expectations accuracy. Thus, we can compare what levels inflation expectations reach in Fig. 10.1, and whether those levels are higher or lower than actual inflation in Fig. 10.2. We can thus categorise subjects as relatively more or less accurate. In general, the one-year and three-year inflation expectations of financial analysts seem to be lower on average compared to those of company managers. The average level of inflation expectations among financial analysts in a one-year horizon is 2.76% (with a standard deviation of 1.11), while in a three-year horizon it is 2.46% (with a standard deviation of 0.54). Among company managers, the one-year mean is 2.96% (with a standard deviation of 1.66), while the three-year mean is 3.01% (with a standard deviation of 1).

Looking at the inflation expectations gap (see Fig. 10.2), expectations were more accurate over shorter horizons among both financial analysts and company managers. However, the difference between the time periods before and after the start of the Ukraine war is worth pointing out. Considering the whole period, the average expectations gap was higher among financial analysts (−0.302 vs. −0.24 for one-year expectations, and −0.395 vs. −0.32 for three-year expectations). It is clear that expectations on average underestimated the actual inflation rate. The largest gap was observed in 2022, when the Ukraine war started. Still, the expectations gap of company managers appeared modestly lower than that of financial analysts. Considering all years except 2022, Fig. 10.2 shows that the average expectations gap of financial analysts was lower than of company managers (0.314 vs. 0.35 for one-year expectations, and 0.32 vs. 0.48 for three-year expectations). Generally, the expectations of financial analysts seemed to be more accurate relative to the actual inflation rate.

Differences were larger for three-year inflation expectations. In general, the expectations gap of financial analysts was lower than that of company managers. That can likely be explained by the level of expertise and different perspective of the analysts. While financial analysts may look at the economy from the outside, company managers are in direct confrontation with the real economic situation, confusing short-term price fluctuations with the actual development of the price level. They thus seem to be more influenced by past development. This effect was also documented by Candia et al. (2021), who found that the inflation expectations of the US corporate representatives (managers and executives) deviate from those of professional forecasters (analysts).

Considering the difference between inflation expectations and the inflation target, the observations discussed above remain valid. InfExpGAPT at Fig. 10.3 shows the difference between expected inflation and the inflation target for financial analysts for one year (InfExpGAPT_FinY1) and three years ahead (InfExpGAPT_FinY3), as well as values for company managers for one year (InfExpGAPT_CompY1) and three years ahead (InfExpGAPT_CompY3). The solid grey line at zero level represents the equilibrium level where inflation expectations are equal to the inflation target, while the dashed level lines represent the upper and lower limits of the target band.

It is apparent that financial analysts tended to follow the inflation target more than company managers. The mean value of the one-year expectations target gap for financial analysts was 0.11% (standard deviation 1.07), while for company managers it was 1.70% (standard deviation 1.70). For the three-year expectations target gap, the mean for financial analysts was 0.19% (standard deviation 0.48), while for company managers it was 0.54% (standard deviation 1.26). Financial analysts thus produced lower target gaps than company managers for both horizon lengths. We can say that in terms of inflation target trust, financial analysts are more anchored than company managers. The analyst/manager difference in gap values was not large, but looking also at standard deviations, analysts tended to produce both smaller gaps and lower variability, while company managers tended to produce larger gaps with higher variability. For three-year expectations, analysts seem to be more solidly anchored. As mentioned before, this may be due to their different viewpoints. For managers, various sectors of the economy may differ in actual trends driven by market fundaments, and the levels of respondent financial expertise may vary by industry as well.

Fig. 10.4 shows how inflation expectations compared with actual inflation. We can see that inflation expectations of company managers seemed more anchored in past inflation than those of financial analysts, who appeared to base theirs more on current economic trends. Nevertheless, both groups suffered from expectation persistence, with the only difference being the scale of divergence from actual inflation. It seems both groups of agents retained lower expectations, possibly due to long experience of low inflation in prior periods, as well as due to their assessment of the current phase of the economic cycle. Short-term expectations were closer to actual inflation and began growing at the end of the period analysed. Between 2013 and 2016, all agents tended to expect higher inflation than what eventually materialised. The reverse trend can be seen after actual inflation began to rise during and after the COVID-19 pandemic, when expectations were fairly slow to react.

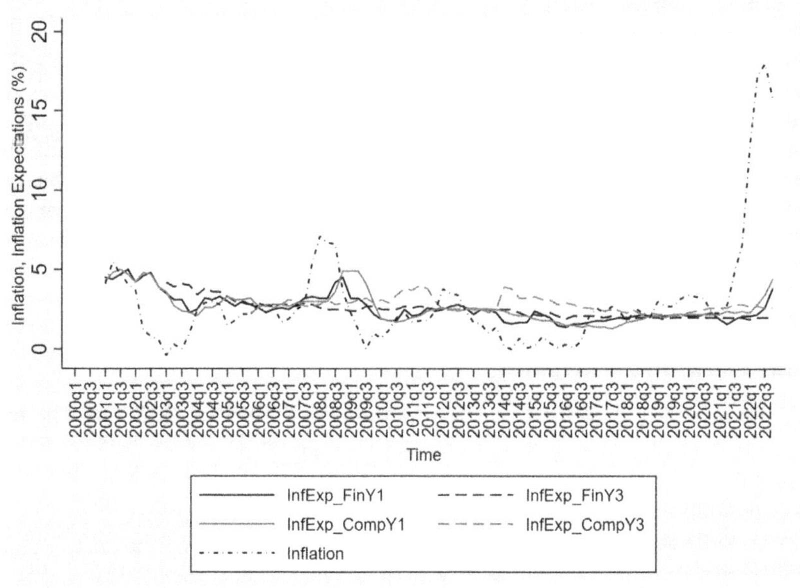

Fig. 10.4. Comparison of Inflation to Inflation Expectations (%). *Notes:* InfExp_FinY1_ and InfExp_FinY3 represent inflation expectations of financial analysts for 1 and 3 years ahead. InfExp_CompY1 and InfExp_CompY3 represent inflation expectations of company managers for 1 and 3 years ahead. *Source:* CNB (2023a, 2023b).

10.4 Macroeconomic Determinants of Inflation Expectations

In our model, we use the consumer price index to capture actual and past inflation, and a set of macroeconomic variables. Cerisola and Gelos (2009) find that the expected inflation rate, past inflation rate, targeted inflation rate, fiscal balance (in per cent of GDP), real policy interest rate, real effective exchange rate and real wages affected inflation expectations in Brazil after inflation targeting was adopted there. They find that the future inflation target and policy rates representing monetary policy instruments, together with a strong fiscal policy, determine inflation expectations and the credibility of the inflation targeting regime in Brazil. Ueda (2010) studies the impact of the output gap, federal fund rate, inflation rate, energy prices and food prices in the United States and Japan, and finds that inflation expectations react to monetary policy shocks quite quickly, and as such are a good predictor of actual inflation changes in these countries. Using a dataset of 42 countries, Feldkircher and Siklos (2019) study whether real GDP, unemployment rate, short- and long-term interest rates, a stock price index, real effective exchange rate, past inflation, oil price inflation, and global oil production and prices have an impact on inflation expectations. The authors identify a short-term effect of domestic demand and supply shocks and a long-term effect of oil price changes on inflation expectations. The fact that inflation expectations (particularly those of households) are significantly sensitive to oil prices is confirmed by Coibion and Gorodnichenko (2015). Public debt is also an important factor affecting the inflation expectations of economic agents (both consumers and professional forecasters), as documented by Łyziak and Mackiewicz-Łyziak (2020). Furthermore, the authors confirm that the past inflation rate, real short-term interest rates, nominal effective exchange rate, output gap, and changes of oil prices contribute to inflation expectations, in line with prior research.

10.5 Data and Variables

We use quarterly data for Czechia over the period 1999:Q2–2022:Q4. The time series is over 20 years long and includes multiple variables we believe may be relevant to Czech economic agents' behaviour. Nonetheless, it is important to keep in mind that even though the time series is over 20 years long, the number of observations is limited due to the use of quarterly data. Information about the dataset and variables including elementary data transformations is provided in Appendix A1.

For the dependent variables, we use data from Czech National Bank surveys among selected economic agents (financial analysts and non-financial company managers). We collect other variables from online databases. We check stationarity using the Augmented Dickey-Fuller test (Dickey & Fuller, 1979). Given the extent of the time series, we control for potential autocorrelation by using robust standard errors, which also help with heteroskedasticity concerns. Furthermore, some of the variables are transformed into differences.

We perform a regression analysis using Eq. (10.1) where our general model specification is as follows:

$$Y_t = \beta_0 + \beta_1 X_t + \ldots + \beta_k X_t + u_t \ldots..,N, t = 1 \ldots T, \tag{10.1}$$

where β_0 denotes the constant, β_1 denotes the regression coefficient for the first explanatory variable X_t and u_t is a random term.

We further specify an empirical model Eq. (10.2) where we estimate the determinants of inflation expectation changes, as well as the impact of inflation persistence on inflation expectations:

$$\begin{aligned} Inf\_exp\_diff_t = {} & \beta_0 + \beta_1 GDP\_gr_t + \beta_2 Nwages\_gr_t + \beta_3 Int_t \\ & + \beta_4 Inf\_diff_t + u_t \ldots..,N, t = 1 \ldots T, \end{aligned} \tag{10.2}$$

where $Inf\_exp\_diff_t$ denotes difference of inflation expectations of surveyed agents at time t, GDP_gr_t is growth of real GDP at time t, $Nwages\_gr_t$ is growth of nominal wages at time t, Int_t is the CNB's two week repo rate at time t, Inf_diff_t is the difference of actual inflation at time t.

Moreover, Eq. (10.3) presents the model for determinants contributing to the divergence/convergence of the inflation expectations of the two surveyed groups of economic agents:

$$\begin{aligned} Diff\_exp\_ana - man_t = {} & \beta_0 + \beta_1 GDP\_gr_t + \beta_2 Nwages\_gr_t + \beta_3 Int_t \\ & + \beta_4 Inf\_diff_t + u_t \ldots..,N, t = 1 \ldots T, \end{aligned} \tag{10.3}$$

where $Diff\_exp\_ana - man_t$ represents the difference between inflation expectations of financial analysts and company managers.

10.6 Results

We present below the results of our modelling of inflation expectation determinants using the specification given in Eq. (10.2) above. Table 10.1 presents the results for inflation expectation determinants of both financial analysts and company managers for one and three-year horizons.

Our first set of models suggests that for both financial analysts and company managers, actual inflation is the key component of building inflation expectations. Other variables, representing the state of the economy (GDP growth), changes in nominal wages, or the interest rates set by the Czech National Bank do not seem to play a role in forming expectations.

Next, we focus on the possible existence of inflation persistence. According to the New Hybrid Keynesian Phillips Curve, economic agents are both forward- and backward-looking, i.e. they incorporate information about the current economic situation as well as information about past inflation into their decisions when making inflation predictions. As such, they set the prices of their production by looking backwards and applying a simple rule of thumb (Galí & Gertler, 1999).

Table 10.1. One- and Three-Year Inflation Expectations in Czechia (1999/Q2–2022/Q4).

	1-Year Inflation Expectations (Diff)		**3-Year Inflation Expectations (Diff)**	
Variables	**Financial Analysts (1)**	**Company Managers (2)**	**Financial Analysts (3)**	**Company Managers (4)**
GDP growth	0.011	0.002	−0.001	0.007
	(0.013)	(0.010)	(0.004)	(0.009)
Nominal wages	−0.036	−0.018	−0.005	−0.007
	(0.024)	(0.016)	(0.006)	(0.015)
Interest rate	0.050	0.046	0.001	0.028
	(0.034)	(0.029)	(0.013)	(0.017)
Inflation (diff)	0.117***	0.350***	0.040***	0.181***
	(0.038)	(0.034)	(0.014)	(0.035)
Constant	2.518	1.682	0.612	−0.052
	(2.042)	(1.691)	(0.629)	(1.246)
Observations	88	88	88	88
R-squared	0.191	0.720	0.121	0.444

Source: Author's Calculations.

Robust standard errors in parentheses.
***$p < 0.01$; **$p < 0.05$; *$p < 0.1$.

The results are presented in Tables 10.2 and 10.3. We can see that changes in past inflation affect financial analysts/company managers up to the second/first quarter back. These agents thus incorporate into their expectations past inflation data from the last half year/the last quarter. Candia et al. (2020) obtained similar results for US corporations. Among financial analysts, real GDP growth and nominal wages contribute with weak statistical significance with a three-quarter delay. Among company managers, real GDP growth proves to be a significant determinant of future inflation estimates, though the effect is weaker compared to the effect of past inflation. Nevertheless, it shows that company managers place more significance on the real economic situation than financial analysts do.

Our results concerning inflation persistence indicate that both current and past inflation is responsible for the formation of inflation expectations of the Czech agents surveyed. That is in line with CNB models that assume around 90% of inflation expectations to be based on current inflation (CNB, 2005).

This effect is strong mainly in the short-term horizon, i.e. inflation expectations for the next 12 months. In the three-year horizon, the effect is smaller but still significant. When we compare the results for financial analysts (Table 10.2) and company managers (Table 10.3), it is clear that past inflation is more important to company managers than to financial analysts.

Evidently, these agents' estimates of the future inflation rate are adaptive, i.e. based on past inflation numbers. It may thus be difficult for CNB monetary policy to anchor these expectations successfully, at least early in the monetary policy horizon (four to six quarters in this case), and the inflation rate may remain persistently high. This behaviour may threaten the effectiveness of CNB monetary policy during periods when inflation is high above the target, and costs of monetary policy tightening may be high in these circumstances.

In the final step, we find the drivers of the differences in the expectations of the two surveyed groups, financial analysts and company managers. Table 10.4 presents the estimation results for the Eq. (10.3). The dependent variable is the difference between the expectations of financial analysts and company managers (i.e. analyst expectations less manager expectations).

We find that economic booms, characterised by rising GDP and nominal wages, tend to increase the difference between the expectations of financial analysts and company managers. This likely means the two groups perceive the changes in general economic conditions differently, causing their inflation expectations to diverge. Financial analysts in particular tend to expect higher inflation than company managers. The situation is reversed with interest rates, as both interest rate growth together with rising inflation lower the difference in the two groups' inflation expectations. Their inflation expectations have a tendency to converge here, meaning they tend to form similar expectations in times when inflation and interest rates rise together. Moreover, these results are similar for the one- and three-year horizons.

10.7 Conclusion

In this study, we used quarterly data for Czechia to identify the primary determinants of the inflation expectations of Czech financial market experts and company managers from 1999:Q2 through 2022:Q4. We explored how selected macroeconomic variables including actual and past inflation affected these groups' inflation expectations. We found that both actual and past inflation had a substantial impact. We identified the existence of backward-looking behaviour among these agents, as originally proposed by Galí and Gertler (1999), as we detected persistence in inflation expectations of up to two quarters. Moreover, analysts formed inflation expectations more in line with economic theory, while managers behaved similarly to consumers, suggesting they may be less well informed or financially educated. Therefore, there is a risk that the current disinflation efforts of CNB monetary policy may be weakened by the fact that at least some agents' inflation expectations are anchored above the inflation target.

Table 10.2. One- and Three-Year Inflation Expectations of Financial Analysts and Inflation Persistence in Czechia (1999/Q2–2022/Q4).

	1-Year Inflation Expectations (Diff) Financial Analysts				3-Year Inflation Expectations (Diff) Financial Analysts			
Variables	**(1)**	**(5)**	**(6)**	**(7)**	**(3)**	**(8)**	**(9)**	**(10)**
GDP growth	0.011	0.016	0.021	0.024*	−0.001	0.000	0.002	0.003
	(0.013)	(0.013)	(0.013)	(0.013)	(0.004)	(0.004)	(0.004)	(0.004)
Nominal wages	−0.036	−0.036	−0.041	−0.048*	−0.005	−0.005	−0.006	−0.009
	(0.024)	(0.024)	(0.027)	(0.027)	(0.006)	(0.006)	(0.007)	(0.007)
Interest rate	0.050	0.033	0.046	0.073	0.001	−0.006	−0.004	0.009
	(0.034)	(0.034)	(0.050)	(0.045)	(0.013)	(0.014)	(0.017)	(0.016)
Inflation (diff)	0.117***				0.040***			
	(0.038)				(0.014)			
Inflation$_{t-1}$ (diff)		0.104*				0.039***		
		(0.057)				(0.015)		
Inflation$_{t-2}$ (diff)			0.063*				0.030*	
			(0.034)				(0.016)	
Inflation$_{t-3}$ (diff)				−0.006				−0.003
				(0.036)				(0.013)
Constant	2.518	2.048	2.051	2.499	0.612	0.436	0.389	0.605
	(2.042)	(2.011)	(2.298)	(2.252)	(0.629)	(0.592)	(0.677)	(0.706)
Observations	88	88	88	88	88	88	88	88
R-squared	0.191	0.157	0.115	0.091	0.121	0.101	0.068	0.020

Source: Author's Calculations.

Robust standard errors in parentheses.
***$p < 0.01$; **$p < 0.05$; *$p < 0.1$.

Table 10.3. One- and Three-Year Inflation Expectations of Company Managers and Inflation Persistence in Czechia (1999/Q2–2022/Q4).

	1-Year Inflation Expectations (Diff) Company Managers				**3-Year Inflation Expectations (Diff) Company Managers**			
Variables	**(2)**	**(11)**	**(12)**	**(13)**	**(4)**	**(14)**	**(15)**	**(16)**
GDP growth	0.002	0.021*	0.038**	0.040**	0.007	0.013*	0.023**	0.022**
	(0.010)	(0.013)	(0.017)	(0.017)	(0.009)	(0.009)	(0.011)	(0.010)
Nominal wages	−0.018	−0.027	−0.050	−0.056*	−0.007	−0.013	−0.019	−0.017
	(0.016)	(0.017)	(0.031)	(0.030)	(0.015)	(0.015)	(0.018)	(0.018)
Interest rate	0.046	0.021	0.089	0.117*	0.028	0.027	0.063	0.099**
	(0.029)	(0.039)	(0.067)	(0.065)	(0.017)	(0.039)	(0.046)	(0.040)
Inflation (diff)	0.350***				0.181***			
	(0.034)				(0.035)			
Inflation$_{t\text{-}1}$ (diff)		0.241***				0.099***		
		(0.048)				(0.034)		
Inflation$_{t\text{-}2}$ (diff)			0.053				0.018	
			(0.047)				(0.042)	
Inflation$_{t\text{-}3}$ (diff)				−0.028				−0.089**
				(0.052)				(0.037)
Constant	1.682	0.587	1.261	1.620	−0.052	−0.495	−0.396	−0.552
	(1.691)	(1.573)	(2.799)	(2.776)	(1.246)	(1.310)	(1.557)	(1.601)
Observations	88	88	88	88	80	80	80	80
R-squared	0.720	0.366	0.151	0.143	0.444	0.197	0.130	0.187

Source: Author's Calculations.

Robust standard errors in parentheses.
$^{***}p < 0.01$; $^{**}p < 0.05$; $^{*}p < 0.1$.

Table 10.4. Difference Between Inflation Expectations of Financial Analysts and Company Managers in Czechia (1999/Q2–2022/Q4).

	(Financial Analysts – Company Managers)	
Variables	**1-Year Expectations (17)**	**3-Year Expectations (18)**
GDP	0.034*	0.038*
	(0.018)	(0.020)
Nominal wages	0.072**	0.060*
	(0.033)	(0.034)
Interest rate	−0.315***	−0.414***
	(0.082)	(0.102)
Inflation (diff)	−0.170**	−0.209**
	(0.077)	(0.089)
Constant	−10.650***	−10.235***
	(3.626)	(3.840)
Observations	88	81
R-squared	0.470	0.549

Source: Author's Calculations.

Robust standard errors in parentheses.
***$p < 0.01$; **$p < 0.05$; *$p < 0.1$.

References

Binder, C. (2017). Fed speak on main street: Central bank communication and household expectations. *Journal of Macroeconomics*, *52*, 238–251. https://doi.org/10.1016/j.jmacro.2017.05.003

Blinder, A. S., Ehrmann, M., Fratzscher, M., De Haan, J., & Jansen, D.-J. (2008). Central bank communication and monetary policy: A survey of theory and evidence. *Journal of Economic Literature*, *46*(4), 910–945. https://www.jstor.org/stable/27647085

Brouwer, N., & De Haan, J. (2022). The impact of providing information about the ECB's instruments on inflation expectations and trust in the ECB: Experimental evidence. *Journal of Macroeconomics*, *73*, 103430. https://doi.org/10.1016/j.jmacro.2022.103430

Candia, B., Coibion, O., & Gorodnichenko, Y. (2020). *Communication and the beliefs of economic agents*. NBER Working Paper, 27800. https://doi.org/10.3386/w27800

Candia, B., Coibion, O., & Gorodnichenko, Y. (2021). *The inflation expectations of U.S. firms: Evidence from a new survey*. NBER Working Paper, 28836. https://doi.org/10.3386/w28836

Castelnuovo, E., Nicoletti-Altimari, S., & Rodriguez-Palenzuela, D. (2003). Definition of price stability, range and point inflation targets: The anchoring of long-term inflation expectations. In O. Issing (Ed.), *Background studies for the ECB's evaluation of its monetary policy strategy* (pp. 43–90). European Central Bank.

Cerisola, M., & Gelos, G. (2009). What drives inflation expectations in Brazil? An empirical analysis. *Applied Economics*, *41*(10), 1215–1227. https://doi.org/10.1080/00036840601166892

Coibion, O., & Gorodnichenko, Y. (2015). Is the Phillips curve alive and well after all? Inflation expectations and the missing disinflation. *American Economic Journal: Macroeconomics*, *7*(1), 197–232. https://doi.org/10.1257/mac.20130306

Cornand, C., & Hubert, P. (2022). Information frictions across various types of inflation expectations. *European Economic Review*, *146*, 104175. https://doi.org/10.1016/j.euroecorev.2022.104175

Czech National Bank. (2005). *Inflation expectation in the CNB's modelling system.* https://www.cnb.cz/en/monetary-policy/inflation-reports/boxes-and-annexes-contained-in-inflation-reports/Inflation-expectations-in-the-CNBs-modelling-system-00001/

Czech National Bank. (2023a, April 25). *Financial market inflation expectations.* https://www.cnb.cz/en/financial-markets/inflation-expectations-ft/

Czech National Bank. (2023b, April 26). *Time series database ARAD.* https://www.cnb.cz/cnb/STAT.ARADY_PKG.STROM_DRILL?p_strid=AC&p_lang=EN

Dickey, D. A., & Fuller, W. A. (1979). Distribution of the estimators for autoregressive time series with a unit root. *Journal of the American Statistical Association*, *74*, 427–431. https://doi.org/10.2307/228634

Ehrmann, M. (2021). Point targets, tolerance bands or target ranges? Inflation target types and the anchoring of inflation expectations. *Journal of International Economics*, *132*, 103514. https://doi.org/10.1016/j.jinteco.2021.103514

European Commission. (2023). *Business and consumer surveys.* https://economy-finance.ec.europa.eu/economic-forecast-and-surveys/business-and-consumer-surveys_en

Feldkircher, M., & Siklos, P. L. (2019). Global inflation dynamics and inflation expectations. *International Review of Economics & Finance*, *64*, 217–241. https://doi.org/10.1016/j.iref.2019.06.004

Galí, J., & Gertler, M. (1999). Inflation dynamics: A structural econometric analysis. *Journal of Monetary Economics*, *44*(2), 195–222. https://doi.org/10.1016/S0304-3932(99)00023-9

Łyziak, T., & Mackiewicz-Łyziak, J. (2020). Does fiscal stance affect inflation expectations? Evidence for European economies. *Economic Analysis and Policy*, *68*, 296–310. https://doi.org/10.1016/j.eap.2020.09.010

Reid, M., Siklos, P., & Plessis, S. D. (2021). What drives household inflation expectations in South Africa? Demographics and anchoring under inflation targeting. *Economic Systems*, *45*(3), 100878. https://doi.org/10.1016/j.ecosys.2021.100878

Scharnagl, M., & Stapf, J. (2015). Inflation, deflation, and uncertainty: What drives euro-area option-implied inflation expectations, and are they still anchored in the sovereign debt crisis? *Economic Modelling*, *48*, 248–269. https://doi.org/10.1016/j.econmod.2014.11.025

Ueda, K. (2010). Determinants of households' inflation expectations in Japan and the United States. *Journal of the Japanese and International Economies*, *24*(4), 503–518. https://doi.org/10.1016/j.jjie.2010.06.002

Appendix A1
List of Variables, Definition, Data Source

Variable	Abbreviation	Transformation	Source	Link
1-year inflation expectations financial analysts	Inf_exp1_fin	Difference	Czech National Bank	https://www.cnb.cz/cnb/STAT.ARADY_PKG.PARAMETRY_SESTAVY?p_sestuid=21936&p_strid=ACAC&p_lang=CS
3-year inflation expectations financial analysts	Inf_exp3_fin	Difference	Czech National Bank	https://www.cnb.cz/cnb/STAT.ARADY_PKG.PARAMETRY_SESTAVY?p_sestuid=21936&p_strid=ACAC&p_lang=CS
1-year inflation expectations company managers	Inf_exp1_man	Difference	Czech National Bank	https://www.cnb.cz/cnb/STAT.ARADY_PKG.PARAMETRY_SESTAVY?p_sestuid=21937&p_strid=ACAB&p_lang=CS
3-year inflation expectations company managers	Inf_exp3_man	Difference	Czech National Bank	https://www.cnb.cz/cnb/STAT.ARADY_PKG.PARAMETRY_SESTAVY?p_sestuid=21937&p_strid=ACAB&p_lang=CS
GDP per capita	GDP_gr	Growth	Czech National Bank	https://www.cnb.cz/cnb/STAT.ARADY_PKG.PARAMETRY_SESTAVY?p_sestuid=60783&p_strid=ACCAAB&p_lang=CS
Nominal wages	Nwages_gr	Growth	Czech National Bank	https://www.cnb.cz/cnb/STAT.ARADY_PKG.PARAMETRY_SESTAVY?p_sestuid=21739&p_strid=ACFA&p_lang=CS
Interest rate	Int	–	Czech National Bank	https://www.cnb.cz/cnb/STAT.ARADY_PKG.PARAMETRY_SESTAVY?p_sestuid=377&p_strid=AAAG&p_lang=CS
Inflation	Inf_diff	Difference	Czech National Bank	https://www.cnb.cz/cnb/STAT.ARADY_PKG.PARAMETRY_SESTAVY?p_sestuid=6546&p_strid=ACL&p_lang=CS

Chapter 11

Regional Housing Prices in Czechia: Dynamics, Co-Movements and Drivers

Daniel Pakši and Aleš Melecký

VSB-Technical University of Ostrava, Czechia

Abstract

In this chapter, we aim to analyze the housing market development in Czechia, in particular the development of housing prices over the last 25 years. We quantify and discuss three distinct periods of excessive growth of regional Czech housing prices, identified through the formation of large positive GAPs – (1) before the entrance of Czechia to the European Union (EU), (2) at the onset of the Global Financial Crisis GFC, (3) in 2021. In all these periods, we identify significant differences among regions. We find that GAPs above 15% may be considered an indication of unsustainable long-term housing price growth that will be followed by a correction.

We then employ fixed effect panel data model to determine the drivers of flat and house prices in 14 Czech regions. Our results show that wage growth, migration and crime rate are significant factors affecting the prices of both flats and houses. Nevertheless, the impact of GDP per capita and job market indicators differs between flats and houses. Moreover, we find that higher migration into the region increases the difference between the prices of houses and flats, while increasing GDP per capita growth and crime rate mitigate this difference significantly.

Keywords: Housing prices; Czechia; regional differences; panel data model; excessive growth; determinants

11.1 Introduction

The Russian invasion on Ukraine indirectly impacted European countries through high inflation and consequent monetary tightening that was gradually transmitted to mortgage rates. Together with new macroprudential policy setting

Modeling Economic Growth in Contemporary Czechia, 171–181

Published under exclusive licence by Emerald Publishing Limited
doi:10.1108/978-1-83753-840-920241011

in Czechia, it led to a sudden stop in housing price growth. However, the reaction differed from region to region and types of properties. Other countries in the region experienced similar stories.

Housing prices are closely related to demographic shifts and migration flows as well as urbanization issues. Regional housing prices are influenced by local economic and demographic factors, such as production that creates job opportunities, population changes and availability of housing. Analysis of regional housing prices is therefore important and may reveal areas with overvalued or undervalued housing prices and identify investment opportunities, reveal the impacts of government policies, identify areas of potential gentrification, etc.

Regionally, housing prices in Czechia vary significantly with the traditionally highest prices in the capital city (Prague) and the second largest city (Brno). Prices in rural areas tend to be lower. One might also expect that the dynamic of housing prices differs among regions. Therefore, we analyze trends in housing prices development over more than two decades to reveal the patterns of the development and discuss important milestones in the Czech housing market.

We find three distinct periods of excessive growth in Czech regional housing prices, identified by large positive GAPs but with different impacts across regions. Using a fixed effect panel data model, we identify common drivers of housing prices, including wage growth, migration and crime rate. However, the impacts of GDP per capita and job market indicators vary between flat and house prices. The difference between flat and house prices seems to be led by migration, GDP per capita growth and crime rate.

The rest of the chapter is organized as follows: Section 11.2 presents a literature review focused on the determinants of housing prices, with the focus on Czechia. Section 11.3 describes the data and empirical methodology employed. Section 11.4 discusses the results of trend and gap analysis as well as panel data analysis, and Section 11.5 concludes.

11.2 Literature Review

While research on Czech housing prices has been on the back burner in academic papers for several years, it gained momentum at the onset of GFC and the consequent sudden stop in housing price growth. Papers that appeared include Égert and Mihaljek (2007), Čadil (2009), Zemčík (2009) and Hlaváček and Komárek (2010). Égert and Mihaljek (2007) analyze the factors influencing housing prices dynamics in transition economies of CEE Europe and OECD countries, including Czechia using panel DOLS approach for the period 1999–2006. They find a positive relationship between per capita GDP and housing prices and robust relationships between real interest rates and housing credit with house prices. In CEE countries, demographic factors and labour market developments seem to be crucial drivers of housing prices. Moreover, they recommend considering also transition-specific factors. Čadil (2009) studied the formation of bubbles in the Czech housing market using price-to-income ratio and VAR modelling using data covering the period 1998 2006. He found that housing prices in Czechia are dominantly demand-determined, with speculative demand driving much of the price dynamics. Not surprisingly, he predicts a future correction in housing prices, especially for flats in big cities.

Zemčík (2011) evaluated the relationship between real estate prices and rents in Czechia using regional cross-sectional dependence, panel data unit root tests and panel data causality tests. He found regional inter-dependence between prices and rents. Unit root tests for price-to-rent ratios show evidence of non-stationarity in both datasets, implying overpriced real estate in Czechia. However, the degree of overpricing seems small, suggesting only a minor decline of prices in some locations. The ideas of the present-value model are supported as changes in rents predict the changes in prices. Hlaváček and Komárek (2010) analyzed housing price determinants in Czechia using simple indicators such as price-to-income, price-to-rent and rental income which suggested faster growth of housing prices compared to foreign countries and differences among regions. They identify Prague as the riskiest region for bubble formation. Their panel data analysis reveals the important role of wages, credit, migration and divorce rates as well as land prices on housing prices.

Not surprisingly, the second wave of papers devoted to Czech housing prices appeared in response to extensive growth of housing prices at the beginning of the 2020s and includes Votava et al. (2021) and Kalabiška and Hlaváček (2022). Using Czech data on regional apartments prices over the period 2000–2017, Votava et al. (2021) found that net disposable income, number of inhabitants per completed apartment, average state of the population, number of applicants per job and number of divorces differ in their impact on regional housing prices. However, there were no significant differences regarding the impact of the number of marriages and the number of crimes on apartment prices. Moreover, they find that increasing housing construction may not be an effective tool to correct 'unhealthy' price developments. Kalabiška and Hlaváček (2022) analyze the determinants of apartment prices in Czechia using traditional panel regression models and dynamic panel regression models. They find that apartment prices are mainly driven by wages and unemployment, and apartment stock the only significant supply-side factor. They find positive effects of divorce rate and migration on apartment prices. The effect of building plot prices on apartment prices varied by region. Labour force factors are more important in low-income regions than in Prague. The Granger causality test revealed that apartment prices are not Granger caused by rents and natural population growth.

The dominant role of demand-side factors is confirmed in various contexts, including German regions. For instance, Brausewetter et al. (2022) and Belke and Keil (2018) find that demand-side factors play a dominant role in determining real estate prices, even in German regions. Specifically, using data for Germany over the period 2008–2019, Brausewetter et al. (2022) finds that regional housing prices growth was particularly pronounced in the seven largest cities and in southern districts. They do not find any evidence for widespread price bubbles. They confirm the dominant role of demand-side factors, such as population growth, high-skilled labour and purchasing power and the important role of prices for building land. Belke and Keil (2018) analyzed German regional data over the period 1990–2010 and found significant demand-side drivers of housing prices such as the size of the regional market, age structure and regional infrastructure. The effects of disposable income and interest rates also impact prices, albeit with some variations in statistical significance. Supply-side determinants such as construction activity, housing stock and real estate transactions also significantly contribute to housing prices dynamics. Moreover, interest rates in their sample seem to be strongly associated with housing prices.

11.3 Data and Methodology

We use data for Czechia; hence, our data sources are the Czech National Bank and the Czech Statistical Office. For our trend analysis, we use quarterly data on the housing price growth (prices of flats in particular). Furthermore, in the panel regression, we use annual data for the growth of both flat and house prices. We also incorporate a set of explanatory variables in order to determine the drivers of housing price growth in Czechia. In the regression analysis, all our variables are in differences or growths to control for a potential stationarity problem. We include both supply and demand-side market variables, with the demand side being dominantly represented as suggested by previous research. Moreover, we incorporate variables such as crime rate per 1,000 inhabitants, which has been often neglected in previous research and we assume its significant effect on housing prices.

In terms of methodology, we employ two approaches. First, we analyze the dynamics of housing prices in regions and their co-movements with the use of trend and gap analysis. Specifically, we calculate year on year growth rates, the one-year moving average (1Y_MA) and the three-year moving average (3Y_MA) according to the following Eqs. (11.1 and 11.2).

$$1Y\_MA = \frac{A_1 + A_2 + A_3 + A_4}{4} \tag{11.1}$$

$$3Y\_MA = \frac{A_1 + A_2 + \ldots + A_{12}}{12} \tag{11.2}$$

Moreover, faster growth of 1Y_MA compared to 3Y_MA may indicate excessive growth. We measure this by constructing a GAP indicator as expressed in Eq. (11.3).

$$\text{GAP in } \% = \frac{1Y\_MA - 3Y\_MA}{3Y\_MA} * 100 \tag{11.3}$$

Second, we perform panel data regression analysis Eq. (11.4) using annual data for all 14 Czech regions, including the capital city of Prague.

$$Y_{it} = \beta_0 + \beta_1 X_{it} + \ldots + \beta_k X_{it} + u_{it} \ldots..,N, t = 1 \ldots T \tag{11.4}$$

We consider three dependent variables: prices of flats, prices of houses and the difference between the two price developments. Our explanatory variables include GDP per capita, wage growth, number of job applicants per one job opportunity, economic activity, migration, change in finished buildings and crimes per 1,000 inhabitants. We employ fixed-effects regression to capture the unobservable characteristics of individual regions.

11.4 Regional Housing Prices in Czechia – Empirical Evidence

The recent steep growth of housing prices decreased affordability of properties. According to Property Index Overview of European Residential Markets (Deloitte, 2022), buyers in Czechia pay on average more than 13 gross annual salaries for a new dwelling of 70 sqm, which makes the situation the worst among European countries. Nevertheless, the ownership rate remains high in Czechia compared to western economies, see Fig. 11.1. The Czech mortgage market is well developed and offers a large variety of products to finance properties. Czechia is open to foreign investors who are attracted by the strong economy, low taxes, government regulations that protect investors and attractive investment opportunities as properties are still catching up to other Western European countries. This further contributes to high demand that is not accompanied by a sufficient increase in supply.

The Czech housing market experienced three significant periods of excessive growth of housing prices that we identify in our data through the formation of large positive GAPs, measured as percentage difference between one-year moving average and three-year moving average of housing prices. The first one appeared before the entrance of Czechia to the European Union (EU). At the end of 2003, the GAP reached high levels in all regions, see Fig. 11.2. The highest GAP of more than 30.46% appeared in the Pilsen Region (PI), while the lowest one was in

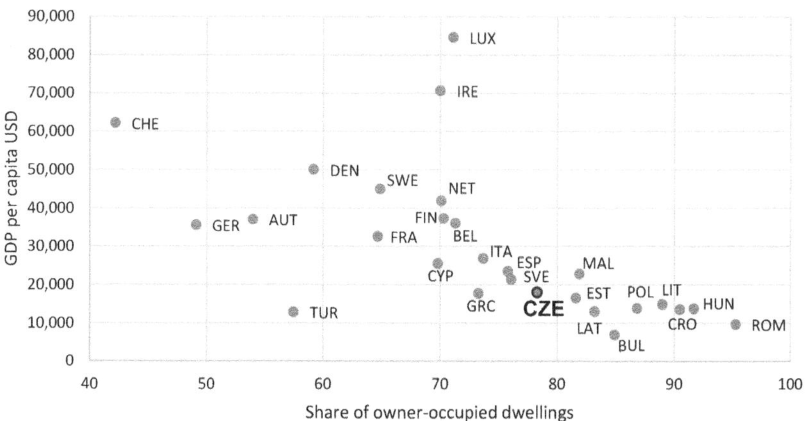

Fig. 11.1. Share of Owner-Occupied Dwellings and Its Relationship to GDP Per Capita in European Countries. *Source:* Authors' calculations based on Eurostat data.

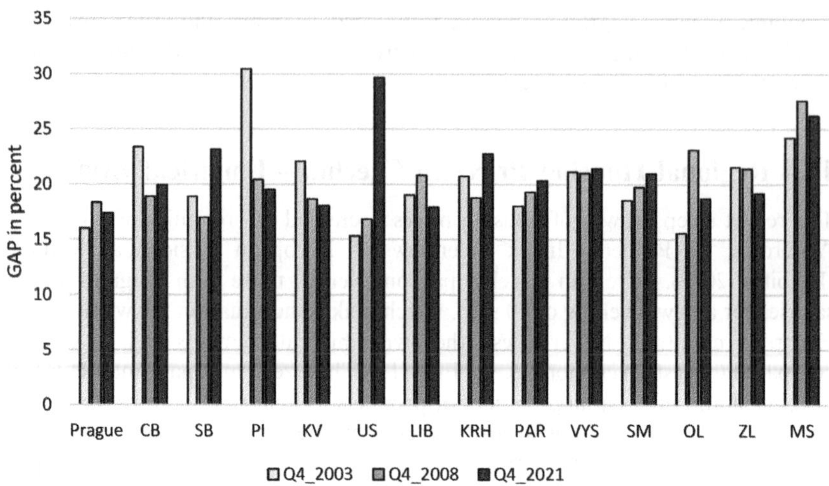

Fig. 11.2. Gaps in Housing Price Growth. *Source:* Authors' calculations.

the Ústí region (15.14%). In all the regions, this disproportional growth was followed by a decrease in housing prices in the following periods.

The second period of excessive housing price growth in Czechia peaked at the onset of the global financial crisis at the end of 2008. As Hlaváček and Komárek (2010) state, the growth of real estate prices continued in Czechia even though real estate prices in other countries had already started to fall due to the GFC. The GAP that materialized in that time reached up to 27.58% in the Moravian-Silesian Region while being the lowest again in the Ústí region (16.83%). This event influenced the housing market for a much longer period (up to 6 years in some of the regions) than the previous one. The reaction to the GFC was different from region to region. One group of regions experienced a rather short decrease in housing prices followed by stagnation or slow growth (Prague, Central Bohemia, South Bohemia, PI, Liberec Region, Olomouc Region and South Moravia Region, while others experienced another drop without a revival of the real estate market (Karlovy Vary Region, Ústí region, Pardubice Region, Vysočina Region, Hradec Králové Region, Moravian-Silesian Region and Zlín Region).

The last formation of high positive GAPs appears at the end of our dataset in the end of 2021 with the largest values in the Ústí region (29.67%) and the lowest in Prague (17.40%). We already know, once again, the large positive GAP has been followed by a decrease in housing prices in the 2022–2023 period, especially due to the consequences of the Russian invasion of Ukraine that caused a rise in inflation and consequent tightening of monetary policy. In Czechia, it was accompanied by the amendment to the Act on the CNB, which entered into force on 1 August 2021, Act No. 219/2021 Coll., which amended Act No. 6/1993 Coll., of the Czech National

Bank. This enabled the CNB to set legally binding macroprudential limits concerning mortgage loans, which helped cool the mortgage market.

In general, this short historical excursion highlights the fact that values of GAPs above 15% seem to be a warning signal that housing price growth is unsustainable in the long term and will soon be followed by a correction. Moreover, there are significant differences from region to region in reaction to such events as the size of the GAP in one region may be up to double compared to other regions.

Regarding regression analysis, we first run the set of regression models with the growth of flat prices as a dependent variable. We steadily add more variables in three separate steps. The results as presented in Table 11.1 indicate four deciding factors that may drive the change in the prices of flats in Czech regions. First, wage growth plays a significant role and contributes to a rise in flat prices. It may be surprizing that GDP per capita growth does not play a significant role in housing market development, but it might be because we are tracking the drivers of change rather than the determinants of nominal prices, where the general economic development may play a more prominent role. Furthermore, we employ a variable of job applicants per one

Table 11.1. Flat Price Determinants.

Variables	**Model 1**	**Model 2**	**Model 3**
GDP per capita growth	0.042	−0.084	0.229
	(0.181)	(0.200)	(0.196)
Wage growth	2.356***	1.722***	1.556***
	(0.229)	(0.432)	(0.233)
Job applicants per one job		−0.227***	−0.117**
		(0.044)	(0.040)
Economic activity		0.197	−0.331
		(1.114)	(0.482)
Migration		1.579***	1.453***
		(0.385)	(0.437)
Finished buildings growth			0.001
			(0.000)
Crime rate per 1,000 inhabitants			−0.801***
			(0.144)
Constant	−3.516***	−14.771	36.933
	(0.843)	(64.682)	(27.236)
Observations	317	317	316
R-squared	0.176	0.249	0.436
Number of id	14	14	14

Source: Authors' calculations.

Robust standard errors in parentheses.

***$p < 0.01$; **$p < 0.05$; *$p < 0.1$.

job available as a proxy for the labour market and we can see that the rise in this indicator (either increase in the number of unemployed or reduction of available jobs) negatively impacts the growth of flat prices. In this model, economic activity does not have a significant impact on housing prices. Nevertheless, it is important to say that this variable does not differ much in time and across the regions. Migration seems to play a significant role in housing market development, where a migration surplus contributes to rising prices on the housing market, putting pressure on the demand side of the market. Concerning the supply side, we can see that within the same year, the growth in the number of finished buildings does not significantly impact the market. Finally, the crime rate might be influencing housing price development, since the variable crimes per 1,000 inhabitants has a negative impact on housing price growth.

Contrary to flats, the drivers of the price of houses seem to differ slightly in their effects. For instance, GDP per capita is significant in primary modelling steps. Wage development has the same impact on house prices as for flat prices, albeit with lesser magnitude. Job applicants per job and economic activity variables are not statistically significant. The insignificance of job applicants is yet another difference from flats. Finally, the migration variable, finished buildings and crime rate have similar impacts on house prices as for flat prices but with smaller coefficients (see Table 11.2). This might be due to a possibly more rigid and stable branch of the housing market when it comes to houses.

Table 11.2. House Price Determinants.

Variables	**Model 4**	**Model 5**	**Model 6**
GDP per capita growth	−0.317***	−0.320**	−0.118
	(0.087)	(0.123)	(0.101)
Wage growth	1.646***	1.287***	1.185***
	(0.149)	(0.245)	(0.155)
Job applicants per one job		−0.048	0.037
		(0.035)	(0.034)
Economic activity		0.595	0.179
		(0.857)	(0.490)
Migration		0.658**	0.561**
		(0.228)	(0.249)
Finished buildings growth			−0.000
			(0.000)
Crime rate per 1,000 inhabitants			−0.620***
			(0.139)

Table 11.2. *(Continued)*

Variables	Model 4	Model 5	Model 6
Constant	0.021	−34.757	5.616
	(0.575)	(50.136)	(26.459)
Observations	317	317	316
R-squared	0.139	0.165	0.418
Number of id	14	14	14

Source: Authors' calculations.

Robust standard errors in parentheses.
$^{***}p < 0.01$; $^{**}p < 0.05$; $^{*}p < 0.1$.

The differences in the effects of drivers for flats and house prices motivate us to the last step of our analysis, in which we analyze the difference between the growth of flat prices and house prices. We provide the results in Table 11.3. We can see that only three variables are statistically significant, and we must keep in mind that we calculate this variable as a difference between growth of flat prices and growth of house prices. We find that increasing GDP per capita growth mitigates the difference in prices together with the increasing crime rate, indicating that increased number of crimes hinders price growth for both segments of the market. What increases the difference in the development between these two branches of the market is the increase of migration into the region, possibly due to newly incoming inhabitants that plan for their first dwelling to be a flat rather than a house, which may come with fewer commitments.

Table 11.3. Drivers of Divergence Between the Price of Flats and Houses.

Variables	Model 7
GDP per capita growth	−0.544**
	(0.205)
Wage growth	0.563
	(0.373)
Job applicants per one job	0.083
	(0.113)
Economic activity	−0.520
	(1.004)
Migration	2.250***
	(0.432)

(Continued)

Table 11.3. *(Continued)*

Variables	Model 7
Finished buildings growth	−0.001
	(0.001)
Crime rate per 1,000 inhabitants	−0.738***
	(0.155)
Constant	45.772
	(61.436)
Observations	316
Number of id	14
R-squared	0.425

Source: Authors' calculations.

Robust standard errors in parentheses.
***$p < 0.01$; **$p < 0.05$; *$p < 0.1$.

As a robustness check, we reestimate our models by adding one lag to all our explanatory variables. In general, our key findings hold. We confirm the key role of crime rate on housing prices in all our models. Moreover, we confirm the effect of the number of job applicants per one job on flat prices and wages on house prices at 5% significance level. The main drivers of the difference between flat and house prices remain the same – migration and crime rate. Full results of robustness tests are available upon request from the authors.

11.5 Conclusion

In this chapter, we quantify and discuss three distinct periods of excessive growth of regional Czech housing prices, identified through the formation of large positive GAPs, calculated as the percentage difference between one-year and three-year moving averages of housing prices. The first period occurred before the entrance of Czechia to the EU. The second peak appeared at the onset of the GFC. The last period of high positive GAPs occurred in 2021. In all these periods, we identify significant differences among regions. We find that GAPs above 15% may be considered an indication of unsustainable long-term housing price growth that will be followed by a correction.

By employing a fixed effect panel data model, we revealed the drivers of the flat prices and house prices in Czech regions. The results show that wage growth, migration and crime rate are significant factors affecting the prices of both flats and houses. Nevertheless, the impact of GDP per capita and job market indicators differs between flats and houses. Moreover, we study factors influencing the difference between flat and house price development. We find that migration into the region increases the difference, while increasing GDP per capita growth and crime rate mitigate this difference significantly.

Our results may help to enrich the understanding of the Czech housing market in terms of identification of excessive growth and drivers of the housing price development. The regional differences should be considered while preparing regional policies.

References

Belke, A., & Keil, J. (2018). Fundamental determinants of real estate prices: A panel study of German regions. *International Advances in Economic Research*, *24*, 25–45. https://doi.org/10.1007/s11294-018-9671-2

Brausewetter, L., Thomsen, S. L., & Trunzer, J. (2022). *Explaining regional disparities in housing prices across German districts*. Halle Institute for Economic Research (IWH). IWH Discussion Papers 13/2022.

Čadil, J. (2009). Housing price bubble analysis—Case of the Czech Republic. *Prague Economic Papers*, *18*(1), 38–47. https://doi.org/10.18267/j.pep.340

Deloitte. (2022, August). *Property index: Overview of European residential markets* (11th ed.). https://www2.deloitte.com/content/dam/Deloitte/cz/Documents/real-estate/Property_Index_2022.pdf

Égert, B., & Mihaljek, D. (2007). Determinants of house prices in Central and Eastern Europe. *Comparative Economic Studies*, *49*(3), 367–388. https://doi.org/10.1057/palgrave.ces.8100221

Hlaváček, M., & Komárek, L. (2010). Rovnovážnost cen nemovitostí v ČR. *Politická Ekonomie*, *58*(3), 326–342. https://doi.org/10.18267/j.polek.733

Kalabiška, R., & Hlaváček, M. (2022). Regional determinants of housing prices in the Czech Republic. *Czech Journal of Economics and Finance (Finance a úvěr)*, *72*(1), 2–29. https://doi.org/10.32065/CJEF.2022.01.01

Votava, L., Komárková, L., & Dvořák, J. (2021). Demand and supply determinants on the property market and their importance in explaining regional differences. *Politická Ekonomie*, *69*(1), 26–47. https://doi.org/10.18267/j.polek.1309

Zemčík, P. (2011). Is there a real estate bubble in the Czech Republic? *Finance a Úvěr*, *61*(1), 49–66.

Chapter 12

Efficiency of the Czech Labour Market: Do Institutions Matter?

Aleš Franc

Mendel University in Brno, Czechia

Abstract

The efficient functioning of the labour market is an important factor that affects long-term economic growth. The interaction of supply and demand on the labour market is influenced by institutions which change the motivations and behaviour of economic actors and, ultimately, the flexibility of the labour market. There is no consensus in the literature on the effect these institutions have on labour market outcomes. This chapter focuses on a set of selective labour market institutions (employment protection legislation, minimum wages, unemployment benefits, labour taxation, trade unions and active labour market policies), compares their relevance to other European Union (EU) countries and through the lens of the Beveridge curve it tries to evaluate their impact on effectiveness of the Czech labour market. The international comparison shows that most of the considered institutions/regulations do not reach such importance (except employment protection legislation) and that they have a significant negative effect on labour market outcomes. Even the model of the Beveridge curve does not indicate that the Czech labour market is characterised by rigidities that would impair the effectiveness of a matching process at the aggregate level.

Keywords: Flexibility of the labour market; unemployment; beveridge curve; regulation; labour market policies; Czech labour market

12.1 Introduction

Labour market institutions include all legal regulations, norms or conventions that influence the form and content of employment contracts and the determination of wages in the economy. In the economic literature, the discussion about

Modeling Economic Growth in Contemporary Czechia, 183–198

Published under exclusive licence by Emerald Publishing Limited
doi:10.1108/978-1-83753-840-920241012

the importance of labour market institutions began to intensify in the 1980s as a reaction to the divergent development of the unemployment rate in developed countries. This debate has intensified as globalisation and technological change have exposed both developed and developing countries to greater competition, sparking debate about the form of a potentially optimal institutional framework (Hayter, 2011).

There are many studies attempting to explain the effect of labour market institutions on unemployment or other labour market outcomes, respectively. According to Nickell (2003), differences in the structure and organisation of the labour market can largely explain country-to-country differences in unemployment. Heavy regulation of the labour market creates rigidities and distortions that make the creation of low-skilled jobs too costly (Krugman, 1994; Nickell, 1997; Scharpf, 2000). Empirical research in the 1990s, largely based on intercountry regressions, typically found that these regulations lead to a higher persistent unemployment rate in many continental European countries (Betcherman, 2012).

Advanced econometric methods and greater data availability began to challenge the dominant emphasis on labour market deregulation as a universal tool for reducing unemployment. According to an alternative view, labour market institutions must be perceived as part of a wider set of complementary institutions (Baker et al., 2003; Bassanini & Duval, 2006; Hall & Soskice, 2001). The impact of these institutions on labour market outcomes is not necessarily negative (on the contrary, some studies report neutral or even positive net effect (see e.g. Bradley & Stephens, 2007) and due to possible institutional complementarities *one-size-fits-all* reform strategies are not necessarily successful (Hall and Soskice, 2001).

This chapter focuses on the role of selective institutions in the Czech labour market: employment protection legislation (EPL), minimum wages, unemployment benefits, labour taxation, trade unions and active labour market policies (ALMPs). The relative importance of each institution will be assessed in context of European Union (EU) member states, for which data are available in the OECD database. The crucial question is to what extent these institutions affect the functioning of the labour market. The model of the Beveridge curve will be used for a rough evaluation of the efficiency of the labour market. Increased frictions or rigidities shift the Beveridge curve towards the right making labour markets less dynamic and flexible (Bhattarai, 2016).

12.2 Labour Market Institutions and Their Effects

Because there is no single measure of institutional setup, theoretical and empirical studies usually use a set of institutional indicators to assess flexibility and rigidity of the labour market (e.g. Fialová & Schneider, 2009; Nickell, 1997, pp. 55–74). For each institution, the estimated impact on labour market outcomes will be summarised and then its importance will be assessed in context with other countries.

12.2.1 Employment Protection Legislation

EPL has been a subject of hot debates since the late 1980s as a result of attempts to explain high and persisting unemployment in European countries. It consists of a set of standards and rules that employers must follow when firing employees. It includes laws and regulations pertaining to severance pay, notification of layoffs, restrictions on individual and collective dismissals and restrictions of temporary contracts. Increased costs, as companies are burdened in complying with these regulations, lead to both a lower rate of job creation and job losses. Calmfors and Holmlund (2000) argue that stringent EPL restricts the flow of workers to growing, high-productivity sectors and reduces employers' willingness to introduce labour-saving technologies. Lower labour market dynamism slows down the reallocation of workers to more productive activities.

EPL also seems to affect the composition of unemployment and employment; countries with strict EPL record a higher unemployment rate of young labour market entrants, women with interrupted work careers and a lower unemployment rate of prime-aged workers (Bertola et al., 2000). Moreover, stricter EPL for permanent contracts is unfavourable for flexible jobs and creates a so-called two-tier system, where firms rely on a core of employees with full-time permanent contracts.

However, as Betcherman (2012) argues, the EPL on the other hand creates a stable job perspective that motivates workers to increase their effort and invest in human capital. At the same time, companies are also induced to make investments at increasing productivity in order to be compensated for the additional costs of EPL.

Fig. 12.1 illustrates intercountry differences in strictness of EPL index published by the OECD for total individual and collective dismissals and how it

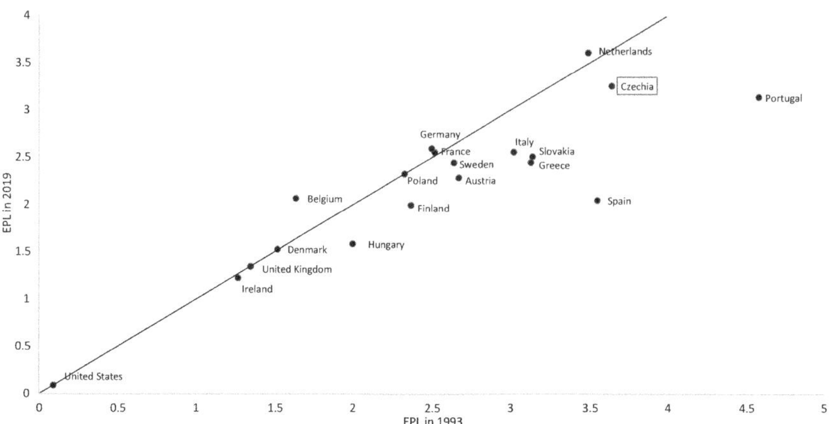

Fig. 12.1. Trends in Strictness of Employment Protection – Individual and Collective Dismissals. *Source:* OECD Employment Protection Legislation Database.

changed in the period 1993–2019. The strictness of regular contracts was eased in many countries, especially with regard to individual dismissals. The same happened in Czechia, but the legislative protection of workers remains rather strict in comparison with other countries. In some countries, there are significant differences between the main components of EPL index, notably between regulations of unfair dismissals and their enforcement. Czechia records the highest score in procedural inconvenience to dismissals (3.8). It can be expected that stricter employment protection for regular workers can result in the increasing share of employment under fixed-term contract, especially when regulations in this area are more relaxed. However, this is not the case of Czechia, because despite strict EPL for permanent contracts, the incidence of temporary contracts is significantly lower than the EU-27 average (23%–47% in 2012 according to Eurostat statistics).

12.2.2 Minimum Wages

There is a great academic controversy over the employment effects of the minimum wage. The simplest economic model of the minimum wage assuming a perfectly competitive labour market predicts that an increase in the minimum wage reduces employment of the most susceptible workers. This consensus broke down in the 1990s as a number of studies introduced different methodology for estimation focusing on the employment effect of minimum wages in specific industries that did not always confirm adverse employment effects (Borjas, 2016). This attracted works on monopsonist labour markets built on Stigler (1946) where minimum wages can increase employment. There is no consensus in either theoretical or empirical literature about the real employment effects of minimum wages.

Acemoglu (2001) argues that high minimum wages increase the costs of low-skilled jobs creation and induce firms to invest in increasing productivity of workers and to create more middle and high-skilled jobs. Higher minimum wages can also invoke a supply-side response through greater job search intensity and investments in human capital. As Acemoglu and Pischke (1999) point out, if a worker's productivity depends on his investment in education and skills, then a binding minimum wage motivates workers to increase their skills so that they are not 'crowded out' by a high minimum wage.

The institute of minimum wages is closely related to other labour market institutions that influence wage distribution. Boeri (2012) finds out that the amount of the minimum wage is influenced by whether it is set by the government or if it is the outcome of collective bargaining. In the latter case, the minimum wage is usually higher. Similarly, Garnero et al. (2015) concludes that government-mandated minimum wages are more common in countries with relatively low levels of collective bargaining coverage.

There are diverse institutional configurations regarding the institute of a minimum wage. In Czechia, the minimum wage is government legislated and in principle applies to all workers who have a legal contract in the private sector. In individual collective agreements, it is possible to agree on a minimum wage that is higher than the legislative minimum. In firms with no collective agreement, the lowest level of the guaranteed wage is applied in addition to the minimum wage. In the public sector, the system of salary schemes is applied in addition to the minimum wage and the lowest levels of the guaranteed wage. As can be seen in Fig. 12.2, despite periodical increases in recent years, the ratio of minimum to median wage is still significantly lower than in most EU countries that apply the national minimum wage.

12.2.3 Unemployment Benefits

The unemployment benefit system is important for motivation of the unemployed to actively look for a job. According to the job search theory, the duration of benefits affects the job finding rate and expected duration of unemployment. Moreover, a rise in the benefit level tends to increase reservation wages of recipients and their search intensity. Holmlund (2014) mentions the 'entitlement effect' having rarely been tested in empirical literature, implying increased search behaviour of the unemployed close to exhausting their benefits so as to qualify for benefits in the future. As Boeri and van Ours (2021) point out, more generous unemployment benefits and a longer search process enable achievement of a higher quality of post-unemployment matching.

The unemployment benefit system consists of three key dimensions: entitlement (rules defining access to the benefits), generosity (duration and level of benefits) and eligibility (rules that the recipient must meet when receiving

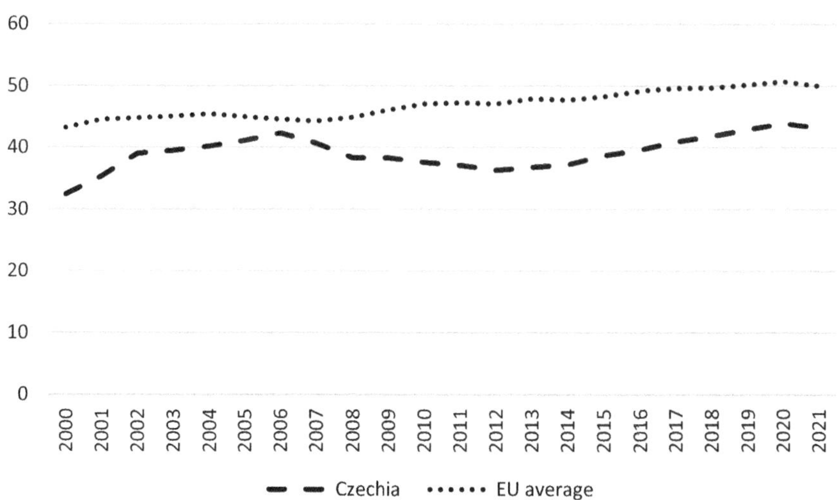

Fig. 12.2. Ratio of Minimum to Median Wage (2000–2021).
Source: OECD Statistics.

benefits). Unemployment benefits in Czechia were provided only for the first 6 months from 2004, with the replacement rate of 50% in the first 3 months and 45% during the following 3 months. In 2008, the duration of unemployment benefits was reduced to 5 months for unemployed people younger than 50 years but extended to 8 months for unemployed workers between the ages of 50 and 55 and to 11 months for people older than 55 years. The replacement rate was modified to 60% for the first 2 months, 50% for the next 2 months and 45% for the last 2 months.

Table 12.1 contains an overview of the main characteristics of the unemployment benefit systems according to the three dimensions across selected EU countries. As can be seen, the entitlement period, as well as the duration of benefits, is at the usual level in Czechia. Some countries also apply a waiting period, which is intended to discourage workers from requesting benefits in case of a short period of unemployment. As for the net replacement ratio (NRR, calculated for a 40-year-old worker with an interrupted working career since age 22, calculated as averages of four family types (for details see Boeri & van Ours, 2021), it drops significantly with the longer time horizon in comparison to other countries. The average level of strictness of eligibility criteria is slightly lower mainly due to rather mild temporary reductions of benefit payments.

12.2.4 Payroll Taxes

Payroll taxes consist of income taxes and social security contributions paid by employees and employers and thereby drive a wedge between total labour costs and the take-home wage of the worker. Growth in the tax burden paid by employers tends to increase costs per worker which leads firms to reduce the amount of workers hired. A lower net wage due to higher taxation of wages leads to a reduced quantity of labour supplied. Payroll taxes thus reduce the size of the labour market. It does not matter whether the tax burden is formally imposed on the workers or the employers, the tax burden in the competitive market is redistributed according to the relative elasticities of labour demand and labour supply (Borjas, 2016). If higher payroll taxes cannot be passed on to workers in form of lower wages, the result is reduced employment. In countries where wages are set in centralised collective bargaining, a stronger impact on employment can be expected due to a flatter labour supply curve (Disney, 2000).

In Czechia, taxation of incomes from labour has constantly changed and developed over time. Initially, a progressive tax rate of 15%, 20%, 25% and 32% and tax deductions were imposed. As a part of social security contributions, the employees were taxed at a rate of 12.5% and the employers 35%. Since 2006, the deductible items have transformed to the form of tax credits. By 2009, the share of social security contributions paid by employees was reduced to 6.5% and the share paid by employers to 25%. In 2008, a linear income tax rate of 15% was introduced and the subject of taxation was total labour costs. Since 2021, only the gross wage has been the subject of taxation, resulting in a significant increase in the net wages of employees. This is the reason why the tax wedge in Czechia is currently lower than in many EU countries (see Fig. 12.3), although social security contributions are among the highest.

Table 12.1. Characteristics of the Unemployment Benefits System.

	Entitlement Conditions		Benefit Generosity				Eligibility Criteria			
				NRR						
Country	**(1)**	**(2)**	**(3)**	**(4)**	**(5)**	**(6)**	**(7)**	**(8)**	**(9)**	**(10)**
Austria	7	0	9	61	60	57	3.0	4.0	1.7	2.9
Belgium	16	0	∞	76	72	63	2.3	3.0	3.5	2.9
Czechia	12	0	11	66	25	7	3.0	2.0	3.0	2.7
Denmark	12	0	24	75	75	47	4.1	3.0	2.2	3.1
Estonia	12	7	12	62	55	20	3.8	4.0	4.7	4.1
Finland	6	5	19	71	67	47	2.5	2.5	3.3	2.8
France	4	7	24	68	68	45	3.4	3.5	3.0	3.3
Germany	12	0	12	66	66	41	3.8	3.5	2.2	3.1
Greece	7	6	12	42	42	17	3.0	1.0	5.0	3.0
Hungary	12	0	3	62	21	11	3.8	2.0	1.7	2.5
Ireland	9	3	9	56	56	57	3.0	3.0	2.1	2.7
Italy	12	8	24	73	66	23	3.5	2.0	4.3	3.3
Latvia	12	0	9	78	48	16	2.6	4.0	3.7	3.4
Lithuania	18	8	9	–	–	–	2.5	3.5	3.0	3.0
Luxembourg	6	0	12	87	87	24	3.3	4.3	5.0	4.2
The Netherlands	6	0	28	75	73	31	3.6	3.0	2.7	3.1

(Continued)

Table 12.1. *(Continued)*

	Entitlement Conditions		Benefit Generosity				Eligibility Criteria			
				NRR						
Country	**(1)**	**(2)**	**(3)**	**(4)**	**(5)**	**(6)**	**(7)**	**(8)**	**(9)**	**(10)**
Poland	12	7	12	48	41	14	4.3	1.0	4.0	3.1
Portugal	12	0	24	76	73	36	3.5	3.0	5.0	3.8
Slovakia	24	0	6	65	38	16	2.8	3.5	3.7	3.3
Slovenia	9	0	12	78	57	22	3.5	3.5	5.0	4.0
Spain	12	0	24	69	62	32	2.5	1.5	4.0	2.7
Sweden	6	7	14	54	54	37	3.8	4.0	2.3	3.4

Source: Boeri and van Ours (2021, p. 519).

Notes: (1) Employment prior to job loss (moths), (2) waiting period (days), (3) maximum duration unemployment insurance benefits (months), (4) initial NRR, (5) NRR average first year, (6) NRR average first five years, (7) availability requirements and suitable work criteria, (8) job-search requirements and monitoring, (9) sanctions, (10) overall.

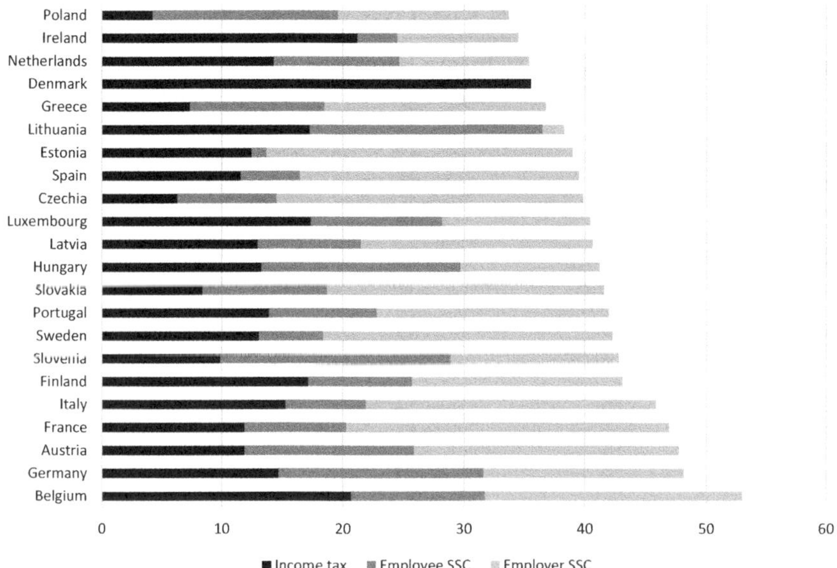

Fig. 12.3. Average Tax Wedge Decomposition (% of Labour Costs). *Source:* OECD Statistics.

12.2.5 Trade Unions

Through their activities, unions cause redistribution in favour of low-skilled workers, which can be positive from the point of view of social justice, but on the other hand, job opportunities for outsiders are limited (Card, 1996). These are low-skilled workers who are pushed out of employment by more egalitarian wage schemes. In addition, the unions support more strict legislative employment protection and thus make it even more difficult for outsiders to return to work.

The impact of trade union activities on labour market outcomes depends both on the way in which collective bargaining is organised and on the degree of coordination of collective bargaining (Aidt & Tzannatos, 2002). The most intuitive indicator of trade union strength, trade union density, does not have sufficient explanatory power in this respect, as it reaches low values in some countries (e.g. France) where collective agreements cover the vast majority of workers (see Table 12.2). Earlier studies (e.g. Layard et al., 1991) concluded that higher collective bargaining coverage leads to an increase in unemployment because unemployed workers find even lower-paying jobs. Garnero (2021) concludes that the relationship between the degree of centralisation and coordination of bargaining systems and labour market outcomes is more complex. Coordinated and uncoordinated but centralised bargaining systems are associated with higher employment than purely decentralised systems.

Table 12.2. Measures of Trade Union Relevance (2019).

Country	Union Density (%)	Collective Bargaining Coverage (%)	Level of Bargaining	Coordination
Austria	26	98	3	4
Belgium	49	96	5	5
Czechia	11	35	1	1
Denmark	67	82	3	4
Estonia	6	6	1	1
Finland	59	89	4	4
France	8	98	3	2
Germany	16	54	3	4
Greece	20	14	2	1
Hungary	8	22	1	1
Ireland	25	34	1	2
Italy	32	100	3	3
Latvia	12	27	1	1
Lithuania	7	8	1	1
Luxembourg	28	57	2	2
The Netherlands	15	76	1	1
Poland	13	13	1	1
Portugal	15	74	3	2
Slovakia	11	25	2	2
Slovenia	20	79	3	2
Spain	13	80	3	3
Sweden	65	88	3	4

Source: OECD Statistics, Visser (2019).

Notes: The Values Refer to 2019 or the Latest Year Available.

Table 12.2 shows that according to all the indicators used, the role of trade unions in Czechia is low. In most other EU countries, a larger proportion of workers are organised in trade unions, and collective agreements also apply to a higher proportion of workers. Collective bargaining is fragmented, confined to individual firms or plants with minimal coordination and predominantly takes place at the company level.

12.2.6 Active Labour Market Policies

ALMP focuses on the most vulnerable groups in the labour market: the long-term unemployed, older workers, workers with inadequate skills and workers with health issues and other disabilities. There has been an increased emphasis on ALMP in Czechia as regards both the number of resources spent on active measures and the number of participants in these programmes. The design of ALMPs has begun to reflect trends in the European labour market – activation and motivation of all participants in the labour market, the emphasis on the employability of the labour force and a motivation system, the pursuit of personalisation and professionalisation of employment services and a higher emphasis on the business environment.

Individual ALMP measures have a specific purpose that determines their influence on unemployed individuals. The most accurate overview of the measures implemented in Czechia is provided by Sirovátka et al. (2005): (1) financing and other support of job creation; (2) programmes increasing/changing qualifications and skills of the unemployed and (3) activation programmes (motivation and rehabilitative measures) that do not meet the nature of any of the previous categories. While retraining programmes are market-conforming measures, financing of job creation is a labour market intervention implemented in economies with a small number of vacancies or low employment of vulnerable groups of workers. In addition to the programmes described below public, employment services are provided. They concern counselling and vocational guidance, job search courses, registration of vacancies and administration of unemployment benefits.

- Job creation: The jobs created by financial support should represent the last resort in the case of the inability to find a job. This measure takes the form of sheltered workshops, socially purposeful jobs and community works. These programmes carry high financial costs as compared to training programmes which are four to five times cheaper. With the decline of investment incentives programme, related expenditures were reduced.
- Retraining programmes: The aim of these programmes is to change the qualification of the unemployed who would not be able to find a job in their field. Retraining courses mostly do not change the level of education of participants and therefore are not suitable for the low-skilled and long-term unemployed people. Even so, it is the most important tool of ALMP.
- Activation programmes: The goal of these programmes is to motivate the unemployed to greater search activity. These programmes are relatively cheap and preparation is not difficult. The disadvantage is that participants must continue with another programme that provides a qualification or work experience.

If they are efficient, ALMPs may reduce mismatch in the labour market because they promote more active search behaviour on the part of the unemployed and enable them to get better jobs through training programmes (Boeri & van Ours, 2021). However, these policies may lead to the opposite results; workers can be locked into training and job creation programmes, which can reduce their search activity. Martin (1998) refers to the substitution effect and deadweight losses as jobs created by ALMP programme can replace other jobs.

The extent to which active labour market measures are implemented is significantly determined by the financial resources available. In this regard, Czechia belongs among the countries with the lowest level of total expenditures on ALMPs even with regard to the level of unemployment. As Fig. 12.4 shows, these expenditures fluctuated around 0.5% GDP, while the EU average (despite significant differences among member states) was roughly three times higher. Approximately half of the ALMP expenditures are allocated on public employment services, the other substantial amount of resources goes to some form of employment support. The sharp increase in 2020 was due to the implementation of targeted programmes to support employment in connection with restrictive anti-epidemic measures.

12.3 The Efficiency of the Labour Market Based on Beveridge Curve

The model of the Beveridge curve contains essential information about the functioning of the labour market and the shocks that affect it (Blanchard et al., 1989). Movements along the Beveridge curve reflect the cyclical fluctuations of the economy, so one can see a decrease in cyclical unemployment during a boom and its rise during a recession. These movements are associated with changes in labour

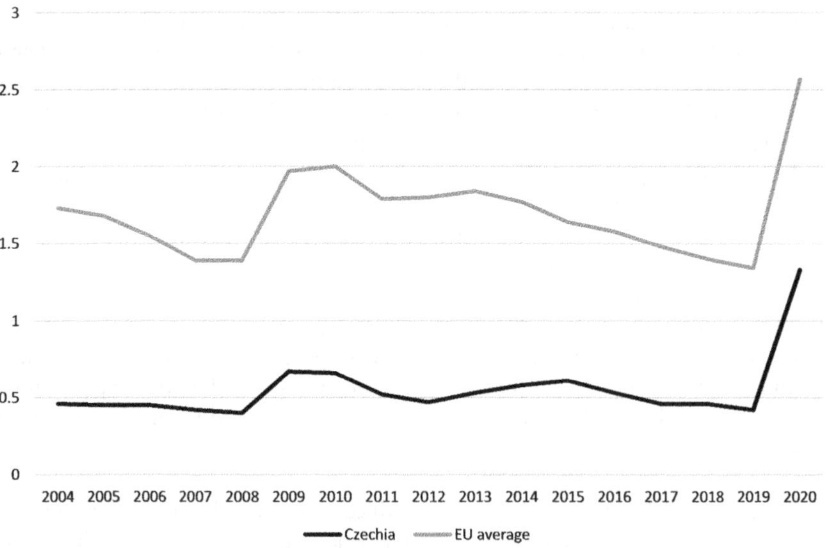

Fig. 12.4. Expenditures on Active Labour Market Policy (% of GDP). *Source:* OECD Statistics.

market tightness measured by the vacancy-unemployment ratio (Consolo & Da Silva, 2019). The shifts of the Beveridge curve reflect changes in the labour market efficiency. According to simple interpretation, the further away the Beveridge curve is from the origin, the lower efficiency of matching process. According to Consolo and Da Silva (2019), the position of the Beveridge curve depends on many factors such as the share of long-term unemployment, geographical dispersion of unemployment and vacancies and structural changes in the labour market.

The following two figures (Figs. 12.5 and 12.6) illustrate the Beveridge curve for Czechia and the 'average' Beveridge curve for the entire EU. Both graphs clearly show the Great Recession at the end of the first decade and the economic boom after 2013. The shift of the Beveridge curve to the right and upwards indicates that in many European countries (unlike Czechia), the Great Recession caused significant structural changes. The position of the Beveridge curve closer to the beginning in the case of Czechia could be mechanically interpreted as evidence of the greater efficiency of the functioning of the Czech labour market. This conclusion is rather simplified because as Boeri and van Ours (2021) point out, the Beveridge curve is an equilibrium condition, potentially capturing both changes in vacancy formation and job search as well as labour demand and labour supply. Nevertheless, the steeper shape of the Beveridge curve in the case of Czechia means that more vacancies are needed for a small decrease in unemployment which can be interpreted as an indicator of labour market shortages.

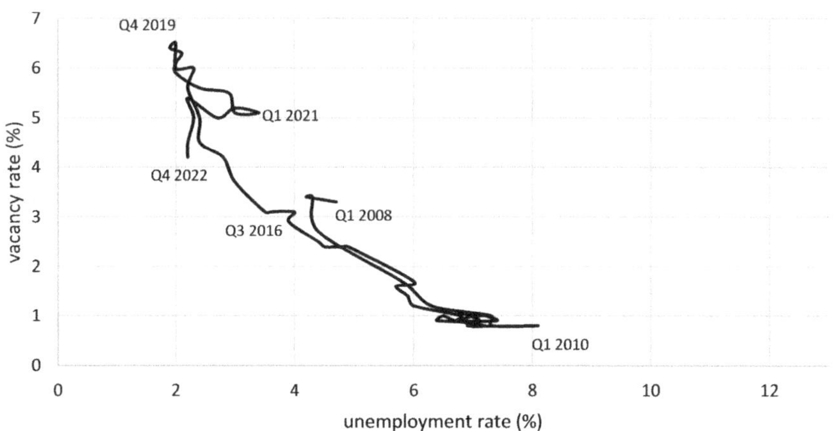

Fig. 12.5. Beveridge Curve in Czechia (2008–2022). *Source:* OECD Statistics.

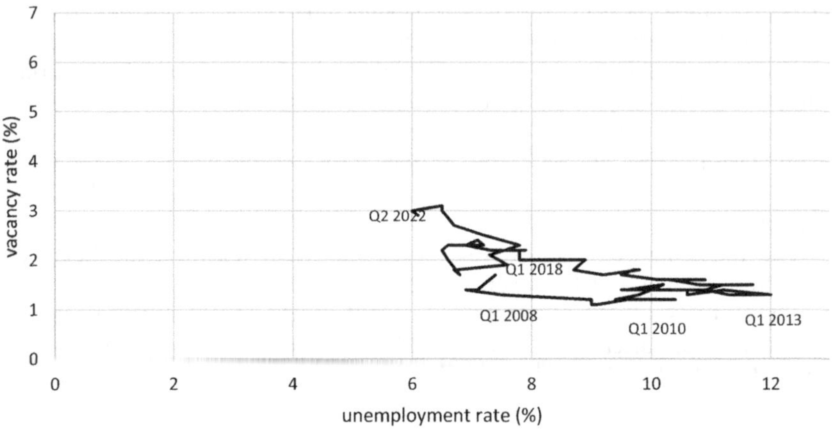

Fig. 12.6. Beveridge Curve in EU Countries (2008–2022). *Source:* OECD Statistics.

12.4 Conclusion

The impact of institutions on labour market outcomes is still a topic of hot debate among economists and policymakers. Proponents of strong regulations argue that they provide essential protection for workers, reduce income inequality and promote social stability. On the other hand, critics contend that they can have unintended consequences, leading to job losses and slower job creation. Although there is no clear definition of a flexible labour market in the literature, some studies (e.g. Laporšek & Dolenc, 2011) prove that Czechia can be characterised by a rather rigid labour market. From the perspective of a selective set of labour market institutions (EPL, minimum wages, unemployment benefits, labour taxation, trade unions and ALMPs), which were analysed in this chapter, it does not seem that the Czech labour market can be characterised by excessive regulations (in terms of international comparison) except EPL. Other institutional barriers are not significant enough to expect a significantly negative impact on unemployment according to standard theory. Despite certain simplification, even the model of the Beveridge curve does not indicate that the Czech labour market is characterised by rigidities that would impair the effectiveness of a matching process at the aggregate level. After all, this follows from the unemployment rate, which has remained at a low level for a long time. On the contrary, the lack of free workers in certain professions can be considered a barrier to economic growth rather than the described labour market institutions.

References

Acemoglu, D. (2001). Good jobs versus bad jobs. *Journal of Labor Economics*, 1–21. https://doi.org/10.1086/209978

Acemoglu, D., & Pischke, J. (1999). The structure of wages and investment in general training. *Journal of Political Economy*, 539–572. https://doi.org/10.1086/250071

Aidt, T., & Tzannatos, Z. (2002). *Unions and collective bargaining: Economic effects in a global environment. Directions in development*. World Bank. http://hdl.handle.net/10986/15241

Baker, D., Glyn, A., Howell, D., & Schmitt, J. (2003). *Labor market institutions and unemployment: A critical assessment of the cross-country evidence*. CES Working Paper No. 98.

Bassanini, A., & Duval, R. (2006). *Employment patterns in OECD countries: Reassessing the role of policies and institutions*. OECD Economics Department Working Papers No. 486.

Bertola, G., Boeri, T., & Cazes, S. (2000). Employment protection in industrialized countries: The case for new indicators. *International Labour Review*, 57–72.

Betcherman, G. (2012). *Labour market institutions: A review of literature*. World Bank Policy Research Working Paper No. 6276. http://hdl.handle.net/10986/16382

Bhattarai, K. (2016). Unemployment-inflation trade-offs in OECD countries. *Economic Modelling*, 93–103. https://doi.org/10.1016/j.econmod.2016.05.007

Blanchard, O. J., Diamond, P., Hall, R. E., & Yellen, J. (1989). The Beveridge curve. In *Brookings papers on economic activity* (pp. 1–76). https://doi.org/10.2307/2534495

Boeri, T. (2012). Setting the minimum wage. *Labour Economics*, 281–290.

Boeri, T., & van Ours, J. (2021). *The economics of imperfect labor markets*. Princeton University Press.

Borjas, G. (2016). *Labor economics*. McGraw-Hill Education.

Bradley, D. H., & Stephens, J. D. (2007). Employment performance in OECD countries: A test of neoliberal and institutionalist hypotheses. *Comparative Political Studies*, 1486–1510. https://doi.org/10.1177/0010414006292609

Calmfors, L., & Holmlund, B. (2000). Unemployment and economic growth: A partial survey. *Swedish Economic Policy Review*, 107–153.

Card, D. (1996). The effect of unions on the structure of wages: A longitudinal analysis. *Econometrica*, *64*(4), 957–979. https://doi.org/10.2307/2171852

Consolo, A., & Da Silva, A. D. (2019). The euro area labour market through the lens of the Beveridge curve. *Economic Bulletin Articles*, *4*. European Central Bank.

Disney, R. (2000). *The impact of tax and welfare policies on employment and unemployment in OECD countries*. IMF Working Papers. WP/00/164. https://doi.org/10.5089/9781451857986.001

Fialová, K., & Schneider, O. (2009). Labor market institutions and their effect on labor market performance in the new EU member countries. *Eastern European Economics*, 57–83. https://doi.org/10.2753/eee0012-8775470303

Garnero, A. (2021). The impact of collective bargaining on employment and wage inequality: Evidence from a new taxonomy of bargaining systems. *European Journal of Industrial Relations*, 185–202. https://doi.org/10.1177/0959680120920771

Garnero, A., Kampelmann, S., & Rycx, F. (2015). Minimum wage systems and earnings inequalities: Does institutional diversity matter? *European Journal of Industrial Relations*, 115–130. https://doi.org/10.1177/0959680114527034

Hall, P. A., & Soskice, D. (Eds.). (2001). *Varieties of capitalism: The institutional foundations of comparative advantage*. Oxford University Press.

Hayter, S. (2011). Introduction. In S. Hayter (Ed.), *The role of collective bargaining in the global economy: Negotiating for social justice* (pp. 1–19). International Labour Organization.

Holmlund, B. (2014). *What do labor market institutions do?* CESifo Working Paper Series No. 4582. https://doi.org/10.2139/ssrn.2390601

Krugman, P. (1994). Past and prospective causes of high unemployment. *Economic Review*, 23–43. https://www.kansascityfed.org/documents/811/1994-Past%20and%20Prospective%20Causes%20of%20High%20Unemployment.pdf

Laporšek, S., & Dolenc, P. (2011). The analysis of flexicurity in the EU members states. *Transylvanian Review of Administrative Sciences*, *7*, 125–145.

Layard, R., Nickell, S., & Jackman, R. (1991). *Unemployment: Macroeconomic performance and the labour market*. Oxford University Press.

Martin, J. (1998). *What works among active labour market policies: Evidence from OECD countries' experiences*. OECD Publishing. OECD Labour Market and Social Policy Occasional Papers, No. 35. https://doi.org/10.1787/267308158388

Nickell, S. (1997). Unemployment and labor market rigidities: Europe versus North America. *Journal of Economic Perspectives*, 55–74. https://ideas.repec.org/a/aea/jecper/v11y1997i3p55-74.html

Nickell, S. (2003). *Employment and taxes*. CESifo Working Paper No. 1109. https://doi.org/10.2139/ssrn.489443

Scharpf, F. W. (2000). Institutions in comparative policy research. *Comparative Political Studies*, 762–790. https://doi.org/10.1177/001041400003300604

Sirovátka, T., Kulhavý, V., Horáková, M., & Rákoczyová, M. (2005). *Směřování české sociální politiky s důrazem na agendu Lisabonské strategie [The direction of Czech social policy with emphasis on the agenda of the Lisbon Strategy]*. VÚPSV, Research Centre Brno.

Stigler, G. J. (1946). The economics of minimum wage legislation. *The American Economic Review*, 358–365. http://www.jstor.org/stable/1801842

Visser, J. (2019). *ICTWSS database, version 6.1*. Amsterdam Institute for Advanced Labour Studies.

Chapter 13

Polarisation of Employment in Czechia and Neighbouring Countries

Radek Náplava

Mendel University in Brno, Czechia

Abstract

The polarisation of employment is a specific structural change in the labour market when the share of high and low-skilled workers increases and, simultaneously, the share of middle-skilled workers decreases. The chapter analyses the effect of polarisation in Czechia and other Central European countries and describes how employment has changed from the perspective of skills regarding gender. The analysis is based on observing the changes in the share of high, middle and low-skilled workers evaluated on the basis of occupational classification over time. Results imply (with a few exceptions) polarisation of employment across all countries during the period between 1998 and 2021, even if we consider the distinction between males and females. Results confirm that employment polarisation has also become a prevalent phenomenon in Central European countries during the last two decades. Finally, this chapter also summarises the economic motivation for studying polarisation phenomenon.

Keywords: Labour market; employment polarisation; structural change; middle class; gender differences; occupational structure

13.1 Introduction

Employment (or job) polarisation represents a specific change in the employment structure regarding skills when the relative share of high and low-skilled workers is increasing while the share of middle-skilled workers is decreasing. The explanation of this phenomenon is primarily based on the nature of technological changes, which have a non-neutral nature, and at the same time, seem to be biased against middle-skilled workers (Goos et al., 2014). Middle-skilled workers

Modeling Economic Growth in Contemporary Czechia, 199–213

Published under exclusive licence by Emerald Publishing Limited
doi:10.1108/978-1-83753-840-920241013

typically perform occupations with a significant content of routine tasks, which lays the foundations for their substitution by technology – algorithms, machines or robots. On the other hand, high and low-skilled workers typically perform occupations with a lower content of routine tasks, making their substitution difficult.

This chapter aims to examine this phenomenon in the context of Czechia. We contribute to the discussion regarding current changes in the labour market. First, we provide evidence about the changing employment structure in the context of employment polarisation in Czechia and neighbouring countries concerning gender during the period 1998–2021. The literature emphasises (Cerina et al., 2021; Jerbashian, 2019) the more important role of females in shaping employment polarisation. In Czechia, our results prove polarisation in female occupations while not in male occupations. In the other selected countries, employment polarisation appears to prevail, typically both in male and female occupations.

Second, we contribute to the broad debate by summarising economic motives for studying polarisation. Abstraction from the argumentation of the causes of research into the polarisation phenomenon is often encountered in empirical studies. Typically, it is research based on the fact that polarisation 'simply is' (see later in the text).

The rest of the chapter is structured as follows: The first section answers why we should care about employment polarisation in the context of economic motives. Second, we describe data and how to evaluate skills to identify employment polarisation. The content of the third section is a descriptive analysis and discussion of the reached results. The last section summarises and concludes the chapter.

13.2 Empirical Evidence and Motives for Studying Employment Polarisation

In the words of Hunt and Nunn (2019), job polarisation is often the focus of researchers – 'for its own sake'. An earlier assumption, formalised by the skill-biased technological change (SBTC) hypothesis, was a directly proportional relationship between the level of skills and the relative labour demand. Card and DiNardo (2002) explain that incorporating a new technology requires more skilled workers to operate them – technologies are thus understood mainly as complementary to qualified workers. Goldin and Katz (2007) demonstrate that this occurred in developed Western countries until the 1980s and 1990s at the aggregate economy level. The decreasing relative demand for middle-skilled workers, accompanied by the growth of the relative demand for high and low-skilled workers (job polarisation), thus does not correspond to the former theoretical assumptions that the SBTC hypothesis established. However, this in itself is not an economic problem. The problem can arise from two other reasons.

First, due to adverse distributional consequences, which can result from disproportionately increasing income inequality (typically measured by the ratio of the upper decile to the median wage) and overall inequality (the ratio of an upper and bottom decile) (Autor et al., 2008; Hunt & Nunn, 2019). Polarisation has been 'revealed' by many efforts to explain rising income inequality in the United States, as income inequality was one of the main research topics in the economics of labour markets. The greater relative demand for the high and low-skilled compared to middle-skilled workers could be reflected in a more dynamic increase in the real wages of the high and low-skilled (high and low-paid workers) compared to the middle-skilled (middle-paid workers).

Rising income inequality is not necessarily problematic as long as there is no decline in real income. Autor et al. (2008) revisit wage inequality in the United States and find increasing overall inequality in the 1980s due to the decline in the real minimum wage. Furthermore, between 1971 and 1995, they document the stagnation and decline of real wages, especially for males, in low and middle-skilled positions. The increase in income inequality due to polarisation, that is, the polarisation of the wage structure (or in other words, wage polarisation), began in the 1990s; however, it is not the case that the real wages of middle-skilled and middle-paid workers fall, but grow relatively more slowly. Naticchioni et al. (2014) show that the decline in real wages of middle-skilled workers occurred at the turn of the millennium in Germany, Spain and Austria. In Spain and Austria, it lasted about two years, while in Germany, this phenomenon was continuous from 2000 until 2006. The decline in real wages of middle-skilled and middle-paid workers was thus an episodic rather than a long-term phenomenon. Although there is a consensus regarding the onset of job polarisation since the 1980s, the actual polarisation of the wage structure occurs roughly a decade later. A similar scenario occurred in Germany; see Spitz-Oener (2006) and Dustmann et al. (2009).

Second, the declining relative demand for middle-skilled workers leads to a shrinking middle class. The shrinking middle class is empirically documented primarily in the United States (Autor & Dorn, 2013a; Jaimovich, 2020; Tüzemen & Willis, 2013) and is one of the economic challenges of the coming years (see Dabla-Norris et al., 2015). The situation in European countries is not as clear as in the United States, as documented by Salido and Carabaña (2019, 2020), whose results at the level of the EU-15 countries do not imply a significant change in the middle class during the last two decades. On the other hand, authors found differences at the level of individual countries, which confirm the conclusions of previous studies, for example, Fernandéz-Macías (2012).

Key are the consequences of the shrinking middle class. First, the middle class is considered the basis of social and political stability (Gimpelson & Kapeliushnikov, 2016). Therefore, the pressure to shrink it due to polarisation presents obvious political and social instability risks. The current circumstances in the form of the election of Donald Trump, Brexit, deglobalisation tendencies and related protectionist tendencies – might be consequences of job polarisation, as mentioned by recent publications (Autor et al., 2020; Kurer & Palier, 2019). Kurer and Palier (2019) elaborate that middle-skilled workers represent a relatively large group threatened by digitisation, automation and offshoring due to the largely routine nature of their jobs. These workers then create a demand of an anti-system nature, to which the political representatives respond accordingly. We can consider these results consistent with the conclusions of Kalleberg (2011), who pointed out that job polarisation reflects the social polarisation that has been occurring in the United States since the 1980s, which corresponds to the onset of job polarisation there.

Autor et al. (2006), Edin et al. (2019) and Fonseca et al. (2018) demonstrate that workers displaced from middle-skilled occupations have a higher probability (and better odds) of finding a job rated as low-skilled. Moreover, the costs associated with potential upskilling are high (Jacobson et al., 1993, 2005). It creates significant pressure for dequalification (deskilling) for many workers, reducing the pressure on their wage growth. If new technologies begin to systematically save labour in a specific area of production, then it can be expected that a worker narrowly specialised in this job will not be able to find a similar occupation. This phenomenon is persistent, and the worker's inability (or unwillingness) to retrain can lead to long-term unemployment, which, as evidenced by Sparreboom and Tarvid (2016), also has adverse effects in the form of psychological deprivation.

Displaced middle-skilled workers thus find employment mainly in low-skilled occupations, for which relative demand is growing, but the expanding supply of low-skilled workers limits the growth of relative wages. Unlike the 19th century, when deskilling occurred due to polarisation in manufacturing and skills improved at the aggregate economy level (see Katz & Margo, 2014), deskilling is now occurring in advanced economies due to polarisation in more sectors of the economy. However, the average skill level at the aggregate economy level is rising (Autor, 2015).

The vast majority of thematic research about polarisation focuses on the United States and Western European countries (most notably Autor et al., 2006; Fernández-Macías, 2012; Goos & Manning, 2007; Goos et al., 2009, 2014), with the onset of polarisation being dated approximately from the 1980s to the 1990s. On the other hand, there are not many studies focusing explicitly on Czechia or neighbouring countries. Let us mention those that deal with Czechia together with other countries, first of all Nchor and Rozmahel (2020) and Martinák (2020). Nchor and Rozmahel (2020) focus on selected countries of Central and Eastern Europe (specifically Bulgaria, Czechia, Hungary, Poland, Romania and Slovakia; they also compare some of the results with the United States) during the period 2000–2016. As part of identifying polarisation, the authors aggregate data for all countries, so the extent of changes for Czechia and other countries is unclear. Their results do not imply polarisation but demonstrate a long-term positive impact of technology on high-skilled workers. In contrast, the long-term impact of technology on middle and low-skilled workers is negative. Martinák (2020) analyses the V4 countries (Czechia, Hungary, Poland, Slovakia) from 1998 to 2016. According to his results, job polarisation did not occur in Czechia or Poland, while Hungary and Slovakia experienced polarisation.

13.3 Data and Methods

This chapter primarily focuses on Czechia and its neighbouring countries – therefore, it covers Czechia, Austria, Germany, Poland and Slovakia. We also add Hungary to these countries, which, together with Czechia, Slovakia and Poland, is part of The Visegrad Group. To these countries, we also add the United Kingdom, which (together with the United States) was, according to empirical evidence (Goos & Manning, 2007), exposed to employment polarisation first and with relatively high intensity.

Employment polarisation refers to the polarisation of the skill structure. The entry problem is, therefore, the measuring and dividing of skills. We can find several approaches to determine the level of skills – as a proxy occupational classifications are used (standard measure in the literature), industrial classifications, wages or achieved education. In this chapter, we use the occupational classification, which presents the thematically most plausible way to identify employment polarisation. Thus, for determining the skill level, we use the ISCO one-digit occupational qualification (level of the major occupational groups), similar to Cirillo (2018), Martinák (2020), Nchor and Rozmahel (2020) and Spareboom and Tarvid (2016). The formation of the major occupational groups implicitly contains the required level of education and should reflect the relative level of wages compared to other main occupational groups.

Following the literature (e.g. Goos et al., 2009, 2014; Martinák, 2020), we define levels of skill as follows:

- High-skilled workers are managers (ISCO major group 01), professionals (02), technicians, and associate professionals (03).
- Middle-skilled workers are clerks (04), skilled workers in agriculture, forestry, and fishing (06), craft and related trades workers (07), plant and machine operators, and assemblers (08).
- Low-skilled workers are services and sales workers (05) and elementary occupations (09).

Data come from the ILOSTAT database (provided by the International Labour Organisation). The examined period 1998–2021 is determined by data availability. Employment polarisation is, in principle, the result of a longer-term tendency. Therefore, striving for as long a time series as possible is desirable. Due to the possible sensitivity of the results to the choice of extreme years, we do not use long differences but multi-year averages. In the empirical literature, we usually encounter only the long difference (e.g. Antón et al., 2022; Autor & Dorn, 2013b; Goos & Manning, 2007; Goos et al., 2009, 2014), which, however, can give biased results. We also want to avoid this bias regarding achieving more robust results. More specifically, instead of the simple difference between the extreme years 1998 and 2021, we observe changes between an aggregation of average shares in 1998–2002 and its change compared to 2017–2021. The exceptions are Slovakia, for which the average of the last three years (2018–2020) is calculated, and the United Kingdom, for which data were available only up to 2018 – for that reason, we use the average of the years 2014–2018.

13.4 Employment Polarisation in Czechia and Neighbouring Countries – Empirical Results

In this section, we present the changes in the employment structure based on skills during the period 1998–2021 – in addition to the analysis of all occupations, we also consider gender. First, we focus on Czechia, the neighbouring countries and the United Kingdom. Let us recall that employment polarisation means increasing the share of high and low-skilled workers and decreasing the share of middle-skilled workers.

Table 13.1 answers whether employment polarisation occurred in Czechia during the observed period. We can see that in the economy as a whole, the share of high-skilled workers increased by 3.23 p.p., the share of middle-skilled workers decreased by 3.48 p.p. and the share of low-skilled workers increased by 0.25 p.p. These values indicate the polarisation of employment.

The table shows the heterogeneity among high, middle and low-skilled workers. In other words, the number of workers increased only in some of the major groups that are among the high-skilled. Similarly, we find an exception for major groups of middle and low-skilled. The increase in the share of clerks compared to other main groups within the group of middle-skilled workers is consistent with Nchor and Rozmahel (2020). The increase in the number of clerks contributed to the fact that their share approached, for example, Austria, the United States and the United Kingdom; however, the difference is that in Czechia, the share of clerks increased (from 8.12% to 9.43%), while in the other named countries, it fell to a similar level. The heterogeneity of results for the group of low-skilled workers is consistent with the conclusions of studies focused on other countries. Goos et al. (2009, 2014) studied selected European countries, Autor and Dorn (2013b) the United States and Fonseca et al. (2018) focused on Portugal, which also showed a decreasing share in elementary occupations (main group 09) and at the same time an increasing share in services and sales (major group 05).

From Table 13.1, it is also clear that the increase in high-skilled workers is mainly a male-caused phenomenon. It is a different conclusion from Tüzemen and Willis (2013) or Cerina et al. (2021), who analyse polarisation in the United States and find a greater increase of high-skilled workers in male occupations. On the other hand, it is consistent with their results about the different contributions by gender to the polarisation process. They address a more important role of female occupations than males. Our results are thus consistent with their findings, implying polarisation in female occupations while not in male occupations.

Table 13.1 also implies relatively high occupational segregation based on gender – for example, in major group 04 (clerks), we see that the initial shares of males and females were 3.01%, resp. 14.65%, and at the end of the period, the shares increased to 3.65%, resp. 16.68%. Similar differences can also be seen in

Table 13.1. Change in Employment Shares in Czechia.

ISCO Major Groups	Males + Females		Males		Females	
	Average Employment Share in (1998–2002) [%]	Percentage Point Change (1998–2002) –(2017–2021)	Average Employment Share in (1998–2002) [%]	Percentage Point Change (1998–2002)–(2017–2021)	Average Employment Share in (1998–2002) [%]	Percentage Point Change (1998–2002) –(2017–2021)
1. Managers	6.52	−1.83	8.64	−2.49	3.80	−0.97
2. Professionals	10.28	6.42	8.71	5.52	12.29	7.53
3. Technicians and associate professionals	18.78	−1.36 3.23	15.54	2.11 5.14	22.92	−5.78 0.78
4. Clerks	8.12	1.31	3.01	0.64	14.65	2.03
5. Skilled workers in agriculture, forestry and fishing	2.04	−0.81	2.08	−0.62	2.00	−1.06
6. Craft and related trades workers	20.60	−4.53	31.09	−5.40	7.17	−3.22
7. Plant and machine operators and assemblers	13.05	0.56 −3.48	17.52	0.34 −5.04	7.33	0.94 −1.31
8. Services and sales workers	12.38	2.76	7.51	1.84	18.62	3.80
9. Elementary occupations	8.23	−2.51 0.25	5.89	−1.94 −0.10	11.21	−3.27 0.53

Source: Author's Calculations Based on the International Labour Organisation.

other major groups, apart from clerks, for example, in major group 05 (services and sales workers) and 07 (craft and related trades workers). According to Verdugo and Allègre (2020), the occupational segregation mentioned above is the cause of the different effects of employment polarisation on gender.

Table 13.2 compares all selected countries and shows a polarisation trend in all countries except Slovakia. In these countries, we can see an increasing share of high and low-skilled workers and a decreasing share of middle-skilled workers. Polarisation in the mentioned countries differs in intensity, expressed by the dynamics of changes in individual qualification groups – for example, Czechia and Slovakia compared to Austria, Germany and the United Kingdom. The common denominator was a decrease in the share of middle-skilled workers. Slovakia, the only country where the results do not imply employment polarisation, has experienced a change that can be perceived as unfavourable for society as a whole – the share of high and middle-skilled workers decreased at the expense of the increase in the share of the low-skilled workers.

From the point of view of the high-skilled workers, there is a noticeable difference in the initial situation in the United Kingdom and Germany compared to Czechia and other countries. The fact that the initial state of this share in Austria was the lowest of all countries at the beginning of the period may seem interesting, although the country was not part of the socialist Eastern Bloc but belonged to the developed countries of Western Europe.

Now, we can examine the differences between males (Table 13.3) and females (Table 13.4). The overall results show similar trends to the previous Table 13.2. For males (Table 13.3), there was polarisation in all countries except Czechia and Poland, where a so-called skill-upgrading tendency was evident (an increase of the high-skilled at the expense of middle and low-skilled). For females, there was no polarisation, only in Germany and Slovakia. Female occupations in Slovakia experienced a decrease in the high-skilled, which was reflected in an overall negative economic change (see Table 13.2). A common denominator was a decrease in the share of middle-skilled males and females.

At first glance, the quantitative difference in the initial and final shares of the groups of the high, middle and low-skilled workers is noticeable; this may be most noticeable in the middle-skilled, where males have a dominant share, and in the low-skilled, where females have a dominant share.

In the context of the nature of the impacts of primarily technological changes, globalisation and periods of recession, the most threatened group is middle-skilled workers. High and low-skilled occupations are the least affected (Fonseca et al., 2018; Jaimovich & Siu, 2020; Verdugo & Allègre, 2020). Verdugo and Allègre (2020) found that the Great Recession in Europe mainly affected male middle-skilled workers, while the high and low-skilled occupations (predominantly female) were less affected. The Great Recession formed the middle part of our selected period, so it can be expected that it should not explicitly affect the achieved results.

Based on the results, we cannot generalise the results of the relationship between gender and dynamics of change in employment. There was a relatively higher decrease in middle-skilled workers in Czechia, Austria, Germany and

Table 13.2. Change in Employment Shares in Czechia and Other Countries Between the Period 1998–2002 and 2017–2021.

	High-Skill		Middle-Skill		Low-Skill	
	Average Employment Share in (1998–2002) [%]	Percentage Point Change (1998–2002)–(2017–2021)	Average Employment Share in (1998–2002) [%]	Percentage Point Change (1998–2002)–(2017–2021)	Average Employment Share in (1998–2002) [%]	Percentage Point Change (1998–2002)–(2017–2021)
Czechia	35.57	3.23	43.82	−3.48	20.61	0.25
Austria	32.31	10.27	44.88	−13.22	22.81	2.95
Germany	38.37	6.89	41.42	−9.20	20.22	2.31
Hungary	31.46	4.60	46.46	−7.01	22.09	2.41
Poland	29.32	11.19	52.00	−11.53	18.67	0.34
Slovakia	33.62	−0.79	43.14	−2.55	23.24	3.34
The United Kingdom	39.39	9.12	35.74	−11.46	24.86	2.34

Source: Author's Calculations Based on the International Labour Organisation.

Note: Due to the unavailability of data, upper period covers years 2018–2020 for Slovakia, and 2014–2018 for the United Kingdom.

Table 13.3. Change in Employment Shares in Czechia and Other Countries Between the Period 1998–2002 and 2017–2021 (Males).

	High-Skill		Middle-Skill		Low-Skill	
	Average Employment Share in (1998–2002) [%]	Percentage Point Change (1998–2002)–(2017–2021)	Average Employment Share in (1998–2002) [%]	Percentage Point Change (1998–2002)–(2017–2021)	Average Employment Share in (1998–2002) [%]	Percentage Point Change (1998–2002)–(2017–2021)
Czechia	32.89	5.14	53.70	−5.04	13.40	−0.10
Austria	32.78	9.61	53.22	−12.74	14.00	3.13
Germany	38.20	5.43	50.12	−9.80	11.69	4.37
Hungary	25.74	4.78	56.81	−6.38	17.45	1.60
Poland	24.51	8.75	62.15	−7.54	13.34	−1.21
Slovakia	27.27	0.32	55.79	−3.83	16.94	3.51
The United Kingdom	42.56	6.46	39.91	−9.10	17.53	2.64

Source: Author's Calculations Based on the International Labour Organisation.

Note: Due to the unavailability of data, the upper period covers years 2018–2020 for Slovakia, and 2014–2018 for the United Kingdom.

Table 13.4. Change in Employment Shares in Czechia and Other Countries Between the Period 1998–2002 and 2017–2021 (Females).

	High-Skill		Middle-Skill		Low-Skill	
	Average Employment Share in (1998–2002) [%]	**Percentage Point Change (1998–2002)–(2017–2021)**	**Average Employment Share in (1998–2002) [%]**	**Percentage Point Change (1998–2002)–(2017–2021)**	**Average Employment Share in (1998–2002) [%]**	**Percentage Point Change (1998–2002)–(2017–2021)**
Czechia	39.01	0.78	31.16	−1.31	29.83	0.53
Austria	31.73	11.07	34.41	−12.68	33.87	1.61
Germany	38.07	8.96	30.03	−7.93	31.90	−1.02
Hungary	38.32	4.36	34.04	−7.74	27.65	3.38
Poland	35.12	14.23	39.78	−16.51	25.09	2.28
Slovakia	41.14	−2.57	28.17	−0.37	30.70	2.94
The United Kingdom	35.64	12.30	30.80	−13.88	33.56	1.59

Source: Author's Calculations Based on the International Labour Organisation.

Note: Due to the unavailability of data, the upper period covers years 2018–2020 for Slovakia, and 2014–2018 for the United Kingdom.

Slovakia. There was a relatively higher decrease in female middle-skilled workers in Hungary, Poland and the United Kingdom. Analogous results can be obtained if we focus similarly on high- and low-skilled workers groups.

13.5 Conclusion

This chapter builds on one of the main topics of labour market research regarding employment polarisation in the context of skills when it analyses Czechia and neighbouring countries. With few exceptions, our results imply polarisation across all countries, even considering the distinction between males and females.

A legitimate 'bogey' of this phenomenon may be the shrinking middle class, which may highlight differences between the ends of the wage and skill distribution. In addition, the distributional effects of new technologies appear to impact policy implications significantly (see Autor et al., 2020; Kurer & Palier, 2019). Further research could lie in the search for answers to how polarisation changes economic (and social) conditions in the country.

Czechia is not in a position like the United States or other countries (the United Kingdom, Germany, Sweden, Norway, and the Benelux countries or Japan) where job polarisation began to show its (negative economic) symptoms first. On the contrary, we find ourselves in a relatively gentle situation where we have been spared by job polarisation at the aggregate economy level and its negative consequences. Like any previous structural change, there is nothing left to do but strive to improve qualifications, that is, to increase the ability to adapt to new conditions.

Even so, economic policymakers should be active in supporting the education system mainly in two aspects. The first is strengthening dexterity and flexibility, which are skills that are, in principle, the most difficult to replace with new technology. The second aspect is the support of retraining programmes, which should ensure the deepening of specialised skills. The given recommendations could contribute to higher flexibility in the labour market and ensure a higher ability to adapt, with which employees would better face the current changes in the labour market.

References

Anton, J. I., Klenert, D., Fernández-Macías, E., Urzì Brancati, M. C., & Alaveras, G. (2022). The labour market impact of robotisation in Europe. *European Journal of Industrial Relations*, *28*(3), 317–339. https://doi.org/10.1177/09596801211070801

Autor, D. H. (2015). Why are there still so many jobs? The history and future of workplace automation. *Journal of Economic Perspectives*, *29*(3), 3–30. https://doi.org/10.1257/jep.29.3.3

Autor, D. H., & Dorn, D. (2013a). How technology wrecks the middle class. *The New York Times*, *24*(2013), 1279–1333.

Autor, D. H., & Dorn, D. (2013b). The growth of low-skill service jobs and the polarization of the US labor market. *The American Economic Review*, *103*(5), 1553–1597. https://doi.org/10.1257/aer.103.5.1553

Autor, D., Dorn, D., Hanson, G., & Majlesi, K. (2020). Importing political polarization? The electoral consequences of rising trade exposure. *The American Economic Review*, *110*(10), 3139–3183. https://doi.org/10.1257/aer.20170011

Autor, D. H., Katz, L. F., & Kearney, M. S. (2006). The polarization of the US labour market. *The American Economic Review*, *96*(2), 189–194. https://doi.org/10.1257/000282806777212620

Autor, D. H., Katz, L. F., & Kearney, M. S. (2008). Trends in US wage inequality: Revising the revisionists. *The Review of Economics and Statistics*, *90*(2), 300–323. https://doi.org/10.1162/rest.90.2.300

Card, D., & DiNardo, J. E. (2002). Skill-biased technological change and rising wage inequality: Some problems and puzzles. *Journal of Labour Economics*, *20*(4), 733–783. https://doi.org/10.1086/342055

Cerina, F., Moro, A., & Rendall, M. (2021). The role of gender in employment polarization. *International Economic Review*, *62*(4), 1655–1691. https://doi.org/10.1111/iere.12531

Cirillo, V. (2018). Job polarization in European industries. *International Labour Review*, *157*(1), 39–63. https://doi.org/10.1111/ilr.12033

Dabla-Norris, M. E., Kochhar, M. K., Suphaphiphat, M. N., Ricka, M. F., & Tsounta, M. E. (2015). *Causes and consequences of income inequality: A global perspective*. International Monetary Fund.

Dustmann, C., Ludsteck, J., & Schönberg, U. (2009). Revisiting the German wage structure. *Quarterly Journal of Economics*, *124*(2), 843–881. https://doi.org/10.1162/qjec.2009.124.2.843

Edin, P. A., Evans, T., Graetz, G., Hernnäs, S., & Michaels, G. (2019). *Individual consequences of occupational decline*. CEPR Discussion Paper No. DP13808. https://ssrn.com/abstract=3428328

Fernández-Macías, E. (2012). Job polarization in Europe? Changes in the employment structure and job quality, 1995–2007. *Work and Occupations*, *39*(2), 157–182. https://doi.org/10.1177/0730888411427078

Fonseca, T., Lima, F., & Pereira, S. C. (2018). Job polarization, technological change and routinization: Evidence for Portugal. *Labour Economics*, *51*, 317–339. https://doi.org/10.1016/j.labeco.2018.02.003

Gimpelson, V., & Kapeliushnikov, R. (2016). Polarization or upgrading? Evolution of employment in transitional Russia. *Russian Journal of Economics*, *2*(2), 192–218. https://doi.org/10.1016/j.ruje.2016.06.004

Goldin, C., & Katz, L. F. (2007). Long-run changes in the wage structure: Narrowing, widening, polarizing/general discussion. *Brookings Papers on Economic Activity*, *2*, 135. https://doi.org/10.3386/w13568

Goos, M., & Manning, A. (2007). Lousy and lovely jobs: The rising polarization of work in Britain. *The Review of Economics and Statistics*, *89*(1), 118–133. https://doi.org/10.1162/rest.89.1.118

Goos, M., Manning, A., & Salomons, A. (2009). Job polarization in Europe. *The American Economic Review*, *99*(2), 58–63. https://doi.org/10.1257/aer.99.2.58

Goos, M., Manning, A., & Salomons, A. (2014). Explaining job polarization: Routine-biased technological change and offshoring. *The American Economic Review*, *104*(8), 2509–2526. https://doi.org/10.1257/aer.104.8.2509

Hunt, J., & Nunn, R. (2019). *Is employment polarization informative about wage inequality and is employment really polarizing?* National Bureau of Economic Research. (No. w26064). https://doi.org/10.3386/w26064

Jacobson, L. S., LaLonde, R. J., & Sullivan, D. G. (1993). Earnings losses of displaced workers. *The American Economic Review*, 685–709.

Jacobson, L., LaLonde, R., & Sullivan, D. G. (2005). Estimating the returns to community college schooling for displaced workers. *Journal of Econometrics*, *125*(1–2), 271–304. https://doi.org/10.1016/j.jeconom.2004.04.010

Jaimovich, N. (2020). *Disappearing middle class: Job polarization and policy approaches*. UBS Center Public Paper Series, (8). https://doi.org/10.5167/uzh-187640

Jaimovich, N., & Siu, H. E. (2020). Job polarization and jobless recoveries. *The Review of Economics and Statistics*, *102*(1), 129–147. https://doi.org/10.1162/rest_a_00875

Jerbashian, V. (2019). Automation and job polarization: On the decline of middling occupations in Europe. *Oxford Bulletin of Economics & Statistics*, *81*(5), 1095–1116. https://doi.org/10.1111/obes.12298

Kalleberg, A. L. (2011). *Good jobs, bad jobs: The rise of polarized and precarious employment systems in the United States, 1970s–2000s*. Russell Sage Foundation.

Katz, L. F., & Margo, R. A. (2014). Technical change and the relative demand for skilled labour: The United States in historical perspective. In *Human capital in history: The American record* (pp. 15–57). University of Chicago Press. https://doi.org/10.7208/chicago/9780226163925.003.0002

Kurer, T., & Palier, B. (2019). Shrinking and shouting: The political revolt of the declining middle in times of employment polarization. *Research and Politics*, *6*(1). 2053168019831164. https://doi.org/10.1177/2053168019831164

Martinák, D. (2020). Vplyv technologického pokroku na štruktúru zamestnanosti v krajinách V4. *Politicka Ekonomie*, *68*(1), 42–61. https://doi.org/10.18267/j.polek.1265

Naticchioni, P., Ragusa, G., & Massari, R. (2014). *Unconditional and conditional wage polarization in Europe*. IZA Discussion Paper No. 8465. http://doi.org/10.2139/ssrn.2502325

Nchor, D., & Rozmahel, P. (2020). Job polarization in Europe: Evidence from Central and Eastern European Countries. *DANUBE*, *11*(1), 52–74. https://doi.org/10.2478/danb-2020-0004

Salido, O., & Carabaña, J. (2019). An increasingly squeezed middle class? Changing income distributions and inequality in the EU15 through the last economic cycle. *Journal of Contemporary European Studies*, *27*(3), 343–356. https://doi.org/10.1080/14782804.2019.1625756

Salido, O., & Carabaña, J. (2020). On the squeezing of the middle class: Overview and prospects for the EU-15. *European Review*, *28*(2), 325–342. https://doi.org/10.1017/S1062798719000462

Sparreboom, T., & Tarvid, A. (2016). Imbalanced job polarization and skills mismatch in Europe. *Journal for Labour Market Research*, *49*(1), 15–42. https://doi.org/10.1007/s12651-016-0196-y

Spitz-Oener, A. (2006). Technical change, job tasks, and rising educational demands: Looking outside the wage structure. *Journal of Labour Economics*, *24*(2), 235–270. https://doi.org/10.1086/499972

Tüzemen, D., & Willis, J. (2013). The vanishing middle: Job polarization and workers' response to the decline in middle-skill jobs. *Economic Review – Federal Reserve Bank of Kansas City*, *5*.

Verdugo, G., & Allègre, G. (2020). Labour force participation and job polarization: Evidence from Europe during the great recession. *Labour Economics*, *66*, 101881. https://doi.org/10.1016/j.labeco.2020.101881

Chapter 14

Institutional Environment, Corruption and Their Impact on Economic Growth

Eva Kotlánová

Silesian University in Opava, Czechia

Abstract

Factors of production (labour, land, capital), technology and technical progress are usually cited as the main sources of economic growth and development. However, there are a number of other factors that have a significant impact on the possibilities and extent of their use or their further improvement and development. These factors undoubtedly include the institutional environment, within which corruption is also a consideration. In this chapter, attention will be focused on the various institutional variables that are used to assess the quality of a country's institutional environment, including corruption. A number of studies have shown that a quality institutional environment and low levels of corruption are prerequisites for long-term economic growth. Using an analysis of individual indicators of the Worldwide Governance Indicators (WGIs), published annually by the World Bank, supplemented by the Corruption Perception Index (published by Transparency International), we look at where Czechia has moved over the last decade or two in terms of institutional quality and corruption.

Keywords: Institutional environment; quality; corruption; economic performance; institutional factors of economic growth; Worldwide Governance Indicators

14.1 Introduction

The institutional environment can influence basic macroeconomic indicators such as real gross domestic product. Thus, the optimal setting of the institutional environment and the elimination of corruption can have a fundamental effect on

Modeling Economic Growth in Contemporary Czechia, 215–230

Published under exclusive licence by Emerald Publishing Limited
doi:10.1108/978-1-83753-840-920241014

economic growth, usually through entrepreneurial activity. This chapter analyses the influence of institutional aspects in Czechia.

Like all countries in Central and Eastern Europe, Czechia has undergone significant institutional changes over the last 30 years. During the transition period, the government of the time had to decide between two paths. The first was to create a market environment first and then to shape institutions on the basis of market needs, and the second was to create an institutional environment first and then to let the market work. Czechoslovakia chose the first option, and although the institutional environment was shaped largely according to the needs of the emerging market economy, not all areas succeeded in setting up institutions to support a healthy and prosperous market environment and the quality of the functioning of the public sector. Especially in the public sector, successive governments have not had the political capital to correct these deficiencies, which is still evident in some areas such as education, health and pension policy. Another significant factor that the emerging economy has had to face is corruption, the degree of which is influenced by the quality of the institutional environment, and at the same time corruption has an impact on the quality of institutions, that is, it is an interaction between these entities.

In the last decade, a number of laws have been adopted in Czechia and a number of new institutions have been created to help improve the quality of the institutional environment and to improve the perception of corruption. Among others, the New Civil Code, the Corporations Act, the Public Procurement Act, Civil Service Act, Freedom of Access to Information Act and the area of Regulatory Impact Assessment (RIA) have been improved.

It is important to note that the quality of the institutional environment is crucial in the long run, as it significantly affects the economic and other indicators, as noted by, for example, Tanzi (1998), Wei (2001), Aidt (2009) and Heckelman and Powel (2010).

A good institutional environment is essential for fostering economic development, social progress, political stability and international competitiveness. It creates an enabling environment for individuals and businesses to thrive, leading to improved living standards and a higher quality of life for the society as a whole. The shortcomings in this area were fully manifested during the COVID-19 pandemic, when many institutions were ineffective, or it was not at all clear how the state and the government should behave and deal with the situation. This was also evident in the following period, when Czechia, despite the inclusion of the effects of the war in Ukraine, was unable to reach the pre-COVID level in many economic indicators.

14.2 Why Institutions Are Important

For a long time, the attention of neoclassical economists was mainly focused on the main sources of economic growth, such as labour, capital, technology and technical progress. However, it has struggled to explain how it is possible that two countries with the same quantity and quality of factors of production do not show the same economic growth. And it was the exponent of the New Institutional Economics, Douglass C. North, who stated that 'Growth and development depend crucially on the institutions currently in place' (North, 1990, p. 5). The impact of quality institutions will show up in the economy with a time lag, not immediately.

Closely related to the concept of institutional quality is the concept of governance, with the World Bank stating that 'Good governance is epitomised by predictable, open, and enlightened policymaking (that is, transparent processes); a bureaucracy imbued with a professional ethos; an executive arm of government accountable for its actions, and a strong civil society participating in public affairs; and all behaving under the rule of law' (IBRD, 1994, p. vii).

A good institutional environment is crucial for the overall well-being and prosperity of a society. A favourable institutional environment provides stability, predictability and security for businesses and investors. It establishes a framework of laws, regulations and property rights that protect private property, enforce contracts and promote fair competition. These factors encourage entrepreneurship, innovation and investment, leading to economic growth and job creation. For example, Heckelman and Powel (2010) state that only after strong economic institutions are in place would reducing corruption be likely to improve growth prospects.

Another area where institutions play an important role is resource allocation. As stated by Volk et al. (2001), strong institutions facilitate the efficient allocation of resources within an economy. They establish transparent and effective mechanisms for market transactions, including fair competition, reliable financial systems and well-functioning regulatory bodies. This enables the allocation of resources based on market signals, reducing wastage and ensuring optimal utilisation.

Good institutions promote social development by ensuring equitable access to basic services such as education, healthcare and infrastructure. They establish social safety nets and regulations that protect vulnerable groups and promote social justice. This fosters social cohesion, reduces inequality and enhances overall quality of life.

A robust institutional environment upholds the rule of law, ensuring that laws are applied fairly and consistently to all individuals and institutions. It establishes an independent judiciary, enforces contracts and protects property rights. This fosters trust and confidence in the legal system, enhances accountability of public officials and reduces corruption. The importance of a good legal framework and law enforcement has been highlighted in studies such as Mauro (1995) and Kaufmann and Wei (1999). It can be concluded that if the institutional environment is set up correctly with law enforcement and judicial independence at a good level, there is no need for excessive regulation of the market environment by the government, because as Tanzi (1998) argues, excessive regulation opens up further room for corruption.

One of the important variables of a good institutional environment is the stability of the government and its accountability to the electorate. Strong institutions contribute to political stability by providing mechanisms for peaceful resolution of conflicts, ensuring democratic governance, and protecting human rights. They establish checks and balances on the exercise of power, promoting a system of governance that is accountable to the citizens. Political stability is vital for attracting investments, maintaining social harmony and avoiding disruptions to economic activities. Just how a government delivers on its pre-election promises and is accountable to its voters can be significantly influenced by its links with the business community, whose interests are usually different from those of the majority of voters. According to Wei (2001), the more a government is connected to and influenced by business, the greater the scope for corruption. As Ades and Di Tella (1999) point out, especially in former transition economies, linkages between key industries and politicians persist to this day, and this is reflected negatively, for example, in corruption levels. Legitimacy of government and public administration also appears to be a key constitutional requirement, as described by Paulovics (2011).

It is impossible to imagine an institutional environment without bureaucracy. The quality of bureaucracy is related to how officials are selected for their positions, how they are motivated and how they are rewarded. Empirical studies by Rauch and Evans (1997) or Van Rijckeghem and Weder (1997) reach the same conclusions in the sense that if the bureaucracy is independent of the government, the selection of officials is based on objective criteria, not on the basis of acquaintances and loyalty to the cabinet currently in power, and salaries are no different from similar positions in the private sector, corruption is lower. This issue has also been partially addressed by Andvig and Moene (1999) who studied the behaviour of bureaucracy in a general equilibrium model.

A good institutional environment enhances a country's competitiveness in the global arena. It creates a favourable business climate, encourages foreign direct investment and enables participation in global trade. This boosts a country's economic performance, integration into the global economy, higher productivity, competitiveness and economic growth. A good institutional environment also encourages the inflow of capital and technology through foreign investment, which further enhances economic growth. In addition, a good institutional environment also contributes to human capital development. For example, a quality education system supported by institutions enables people to acquire the necessary skills and knowledge for entrepreneurship and innovation. This has a positive impact on labour productivity and technological development.

Conversely, a weak or negative institutional environment can hamper economic growth. Corruption, lack of legal certainty, inefficient bureaucracy and political instability will deter investors, limit entrepreneurial activity and reduce confidence in the economy. This can lead to slower growth and worsening economic performance.

14.3 Quality of the Institutional Environment and Its Measurement

Currently, there are a number of approaches to assessing and measuring the quality of the institutional environment that can be used to characterise the impact of institutions on growth performance and competition competitiveness of the economy and which can also be used to compare institutional quality across countries.

However, when assessing institutional quality, it should be taken into account that soft data are used here, which are mostly based on expert surveys. The effective functioning of institutions is primarily influenced by the citizens of a given country, so it is necessary to ascertain their perception of the functioning of institutions and conduct surveys among them, in addition to the opinion of experts. When measuring the quality of institutions, it is also necessary to take into account the characteristics of different population groups, as the application of the law and the perception of the quality of institutions vary systematically according to these characteristics. For example, younger, less educated, low-income groups are less likely to participate in elections, according to research.

Organisations working on these processes include the Fraser Institute, the Heritage Foundation and the World Economic Forum. For the purposes of this article, the Worldwide Governance Indicators (WGIs), compiled and published annually since 2002 by the World Bank, were chosen. Previously, this group of indicators was known as Governance Matters and is authored by Kaufmann et al. (2010). The authors struggled to find an acceptable definition of governance, which they define as 'the traditions and institutions by which authority in a country is exercised' (Kaufmann et al., 2010, p. 3). They divided the field of governance into three groups of indicators that reflect (A) the process by which governments are selected, monitored and replaced; (B) the capacity of the government to effectively formulate and implement sound policies and (C) the respect of citizens and the state for the institutions that govern economic and social interactions among them. Then they construct two measures of governance corresponding to each of these three areas, resulting in a total of six dimensions of governance (Kaufmann et al., 2010, pp. 3–4):

- Voice and Accountability (VA) assesses the quality of political, civil and human rights and political process mechanisms. This indicator also reflects the independence of the media. Political Stability and Absence of Violence/Terrorism (PV) reflects the possibility of destabilisation of government power and the likelihood of the government being overthrown by unconstitutional means or violence, including the possibility of terrorism. It also shows whether changes in government have implications not only for policy continuity but also whether they undermine the ability of citizens to peacefully select and replace government and politicians.
- The second pair of indicators reflects the government's ability to formulate and implement appropriate policies, including regulatory quality. Government Effectiveness (GE) captures perceptions of the quality of public services, the quality of the civil service and the degree of its independence from political pressures, the quality of policy formulation and implementation and the credibility of the government's commitment to such policies. The Regulatory Quality (RQ) indicator captures perceptions of the ability of the government to

formulate and implement sound policies and regulations that permit and promote private sector development.

- The third pair shows the quality of institutional interactions. The willingness of actors to obey the law, the efficiency and predictability of the judiciary, the protection of property rights, the quality of contract enforcement, the functioning of the police and the likelihood of violent and non-violent crime constitute the Rule of Law (RL) indicator. The Control of Corruption (CC) indicator shows the extent to which public power is perceived to be used for private gain, both in the case of grand (political) and petty (bureaucratic) corruption, and in the case of the ability to influence policies and laws, referred to as state control.

The individual indicators, as well as the aggregated one, can take values from −2.5 (worst result) to 2.5 (best result). In this text, we will work with both the individual indicators and the aggregated index of the quality of governance and institutional environment, which is constructed on the basis of the above-mentioned six indicators as an arithmetic average.

14.4 Institutional Environment in Czechia

Like many other economies in Central and Eastern Europe that were part of the so-called Eastern Bloc, Czechia underwent a significant transformation in the 1990s during the transition from a centrally planned economy to a market economy. If we focus on the institutional environment, the period of about 30 years can be divided into several stages. As already mentioned above, the leaders of the time chose a path where the market was first given room to operate and institutions were created on the basis of its needs.

In the first phase of the transition, it was necessary to ensure that the basic elements of a market economy could function. The operation of the market mechanism had to be resolved and the transition from common ownership to private ownership had to be ensured. In addition to restitution, large-scale privatisation of state property was carried out, divided into 'small' and 'large'. However, this process was not always completely transparent and fair, which left its mark on the institutional environment. At the same time as price liberalisation and privatisation, Czechia carried out extensive legislative reforms to create a legal framework for a market economy. A new constitution was adopted and laws were created on commercial law, property law, the tax system and other areas. These steps were designed to strengthen legal certainty, transparency and trust in institutions. It should be noted here that in the 1990s, the most necessary adjustments were made to a number of key laws, when their shortcomings gradually began to become apparent, and therefore legislators proceeded to create completely new legal codes that came into force after 2000 (Criminal Code – 2010, Civil Code – 2014, Law on Commercial Corporations – 2014). A significant milestone in the institutional environment was Czechia's accession to the European Union (EU) in 2004, as EU membership brought additional requirements for legal norms, regulations and standards in various areas, which led to further legislative and institutional changes. Already in the pre-accession phase, Czechia faced criticism in the area of anti-corruption, and although there has been a slight improvement over a period of time, the focus has been on fighting corruption and strengthening the transparency of institutions with intermittent success. A number of measures have been taken, such as the establishment of specialised anti-corruption units, the introduction of a register of beneficial owners, amendments to criminal legislation, etc.

This was a very brief overview of the evolution of the institutional environment and we will now look at it in more detail in the context of the WGI institutional quality assessment, which is compiled and published by the World Bank. Fig. 14.1 shows a cross-section of the values for each EU country, with values selected for 2000, 2010 and 2021. While Czechia shows that the quality of the institutional environment has gradually improved over time, Greece, Hungary and Italy, for example, have seen a decline over the years. The figure also shows that the group of Scandinavian countries, the Netherlands or Luxembourg have long-standing stable institutions at a high level and are well above the EU average.

Since the Visegrad Four countries are the closest to us in terms of the institutional environment, historically and otherwise, we will focus on them in more detail and complement them with a comparison with the EU-27 average.

As can be seen in Fig. 14.2, which shows the evolution of the overall averaged WGI for Czechia, Hungary, Poland, Slovakia and the EU27 average, the quality of the institutional environment in Czechia has been improving over time with some fluctuations, and between 2020 and 2021, it has reached the EU average. In the other V4 countries, the overall average WGI shows a downward trend. In Hungary, it dropped from 0.96 to 0.49 over the period under review, with the

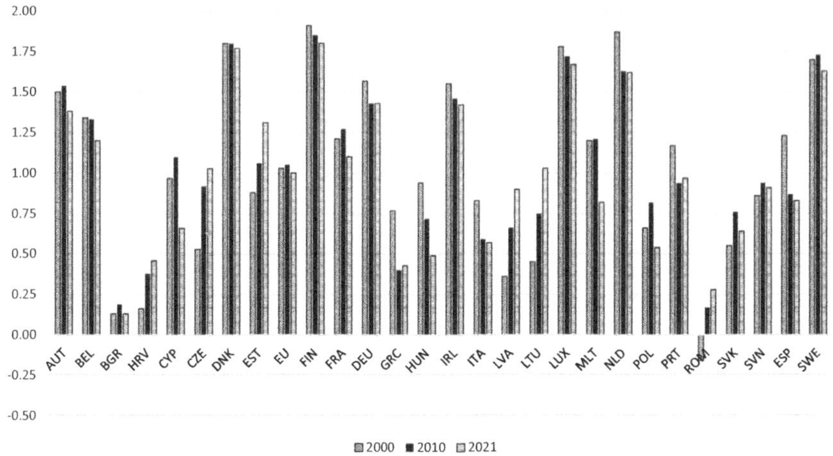

Fig. 14.1. Aggregate WGI Index in EU Countries. *Source:* World Bank (2023).

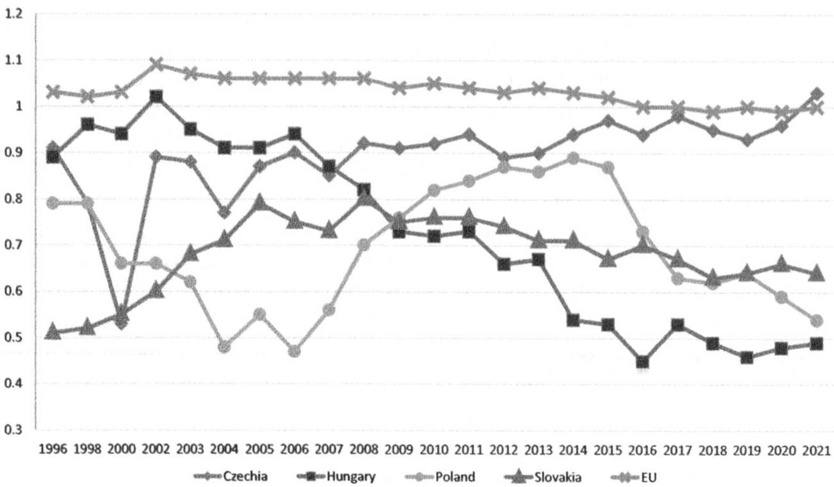

Fig. 14.2. Aggregate WGI Index (1998–2021). *Source:* World Bank (2023).

worst performance in recent years in the areas of CC and quality of the legal framework and judiciary (RL). Slovakia gradually improved until 2008, when the WGI took a downward trend until 2018. During this period, as in Hungary, CC and the area of law (RL) were among the worst-rated areas. The institutional environment in Poland underwent a very interesting development. After an initial decline, the WGI rebounded from an imaginary bottom in 2006, rose until 2014 and started to decline sharply in 2015. The areas of greatest decline are the role of the law and the judiciary (probably related to the reform of the judiciary in Poland, which is also being addressed by the EU), the quality of governance (GE) and the Voice and Accountability (VA) indicator, which assesses the quality of political, civil and human rights and the mechanism of political processes (here one can mention the Polish government's long-standing attitude towards minorities, the LGBT community, abortion, the teaching of certain subjects in schools, etc.).

In 2000, there was a sharp decline in the value of the aggregate WGI index for Czechia. There were also declines in Poland and Hungary, but the decline was not as dramatic. If we look at the individual components of the WGI (there are 6 in total), we find that all of them have deteriorated (see Table 14.1). However, the biggest drops were in CC (from 0.52 to 0.15) and Political Stability and Absence of Violence (from 0.90 to 0.33). The area of corruption will be discussed separately later, but we can already say that this indicator is not rated very positively in the long term and significantly reduces the value of the overall average index in all years under review. It is the CC value that shows that in Czechia, there is a long-standing strong interdependence between the market and the state, complex

Table 14.1. GWI Index Czechia.

	1998	**2000**	**2010**	**2011**	**2012**	**2013**	**2014**	**2015**	**2016**	**2017**	**2018**	**2019**	**2020**	**2021**
VA	0.97	0.76	1.01	1.02	0.97	0.98	1.03	1.04	1.03	0.88	0.81	0.84	0.98	1.02
PV	0.90	0.33	0.99	1.11	1.05	1.08	0.99	0.98	0.98	1.00	1.03	0.94	0.92	0.96
GE	0.59	0.59	0.91	0.93	0.93	0.92	1.03	1.06	1.04	1.06	0.98	0.95	0.95	1.11
RQ	0.92	0.74	1.30	1.20	1.05	1.08	1.00	1.09	0.98	1.23	1.27	1.24	1.24	1.35
RL	0.87	0.61	0.93	1.02	1.02	1.02	1.14	1.13	1.01	1.12	1.05	1.05	1.05	1.13
CC	0.52	0.15	0.38	0.38	0.31	0.30	0.43	0.50	0.59	0.60	0.54	0.56	0.58	0.64
GWI	**0.79**	**0.53**	**0.92**	**0.94**	**0.89**	**0.90**	**0.94**	**0.97**	**0.94**	**0.98**	**0.95**	**0.93**	**0.96**	**1.03**

Source: World Bank (2023).

legal processes and non-transparent regulation expand the space for corrupt behaviour, all of which is complemented by a number of political corruption cases. In the case of the PV sub-index, the cause was the so-called Tolerance Patent, which was an amendment to the Opposition Agreement that the then two largest parties, ČSSD and ODS, concluded together after the 1998 elections. The consequence of this amendment was, among other things, a change in the electoral system for the Chamber of Deputies, which eliminated the influence of small parties. Another factor that may have affected political stability and also another indicator of GE was the resignation of 6 ministers out of a total of 19 members of the government, and in some departments, ministers were replaced repeatedly in 2000.

Despite the fact that Czechia joined the EU, there was a further significant decline in 2004, when deterioration was recorded in all monitored areas except for the Governance Effectiveness indicator. The most significant decline was recorded in the indicator of Political Stability, which was due to the increasing preferences of the Communist Party and also its result in the elections. Although ODS won the election with 36.36% of the vote, the Communist Party of Bohemia and Moravia came in right behind (19.68%) and ahead of the Czech Social Democratic Party (14.03%). Since 2004, there has been a gradual improvement in the GWI indicators.

Czechia is considered a relatively politically stable country, with no political upheavals. Political, civil and human rights are guaranteed by the Constitution. This is also evidenced by the development of the Voice and Accountability (VA) sub-index, which is without major fluctuations until 2016. Among other things, it also assesses the independence of the media, and it was this area that had an impact on its development between 2017 and 2019. The reason for this deterioration may have been the fear of media influence by the then election winner and Prime Minister Andrej Babiš, in whose ownership some media were located. In the area of civil rights, there was a significant change in 2017, when the Constitutional Court somewhat restricted the right to information on the management of public institutions or on salaries in public administration due to conflicts with other rights. All of this is reflected in a worse rating in this area.

The indicator of Political Stability and Absence of Violence/Terrorism (PV) has been around 1 since 2010. A larger decline occurred in 2014 and 2019. In both years, the effects of post-election negotiations were felt, with elections to the Chamber of Deputies taking place in 2013 and 2017. In 2013, there was a complete change of political representation, with the hitherto ruling right completely losing the early elections, threatening the continuity of economic policy. Long before the elections, the then opposition had already expressed the view that it would abolish a number of key measures if it won the elections (see, for example, the second pension pillar). In 2017, the ANO movement won the elections, but was unable to form a viable coalition and its minority government failed to win the confidence of the Chamber of Deputies in January 2018. This was only obtained in July 2018 with the support of ČSSD, which was part of the ruling coalition, and the tacit approval of KSČM (Communist Party).

We see a gradual improvement in GE between 2010 and 2017. A number of laws and measures have been enacted to improve the quality of public services and reduce political pressure on public administration performance. The Public Procurement Act came into force in 2012, and the Civil Service Act came into force in January 2015 to depoliticise the civil service. Mechanisms for screening RIA when legislative proposals were considered were strengthened. In terms of quality and accessibility of health care, Czechia is among the better average EU countries, but recent shortcomings and neglect of long-term systemic changes in individual fields (psychiatry, paediatric general medicine, dentistry) have started to show, leading to limitations in access to care. In the field of education, there is still a failure to streamline inclusion at all levels. The inefficiency of the whole system is becoming fully apparent at a time when the so-called ‘strong classes’ are entering schools. Another area that should be addressed at government level is inequalities in access to education. Problems in these areas are caused by a long-standing underestimation of the system's set-up, the role of individual institutions and their competences.

RQ is related to, among other things, the aforementioned RIA. Another important area in the quality of regulation is the digitisation of public administration services, which is very slow, often uncoordinated and very costly in Czechia. Nevertheless, we can state that in the RQ sub-index, Czechia is on a par with the EU average, as is the case for the RL indicator.

The assessment of the quality of the institutional environment in terms of corruption will be carried out using the CPI Corruption Perceptions Index, as it is also a major component of the CC subindex.

14.5 Institutional Environment and Corruption

The quality of the institutional environment is to some extent linked to the perception of corruption, not only from the perspective of experts and public administration experts but also from the perspective of citizens, because only institutions that citizens trust can have the expected influence on their behaviour.

The Corruption Perception Index (CPI) has been published annually by Transparency International since 1995. As stated by Transparency International (2023), the Index ranks countries according to the degree of perceived corruption in the public sector and business using a 0–100 scale, where 100 points indicates a country with almost no corruption and 0 points indicates a high level of corruption. The number of countries varies slightly from year to year. Therefore, it is important to focus on the index value rather than the ranking position in the analysis.

The rankings are compiled on the basis of surveys among experts in which respondents (whether individuals or organisations that are able to assess the level of corruption in the public sector based on their position and experience) assess, among other things, the ability of government institutions to suppress and punish corruption, the effectiveness of anti-corruption measures, the extent of corruption in various areas of public administration, the degree of transparency of its functioning and the degree of abuse of public functions and public funds.

The individual surveys are conducted independently by 12 international professional organisations in 13 rankings, although not all countries always have a full set of them. They then provide the data to TI. The combination of these indices produces the final CPI value.

The data for the current Index are collected roughly a year and a half before its publication, so the result does not reflect a single recent event or policy decision, but rather a reflection of a longer-term trend over a given time period.

Czechia was first included in the assessment in 1996, but since the methodology has changed since 2012, the period 2012–2022 will be analysed.

It should be mentioned only briefly that in the period 1996–2011, with the exception of about 3 years, the situation in the area of perceived corruption was not very good; in 2011, Czechia scored 44 out of 100. Despite the fact that a number of laws and norms were discussed to reduce corruption, the process of their adoption could not be accelerated and the reforms were not completed. The most problematic areas were considered to be making the financing of political parties more transparent, adopting rules on the status of civil servants and depoliticising the public administration, ensuring greater independence of the judiciary and prosecution, specialising prosecutors and much more effective control of the use of EU funds. Corruption in these areas undermines the independent functioning of institutions, the efficiency of public investment, a fair business environment and public confidence in the political system.

In 2012, there was a slight improvement, but within the EU countries, Czechia is still among the worst with 49 points, and only Slovakia was worse in the V4 countries. In addition to problems from the past, other areas such as EU funds, oversized state IT contracts and the lack of regulation of the water sector or inefficient management of the State Material Reserves are mentioned. It is in these sectors that corruption leads to a waste of public resources.

In 2013, there was a slight drop to 48 points, putting Czechia on a par with Croatia and Namibia. It was ranked 25th among EU countries, which is not very flattering and one of the main reasons for this is the lack of a concept and priorities in the fight against corruption. The main recommendations to improve the situation included holding accountable decision-making at all levels of politics and public administration, good governance of state-owned companies and rigorous and independent investigations into serious corruption.

The chart also shows an improving trend in the perception of corruption in Czechia since 2013, which persisted until 2018 (Fig. 14.3). In 2014, the country was rated 51 points, with positive signs of the adoption and functioning of the law on free access to information, efforts to self-regulate some lobbying firms and the existence of an RIA system. However, there is still a lack of a law on political party financing and an effective system for securing the proceeds of crime and tax evasion. In 2014, an amendment to the Public Procurement Act also started to be discussed.

In 2015, Czechia, with a CPI score of 56, managed to improve 16 places in the global ranking and moved up to 22nd place in the EU, surpassing Hungary. This

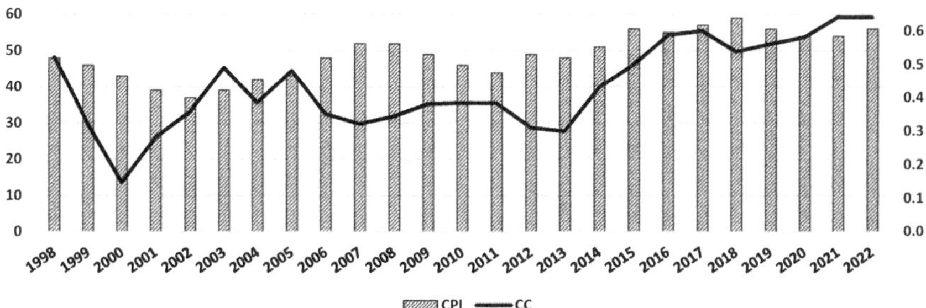

Fig. 14.3. Czechia CPI and CC 1998–2022. *Source:* Transparency International (2023) and World Bank (2023).

is because the measures taken in the fight against corruption in earlier years had begun to take effect. These measures include the adoption of a civil service law or a law on the publication of contracts, personnel and systemic changes in the public prosecutor's office, the dismantling of clientelistic systems in which important public affairs were decided by persons from the so-called grey zone, greater citizen involvement at the local level of municipal politics, increased emphasis on the quality and integrity of public institutions and a greater focus on the efficient management of public finances.

In 2016, there was a slight deterioration to 55 points, where the main reasons could be the failure to adopt the law on whistleblowing or the expansion of the powers of the Supreme Audit Office. On the other hand, the law on the register of ultimate owners, the law on conflict of interest and the law on financing of political parties were adopted, but unfortunately, these norms were perceived by experts as ineffective or even inadequate. In the judiciary, major corruption cases were not closed, which significantly weakened public confidence in a transparent and efficient judicial system. The stagnation continued in 2017, with Czechia's score dropping to 57. This showed that it is not enough to pass anti-corruption laws, but it is also important to enforce them consistently.

In 2018, there was an improvement to 59 points, which was a positive trend, but Czechia was still below the EU average of 65 points. In addition, Czechia was identified as a country to watch in the area of corruption, not least because Prime Minister Andrej Babiš was found guilty of a conflict of interest in relation to his media outlets and was accused of a conflict of interest regarding his association with a company that received millions of euros in EU subsidies. According to David Ondráčka of TI Czechia (TI, 2022), the privatisation of the public interest (state capture) is also continuing, with economic influence groups no longer seeking support for their interests only in politics, but regulating the operation of institutions themselves and creating conditions that are suitable for their business. This could be countered by a professional and respected public administration, but this is lacking in Czechia and has not been helped (or rather worsened) by the adoption of the amendment to the Civil Service Act, which allows politically motivated personnel interference in the staffing of individual offices and ministries.

In 2019, a downward trend started, which lasted for 3 years, during which time Czechia's rating dropped to 54 in 2021. During this period, the lack of legislative action in the fight against corruption from the previous 2 to 3 years and the shortcomings of the Civil Service Act, which led to a dysfunctional civil service, became fully apparent. The reasons for this dysfunction are stronger political influence on the civil service, a reduction in efficiency and professionalism and the departure of experienced people from the civil service. As an example, the Ministry of Regional Development was unable to develop a new construction law due to a lack of in-house experts and had to outsource this agenda. The problems of the state and public administration in failing to attract experienced professionals or to modernise and remove unnecessary bureaucracy were fully manifested during the COVID-19 pandemic in the form of expensive purchases of medical supplies, dysfunctional routing, poor communication between the government and the public, confusing vaccination strategies and frequent changes of ministers in key positions at the time. All of this led to a renewed distrust of the state and institutions by the citizens, as it is the quality of institutions, public administration and building citizens' trust in the state that is crucial to the prosperity of the country. In 2021, all V4 countries except Slovakia confirmed the long-term stagnation or decline in CPI scores. As TI Czechia (2022) points out, 'in most areas, there can be no change for the better until existing leaky laws are amended or completely new legal norms are adopted. Czechia's poor CPI scores in recent years accurately reflect the inability of Andrej Babiš's government to get anything meaningful passed in the fragmented House of Commons'. The CPI result also reflects the already mentioned fact that some corruption cases take too long in Czechia and often end up in court decisions that are not well understood by the public (e.g. the cases concerning the Prague Transport Company and Ivo Rittig, Andrej Babiš and the subsidies for the Čapí hnízdo subsidy, corruption in sports or the behaviour of the Chancellor of the President Vratislav Mynář).

In 2022, the CPI score improved slightly to 56 points, and this improvement is attributed to the expectations of the new government, which was strongly opposed to corruption before the elections. However, it cannot be said that these expectations have been met by the ruling coalition. As a result of the war in Ukraine and the need to address mainly security and economic threats, all anti-corruption activity has been significantly curtailed and, moreover, the new coalition's rule has been accompanied by a number of corruption scandals within its own ranks. All this has resulted in inadequate anti-corruption legislation and weakening political integrity, not least the failure to sanction the laundering of mainly Russian money.

The evolution of experts' perception of corruption in Czechia shows that better periods alternate with worse ones. Sometimes this development is compared to a roller coaster ride, because there is no long-term concept of fighting corruption. It is precisely the absence of such a concept, together with the inability of individual governments to consistently comply with the rules already set and to further deepen, improve and develop them, that is, preventing Czechia from improving the situation in the area of corruption to at least the average of EU countries.

14.6 Conclusion

There is no doubt that focusing only on the basic factors of production is not enough for long-term economic growth, but the institutional environment is equally important. In the 30 years of its existence, Czechia has undoubtedly made great progress in the development and quality of the institutional environment, but there are still areas for improvement. Several principles need to be followed when designing, reforming and improving the quality of the institutional environment. The institutional environment should be transparent and predictable, so any change to it should be in line with the values that society perceives and identifies with. This is where not only the communication of the government is important but also the role of the civil sector, which, by accepting these changes, helps to remove the elements of uncertainty that these changes bring.

Governments should only introduce institutional changes to which they can credibly commit and for which they have the support of the wider political spectrum. A situation in which one government introduces a major change and the next government reverses it creates chaos in society and public distrust in the functioning of institutions. Before a new institution is initiated, the existing situation needs to be thoroughly analysed and the costs of a new institution compared to a situation where the agenda could be integrated into existing structures. Equally important is the legislative process itself, the quality of regulation and a lean and efficient civil service.

Perception of corruption is an integral part of the quality of the institutional environment. Over the last decade (since about 2010), there has been some improvement in this area, followed by stagnation, which has been replaced by a decline in 2019. Czechia still lacks strategic solutions to anti-corruption legislation, but also amendments to the Conflict of Interest Act or the Public Prosecutor's Office Act. Among other things, we are not able to complete European legislation, such as the law on the protection of whistleblowers, where the two-year deadline to implement the directive in our legislation has already expired. The law was finally adopted at the beginning of June 2023, but it will not take effect until August 2023, and it is now being decided how much of the total amount Czechia will have to pay.

The reason why a good institutional environment and the lowest possible level of corruption are important for the economy is clear. If institutions are set up correctly, efficiently and transparently, the economy can thrive, cope much better with shocks like the COVID-19 pandemic, various economic crises and face the challenges ahead.

References

Ades, A., & Di Tella, R. (1999). Rents, competition, and corruption. *The American Economic Review*, *89*(4), 982–993.

Aidt, T. S. (2009). Corruption, institutions and economic development. *Oxford Review of Economic Policy*, *25*(2), 271–291.

Andvig, J. C., & Moene, O. K. (1999). How corruption may corrupt. *Journal of Economic Behavior Organization, & Organization*, *13*(1), 63–76.

Heckelman, J. C., & Powel, B. (2010). Corruption and the institutional environment for growth. *Comparative Economic Studies*, *52*(3), 351–378.

International Bank for Reconstruction and Development. (1994). *Governance: The World Bank's experience* (p. vii). The World Bank.

Kaufmann, D., Kraay, A., & Mastruzzi, M. (2010). *The Worldwide Governance Indicators: Methodology and analytical issues.* World Bank Policy Research Working Paper No. 5430.

Kaufmann, D., & Wei, S. J. (1999). *Does grease payment speed up the wheels of commerce?* Working Paper No. 2254. The World Bank.

Mauro, P. (1995). Corruption and growth. *Quarterly Journal of Economics*, *110*(3), 681–712.

North, D. C. (1990). *Institutions, institutional change and economic performance.* Cambridge University Press.

Paulovics, A. (2011). Guarantees of the legality of administration and administrative procedure in Hungary. *Danube: Law and Economics Review*, (2), 43–53.

Rauch, J. E., & Evans, P. B. (1997). *Bureaucratic structure and bureaucratic performance in less developed countries.* University of California-San Diego and University of California-Berkeley.

Tanzi, V. (1998). *Corruption around the world: Causes, consequences, scope, and cures.* Working Paper 98/63, Washington. International Monetary Fund.

Transparency International. (2023). *Corruption Perception Index.* https://www.transparency.org/en/cpi/

Transparency International Czech Republic. (2022). *Česko si stále neví rady s korupcí, ukazuje nejnovější Index vnímání korupce. Zastaví vláda Petra Fialy negativní trend?* https://www.transparency.cz/cpi2021/

Van Rijckeghem, C., & Weder, B. (1997). *Corruption and the rate of temptation – Do low wages in the civil service cause corruption?* Working Papers No. 97/73. International Monetary Fund.

Volk, C. S., Slaughter, S., & Thomas, S. L. (2001). Models of institutional resource allocation. *The Journal of Higher Education*, *72*(4), 387–413. https://doi.org/10.1080/00221546.2001.11777106

Wei, S. J. (2001). Corruption in economic transition and development: Grease or sand? Working Paper for UNECE Spring Seminar in Geneva.

World Bank. (2023). *Worldwide governance indicators.* https://info.worldbank.org/governance/wgi/

Chapter 15

Sectoral Indebtedness and Its Influence on Output of the Czech Economy

Ladislava Issever Grochová[a] *and Michal Škára*[b]

[a]Mendel University in Brno, Czechia
[b]Czech National Bank, Czechia

Abstract

This chapter examines the impact of sectoral indebtedness on GDP in Czechia, initially a low-indebted small open economy in which debt dynamics are becoming a major concern. The impact of household debt, non-financial corporation debt and public debt is analysed with the use of local projections based on instrumental variable estimations. The results show a more pronounced influence of household debt compared to non-financial corporation and government debt. Initially, increasing household debt stimulates short-run economic activity, but in the medium run, it limits household consumption and negatively affects output. This negative impact gradually turns into a positive effect in the long run. Non-financial corporation debt has a negative short- to medium-run impact but can have a small positive effect in the long run due to the prevalence of tradable industries. Public debt initially has a short-run negative impact, but then gradually becomes positive. Overall, the findings have implications for macroeconomic policies and the importance of monitoring financial stability.

Keywords: Sectoral indebtedness; credit boom; credit shock; economic growth; short-run effects; long-run effects

15.1 Introduction

In the early 2000s, a global financial crisis erupted from the United States due to high financial sector globalisation. The crisis was preceded by a long-standing accumulation of private and public debt. The housing bubble, fuelled by increased mortgage loans, burst in 2008, causing severe disruptions in the financial sector

Modeling Economic Growth in Contemporary Czechia, 231–250

Published under exclusive licence by Emerald Publishing Limited
doi:10.1108/978-1-83753-840-920241015

and necessitating government bailouts of major banks (BIS, 2018). Changes in institutional settings and the significance of debt liabilities for economic development have gained international attention. Higher credit activity is associated with lower output volatility but also increases the risk of deepening recessions and financial crises (Jordà et al., 2017). Countries with higher debt levels experience greater vulnerability to shocks and fluctuations in business and consumer expectations (Jordà et al., 2013). Indebtedness leads to less frequent but more severe and prolonged economic expansions or recessions (Bernardini & Forni, 2020; Jordà et al., 2013; Schularick & Taylor, 2012). Currently, various sectors and economies are experiencing historically high levels of indebtedness, accelerated by the COVID-19 pandemic, the war in Ukraine and relaxed monetary policies (Boone et al., 2022).

This chapter focuses on analysing the causes and effects of increasing private and public debt on the Czech economy, which has seen dynamic growth in public indebtedness compared to other European countries. Czechia is a small developed open economy; it is an export-oriented country with a prevalence in the tradable sector. Income among Czech households is still relatively equally distributed, although there is a growing social gap. As for most European countries, an ageing population is becoming a serious concern for the country. In terms of financial development, Czechia's financial sector is slightly below the European Union (EU) average. However, it adheres to the Basel III framework, ensuring compliance with international banking standards. The chapter examines how these aspects frame sectoral debt and how the indebtedness influences economic development in the short, medium and long run. The analysis draws upon relevant literature by Jordà et al. (2013), Mian et al. (2017, 2020), Mian and Sufi (2018), Reinhart and Rogoff (2010), and Schularick and Taylor (2012), which provide a foundational framework for understanding the impact of debt on the Czech economy.

15.2 Private and Public Indebtedness and Its Dynamics in Czechia

A certain degree of indebtedness is necessary for an economy to achieve its full potential by enabling sustainable levels of consumption, investment and production (Minsky & Kaufman, 2008). However, total national debt all over the world has experienced a substantial increase in the past two decades, encompassing both public and private sectors. This rise in debt levels has raised concerns regarding the potential negative consequences for the global economy and the overall stability of countries in terms of macroeconomic, financial and fiscal stability (Heridotu, 2023).

Excessive indebtedness of individual sectors – government, households and non-financial corporations can impede their ability to obtain additional loans for financing consumption or investment needs (for details see the following subchapters). This has a detrimental impact on economic growth (Minsky & Kaufman, 2008). Furthermore, elevated overall debt levels raise concerns about debt sustainability, posing further risks to the economy.

Excessive indebtedness risks have increased due to recent supply-side shocks: the COVID-19 pandemic and the ongoing war in Ukraine. These shocks led to a significant global rise in public but also private debt as governments provided support through credit guarantees and subsidies. The elevated indebtedness thus poses a threat to future economic growth and vulnerability to external shocks. Despite lower initial debt levels in post-communist countries, a combination of low interest rates, irresponsible fiscal policies and the recent shocks has driven significant growth in total indebtedness in Czechia over the past three decades. Moreover, in 2022, the Czech National Bank (CNB) initiated a tightening of monetary policy to address concerns of excessive demand and inflationary pressures, posing further risks to debt sustainability and its effects on economic growth.

15.3 Household Indebtedness: Demand for Housing

Households typically borrow money to smooth their consumption overtime which in itself should enhance economic output. However, the subsequent debt service reduces disposable income, leading to lower consumption and output. The time aspect is crucial in studying household indebtedness. Specifically, credit expansion might have a positive short-run impact on income through increased domestic aggregate demand (Drehmann et al., 2017; Mian & Sufi, 2018). Studies have shown that after 3–4 years, consumption expenditure declines, primarily driven by increased loan repayments (Drehmann et al., 2017; Mian et al., 2017, 2020; Mian & Sufi, 2018). Furthermore, household indebtedness is ruled by demand for non-tradable goods such as real estate, representing the major share of household debt, leading to an inflationary environment.

However, when the real estate bubble bursts, collateral values decline, posing significant challenges for an economic slowdown (Justiniano et al., 2019; Mian & Sufi, 2018). Reduced collateral values trigger credit restrictions, further dampening housing demand, decreasing households' wealth and resulting in deflationary recessions. During these recessions, disposable income decreases, unpaid mortgages rise (see Fig. 15.1), impacting bank capital, and creating a scenario similar to Minsky's debt deflation (Minsky & Kaufman, 2008). In the long run, it results in deflationary effects on demand and income (Jordà et al., 2013; Mian et al., 2017).

In summary, a credit boom can temporarily stimulate consumption and delay a recession. However, this postponement is not permanent, and the subsequent recession tends to be deeper and longer. Increased loan dynamics lead to greater fluctuations in the business cycle, particularly when there is excessive debt accumulation prior to a crisis or recession, increasing the likelihood of a financial crisis (Jordà et al., 2013). In economies with higher income inequality, an income shock results in a significant decline in consumer spending. High-income households are unable to fully compensate for the consumption shortfall of low-income households, leading to an overall decline in aggregate consumption (Eggerston & Krugman, 2012; Korinek & Simsek, 2016). This amplifies the business cycle,

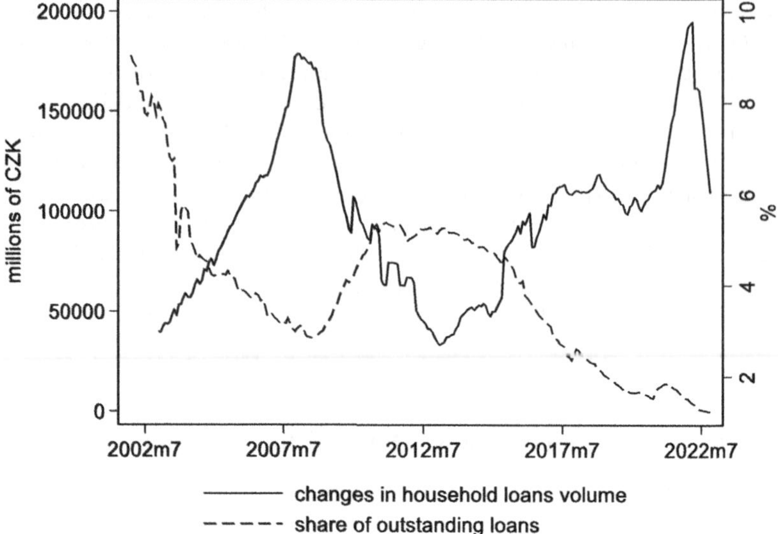

Fig. 15.1. Czech Household Loans and the Share of Outstanding Loans. *Source*: CNB ARAD (2023).

especially when accompanied by a high loan-to-value ratio or high total debt liabilities to household income ratio. As debt begins to limit household consumption expenditures, it also reduces the output of the economy (Alter et al., 2018).

If we focus on the current situation in Czechia but also other European countries, there is evidence of rapidly increasing household indebtedness and a rise in real estate prices dating from the outbreak of the pandemic to approximately the first half of the following year. After the outbreak of the pandemic, central banks across the continent feared deflationary pressures caused by a drop in disposable income. In response they began to rapidly reduce interest rates and use the unconventional tool of quantitative easing. A large volume of liquidity accumulated in the economy without a subsequent consideration, leading ex-ante to pro-inflationary pressures and ex-post to increasing interest rates. Not only in connection with rising debt service, household indebtedness began to slow from around mid-2021, associated with the cooling of the mortgage market, leading to a decrease in real estate prices (see Fig. 15.2).

15.4 Non-financial Corporate Debt

Non-financial corporate debt provides firms with increased access to funding for investment ventures and allows them to broaden their financing options. However, elevated levels of non-financial corporation debt can pose risks to the economy and

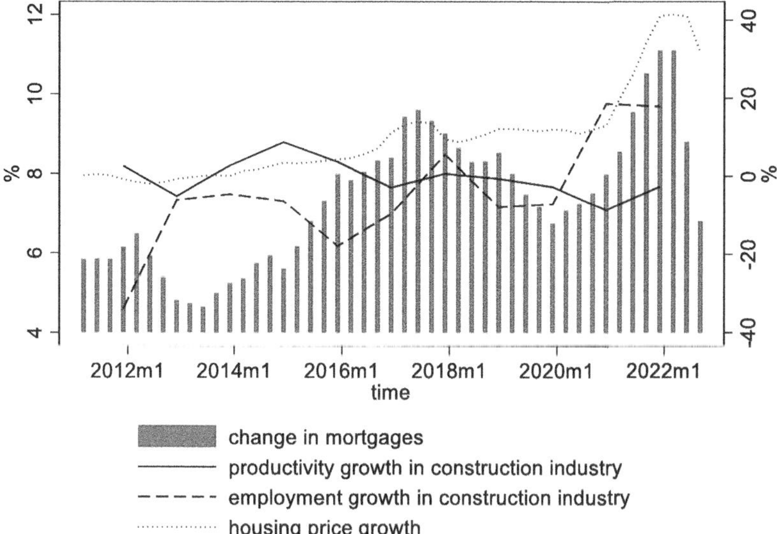

Fig. 15.2. Growth of Mortgages and Housing Prices in Czechia. *Source*: CNB ARAD (2023).

contribute to financial instability. It reduces overall input productivity, price competitiveness, and raises uncertainty and risks. Consequently, it diminishes expected investment returns and long-run investments (Jordà et al., 2022). The COVID-19 pandemic has heightened concerns regarding firms' ability to handle their debt burdens and the potential adverse effects on economic recovery.

Compared to households, the business sector exercises more caution in evaluating opportunities and risks and is less susceptible to optimistic income expectations. Firms are also less affected by real estate price developments, as they rely on a variety of collateral types. Additionally, there are differences in bankruptcy resolution, with greater regulation for firms and easier loan recovery for banks compared to households (Mian et al., 2017). The maturity period for debt repayment also varies, with households averaging around 18 years and non-financial corporations having a shorter period, primarily due to a lower share of real estate loans (Drehmann et al., 2017). These differences suggest that company debt has a less pronounced impact on amplifying the business cycle compared to households.

The effects of non-financial corporate debt over time are influenced by industry-specific factors (Müller & Verner, 2023). Non-tradable industries, which depend solely on domestic demand and face weaker competition, tend to invest less in technology and innovation, negatively affecting productivity. They are more reliant on changes in loan supply and interest rates, with limited external financing options. Indebtedness in the non-tradable sector, particularly through the real estate price channel, can lead to a decline in overall productivity. Positive demand shocks initially stimulate production, prices and employment, resulting in wage increases. However, this leads to an increased price level, exchange rate appreciation and reduced price competitiveness in the medium run. Moreover, higher wages attract workers away from more productive sectors, further dampening productivity in non-tradable industries (Schularick, 2021). The indebtedness of the non-tradable sector increases the economy's financial fragility, with falling real estate prices reducing collateral value and increasing outstanding loans, thus impacting the capital of financial institutions. This decline in liquidity results in reduced loans to both the non-tradable sector and households, leading to decreased consumption and the onset of a recession (Minsky & Kaufman, 2008; Müller & Verner, 2023). Labour reallocation due to higher wages in the construction industry has severe implications for the long-run economic performance as it reduces overall labour productivity (Borio et al., 2016; Cecchetti & Kharroubi, 2015; Gopinath et al., 2017; Mian et al., 2020; Müller & Verner, 2023).

Loans granted to tradable industries have a diametrically different effect on output. Export-oriented firms face intense competition and thus invest in production factors, technology and innovation to remain competitive with foreign counterparts. These firms have better access to liquidity, capital market funds, more favourable loan negotiations, diversified collateral and easier bond issuance (Müller & Verner, 2023) that provide benefits in terms of the productivity of the entire economy, supporting long-run national economic development (Müller & Verner, 2023).

Empirical studies show insignificant or marginal negative effects of company debt on the final product, with some studies indicating a positive initial impulse on employment that diminishes over time (Alter et al., 2018; Boone et al., 2022; Drehmann et al., 2017; Kim & Zhang, 2021; Mian et al., 2017, 2020). The impact of company debt on GDP growth appears to be less pronounced compared to increasing household indebtedness. Furthermore, the sectoral distribution of debt plays a crucial role, with a greater share of loans to the non-tradable sector having an overall negative effect on economic activity compared to the tradable sector.

The overall size of the impact of non-financial corporation indebtedness is influenced by various factors, including the institutional framework of the bankruptcy regime and the effectiveness of property rights and their enforcement. In the presence of a well-designed bankruptcy system and robust property rights enforcement, non-financial corporation debt does not exacerbate economic cycles. When an indebted company faces insolvency, its existing obligations are settled through the sale of its assets. In this scenario, strong property rights enforcement benefits creditors as their claims are effectively resolved through the liquidation of the company and the restructuring of the initially misallocated debt (Müller, 2022). However, if transaction costs associated with poor contract enforcement or lengthy liquidation processes are high, a situation similar to household indebtedness can arise. Furthermore, a higher number of 'zombie firms' may persist in the economy (Adalet McGowan et al., 2018; Jordà et al., 2022).

Since the 1980s, there has been an increase in loans flowing to the service and construction sectors in advanced economies, primarily driven by mortgage expansion. This, coupled with rising household indebtedness, has led to a decline in productivity in the medium- and long run. The growing share of loans in the construction industry comes at the expense of manufacturing and mining industries, further hampering overall productivity (Müller & Verner, 2023). The increased reliance on the construction industry in loan allocation also amplifies the economy's vulnerability to fluctuations in real estate prices (Boone et al., 2022). In the case of Czechia, in the last decades, there has been a significant overall increase in non-financial corporate sector debt. This trend continued in the years after the crisis, and particularly in 2020, as companies took on debt to mitigate the financial impact of the pandemic. This raises a question about whether the high levels of non-financial corporation debt will amplify the severity of recessions caused by the pandemic. However, there is a notable disparity in the share of tradable to non-tradable industries and in loans between the tradable and non-tradable sectors, with a higher proportion allocated to the tradable sector accounting for 64% on average. The construction industry, along with real estate sales, represents only 8.5% of total loans.

The prevalence of tradable industries in terms of output is a typical feature of the Czech economy. The tradable sector attracts more employees which might positively affect overall productivity which is in line with Müller and Verner (2023) (see Fig. 15.3).

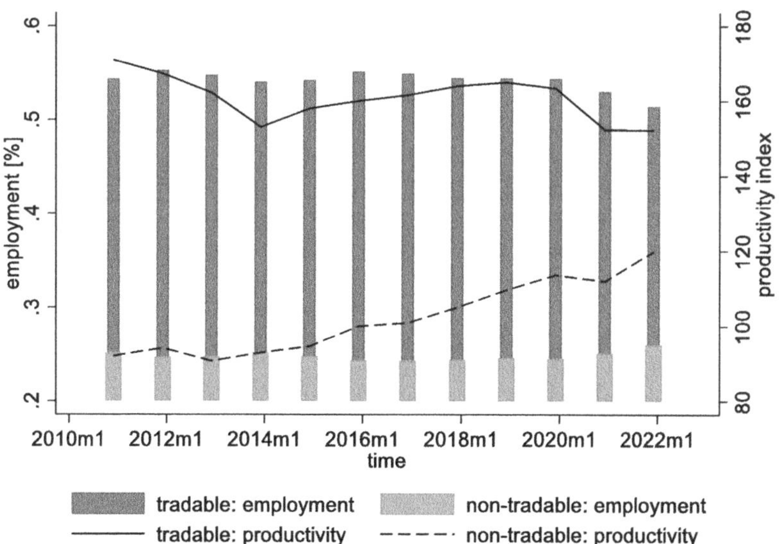

Fig. 15.3. Changes in Employment and Productivity in Tradable and Non-tradable Industries. *Source*: CNB ARAD (2023).

15.5 The Public Debt and the Risks Entailed

Government debt rises due to increased spending, lower tax revenues or other fiscal changes. During economic slowdowns, indebted governments face severe financial distress. This is caused not only by increased payments on social benefits but also by guarantees issued for defaulted loans and the need to recapitalise banks and rescue the financial sector (Jordà et al., 2016). Consequently, fiscal policy has limited capacity to invest, affecting future economic output (Bernardini & Forni, 2020; de Soyres et al., 2022; Heimberger, 2021).

Government bonds are the primary financial instrument to obtain the necessary liquidity in most EU countries, including Czechia (Campos-Martins & Amado, 2022). This makes public debt diametrically different compared to the debt of the private sector. Although government bonds are recognised as assets of high quality and liquidity, they carry risks. During financial instability, less liquid government bond markets face discrimination (Frait et al., 2021). Concerns about governments' solvency increase yields and risk premiums, potentially limiting their access to financial markets and hampering fiscal policy, dampening economic growth. The impact of government indebtedness on real GDP is thus crucial for assessing the sustainability of public debt (Heimberger, 2023).

Despite numerous theoretical and empirical studies on the impact of public debt on economic growth, there is no consensus on the magnitude and direction of this relationship. While initial increases in public debt and government expenditures may provide a positive impulse by increasing disposable incomes, empirical evidence suggests insignificant or negative effects on economic development because public debt crowds out private investment and reduces national savings (Bernardini & Forni, 2020; Jordà et al., 2016; Liaqat, 2019). Specifically, the public debt shock increases interest rates affecting investments, exchange rate impacting exports and uncertainty leading to expectations of economic repression (Ash et al., 2017). Consequently, a significant increase in the government debt-to-GDP ratio is likely to result in reduced infrastructure expenditures as the government seeks to manage debt levels and mandatory spending (Mian et al., 2017). Some studies conclude that there is either a negative or no correlation between public debt and real GDP growth in OECD countries (Panizza & Presbitero, 2014). On the other hand, other studies identify a significantly positive response of real GDP (Marcelino & Hakobyan, 2014; Pattillo & Ricci, 2011), often attributed to hysteresis effects (Fazzari et al., 2020).

The level of public debt is crucial in determining its nonlinear impact on growth. Reinhart and Rogoff (2010) find that when public debt-to-GDP exceeds 90%, it can have a detrimental effect on economic growth. Similarly, Cecchetti et al. (2011) reach a similar conclusion using a growth model approach. However, no specific threshold for debt-to-GDP ratios that significantly compromise medium-run growth has been identified (Pescatori et al., 2014). Additionally, the pace of debt accumulation also matters, as increasing debt trajectories have shown a minor negative impact on growth in certain countries (Pescatori et al., 2014).

After splitting with Slovakia, Czechia inherited a relatively low public debt both in absolute and relative terms (see Fig. 15.4, Panel A and B). From 1997, the

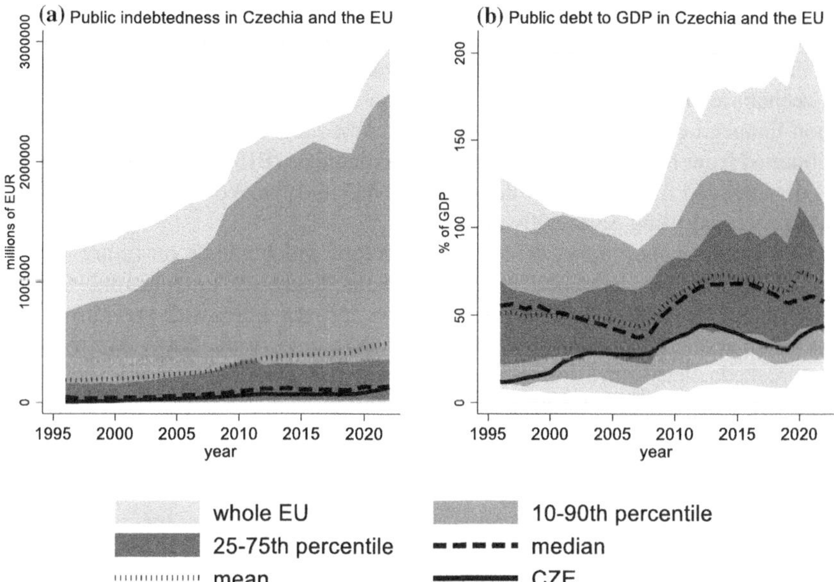

Fig. 15.4. Czech Public Indebtedness in the European Context. *Source*: Eurostat (2023).

debt grew steadily, reaching around 41% in 2014 before declining. Between 2016 and 2019, indebtedness decreased to 29%. However, the COVID-19 pandemic and the post-pandemic period put significant pressure on public finance sustainability globally, with increased spending on healthcare and employment support during lockdowns. Supportive programmes and state guarantees for private sector loans also played an important role. In Czechia, the need to finance the deficit and repay debt led to a significant increase in the debt-to-GDP ratio, reaching 40% in 2021. This trend is expected to persist due to ongoing budget deficits. Even though the Czech public debt is still below the European average, its dynamics are alarming.

The public debt in Czechia is primarily held by domestic residents in the form of medium- and long-term government bonds. Another burden for the Czech state budget is the problem of population ageing and a still unimplemented pension system reform which hampers the state budget via mandatory expenditure without adequate revenue inflow.

15.6 Effects of Indebtedness on GDP Growth in Czechia

Czechia is a typical small open economy. The country inherited quite low public debt and relatively equal income distribution among Czech households. Both have, however, been catching up to European levels. Thus, an initially low-indebted country ultimately elevated the pace of indebtedness which has been accentuated by the recent COVID-19 pandemic and the ongoing war in Ukraine. The indebtedness dynamics are alarming for future output growth.

The individual effects of increasing sectoral indebtedness on GDP growth in Czechia are presented in this section. We use quarterly data on GDP, household, non-financial corporation and government debt ranging from 2005q4 to 2021q3 obtained from the Bank for International Settlements (BIS), the remainder of data is downloaded from the CNB database ARAD and the World Bank (WB). Data are processed using Stata software.

To examine the impact of individual sectors' indebtedness on future 10-year GDP growth, we estimated local projections based on instrumental variable regressions to account for endogeneity. This approach aligns with previous studies by Mian et al. (2017, 2020), Bahadir et al. (2020), and Jordà (2005). We utilised a heteroskedasticity- and autocorrelation-consistent (HAC) weighting matrix in conjunction with the generalised method of moments (GMM) estimator. By computing impulse responses based on local projections, we were able to demonstrate the effects of sectoral indebtedness increases on the economy's output over time.

Given that household demand is considered the primary channel through which debt impacts economic output (Bahadir et al., 2020; Mian et al., 2017), time series are differentiated by 12 lags (equivalent to 3 years) to capture the expansionary phase of household borrowing. The coefficients of the explanatory variables (β) were collected over time (k) conducting h instrumental variables regressions to assess their impact (15.1):

$$\Delta_{12}y_{t+k} = \alpha + \beta^{\mathrm{hh}}\Delta_{12}\mathrm{hhdebt}_{t-4} + \beta^{\mathrm{nfc}}\Delta_{12}\mathrm{nfcdebt}_{t-4} + \beta^{\mathrm{gg}}\Delta_{12}\mathrm{ggdebt}_{t-4} + \varepsilon_{t+k} \quad (15.1)$$

where

$\Delta_{12}y_{t+k} = \ln\left(\frac{y_{t+k}}{y_{t+k-12}}\right)$ is the past 3-year change in real GDP expressed in quarters t, with forward leads $k = -4, -3, \ldots h-4$. The set of h regressions consists then of 10-year local projections to assess a 10-year effects on GDP growth,

$\Delta_{12}\mathrm{hhdebt}_{t-4} = \left(\frac{\mathrm{hhdebt}}{y}\right)_{t-4} - \left(\frac{\mathrm{hhdebt}}{y}\right)_{t-16}$ is the past 3-year change in household debt to GDP ratio expressed in quarters; in line with the financial instability hypothesis (Minsky, 1992), we expect that credit expansion can initially stimulate the economy by encouraging consumption and investment, but in the medium run, we expect negative correlation due to increased repayments,

$\Delta_{12}\mathrm{nfcdebt}_{t-4} = \left(\frac{\mathrm{nfcdebt}}{y}\right)_{t-4} - \left(\frac{\mathrm{nfcdebt}}{y}\right)_{t-16}$ is the past 3-year change in non-financial corporation debt to GDP ratio expressed in quarters; given the Czech context, the effect of corporate debt on the final product is not entirely clear a priori. However, we lean slightly towards a positive impact, considering the significant presence of the tradable sector, which suggests that productive investments financed by loans could have a predominant influence,

$\Delta_{12}\mathrm{ggdebt}_{t-4} = \left(\frac{\mathrm{ggdebt}}{y}\right)_{t-4} - \left(\frac{\mathrm{ggdebt}}{y}\right)_{t-16}$ is the past 3-year change in government debt to GDP ratio expressed in quarters; even though the development of the Czech government debt is one of the most dynamic, the level of indebtedness is still among the lowest in the EU, we can thus expect a below-threshold state and thus moderately positive effects on growth,

ε_{t+k} is the error term.

The 1-year and 3-years changes in GDP and household, non-financial firm and government debt to GDP are shown in Table 15.1. Household sector debt to GDP has been increasing by approximately 1 percentage points a year on average driven mainly by demand for housing, while non-financial corporation debt decreased by more than 1% over the same period. A reason can be found in historical development. non-financial corporation had high net borrowing before the 2008 global crisis, driven by significant investment growth. For example, in 2007, year-to-year investment growth was 23%. Consequently, in response to the crisis, non-financial corporation adjusted quickly, increasing savings and reducing net borrowing. Thus, for example, in 2008, there was a year-to-year increase of the gross saving rate of 4%, while the investment growth reduced to 1% (CNB). The change in non-financial company debt is about two times as volatile as household debt, probably due to stabile household preferences for housing on one hand and non-financial corporations' flexible behaviour on the other. Other characteristics were consistent with the small open economy business cycle literature. Household indebtedness is approximately as volatile as output, while government debt volatility is even greater than the non-financial corporation sector.

The effects of the increasing indebtedness of households, non-financial corporation and the government are monitored in connection with the future output of the economy. For clarity, Table 15.2 reports the effects at the end of each year ($m = k/4$). The regression analysis highlights the significant impact of household debt on the economy, surpassing other sectors' indebtedness. Initially, increasing household debt positively affects short-run output growth. However, over time, the positive effect weakens as borrowers face repayment obligations, leading to a medium-run decline. The increase in household debt has the most substantial negative impact on output growth over the next 3 years. The negative effect diminishes afterwards, and in the long run, debt starts contributing positively to economic activity as borrowers have lower repayments and thus more of their disposable income remains for consumption expenditures.

For non-financial corporation, the initial impact of debt on economic growth is negative, but it switches after 5 years. The initial burden of loans proves to be a worthwhile investment, supporting long-run economic growth, possibly due to the prevalence of tradable industries in Czechia.

In contrast, public debt initially hampers short-run output growth. However, in the medium run, the financial resources provided by the state have a positive effect on the economy, such as infrastructure development, which takes time to be addressed by the final output. Nevertheless, in the long run, state indebtedness limits the government's ability to implement effective fiscal policies, especially during downturns, resulting in a negative long-run effect.

Results for Czechia are in line with panel studies by Mian et al. (2017), Kim and Zhang (2021) and Alter et al. (2018) but are more accentuated. This goes hand in hand with the Müller and Verner (2023) explanation that in small open

Table 15.1. Descriptive Statistics.

Variables	Obs	Mean	Std. Dev.	Min	Max	$p1$	$p99$	Skew.	Kurt.
$\Delta_4\ y$	104	2.332	1.301	0.552	4.96	0.556	4.949	0.53	2.162
$\Delta_{12}\ y$	96	7.282	3.636	1.974	14.301	1.974	14.301	0.43	2.12
Δ_4 hhdebt	100	0.969	1.467	−3	4.1	−2.85	4.1	−0.038	2.859
Δ_{12} hhdebt	92	3.23	3.221	−4.7	9.8	−4.7	9.8	0.442	2.733
Δ_4 nfcdebt	100	−1.109	3.562	−11.6	8.8	−10.55	6.8	−0.385	3.217
Δ_{12} nfcdebt	92	−2.938	8.012	−17.9	8.5	−17.9	8.5	−0.281	1.868
Δ_4 ggdebt	92	1.091	3.703	−6.4	10.1	−6.4	10.1	0.35	2.436
Δ_{12} ggdebt	84	3.319	8.058	−11.4	17.1	−11.4	17.1	−0.241	1.914

Source: Authors' Calculations.

Note: y stands for log real GDP, while Δ_4 and Δ_{12} stand for year-on-year and 4-year differences.

Table 15.2. Estimated Sectoral Effects.

y_{t-m}, m =	−1	0	1	2	3	4	5	6	7	8	9	10
hhdebt	0.652***	0.257**	−0.135	−0.433***	−0.511***	−0.372***	−0.104	0.254**	0.545***	0.450***	0.141**	0.174
	(0.075)	(0.108)	(0.098)	(0.057)	(0.019)	(0.050)	(0.081)	(0.108)	(0.176)	(0.148)	(0.065)	(0.279)
nfcdebt	−0.367***	−0.419***	−0.422***	−0.336***	−0.211***	−0.084***	0.030	0.103***	0.116***	0.111***	0.087***	−0.056
	(0.036)	(0.050)	(0.034)	(0.026)	(0.023)	(0.024)	(0.031)	(0.029)	(0.024)	(0.024)	(0.007)	(0.049)
ggdebt	−0.227***	−0.101***	0.083**	0.227***	0.314***	0.348***	0.296***	0.199***	0.074*	−0.130***	−0.292***	−0.283***
	(0.020)	(0.026)	(0.038)	(0.025)	(0.016)	(0.027)	(0.032)	(0.024)	(0.042)	(0.044)	(0.012)	(0.032)
N	81	81	77	73	69	65	61	57	53	49	45	41
R2	0.820	0.685	0.755	0.868	0.903	0.829	0.621	0.512	0.719	0.918	0.946	0.757

Source: Authors' Calculations.

Note: Standard errors in parentheses, $^{***}p < 0.01$, $^{**}p < 0.05$, $^{*}p < 0.1$.

economies, the effects are elevated as in the medium run, domestic demand falls, uncompensated by foreign demand due to the appreciation of the real exchange rate which negatively affects output growth. A more pronounced effect can be also caused by economic and institutional factors such as lower financial development and property rights score, higher openness or increased employee protection compared to the European average (see Table 15.3). More specifically, higher regulatory measures by central banks can mitigate the negative impact of debt through macroprudential limits. Well-designed limits reduce excessive credit supply, risky lending and the vulnerability of low-income borrowers (Alter et al., 2018; Jordà et al., 2016; Mian et al., 2020). Regulations also prevent the emergence of undercapitalised banks and 'zombie' firms (Schularick, 2021). Factors such as financial sector maturity and debtor registry transparency further mitigate negative effects (Alter et al., 2018; Bahadir et al., 2020). Conversely, openness and labour market rigidities deepen the negative impact of debt on output (Mian et al., 2020; Müller & Verner, 2023). Despite the gradual widening of social disparities, income inequality remains among the lowest in Europe which favours economic development.

The sectoral indebtedness effects are presented also graphically. Fig. 15.5 illustrates a more pronounced impact of GDP growth on household debt compared to non-financial corporation and government indebtedness. Initially, increasing household debt stimulates economic activity in the short run. However, after approximately 2 years, the burden of repayment begins to limit household consumption expenditures, resulting in a negative impact on final output. This negative effect reaches its lowest point around the fifth year, after which the negative impact gradually decreases and turns into a positive effect from the seventh year onwards. This transition from a weakening negative effect to a moderate positive effect on the final product is supported by Drehmann et al. (2017), who suggest that repayments peak around 4 years after the expansionary phase of credit activity, which typically lasts for about 3–4 years. As household budgets become less constrained, consumer expenditures increase which encourages economic growth.

On the other hand, non-financial corporation debt has a negative short- to medium-run effect on economic activity as the debt accumulates. However, in the long run, a small positive effect can be expected due to the prevalence of tradable industries in the Czech economy and productive investments and innovations financed by loans. A long-run positive effect of non-financial corporation debt does not indicate a visible workforce reallocation to the non-tradable sector. Therefore, considering Czechia's export-oriented nature and the dominance of tradable industries, overall labour productivity is not expected to decrease. A possible danger is a real estate bubble burst which would put pressure on the reduction of household consumption expenditure in accordance with the reduction of their wealth precisely through the fall in real estate prices and the possibility of the outbreak of Fisher debt deflation and a decline in output. However, overheated distribution channels, associated with outages during the pandemic, and the war in Ukraine, causing energy and fuel prices to rise, are pushing up the prices of goods and services. In this situation, we can hardly expect that the prices adjust to pre-pandemic levels.

Table 15.3. Variables Amplifying Debt Effects.

Variable	Europe				Czechia			
	Mean	Std. Dev.	Min	Max	Mean	Std. Dev.	Min	Max
FDI	50.829	21.436	9.587	100.000	40.740	5.569	30.813	46.889
Exports to GDP	48.408	30.061	14.287	205.482	61.300	14.793	38.133	81.954
Openness	96.349	55.909	30.099	380.104	120.338	26.024	81.098	157.575
Empl_protection	2.399	0.748	1.103	5.000	3.466	0.175	3.258	3.639
Property Right Score	77.447	10.717	44.1	91.9	70.781	2.775	65	76.8
Gini	34.713	5.797	16.217	59.896	25.706	0.880	23.790	28.006

Source: Authors' Calculations.

Note: FDI is financial development index * 100; Empl_protection stands for employment protection index developed by OECD, Gini is post-tax national income gini coefficient over age 20.

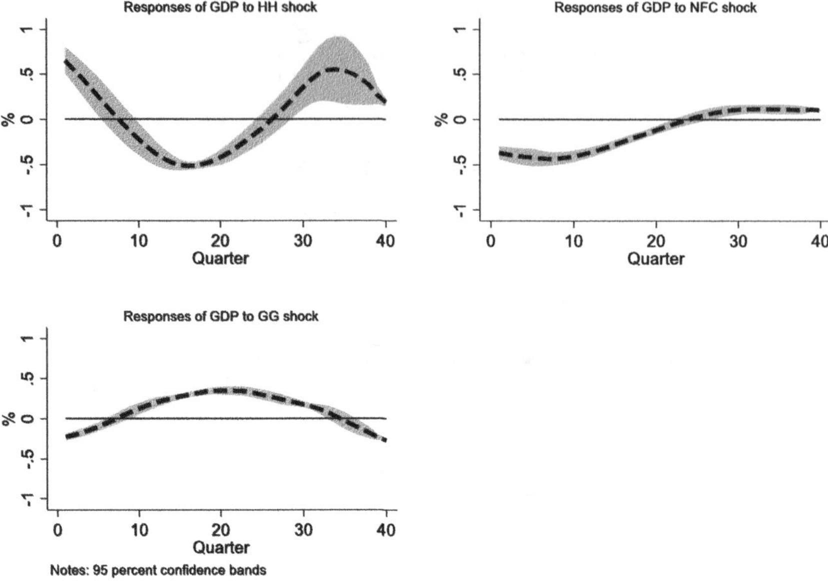

Fig. 15.5. Schedules of the Effects of Sectoral Indebtedness on GDP Growth. *Source*: Own calculations.

The initial negative impact of a public sector debt shock becomes evident for a period of 2 years. However, thereafter, the public indebtedness has a positive effect, reaching its peak in the fifth year following the increase in public debt. Subsequently, the positive effect gradually diminishes. The gradual fading of the positive effect may be attributed to factors such as the reduced ability to implement effective fiscal policies during recessions. Here, it is worth mentioning that Czechia's public debt-to-GDP ratio does not approach the critical threshold of 90% where it would significantly hinder future output (Woo & Kumar, 2015), as well as it is not below 30% when it can contribute to the growth of the economy (Reinhart et al., 2012). As the Czech public indebtedness approaches the debt levels of 47%–70% of GDP identified by Checherita-Westphal and Rother (2012), we draw attention to a possible decline in public investment, as cuts in state budgets primarily affect public investment when the government tries to maintain a reasonable level of debt and procure mandatory spending. Nonetheless, insofar the cumulative effect is positive by the end of the scheduled period supporting the hysteresis effect hypothesis.

The analysis further points to various challenges and implications for macroeconomic policies, including a potential real estate bubble burst, which could put pressure on reducing household consumption expenditure, wealth reduction due to falling real estate prices and the possible emergence of Fisher debt deflation; or the growing demand on the welfare state, which increases mandatory expenses and puts pressure on budget deficit management. The ageing population and the unsustainability of the pension system also pose challenges for policymakers. These challenges can lead to higher government expenditures and indebtedness, hampering the economy's output, particularly in the long run. The growing proportion of foreign investors holding Czech debt could introduce the risk of exchange rate fluctuations. Low interest rates have facilitated low debt servicing in many countries, Czechia included, but rising real interest rates worldwide and elevated public debt service costs create a challenging environment for sustaining fiscal policy. The dynamics of public debt in Czechia accentuate the importance of sustaining high deficits potentially increasing the risk premium.

The central bank plays a crucial role in monitoring the fiscal situation and its impact on financial stability. With ongoing public debt dynamics, there is a risk of fiscal dominance, when the CNB could potentially maintain accommodative monetary policy to avoid increasing the costs of servicing high government debt, despite inflationary pressures. The interconnectedness between the financial and government sectors is controlled, and concentration risks are assessed to prevent systemic risk. The CNB closely monitors the dynamics of public debt and market expectations to mitigate the risks.

15.7 Conclusion

This chapter explores the relationship between sectoral indebtedness in Czechia and future economic output. It discusses the causes and origins of increasing household, non-financial corporation and government debt, as well as the mechanisms through which indebtedness affect the economy. It highlights the short- and long-run effects of credit shocks on consumption, public and private investments, labour productivity and economic growth.

The empirical analysis reveals that the impact of debt on future economic activity varies across different time horizons and economic sectors. Household debt has a positive short-run effect on the economy but becomes negative in the medium run. The negative effect peaks in the 5th year after the household debt boom, gradually fading over time. Over the long run, there is a modestly positive effect as household budgets become less restrictive, leading to increased consumer spending and moderate stimulation of economic growth. Non-financial corporation debt has a negative short- to medium-run effect on economic activity, but in the long run, a small positive effect is expected due to an increased share of tradable industries and productive investments financed by loans. Public sector debt initially has a negative impact but turns positive after 2 years, reaching its peak in the 5th year, and gradually diminishes thereafter.

The chapter emphasises the importance of the interaction between different sectors' debt exposures and the role of formal institutions and other socio-economic aspects such ageing, increasing income inequality, competition in the credit market and job protection, on the debt-output relationship. It also points out the potential consequences of recent events, such as the COVID-19 pandemic, the war in Ukraine and ongoing banking sector reforms. Policy recommendations include monitoring the real estate market, maintaining fiscal discipline, addressing the challenges posed by ageing populations and growing mandatory expenditures and considering the impact of interest rates and debt servicing costs on fiscal sustainability. The CNB should closely monitor the fiscal situation to prevent adverse effects on financial stability and systemic risk.

References

Adalet McGowan, M., Andrews, D., & Millot, V. (2018). The walking dead? Zombie firms and productivity performance in OECD countries. *Economic Policy*, *33*(96), 685–736.

Alter, A., Feng, A. X., & Valckx, N. (2018). *Understanding the macro-financial effects of household debt: A global perspective*. International Monetary Fund.

Ash, M., Basu, D., & Dube, A. (2017). *Public debt and growth: An assessment of key findings on causality and thresholds (No. 2017–10)*. Working Paper.

Bahadir, B., De, K., & Lastrapes, W. D. (2020). Household debt, consumption and inequality. *Journal of International Money and Finance*, *109*, 102240.

Bernardini, M., & Forni, L. (2020). Private and public debt interlinkages in bad times. *Journal of International Money and Finance*, *109*, 102239.

BIS. (2018). *Structural changes in banking after the crisis*. CGFS Papers, no. 60.

Boone, L., Fels, J., Jordà, Ò., Schularick, M., & Taylor, A. M. (2022). *Debt: The eye of the storm*. ICMB International Center for Monetary and Banking Studies.

Borio, C. E., Kharroubi, E., Upper, C., & Zampolli, F. (2016). Labour reallocation and productivity dynamics: Financial causes, real consequences. https://ssrn.com/abstract=2711258

Campos-Martins, S., & Amado, C. (2022). Financial market linkages and the sovereign debt crisis. *Journal of International Money and Finance*, *123*, 102596.

Cecchetti, S. G., & Kharroubi, E. (2015). Why does financial sector growth crowd out real economic growth? https://ssrn.com/abstract=2615882

Cecchetti, S. G., Mohanty, M. S., & Zampolli, F. (2011). The real effects of debt. https://ssrn.com/abstract=1946170

Checherita-Westphal, C., & Rother, P. (2012). The impact of high government debt on economic growth and its channels: An empirical investigation for the euro area. *European Economic Review*, *56*(7), 1392–1405.

Drehmann, M., Juselius, M., & Korinek, A. (2017). Accounting for debt service: the painful legacy of credit booms. https://doi.org/10.2139/ssrn.2993859

Eggertsson, G. B., & Krugman, P. (2012). Debt, deleveraging, and the liquidity trap: A Fisher-Minsky-Koo approach. *Quarterly Journal of Economics*, *127*(3), 1469–1513.

Fazzari, S. M., Ferri, P., & Variato, A. M. (2020). Demand-led growth and accommodating supply. *Cambridge Journal of Economics*, *44*(3), 583–605.

Frait, J., Komárková, Z., & Szabo, M. (2021). *Rostoucí zadlužení státu, provázanost mezi vládním a finančním sektorem a rizika pro finanční stabilitu*. ČNB.

Gopinath, G., Kalemli-Özcan, Ş., Karabarbounis, L., & Villegas-Sanchez, C. (2017). Capital allocation and productivity in South Europe. *Quarterly Journal of Economics*, *132*(4), 1915–1967.

Heimberger, P. (2021). Do higher public debt levels reduce economic growth? *Journal of Economic Surveys*. https://doi.org/10.1111/joes.12536

Heimberger, P. (2023). *Debt sustainability analysis as an anchor in EU fiscal rules*. IPOL, Economic Governance and EMU Scrutiny Unit. PE 741.504 - March 2023. https://www.europarl.europa.eu/RegData/etudes/IDAN/2023/741504/IPOL_IDA(2023)741504_EN.pdf

Heridotu, C. (2023). BIS – Central bankers' speeches: Constantinos Herodotou: The global debt trap – The implications for growth and possible solutions to tackle it Speech by Mr Constantinos Herodotou, Governor of the Central Bank of Cyprus, at the YPO – Cyprus Chapter event. *Nicosia*, 19 January 2023.

Jordà, Ò. (2005). Estimation and inference of impulse responses by local projections. *The American Economic Review*, *95*(1), 161–182.

Jordà, Ò., Kornejew, M., Schularick, M., & Taylor, A. M. (2022). Zombies at large? Corporate debt overhang and the macroeconomy. *Review of Financial Studies*, *35*(10), 4561–4586.

Jordà, Ò., Schularick, M., & Taylor, A. M. (2016). Sovereigns versus banks: Credit, crises, and consequences. *Journal of the European Economic Association*, *14*(1), 45–79.

Jordà, Ò., Schularick, M., & Taylor, A. M. (2017). Macrofinancial history and the new business cycle facts. *NBER Macroeconomics Annual*, *31*(1), 213–263.

Jordà, Ò., Schularick, M., & Taylor, A. M. (2013). When credit bites back. *Journal of Money. Credit and Banking*, *45*(2), 3–28.

Justiniano, A., Primiceri, G. E., & Tambalotti, A. (2019). Credit supply and the housing boom. *Journal of Political Economy*, *127*(3), 1317–1350.

Kim, Y. J., & Zhang, J. (2021). The relationship between debt and output. *IMF Economic Review*, *69*, 230–257.

Korinek, A., & Simsek, A. (2016). Liquidity trap and excessive leverage. *The American Economic Review*, *106*(3), 699–738.

Liaqat, Z. (2019). Does government debt crowd out capital formation? A dynamic approach using panel VAR. *Economics Letters*, *178*, 86–90.

Marcelino, M. S., & Hakobyan, M. I. (2014). *Does lower debt buy higher growth? The impact of debt relief initiatives on growth*. International Monetary Fund.

Mian, A., & Sufi, A. (2018). Finance and business cycles: The credit-driven household demand channel. *The Journal of Economic Perspectives*, *32*(3), 31–58.

Mian, A., Sufi, A., & Verner, E. (2017). Household debt and business cycles worldwide. *Quarterly Journal of Economics*, *132*(4), 1755–1817.

Mian, A., Sufi, A., & Verner, E. (2020). How does credit supply expansion affect the real economy? The productive capacity and household demand channels. *The Journal of Finance*, *75*(2), 949–994.

Minsky, H. P. (1992). *The financial instability hypothesis* (Working paper No. 74). The Jerome Levy Economics Institute of Bard College.

Minsky, H. P., & Kaufman, H. (2008). *Stabilizing an unstable economy* (Vol. 1). McGraw-Hill.

Müller, K. (2022). Busy bankruptcy courts and the cost of credit. *Journal of Financial Economics*, *143*(2), 824–845.

Müller, K., & Verner, E. (2023). Credit allocation and macroeconomic fluctuations. https://doi.org/10.2139/ssrn.3781981

Panizza, U., & Presbitero, A. F. (2014). Public debt and economic growth: Is there a causal effect? *Journal of Macroeconomics*, *41*, 21–41.

Pattillo, C., & Ricci, L. A. (2011). External debt and growth. *Review of economics and institutions*, *2*(3), 30.

Pescatori, M. A., Sandri, M. D., & Simon, J. (2014). *Debt and growth: Is there a magic threshold?* International Monetary Fund. https://doi.org/10.5089/9781484306444.001

Reinhart, C. M., Reinhart, V. R., & Rogoff, K. S. (2012). Public debt overhangs: Advanced-economy episodes since 1800. *The Journal of Economic Perspectives*, *26*(3), 69–86.

Reinhart, C. M., & Rogoff, K. S. (2010). Growth in a Time of Debt. *The American Economic Review*, *100*(2), 573–578.

Schularick, M. (2021). *Corporate indebtedness and macroeconomic stabilisation from a long-term perspective (No. 024)*. ECONtribute Policy Brief.

Schularick, M., & Taylor, A. M. (2012). Credit booms gone bust: Monetary policy, leverage cycles, and financial crises, 1870–2008. *The American Economic Review*, *102*(2), 1029–1061.

de Soyres, C., Kawai, R., & Wang, M. (2022). *Public Debt and Real GDP: Revisiting the Impact*. International Monetary Fund.

Woo, J., & Kumar, M. S. (2015). Public debt and growth. *Economica*, *82*(328), 705–739.

Chapter 16

The Contribution of Financial Institutions to Economic Growth

Iveta Palečková, Lenka Přečková and Roman Hlawiczka

Silesian University in Opava, Czechia

Abstract

This chapter explores the influence of the banking and insurance sectors on the economic growth of Czechia, a nation with unique financial dynamics ideal for this study. Our aim is to ascertain the contribution of these financial institutions to economic growth, addressing the divergence in empirical findings that have marked this research area for decades. We scrutinise the impact of various factors, including sectoral development and the efficiency and stability of these institutions, all within the Czech context. Utilising the Granger causality test, we assess the role of several indicators related to the development of the banking and insurance sectors. Our findings reveal that in Czechia, the evolution and operational efficiency of these financial institutions significantly drive economic growth. This study provides an in-depth understanding of the role these sectors play in the Czech economic landscape, affirming their crucial contribution to the nation's economic prosperity.

Keywords: Banking sector; insurance sector; financial stability; efficiency; economic growth; Data Envelopment Analysis

16.1 Introduction

The banking and insurance sectors play an important role in economic development. The important role of the banking sector in the economy is to channel resources from primary savers to investment opportunities. Therefore, the role of financial institutions is crucial in a bank-based system. In addition, an efficient banking system facilitates better mobilisation and use of resources and accelerates the process of economic growth (Saqib, 2016). On the other hand, banks are more

Modeling Economic Growth in Contemporary Czechia, 251–263

Published under exclusive licence by Emerald Publishing Limited
doi:10.1108/978-1-83753-840-920241016

biased towards conservative investments and thus will be less effective at promoting innovation and growth compared to markets (Haini, 2020; Morck & Nakamura, 1999).

Nevertheless, the relationship between financial institutions and economic growth is important. The earliest proponent of the importance of financial development in economic growth is Schumpeter (1911). Schumpeter (1911) suggested that financial intermediaries are important for technical innovation and economic growth. Subsequently, empirical studies by Goldsmith (1969) and King and Levine (1993) supported the view that financial development is a good predictor of economic growth. Over the last several decades, several empirical studies have examined the relationship between finance or financial institutions and economic growth. Although the impact of financial development on economic growth has received considerable attention in empirical literature, the results of the studies are not unambiguous. Moreover, only several studies (Adams et al., 2009 or Pradhan et al., 2017) examined the impact of banks and insurance companies on economic growth.

This chapter aims to assess how financial institutions contribute to economic growth. We consider the impact of banks and insurance companies, the development of the banking sector and insurance development on economic growth in Czechia. In addition, we assess whether the efficiency and stability of the banking and insurance sectors are significant factors of economic growth. The dataset covers the period 2004–2021; therefore, the study includes the period of the global financial crisis and partly the period of the COVID-19 pandemic.

16.2 Literature Review

Pradhan et al. (2017) mentioned that a significant number of studies have examined the dynamics between a broad measure of financial development and economic development. While there is extensive research on the nexus between financial sector development and economic growth, the existing literature provides narrow coverage on the impact of the insurance market activities on economic growth or the nexus between economic growth and financial stability and efficiency of the banking and insurance sectors.

The development and stability of the banking sector have a significant impact on economic growth. Financial institutions, especially banks, play a key role in economic growth. Moreover, the efficiency of banks and insurance companies is linked to financial stability. These crucial influences have been addressed by some authors in their studies, and their results are significant and a challenge for further research. Reduced bank competition, increased banking stability and the exploitation of the potential of the banking sector are essential factors in promoting economic growth. This area was addressed in the study by Ijaz et al. (2020). They examined the relationship between bank competition, financial stability and economic growth in 38 European countries. Empirical results show that bank stability contributes significantly to economic growth in Europe. The study also highlights the importance of a resilient banking system in times of stress, as these are periods when economic growth declines. Bank competition is also addressed in the study by Pradhan et al. (2020). The research focused on the causal links between bank competition, stock and insurance market developments and economic growth in Europe between 1996 and 2016. The study found short-run bidirectional causality between stock market development and insurance market development, and strong evidence of Granger causality from bank competition, insurance market development and stock market development to economic growth in the long run. The impact of banking sector development on economic growth is addressed in a study conducted by Rushchyshyn et al. (2021). The study compares the development of the banking sector in Ukraine with some European Union (EU) countries (also Czechia) over the period 2000–2019. The results show a strong positive relationship between the level of development of the banking sector in Ukraine and GDP per capita, a moderate relationship with foreign direct investment, and an inverse relationship with the level of poverty in the country.

Several authors have researched the relationship between insurance and economic growth. As stated by some authors (Niavand & Mahesh, 2018; Njegomir & Stojić, 2010; Oke, 2012; Pradhan et al., 2020; Ul Din et al., 2017), the development of the insurance sector is an important prerequisite for stimulating economic growth. However, most research studies are conducted in developing countries, which motivates other authors to look at this area in Europe, not excluding Czechia. The relationship between the insurance industry and a country's economic development goes beyond insurance, as the insurance and banking sectors are increasingly integrated. This interconnection brings a number of advantages, but unfortunately also disadvantages and new risks (see Szewieczek, 2013). Cooperation between banks and insurance companies has been the focus of publications such as Dicevska et al. (2018) and Al-Khalifah (2018). The cooperation between banks and insurance companies can make the impact on a country's economic development more intense, as discussed in the research of Webb et al. (2002) and Balcilar et al. (2018) or Haini (2020). As in the study by Webb et al. (2002), banks and insurance companies should contribute to economic growth by facilitating efficient capital allocation. The authors focus on the financial intermediation factor and find that financial institutions can have a joint role in stimulating the economy and work better together than separately. The more efficient banking payment systems are, the lower the associated administrative costs for insurance companies.

A country's economic growth is measured by GDP growth or GDP per capita growth (e.g. Dash et al., 2018; Haiss & Sümegi, 2008; or Oke, 2012). In the empirical literature, banking or financial development is measured using three main indicators: (i) The ratio of bank credit to the private sector to GDP (Ductor & Grechyna, 2015; Duramany-Lakkoh et al., 2022; Hou & Cheng, 2017; Pradhan et al., 2017; Ruiz, 2018; Samargandi et al., 2015). (ii) The ratio of commercial bank assets divided by the sum of commercial bank assets and central bank assets (Ang & McKibbin, 2007; Duramany-Lakkoh et al., 2022; Samargandi et al., 2015). The variable measures the relative importance of a specific type of financial institution (commercial banks) in the financial system. Ang and McKibbin (2007) argue that the advantage of this measure is that commercial banks make more efficient use of funds than central banks by channelling savings to profitable investment opportunities. (iii) The ratio of liquid liabilities (or M3) to nominal GDP (Ductor & Grechyna, 2015; Samargandi et al., 2015). Ibáñez-Hernández et al. (2015) concluded that high growth in lending leads to instability in the financial sector and thus negatively influences economic development. On the other hand, Takáts and Upper (2013) found that decreasing bank lending to the private sector does not necessarily hinder economic recovery after a financial crisis. De Gregorio and Guidotti (1995) found a positive correlation between the growth rate of bank loans to the private sector and the growth of GDP, but the impact varies in different countries. In addition, Černohorský (2017) concluded that different types of bank loans have an impact on economic growth. The only exception was consumer loans, where this relationship was not confirmed.

The ratios used to evaluate development in the insurance market are the growth rate of written premiums and penetration or density (e.g. Oke, 2012 or Ul Din et al., 2017). The authors conducted research from the perspective of total insurance, but separately on life and non-life insurance (see, e.g. Oke, 2012). This is due to the specificities of life and non-life insurance. The authors Pradhan et al., (2020) focused on European countries and investigated the relationship between economic growth, banking competition, insurance market development and stock market development over a 20-year period. It was found that the long-term economic growth of European countries depends on competition in the banking sector coupled with a developed insurance market and a dynamic stock market. The study also found that the development of the insurance market, competition in the banking sector and economic growth have a long-term effect on stock market development in these countries. In a study by Dash et al. (2018), the authors confirm that there is mixed evidence of a correlation between insurance market penetration and per capita growth in 19 Euro area countries. Financial markets and the insurance industry can help allocate capital to its most productive use, which promotes economic growth and benefits society.

In addition, several studies (Levine, 1997 or Saqib, 2016) linked the efficiency of financial institutions with economic growth. Besides, Diallo (2018) stated that bank efficiency relaxed credit constraints and increased the growth rate for financially dependent industries during the crisis. Furthermore, financial stability helps stakeholders manage their risks promptly and enables them to use their financial resources efficiently, which ultimately increases economic growth (Creel et al., 2015; Hoggarth et al., 2002; Ijaz et al., 2020; Jokipii & Monnin, 2013). Moreover, Ijaz et al. (2020) argue that financial stability and economic growth reinforce each other. Countries facing economic decline, notably, have hindered banking operations and business activities. For such countries, it is difficult to get foreign financing, which lowers GDP growth and credit. Therefore, economic growth promotes financial stability (Dell'Ariccia et al., 2008; Cave et al., 2020; Wang et al., 2019).

As is evident from the literature review, the relationship between financial development and economic growth has been widely examined in empirical literature. As mentioned in Ruiz (2018), many econometric techniques have been employed, such as co-integration analysis (e.g. Saqib, 2016), VAR modelling with the Granger causality test (e.g. Adams et al., 2009; Pradhan et al., 2017 or Pradhan et al., 2020), panel data analysis using ordinary least squares (Diallo, 2018; Ductor & Grechyna, 2015) or the generalised method of moments model (Haini, 2020; Ijaz et al., 2020 or Creel et al., 2015; Petkovski & Kjosevski, 2014; Ruiz, 2018).

16.3 Data and Methodology

Financial development is commonly defined in terms of aggregate size of the financial sector, its sectorial composition and a range of attributes of its individual sub-sectors that determine their effectiveness in meeting the various economic agents' requirements to enhance their wealth (Pradhan et al., 2017). As Samargandi et al. (2015) mentioned, the construction of the variables to capture financial development is a difficult task. Financial services are provided by a wide range of financial institutions and agents. We consider that the Czech financial system is bank-based; therefore, we used bank-based financial proxies.

The dataset used in this chapter was obtained from the annual reports of the individual commercial banks and insurance companies. The dataset consists of 20 commercial banks and 32 commercial insurance companies in Czechia. We distinguish between the insurance companies with life and non-life insurance predomination. Therefore, the dataset consists of 20 insurance companies with the predomination of non-life insurance and 12 insurers with the predomination of life insurance. The analysis covers the period 2004–2021, and all data are collected on an unconsolidated basis.

The dependent variable is economic growth, measured as the growth rate of real GDP in Czechia. We selected several independent variables. We focus on banking sector development and insurance market development, the financial stability of the Czech banking and insurance sector and efficiency of financial institutions (commercial banks and insurance companies). Banks are the primary supplier of credit especially for households and companies. Banks also provide depositors with a safe place to keep their money, and the banking sector is also an employer. Therefore, we measure the banking sector development using bank credit to the private sector and the ratio of commercial bank assets divided by the sum of commercial bank assets and central bank assets. The insurance market development is measured by the growth rate of written premiums and density.

We measure the financial stability of banks and insurers using the summary index of financial stability. The construction of the aggregate index is detailed as described in Klepková Vodová et al. (2022). Briefly, the summary index was constructed as a weighted sum of selected indicators (performance, liquidity, solvency and asset quality). The aggregate index for insurers is constructed as a weighted sum of selected indicators, namely: profitability, liquidity, cost, technical provisions and solvency. The aggregate financial stability index is calculated for each insurance company for each year. A more detailed description of the summary index of financial stability is provided by Přečková and Palečková (2023).

The financial efficiency of banks and insurance companies is measured by the traditional Data Envelopment Analysis (DEA) model. We used the input-oriented DEA model under the assumptions of variable returns to scale. For the estimation of bank efficiency, it is necessary to define used inputs and outputs. Consistently with the intermediation approach, we assume that banks use three inputs: labour measured by total number of employees, physical capital measured by fixed assets and total deposits, and one output: total loans. In the case of efficiency of insurance companies, following Zimková (2015) we used two inputs: the total operating expenses and capital and two outputs: gross premium written and profit after tax.

For empirical analysis we use the Granger causality test. The Granger (1969 and 1980) causality test is based on the following idea: If the predictability of a time series can be improved by the incorporation of a second time series, it can be stated that the second time series has a causal effect on the first one. The process of the Granger causality test essentially consists of estimating a bivariate linear model, determining the optimal lag length, and testing the significance of the lags of the exogenous variable(s).

However, this test ignores the possibility that the strength/direction/existence of the Granger causality could vary over different frequencies as mentioned by Lemmens et al. (2008), and in the case of nonstationary variables, it is necessary to take the differences to make them stationary which causes the loss of long-run information (Bozoklu & Yilanci, 2013). Dolado and Lütkepohl (1996) and Bozoklu and Yilanci (2013) suggested using the vector autoregressive model (VAR) with one lag to eliminate the need for pretesting the unit root characteristics of the variables and also to avoid taking the differences of the nonstationary variables.

16.4 Empirical Analysis and Results

First, we tested the stationarity of data using the Augmented Dickey Fuller (ADF) test for unit roots. We transformed data using differencing to stationarity time series data. We employed the VAR model and used the Granger causality test to estimate how banks and insurance companies contribute to the economic growth.

We tested how the development of the banking sector, banking stability and banking efficiency affected economic growth. The results of the impact of the banking sector on economic growth are presented in Table 16.1. We found that banking efficiency contributed to economic growth in Czechia during the period 2004–2021. This result is in line with our estimation because the efficient banking sector contributes to an efficient economy and therefore to economic growth. Belke et al. (2016) concluded that more efficient banks promote growth in EU countries. The authors found that this relationship held even during the recent financial crisis suggesting that bank efficiency also improves a region's resilience to adverse economic shocks. The analysed period in this chapter included the financial crisis as well as the crisis connected with the pandemic COVID-19.

Table 16.1. The Relationship Between Banking Sector Development and Economic Growth.

Banking Sector			
	Chi-sq	**df**	**Prob.**
Efficiency to GDP growth	5.320190	2	0.0699
Assets to GDP growth	6.227992	2	0.0444
Financial stability to GDP growth	0.849479	2	0.6539
Credit to GDP growth	2.504158	2	0.2859
GDP growth to financial stability	6.505130	2	0.0387
GDP growth to efficiency	3.342890	2	0.1880
GDP growth to credit	11.19107	2	0.0037
GDP growth to assets	11.19107	2	0.0037

Source: Authors' Calculation.

Moreover, we found that banking development (proxied by the ratio of commercial bank assets to the sum of commercial bank assets and central bank assets) influenced economic growth. The assets of commercial banks are an important factor for the efficiency and performance of GDP. A strong financial sector with a high share of bank assets can have a positive impact on the economy, as banks provide a significant source of loans for businesses and consumers. The efficiency of the banking sector also has a positive impact on the overall productivity of the economy when financial resources are allocated to different areas of the economy. On the other hand, high concentration in the banking sector and associated risky activities can represent a risk to the stability of the economy, leading to regulation and supervision by central banks and other financial institutions. Therefore, we can confirm that banks play an important role in economic growth and banks support economic growth in Czechia.

On the other hand, we do not confirm the influence of banking sector stability on economic growth in Czechia. We confirm only that economic growth supports the banking sector's financial stability. This is an interesting finding because in the economic theory, economic growth is connected with the stability of the economy.

Using the Granger causality test, we estimate the contribution of financial stability and efficiency of insurance companies to the evolution of the insurance market (Table 16.2). Controlling for two lags, we found that the efficiency of the insurance market affects economic development. Additionally, we also found that economic growth affects the efficiency of the insurance market. We found that insurance development, as measured by written premiums and density, contributed to economic growth. The efficiency of the insurance market affected economic development. These findings confirm the results of some authors, for example, Webb et al. (2002) or Bayar et al. (2021). Based on causality tests, Bayar et al. (2021) found unidirectional causality leading from economic growth to both

Table 16.2. The Relationship Between Insurance Sector Development and Economic Growth.

	Chi-sq	df	Prob.
Whole Insurance Market			
Density to GDP growth	7.139120	2	0.0282
Premium written total to GDP growth	5.680386	2	0.0584
Efficiency to GDP growth	5.560876	2	0.0620
Financial stability to GDP growth	4.270431	2	0.1182
GDP growth to density	5.694765	2	0.0580
GDP growth to financial stability	7.711599	2	0.0212
GDP growth to premium written total	1.884279	2	0.3898
Life Insurance (LI) Market			
Density LI to GDP growth	4.105758	2	0.1284
Premium written LI to GDP growth	4.117051	2	0.1276
Financial stability LI to GDP growth	2.721048	2	0.2565
GDP growth to premium written LI	4.747879	2	0.0931
GDP growth to financial stability LI	4.855376	2	0.0882
Non-Life Insurance (NLI) Market			
Financial stability NLI to GDP growth	4.094061	1	0.0430
Density NLI to GDP growth	7.139120	2	0.0282
GDP growth to premium written NLI	1.210751	2	0.5459
GDP growth to financial stability NLI	9.572849	2	0.0083
GDP growth to density NLI	7.139120	2	0.0282

Source: Authors' Calculation.

life and non-life insurance and conclude that economic growth is positively related to both life and non-life insurance. However, the conclusions of the studies also point out from a general perspective that the correlation between insurance market development and a country's economic level is determined by the environment of a particular country. These conclusions were reached by the authors Skalská (2018) and Peleckienė et al. (2019). Peleckienė et al. (2019) investigated the relationship between insurance and economic growth in the countries of the EU. According to their results, the development of the insurance industry is higher in economically rich countries in Europe and that as the economy of a country grows, the insurance industry grows as well. In Czechia, the relationship between insurance development and economic growth was found to be low.

In our research, we distinguish between insurance companies with a predominance of non-life insurance and insurance companies with a predominance of life insurance. The reason for this separation is the specific characteristics of the insurance risks. The results on the impact of life and non-life insurance in Czechia differ. Skalská (2018) reached a similar conclusion, whose research provides new evidence that it is appropriate to analyse separately the different parts of the insurance market and focus on each of them. That is, to examine selected life and non-life insurance products separately. Our findings are different for the life and non-life insurance companies examined. In the case of life insurance, we find that the development of the insurance market and the financial stability of the life insurance market are not affected by economic growth. We only found the opposite effect; we found that economic growth affects financial stability. The development and current state of life insurance in Czechia cannot be overlooked. The life insurance market is less developed compared to the non-life insurance market, but also compared to other European countries. Interest in life insurance is still declining due to low interest rates. As Kábrt (2016) points out, if financial markets do not offer the possibility of profitable appreciation of funds, the public interest in investment life insurance decreases and clients seek appreciation in alternative assets. Another factor hindering the upward development of demand for life insurance is the unattractive tax advantage in the form of a low deductible item from the personal income tax base. As life insurance is not sufficiently developed in Czechia, it can be concluded that life insurance does not have an impact on economic growth.

As regards non-life insurance, the Granger causality test confirmed that financial stability affects economic growth. Furthermore, we found that the development of the non-life insurance market contributed to economic growth, which is also confirmed by Bayar et al. (2021) on this relationship in Central and Eastern European countries. On the contrary, we found that economic growth influenced the premiums written and financial stability of the insurance market and non-life insurers in Czechia.

16.5 Conclusion

This chapter has demonstrated the significant roles that the banking and insurance sectors played in contributing to the economic growth of Czechia between 2004 and 2021, even during periods of financial and health crises. Our findings indicate that the development of the banking sector, represented by bank credits to the private sector and the ratio of commercial bank assets to total banking assets, has positively impacted economic growth. Importantly, banking efficiency emerged as a significant factor in this economic progress, highlighting its critical role in the country's financial landscape.

While the study did not reveal a direct impact of banking stability on economic growth, it became evident that economic conditions do, in fact, influence banking stability. This underscores the interconnectedness of the economy and the banking sector.

In terms of insurance, our assessment based on written premiums and density revealed that the financial stability and efficiency of insurance companies are vital for the sector's development. Intriguingly, a reciprocal relationship was discovered between the efficiency of the insurance market and economic growth. The development of the insurance sector, thus, has been found to contribute to economic growth, further emphasising the importance of efficiency in the market. Overall, these results provide valuable insights for policymakers, pointing to the crucial roles of efficiency in the banking and insurance sectors for the economic growth of Czechia.

References

Adams, M., Andersson, J., Andersson, L. F., & Lindmark, M. (2009). Commercial banking, insurance and economic growth in Sweden between 1830 and 1938. *Accounting Business and Financial History*, *19*(1), 21–38.

Al-Khalifah, A. (2018). The strategic stabilization of private banks and insurance company in the financial service sector. *Journal of Humanities Insights*, *2*(04), 161–166.

Ang, J. B., & McKibbin, W. J. (2007). Financial liberalization, financial sector development and growth: Evidence from Malaysia. *Journal of Development Economics*, *84*(1), 215–233.

Balcilar, M., Gupta, R., Lee, C. C., & Olasehinde-Williams, G. (2018). The synergistic effect of insurance and banking sector activities on economic growth in Africa. *Economic Systems*, *42*(4), 637–648. https://doi.org/10.1016/j.ecosys.2018.08.002

Bayar, Y., Gavriletea, M. D., & Danuletiu, D. C. (2021). Does the insurance sector really matter for economic growth? Evidence from Central and Eastern European countries. *Journal of Business Economics and Management*, *22*(3), 695–713. https://doi.org/10.3846/jbem.2021.14287

Belke, A., Haskamp, U., & Setzer, R. (2016). *Bank efficiency and regional growth in Europe: new evidence from micro-data*. Working paper series. European Central Bank. https://www.ecb.europa.eu/pub/pdf/scpwps/ecbwp1983.en.pdf

Bozoklu, S., & Yilanci, V. (2013). Energy consumption and economic growth for selected OECD countries: Further evidence from the Granger causality test in the frequency domain. *Energy Policy*, *63*, 877–881. https://doi.org/10.1016/j.enpol.2013.09.037

Cave, J., Chaudhuri, K., & Kumbhakar, S. C. (2020). Do banking sector and stock market development matter for economic growth? *Empirical Economics*, 1–23. https://doi.org/10.1007/s00181-019-01692-7

Černohorský, J. (2017). Types of bank loans and their impact on economic development: A case study of the Czech Republic. *E & M*, *20*(4), 34–48. https//doi.org/10.15240/tul/001/2017-4-003

Creel, J., Hubert, P., & Labondance, F. (2015). Financial stability and economic performance. *Economic Modelling*, *48*, 25–40. https://doi.org/10.1016/j.econmod.2014.10.025

Dash, S., Pradhan, R. P., Maradana, R. P., Gaurav, K., Zaki, D. B., & Jayakumar, M. (2018). Insurance market penetration and economic growth in Eurozone countries: Time series evidence on causality. *Future Business Journal*, *4*(1), 50–67.

De Gregorio, J., & Guidotti, P. (1995). Financial development and conomic Growth. *World Development*, *23*(3), 433–448. https://doi.org/10.1016/0305-750X(94)00132-I

Dell'Ariccia, G., Detragiache, E., & Rajan, R. (2008). The real effect of banking crises. *Journal of Financial Intermediation*, *17*(1), 89–112. https://doi.org/10.1016/j.jfi.2007.06.001

Diallo, B. (2018). Bank efficiency and industry growth during financial crises. *Economic Modelling*, *68*, 11–22. https://doi.org/10.1016/j.econmod.2017.03.011

Dicevska, S., Karadjova, V., & Jolevski, L. (2018). Advantages and disadvantages of cooperation between banks and insurance companies. In *Conference Proceedings: 2nd International Scientific Conference ITEMA 2018*. http://eprints.uklo.edu.mk/id/eprint/1533

Dolado, J. J., & Lütkepohl, H. (1996). Making Wald tests work for cointegrated VAR systems. *Econometric Reviews*, *15*, 369–386.

Ductor, L., & Grechyna, D. (2015). Financial development, real sector, and economic growth. *International Review of Economics & Finance*, *37*, 393–405. https://doi.org/10.1016/j.iref.2015.01.001

Duramany-Lakkoh, E. K., Jalloh, M. S., & Jalloh, A. (2022). An Empirical Examination of the Impact of Banks on Economic Growth in Sierra Leone (2001–2017). *Journal of Financial Risk Management*, *11*(2), 258–276. https//doi.org/10.4236/jfrm.2022.112013

Goldsmith, R. (1969). *Financial structure and development*. Yale University Press.

Haini, H. (2020). Examining the relationship between finance, institutions and economic growth: Evidence from the ASEAN economies. *Economic Change and Restructuring*, *53*(4), 519–542. https://doi.org/10.1007/s10644-019-09257-5

Haiss, P., & Sümegi, K. (2008). The relationship between insurance and economic growth in Europe: A theoretical and empirical analysis. *Empirica*, *35*, 405–431. https//doi.org/10.1007/s10663-008-9075-2

Hoggarth, G., Reis, R., & Saporta, V. (2002). Costs of banking system instability: Some empirical evidence. *Journal of Banking & Finance*, *26*(5), 825–855. https://doi.org/10.1016/S0378-4266(01)00268-0

Hou, H., & Cheng, S.-Y. (2017). The dynamic effects of banking, life insurance, and stock markets on economic growth. *Japan and the World Economy*, *41*, 87–98. https://doi.org/10.1016/j.japwor.2017.02.001

Ibáñez-Hernández, F. J., Peña-Cerezoa, M. Á., & Araujo, A. (2015). Countercyclical capital buffers: Credit-to-GDP ratio versus credit growth. *Applied Economics Letters*, *22*(5), 385–390. https//doi.org/10.1080/13504851.2014.946174

Ijaz, S., Hassan, A., Tarazi, A., & Fraz, A. (2020). Linking bank competition, financial stability, and economic growth. *Journal of Business Economics and Management*, *21*(1), 200–221. https://doi.org/10.3846/jbem.2020.11761

Jokipii, T., & Monnin, P. (2013). The impact of banking sector stability on the real economy. *Journal of International Money and Finance*, *32*, 1–16. https://doi.org/10.1016/j.jimonfin.2012.02.008

Kábrt, T. (2016). Analýza vlivu makroekonomických veličin na předepsané pojistné u životního pojištění v České republice, Německu a Spojených státech amerických. *Český finanční a účetní časopis*, *11*(2), 49–72.

King, R. G., & Levine, R. (1993). Finance and growth: Schumpeter might be right. *The Quarterly Journal of Economics*, *108*(3), 717–737. https://doi.org/10.2307/2118406

Klepková Vodová, P., Palečková, I., & Stavárek, D. (2022). *Banking stability and financial conglomerates in European emerging countries*. Elements in the Economics of Emerging Markets. Cambridge University Press. https//doi.org/10.1017/9781009092166

Lemmens, A., Croux, C., & Dekimpe, M. G. (2008). Measuring and testing granger causality over the spectrum: An application to European production expectation surveys. *International Journal of Forecasting*, *24*, 414–431.

Levine, R. (1997). Financial development and economic growth: Views and agenda. *Journal of Economic Literature*, *35*(2), 688–726.

Morck, R., & Nakamura, M. (1999). Banks and corporate control in Japan. *The Journal of Finance*, *54*(1), 319–339. https//doi.org/10.1111/0022-1082.00106

Niavand, H., & Mahesh, R. (2018). The role of insurance development in financial and economic growth in Iran. *International Journal of Management Studies*, *3*(3), 133–136. https://doi.org/10.2139/ssrn.3436958

Njegomir, V., & Stojić, D. (2010). Does insurance promote economic growth: The evidence from ex-Yugoslavia region. *Ekonomska misao i praksa*, *19*(1), 31–48. https://hrcak.srce.hr/54655

Oke, M. O. (2012). Insurance sector development and economic growth in Nigeria. *African Journal of Business Management*, *6*(23), 7016–7023. https//doi.org/10.5897/AJBM11.2853

Peleckienė, V., Peleckis, K., Dudzevičiūtė, G., & Peleckis, K. (2019). The relationship between insurance and economic growth: Evidence from the European Union countries. *Economic research-Ekonomska Istraživanja*, *32*(1), 1138–1151. https://doi.org/10.1080/1331677X.2019.1588765

Petkovski, M., & Kjosevski, J. (2014). Does banking sector development promote economic growth? An empirical analysis for selected countries in Central and South Eastern Europe. *Economic Research-Ekonomska Istraživanja*, *27*(1), 55–66. https//doi.org/10.1080/1331677X.2014.947107

Pradhan, R. P., Arvin, M. B., Nair, M., & Bennett, S. E. (2020). Unveiling the causal relationships among banking competition, stock and insurance market development, and economic growth in Europe. *Structural Change and Economic Dynamics*, *55*(2020), 74–87. https://doi.org/10.1016/j.strueco.2020.08.006

Pradhan, R. P., Arvin, M. B., Nair, M., Hall, J. H., & Gupta, A. (2017). Is there a link between economic growth and insurance and banking sector activities in the G-20 countries? *Review of Financial Economics*, *33*, 12–28. https://doi.org/10.1016/j.rfe.2017.02.002

Přečková, L., & Palečková, I. (2023). Financial stability of the Czech insurance companies. *Ekonomický časopis*, *71*(1), 65–86. https://doi.org/10.31577/ekoncas.2023.01.04

Ruiz, J. L. (2018). Financial development, institutional investors, and economic growth. *International Review of Economics & Finance*, *54*, 218–224. https://doi.org/10.1016/j.iref.2017.08.009

Rushchyshyn, N., Mulska, O., Vasyltsiv, T., Nikolchuk, Y., & Rushchyshyn, M. (2021). The impact of banking sector development on economic growth: Comparative analysis of Ukraine and some EU countries. *Investment Management and Financial Innovations*, *18*(2), 193–208. https//doi.org/10.21511/imfi.18(2).2021.16

Samargandi, N., Fidrmuc, J., & Ghosh, S. (2015). Is the relationship between financial development and economic growth monotonic? Evidence from a sample of middle-income countries. *World Development*, *68*, 66–81. https://doi.org/10.1016/j.worlddev.2014.11.010

Saqib, N. (2016). Banking sector liberalization and economic growth: Case study of Pakistan. *Journal of Business Economics and Management*, *17*(1), 125–139. https// doi.org/10.3846/16111699.2013.804874

Schumpeter, J. A. (1911). *The theory of economic development*. Harvard University Press.

Skalská, M. (2018). The relationship between insurance development and economic growth: The motor third party liability insurance in the Czech Republic in years 2000–2017 in relation to macroeconomic determinants in the Czech Republic. In *The 12th International Days of Statistics and Economics: Conference Proceedings*. Melandrium.

Szewieczek, D. (2013). The risk of cooperation between banks and insurance companies. *Studia Ekonomiczne*, *127*, 137–151. https://cejsh.icm.edu.pl/cejsh/element/bwmeta1.element.desklight-c2214452-e4c5-4c9e-84aa-2d69295092fb?q=bwmeta1.element.desklight-d2119aac-5aa9-4617-b377-0d9b5bf5cb97;8&qt=CHILDREN-STATELESS

Takáts, E., & Upper, C. (2013). *Credit and growth after financial crises*. BIS Working Paper No 416. Bank for International Settlements.

Ul Din, S. M., Abu-Bakar, A., & Regupathi, A. (2017). Does insurance promote economic growth: A comparative study of developed and emerging/developing economies. *Cogent Economics & Finance*, *5*(1), 1–12. https://doi.org/10.1080/23322039.2017.1390029

Wang, S., Chen, L., & Xiong, X. (2019). Asset bubbles, banking stability, and economic growth. *Economic Modelling*, *78*, 108–117. https://doi.org/10.1016/j.econmod.2018.08.014

Webb, I., Grace, M. F., & Skipper, H. D. (2002). *The effect of banking and insurance on the growth of capital and output* (Vol. 1). Working Paper No 02. Centre for Risk Management and Insurance.

Zimková, E. (2015). Technical efficiency and super-efficiency of the insurance sector in Slovakia. *Acta Universitatis Agriculturae et Silviculturae Mendelianae Brunensis*, *63*(6), 2205–2211. https://doi.org/10.11118/actaun201563062205

Chapter 17

The Information and Communication Technology Sector in Czechia and Its Contribution to Innovation and Economic Growth

Dennis Nchor

Mendel University in Brno, Czechia

Abstract

The growing use of internet communication technology has led to increased economic growth across the world, and this chapter seeks to assess the case of Czechia. The study also examines the changing employment distribution in the labour market with the growing influence of information and communication technology (ICT). The multiple indicators and multiple causes model as well as changes in employment or earnings shares of occupations are used for the analysis. The findings show that increased use of ICT contributes to growth in GDP and employment. It also shows that ICT has contributed to rising labour and factor productivity through increased innovation. There is also increased demand for highly educated labour leading to growth in employment in high skill occupations, while the share of low and middle skill occupations declines. The situation, however, does not indicate job polarisation in the labour market and total employment is still increasing. The study also finds that investment and use of ICT has led to progressive development in the human development index of the Czech Republic and a decline in the gender inequality index.

Keywords: Economic growth; ICT; job polarisation; human development; labour productivity; digitalisation

Modeling Economic Growth in Contemporary Czechia, 265–279

Published under exclusive licence by Emerald Publishing Limited
doi:10.1108/978-1-83753-840-920241017

17.1 Introduction

Investment and development in information and communication technology (ICT) has increased over the years around the world (Akande et al., 2019). Czechia has the third highest ICT investment as a share of gross domestic product (GDP) (3.96%) among the organisation for economic cooperation and development (OECD) countries (OECD, 2023). The high investment in ICT and progressive development has brought increased competition in markets. It has also provided strong incentives for replacing some capital and labour (Jorgenson, 2001). There has been a paradigm shift in production processes with the spread of ICT such as fixed telephone subscriptions, the internet and broadband subscriptions (EUROSTAT, 2020). There has also been an increase in the efficiency of resource allocation, a decrease in production costs and increased demand across economic sectors due to increased adoption of ICT (Grimes et al., 2012; Jorgenson & Stiroh, 2000; Pradhan et al., 2016; Vu et al., 2020). As at the end of 2020, the value added by the ICT sector in the European Union (EU) was estimated to be 5.2% of GDP (EUROSTAT, 2020).

There is a vast amount of literature on the linkage between development in the ICT sector and economic growth of countries; however, the empirical evidence provided is mixed and conflicting. Some studies have provided positive linkage (Cheng et al., 2021; Inklaar et al., 2003; Ishida, 2015; Venturini, 2009), whereas others found ambiguous or even negative linkage (Dewan & Kraemer, 2000; Yousefi, 2011). This chapter aims to contribute to this important academic discourse with emphasis on Czechia. Most literature has limited the impact of ICT to only economic growth (Kurniawati, 2020; Pradhan et al., 2019; Remeikienė et al., 2022). This chapter, however, apart from studying the impact on economic growth also measured the impact from the perspective of human development and gender equality. The use of the combination of indicators to measure the impact of ICT makes it more robust in that, the human development index (HDI) combines data for life expectancy, adult literacy and GDP per capita whereas the gender inequality index (GII) measures inequality between men and women.

There are two main motivations for this chapter. First, Czechia is a country with high potential for ICT diffusion; however, research examining the contributions of ICT to economic growth has provided rather mixed results and most research focused on the narrow scope of economic growth. Second, the adoption of ICT in the workplace has changed the demand for labour in the performance of tasks and this has led to rising fears of technologically induced unemployment and job polarisation where employment growth is concentrated in low and high skill occupations, whereas jobs in the middle of the skill distribution are diminished (Goos & Manning, 2007; Nchor & Rozmahel, 2020). The goal of this study is therefore twofold. First, to assess the impact of ICT on economic growth, human development and gender equality. Second, to examine the changing employment distribution in the labour market with growth in ICT use.

17.2 Literature Review

The world has progressed tremendously in its investment and use of ICT. Economic growth and globalisation have largely been propelled by the development of new and advanced technology. Prior theories have recognised the increasing role of ICT in economic growth within countries. For example, Solow (1956) argued in favour of ICT regarding its contribution to economic growth. According to this theory, ICT influences growth in the form of capital and transforms production processes. It also contributes to increased value addition resulting in increased productivity and economic growth (Aghaei & Rezagholizadeh, 2017). The benefit of ICT is that it makes it easier for the exchange of information. Its presence has led to a huge paradigm shift in human development in several areas in that, it has helped to expand the range of choices for consumers (Yakunina & Bychkov, 2015).

The impact of ICT has been viewed in two different ways: direct and indirect. The direct connection is through improved productivity and efficiency in production processes such as observed in the original works of Solow (1956). The indirect impact on growth occurs through improved processes of revenue generation, increased employment opportunities and reduced transactions cost (see Dewan & Kraemer, 2000; Haftu, 2019). This chapter measures ICT following the approaches of Donou-Adonsou et al. (2016) as well as Asongu and Odhiambo (2020). It considers other factors contributing to the economic growth of countries which include the labour force participation (LFP) rate in official activities, capital, trade openness (TO), foreign direct investment (FDI) and financial development (FD) following the approaches of Chien et al. (2020).

Some studies have considered a causality analysis between ICT and economic growth. The results have been mixed so far. Whereas some found unidirectional Granger causality from increased ICT use to economic growth (see Koutroumpis et al., 2020; Shahiduzzaman & Alam, 2014), other studies have reported unidirectional Granger causality from economic growth to ICT (see Beil et al., 2005). Studies that found bidirectional relationships include Pradhan et al., 2014), as well as Kumar et al. (2016). Results have also shown that ICT's impact on economic growth depends on the proxies of ICT. Vu et al. (2020) argue that ICT – economic growth linkage is an established one and studies should now be focused on explaining how ICT directly or indirectly affects economic growth.

17.3 Methodology and Data

The analysis applies the multiple indicators and multiple causes (MIMIC) model as well as changes in employment shares. The MIMIC model is used to fulfil the first goal, whereas analysis of changing employment and earnings shares are used to achieve the second goal. The data for the MIMIC model is obtained from the World Bank's world development indicators and the United Nations Development Program covering the period 1990–2021. I checked the time series properties of the dataset. First, the degree of integration using the Augmented Dickey–Fuller (Dickey & Fuller, 1979) unit root test. Second, cointegration using the Johansen test of cointegration (Johansen, 1988). I considered three indicators as the impact of ICT namely, economic growth, the HDI and the GII. The use of a combination of indicators makes it more robust. The HDI combines data for life expectancy, adult literacy and GDP per capita to produce a measure from zero to one. Scores closer to one indicate higher levels of development. The GII is a measure comparing the impact of development on women and men. It varies between 0 and 1. A value of zero implies women and men fare equally and vice versa. Economic growth is measured using annual growth in GDP.

This chapter considered a set of independent variables including LFP rate, gross fixed capital formation (GFF), TO, FD, FDI and ICT following the approach of Meta (2020). ICT is subdivided into three variables namely, fixed broadband subscriptions per 100 inhabitants, fixed telephone lines per 100 inhabitants and internet users as a percentage of the population. I used LFP rate to proxy labour participation in official production, GFF is used to measure capital, FD is measured using the percentage of credit from financial institutions to the private sector, FDI is measured using the percentage of net foreign direct inflows. TO is measured using the ratio of the sum of imports and exports to GDP. First order differences were taken for all non-stationary variables. The MIMIC model, which is a variant of the structural equation model (SEM), is used due to its ability to model multiple dependent variables. An SEM has two components namely, the structural equation part and the measurement part. The structural equation part measures the relationship between a set of causal variables, in this case the independent variables with the latent variable. The measurement part covers the relationship between the latent variable and the three indicators. Eq. (17.1) shows the structural equation part of the MIMIC model.

$$\eta_i = \alpha_i + \beta X_i + \varepsilon_i \tag{17.1}$$

where η_i is a vector of latent endogenous variables, α_i is a vector of intercept terms, β is the matrix of coefficients of the independent variables X_i and ε_i is the vector of error terms. The subscript i is the ith case in the sample. I assume that $E(\varepsilon_i) = 0$, $\mathrm{COV}(\widehat{X}'_i, \varepsilon_i) = 0$. Eq. (17.2) shows the measurement part of the MIMIC model.

$$y_i = \gamma + \rho_1 \eta_i + \omega_i \tag{17.2}$$

where η_i is a vector of the observed causes of y_i, γ is an intercept vector, ρ_1 is a matrix of regression coefficients giving the impact of η_i on y_i and ω_i is vector of error terms with expected values of zero, covariance matrices of $\Sigma_{\omega\omega}$ uncorrelated with each other and with ε_i. The parameters of the model are analysed in a vector, θ. If a model is correctly specified, then the following mean (μ) and covariance (Σ) is observed (Eqs. 17.3 and 17.4)

$$\mu = \mu(\theta) \tag{17.3}$$

and

$$\Sigma = \Sigma(\theta) \tag{17.4}$$

There are a number of estimators of the SEM, but the most preferred is the maximum likelihood (ML) estimator which I employed. The ML equation in SEMs is given in Eq. (17.5).

$$F_{\mathrm{ML}} = \ln|\boldsymbol{\Sigma}(\boldsymbol{\theta})| - \ln|M| + \mathrm{tr}[[\Sigma^{-1}(\theta)M]] - H_z \tag{17.5}$$

M represents the sample covariance matrix, $\overline{Z}$ is the sample means vector of the observed variables, H_z is the number of observed variables, ln represents natural log, |.| depicts a matrix determinant and the trace of a matrix is represented by tr. $\widehat{\theta}$ is chosen as the ML estimator to minimise F_{ML}. $\widehat{\theta}$ is consistent, unbiased, efficient and normally distributed asymptotically.

Regarding the second research question, I applied changes in employment shares of ISCO08 occupations to assess the changing employment distribution in the labour market in Czechia following the approach of Goos and Manning (2007). The source of the data is the harmonised individual European Union Labour Force Survey (ELFS). The data are annual and cover the period from 1997 to 2021. It is measured in thousands of people. The classification of occupations into skill groups is done according to the international standard classification of occupations (ISCO-08) by the International Labour Organization (ILO, 2022) and according to the approach of Acemoglu and Autor (2011) based on two main concepts namely the nature of work performed and the concept of skill. Occupations in this classification include managers, professionals, technicians and associate professionals, clerical support workers, services and sales workers, skilled agriculture, fishery and forestry, craft and other trade related activities, plant and machine operators, the armed forces and elementary occupations. According to this classification, low skill occupations consist of all elementary occupations. Middle skill occupations include clerical support workers, services and sales workers, skilled agriculture, fishery and forestry, craft and other trade related activities, plant and machine operators as well as the armed forces. High skill occupations include managers, professionals as well as technicians and associate professionals. Employment shares are calculated as the total employment within an occupation as a ratio of total employment in the country. An observation of a u-shaped employment distribution indicates job polarisation. The results are discussed in the subsequent chapter.

17.4 The Contribution of ICT Sector in Czechia to Innovation and Economic Growth – Empirical Results

This section interprets and discusses the results. Results are displayed in the form of graphs and tables. Fig. 17.1 shows the development in the internet variables over the years in Czechia. It is observed that fixed broadband subscriptions per 100 people, cellular phone subscriptions per 100 people and internet use have been rising over the years. Fixed telephone subscriptions per 100 people are, however, declining largely because of the rise in the use of mobile phones.

Fig. 17.2 shows the trend in ICT as a percentage of GDP and the percentage of ICT personnel in total employment. It also shows development in the HDI, GII

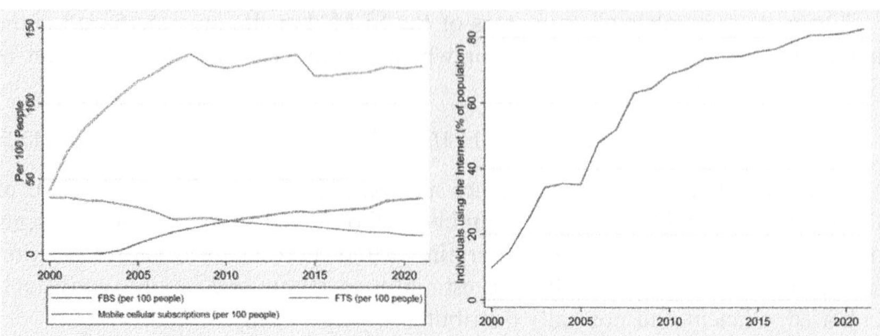

Fig. 17.1. ICT Use in Czechia. *Source:* Author's Own Work Using Data from the World Development Indicators and Eurostat. *Note:* FBS per 100 people represents fixed broadband subscriptions per 100 inhabitants, FTS per 100 people represents fixed telephone subscriptions per 100 people.

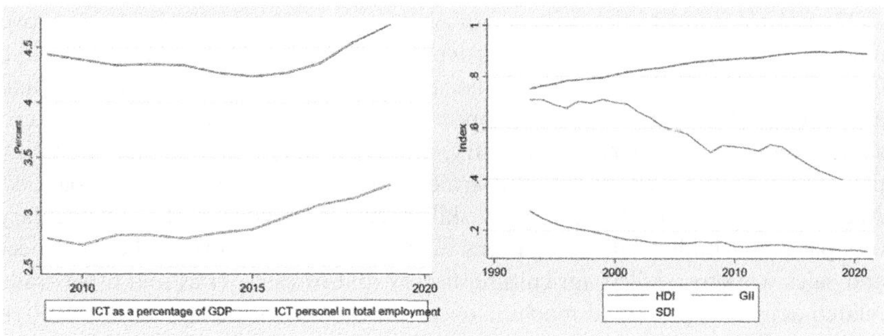

Fig. 17.2. Indicators of ICT Sector Development. *Source:* Author's Own Work Using Data from Eurostat and The United Nation's Development Program.

and sustainable development index (SDI) over the years. It is observed that the contribution of ICT to GDP in Czechia has been rising and so is the share of employment of ICT personnel in total employment. Also, the HDI in Czechia is rising, whereas the GII declines, thus showing cases of progressive development. The SDI, however, is declining given concerns of development not being sustainable and this can be attributed to the fact that only a few firms in Czechia take into consideration the impact of ICT equipment on the environment when procuring such services.

Fig. 17.3 shows the developments in labour and factor productivity over the years. Labour productivity is an important economic indicator closely linked to

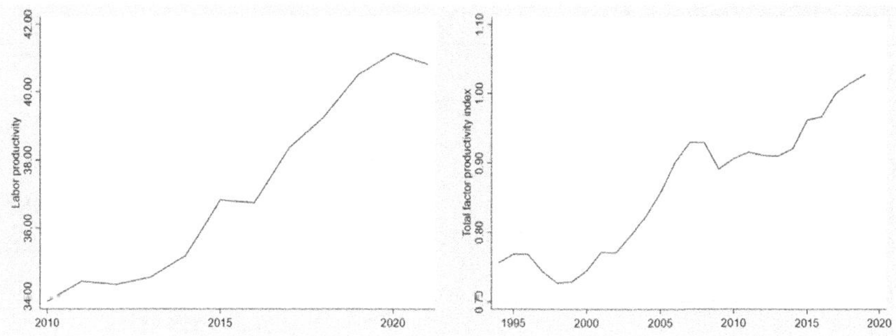

Fig. 17.3. Labour and Total Factor Productivity. *Source:* Author's Own Work Using Data from Eurostat.

economic growth. It provides information about the efficiency and quality of human capital in the production process. Both have been rising over the years. This implies that Czechia produces more goods and services using the same or less amount of work as compared with previous efforts. The increase in output also has a significant positive effect in lowering the prices of consumer goods and services.

Table 17.1 shows the results of the MIMIC model. LFP rate, GFF, TO, FD, FDI and ICT variables are statistically significant showing that they impact on

Table 17.1. The MIMIC Model.

Variable	Coefficient
Structural	
L1	
Labour force participation rate	0.01445*** (0.0021023)
Trade openness	0.009866*** (0.001561)
Gross fixed capital formation	0.006351*** (0.0011655)
Fixed broadband subscriptions per 100 inhabitants	0.013 *** (0.0013054)
Fixed telephone subscriptions per 100 inhabitants	0.0146 *** (0.000927)
Financial development	−0.0024*** (0.0003005)
Foreign direct investment	0.001325** (0.0005638)
Internet use	0.001095*** (0.0003173)
Measurement	
HDI	
L1	1(constrained)

Table 17.1. *(Continued)*

Variable	Coefficient
Constant	0.832966*** (0.0034979)
GII	
L1	−0.89961*** (0.0694982)
Constant	0.177186*** (0.0029748)
Economic Growth	
L1	0.7645327*** (0.06114372)
Constant	0.13139

Source: Author's Own Calculations.

*** depicts statistical significance at 1% level. Standard errors are in brackets. Significant regression coefficients have * by them.

economic growth, human development and gender equality. The measurement part of the model shows that the three indicator variables are also statistically significant and 93% of the model is explained by the observed variables. Regression results are produced after a series of iterations when convergence is achieved. The reliability and correct specification of the model was checked using model fit indices such as the chi square (χ^2), root mean square error of approximation (RMSEA), standardised root mean square residual (SRMR) and the comparative fit index (CFI). All the criteria were met.

Regarding the changing employment distribution in Czechia, the chapter first looks at whether total employment in Czechia is declining due to the increased role of ICT. Results in Fig. 17.4 show otherwise as total employment has been increasing over the years except for 2020 where it dipped largely due to the coronavirus pandemic. I also looked at whether firms and companies take into consideration the impact of procured ICT equipment on the environment. The results show that only 60% of firms in Czechia do so.

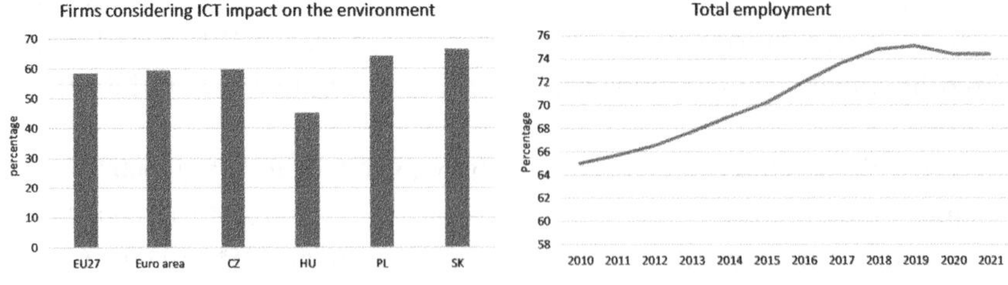

Fig. 17.4. Total Unemployment in Czechia. *Source:* Author's Own Work Using Data from Eurostat. *Note:* Where EU (European Union), CZ (Czechia), PL (Poland), HU (Hungary), SK (Slovakia).

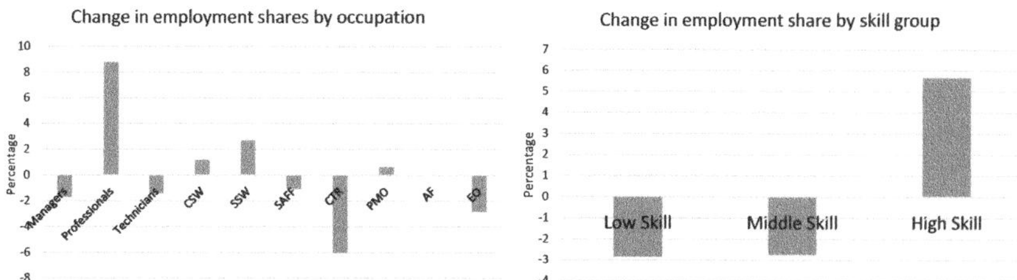

Fig. 17.5. Changes in Employment Shares of Occupations. *Source:* Author's Own Work Using Data from Eurostat.

We proceeded to examine changes in employment shares of occupations over the years. Fig. 17.5 shows the results. It is observed that the share of employment of professionals, clerical support workers, services and sales workers as well as plant and machine operators increased, whereas the share of employment of managers, technicians and associate professionals, skilled agriculture, fishery and forestry, armed forces and elementary occupations decreased. Classifying the occupations into three skill groups using the criteria of the International Labour Organization, I observed a decline in the share of employment of both low skill and middle skill employment while high skill employment increased. The employment distribution, however, does not indicate job polarisation. Growth in ICT and digitalisation might be contributing to the decline in the demand for labour in certain occupations, but the overall effect of technological displacement has not resulted in increased total unemployment. This is attributed to labour relocations within occupations and skill groups. For example, in the high skill group, the decline in the share of employment of managers and technicians is offset by the rise in the share of professionals. Similarly, in the middle skill group, the decline in the share of employment of skilled agriculture, forestry and fishery as well as craft and trade related is offset by the rise in the employment share of clerical and support workers, services and sales workers as well as plant and machine operators. There is also the possibility of education and retraining of displaced workers relocating to higher skill employment.

Fig. 17.6 shows the changes in shares of earnings of occupations and skill groups. It is observed that the share of earnings of all occupations increased

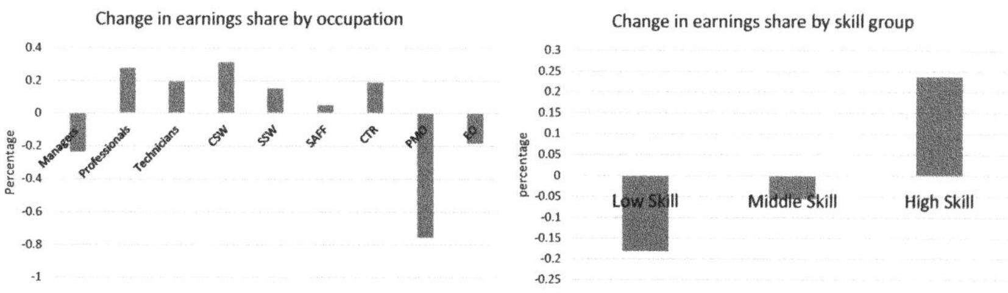

Fig. 17.6. The Changing Shares of Earnings. *Source:* Author's Own Work Using Data from Eurostat.

except for managers, plant and machine operators as well as elementary occupations which experienced declines. I observed a decline in the share of earnings of low and middle skill occupations just like in the case of employment. Though the overall share of earnings in the middle skill group declined, the respective shares of most occupations increased except in the case of plant and machine operators which experienced a decline. Thus, the decline in the share of earnings in the middle skill group is accounted for by the large impact of the decline in the share of earnings of plant and machine operators. The rise in the share of earnings of the high skill group is accounted for by a rise in the share of professionals, technicians and associate professionals. There is no clear case of a u-shaped earnings distribution to indicate job polarisation.

17.5 Discussion

We found a significant positive relationship between economic growth and ICT. All ICT variables were statistically significant. I also found that the contribution of ICT to GDP and employment has increased over the years. Labour productivity and total factor productivity also increased correspondingly. Total employment in Czechia also increased. No clear case of job polarisation was observed though the shares of employment of both low skill and middle skill groups have declined. The overall share of employment in the middle skill group declined, but occupations such as clerical and support workers, services and sales workers as well as plant and machine operators within this skill group experienced a rise in their employment shares. The overall decline in the share of employment was therefore accounted for by a decline in the share of employment of skilled agriculture, forestry and fishery as well as craft and trade-related activities. Similarly, the overall share of employment of the high skill group increased, whereas the share of employment of some occupations within this skill group declined, for example, managers, technicians and associate professionals. The rise in the employment share of the group is accounted for by the rise in the share of employment of professionals. This serves as evidence of labour relocations within occupations and skill groups thus offsetting the impact of technological displacement.

The rise in employment in the face of mass digitalisation is attributed to the job creation potential of the ICT sector. ICT creates opportunities through the generation of completely new goods and services (OECD, 2013; Evangelista & Vezzani, 2010). Enrico and Wilson (2013) argues that the job multiplier of ICT is high. The decline in the low and middle skill share of employment is explained by the de-skilling process where high-skill workers are taking up jobs normally performed by lower-skill workers thus pushing low-skill workers even further down the occupational ladder and out of the labour force. The mechanism through which ICT impacts on the economy is partly through labour productivity as found in the studies of Henry-Nickie et al. (2019) and Basl and Doucek (2012), the lessening of information asymmetry (Al Nawayseh, 2020; Asongu & Moulin, 2016; Maruta et al., 2020) and improved FD (Henderson et al., 2012). Roller and

Waverman (2001) found a positive linkage between investment in telecommunication infrastructure and economic growth. Vu (2011) argues that the introduction of personal computers, mobile phones and internet use has had an effect on economic growth. Pradhan et al. (2016) found a significant relationship between economic growth and ICT infrastructure. Other studies that find a positive association between ICT and economic growth include Gómez-Barroso and Marbán-Flores (2020). The creative-destruction proponents suggest that the growing use of ICT leads to more innovation (Basl & Doucek, 2012) which creates more opportunities that make up for the destroyed ones.

We also found that gender inequality in Czechia is declining with growing use of ICT corresponding with the findings of Valberg (2020) and Graf (2020). Gender-based discrimination occurs in several ways ranging from work, education to mention but a few and this causes profound damage to society. However, ICT is an enormous tool which creates opportunities for all entrepreneurs to compete in global markets without discrimination. It provides a level-playing field that enables all businesses, regardless of size, location or sector, to operate. It has also provided opportunities for remote work for women with family duties at home to be able to participate productively thus boosting inclusive development and reducing the gender inequality gap significantly. This helps to push towards the achievement of goal five of the sustainable development goals calling for action to promote gender parity through technology.

There could be spillover effects of ICT diffusion in the form of job polarisation; however, I conclude that changes in the employment distribution in Czechia over the past years do not show polarisation and cannot be understood as being dominated by ICT alone. Growing demand for education has also contributed significantly to the changing dynamics of the employment process. In other words, the reallocation of employment from middling to top occupations is influenced by the demand for labour with higher education. The high growth in high skill employment and the sharp decline in middle skill and low skill employment could be indicative of the gain high skill occupations have made from the decreased employment shares of the low and middle skill groups as also concluded in the studies of Davis and Haltiwanger (2014) and Atkinson et al. (2010). I note that though ICT serves as a key driver of economic growth in Czechia, its impact will further be strengthened through stronger institutions and developed human capital.

17.6 Conclusion

There is a large body of literature investigating the impact of ICTs on economic growth; however, the empirical evidence on growth has provided mixed results. We contribute to this debate by examining the case of Czechia by including the HDI and the GII. We found that all proxies for ICT show an impact on economic growth, human development and gender equality. We also found that ICT contributes to increased labour and factor productivity. Its impact on gross value added and total employment is immense. The mechanism of impact is the fact that it provides access to information and allows for collaboration globally thus creating opportunities for job creation and increased production, transfer of skills, greater efficiency and transparency. Given the percentage of firms in Czechia that take into consideration the impact of ICT equipment on the environment before procuring, we recommend action and stricter enforcement to cover all actively participating firms since the spillover effect of such procured ICT tools could spell problems in terms of sustainable development. The findings do not show a case of job polarisation in Czechia, but there is an obvious trend of increased demand for labour with higher education partly due to increased ICT use. Other factors also contribute to the labour market dynamics and the changing employment distribution cannot be solely attributed to growth in ICT.

References

Acemoglu, D., & Autor, D. H. (2011). Skills, tasks and technologies: Implications for employment and earnings. *Handbook of Labour Economics*, 1043–1171.

Aghaei, M., & Rezagholizadeh, M. (2017). The impact of information and communication technology (ICT) on economic growth in the OIC Countries. *Economic and Environmental Studies*, *17*(2 (42)), 257–278.

Akande, A., Cabral, P., & Casteleyn, S. (2019). Assessing the gap between technology and the environmental sustainability of European cities. *Information Systems Frontiers*, *21*(3), 581–604. https://doi.org/10.1007/s10796-019-09903

Al Nawayseh, M. K (2020). Fintech in COVID-19 and beyond: What factors are affecting customers choice of fintech applications? *Journal of Open Innovation: Technology Market, and Complexity*, *6*(4), 1–15.

Asongu, S. A., & Odhiambo, N. M. (2020). Foreign direct investment, information technology and economic growth dynamics in Sub-Saharan Africa. *Telecommunications Policy*, *44*(1).

Asongu, S., & Moulin, B. (2016). The role of ICT in reducing information asymmetry for financial access. *Research in International Business and Finance*, *38*(C), 202–213.

Atkinson, A. B., Piketty, T., & Saez, E. (2010). Top incomes in the long run of history. *Journal of Economic Literature*, *49*(1), 3–71.

Basl, J., & Doucek, P. (2012). ICT and innovations in context of sustainable development. In *IDIMT-2013 information technology human values, innovation and economy* (pp. 87–96). Trauner Verlag.

Beil, R., Ford, G., & Jackson, J. (2005). On the relationship between telecommunications investment and economic growth in the United States. *International Economic Journal*, *19*(1), 3–9.

Cheng, C.-Y., Chien, M.-S., & Lee, C.-C. (2021). ICT diffusion, financial development, and economic growth: An international cross-country analysis. *Economic Modelling*, *94*, 662–671. https://doi.org/10.1016/j.econmod.2020.02.008

Chien, M., Cheng, C., & Kurniawati, M. A. (2020). The non-linear relationship between ICT diffusion and financial development. *Telecommunications Policy*, *44*(9). https://ideas.repec.org/a/eee/telpol/v44y2020i9s0308596120301154.html

Davis, S. J., & Haltiwanger, J. (2014). *Labour market fluidity and economic performance NBER Working Paper No. 20479*. National Bureau of Economic Research.

Dewan, S., & Kraemer, K. L. (2000). Information technology and productivity: Evidence from country-level data. *Management Science*, *46*(4), 548–562. https://ideas.repec.org/a/inm/ormnsc/v46y2000i4p548-562.html

Dickey, D. A., & Fuller, W. A. (1979). Distribution of the estimators for autoregressive time series with a unit root. *Journal of the American Statistical Association*, *74*, 427–431. https://doi.org/10.2307/2286348

Donou-Adonsou, F., Lim, S., & Mathey, S. A. (2016). Technological progress and economic growth in Sub-Saharan Africa: Evidence from telecommunications infrastructure. *International Atlantic Economic Society*, *22*(1), 65–75. https://ideas.repec.org/a/kap/iaecre/v22y2016i1d10.1007_s11294-015-9559-3.html

Enrico, M., & Wilson, D. (2013). State incentives for innovation. Star scientists and jobs: Evidence from biotech. *The Journal of Urban Economics*, *79*.

EUROSTAT. (2020). *ICT sector - value added, employment and R&D*. https://ec.europa.eu/eurostat/statistics-explained/index.php?title=ICT_sector_-_value_added,_employment_and_R%26D&oldid=551753#Employment

Evangelista, R., & Vezzani, A. (2010). The economic impact of technological and organizational innovations. A firm-level analysis. *Research Policy*, *39*(10), 1253–1263. https://econpapers.repec.org/article/eeerespol/v_3a39_3ay_3a2010_3ai_3a10_3ap_3a1253-1263.htm

Gómez-Barroso, J. L., & Marbán-Flores, R. (2020). Telecommunications and economic development – The 21st century: Making the evidence stronger. *Telecommunications Policy*, *44*(2). https://econpapers.repec.org/article/eeetelpol/v_3a44_3ay_3a2020_3ai_3a2_3as0308596119304513.htm

Goos, M., & Manning, A. (2007). Lousy and lovely jobs: The rising polarization of work in Britain. *The Review of Economics and Statistics*, *89*(1), 118–133. https://econpapers.repec.org/article/tprrestat/v_3a89_3ay_3a2007_3ai_3a1_3ap_3a118-133.htm

Graf, V. (2020). *Inclusiveness in a Digitizing World – Investigating ICT and Women's Empowerment Research Papers* (p. 114).

Grimes, A., Ren, C., & Stevens, P. (2012). The need for speed: Impacts of internet connectivity on firm productivity. *Journal of Productivity Analysis*, *37*(2), 187–201.

Haftu, G. G. (2019). Information communications technology and economic growth in Sub-Saharan Africa: A panel data approach. *Telecommunications Policy, Elsevier*, *43*(1), 88–99. https://ideas.repec.org/a/eee/telpol/v43y2019i1p88-99.html

Henderson, J., Vernon, A. S., & Weil, D. N. (2012). Measuring economic growth from outer space. *American Economic Review*, *102*(2), 994–1028.

Henry-Nickie, M., Frimpong, K., & Sun, H. (2019). *Trends in the information technology sector*. The Brookings Institute. https://www.brookings.edu

Inklaar, R., O'Mahony, M., & Timmer, M. P. (2003). *ICT and Europe's productivity problem, industry-level growth account comparisons with the United States*. GGDC Research Memorandum. GD-68.

International Labour Organization (ILO). (2022). https://www.ilo.org/public/english/bureau/stat/isco/isco08/index.htm

Ishida, H. (2015). The effect of ICT development on economic growth and energy consumption in Japan. *Telematics and Informatics*, *32*(1), 79–88. https://doi.org/10.1016/j.tele.2014.04.003

Johansen, S. (1988). Statical analysis of cointegration vectors. *Journal of Economic Dynamics and Control*, *12*, 231–254.

Jorgenson, D. W. (2001). Information technology and the U.S. economy. *American Economic Review*, *91*(1), 1–32.

Jorgenson, D. W., & Stiroh, K. (2000). *Raising the speed limit: US economic growth in the information age* (pp. 161–67). Brookings Papers on Economic Activity: 1. Brookings Institution.

Koutroumpis, P., Leiponen, A., & Thomas, L. D. W. (2020). Small is big in ICT: The impact of R&D on productivity. *Telecommunications Policy*, *44*(1). https://ideas.repec.org/a/eee/telpol/v44y2020i1s0308596119301004.html

Kumar, R. R., Stauvermann, P. J., & Samitas, A. (2016). The effects of ICT on output per worker: A study of the Chinese economy. *Telecommunications Policy*, *40*(2), 102–115. https://ideas.repec.org/a/eee/telpol/v40y2016i2p102-115.html

Kurniawati, M. A. (2020). ICT infrastructure, innovation development and economic growth: A comparative evidence between two decades in OECD countries. *International Journal of Social Economics*, *48*(1), 141–158. Emerald Group Publishing Limited.

Maruta, A. A., Banerjee, R., & Cavoli, T. (2020). Foreign aid, institutional quality and economic growth: Evidence from the developing world. *Economic Modelling*, *89*(C), 444–463. https://ideas.repec.org/a/eee/ecmode/v89y2020icp444-463.html

Meta, A. K. (2020). ICT infrastructure, innovation development and economic growth: Comparative evidence between two decades in OECD countries. *International Journal of Social Economics*. *48*(1), 141–158. https://ideas.repec.org/a/eme/ijsepp/ijse-05-2020-0321.html

Nchor, D., & Rozmahel, P. (2020). Job polarization in Europe: Evidence from Central and Eastern European Countries. *DANUBE: Law, Economics and Social Issues Review*, *11*(1), 52–74. https://doi.org/10.2478/danb-2020-0004

OECD. (2013). *Investment in ICT, in OECD Factbook 2013: Economic, Environmental and Social Statistics*. OECD Publishing.

OECD. (2023). *ICT Investment as a share of GDP*. https://goingdigital.oecd.org/en/indicator/30

Pradhan, R., Arvin, M. B., Nair, M., Bennett, S. E., & Bahmani, S. (2019). Short-term and long-term dynamics of venture capital and economic growth in a digital economy: A study of European countries. *Technology in Society*, *57*(C), 125–134. https://ideas.repec.org/a/eee/teinso/v57y2019icp125-134.html

Pradhan, R. P., Arvin, M. B., Norman, N. R., & Bele, S. K. (2014). Economic growth and the development of telecommunications infrastructure in the G-20 countries: A panel-VAR approach. *Telecommunications Policy*, *38*(7), 634–649. https://ideas.repec.org/a/eee/telpol/v38y2014i7p634-649.html

Pradhan, R. P., Arvin, M. B., Hall, J. H., & Nair, M. (2016). Innovation, financial development and economic growth in Eurozone countries. *Applied Economics Letters*, *23*(16), 1141–1144.

Remeikienė, R., Gasparėnienė, L., Bayar, Y., Ginevičius, R., & Ragaišytė, J. M. (2022). ICT development and shadow economy: Empirical evidence from the EU transition economies, Economic. *Research-Ekonomska Istraživanja*, *35*(1), 762–777.

Roller, L. H., & Waverman, L. (2001). Telecommunications infrastructure and economic development: A simultaneous approach. *American Economic Review*, *91*(4), 909–923.

Shahiduzzaman, M., & Alam, K. (2014). The long-run impact of Information and Communication Technology on economic output: The case of Australia. *Telecommunications Policy, Elsevier*, *38*(7), 623–633. https://ideas.repec.org/a/eee/telpol/v38y2014i7p623-633.html

Solow, R. (1956). A contribution to the theory of economic growth. *Quarterly Journal of Economics*, *70*, 65–94.

Valberg, S. (2020). ICT, gender, and the labor market: A cross-country analysis. In D. Maiti, F. Castellacci, & A. Melchior (Eds.), *Digitalisation and development* (pp. 375–405). Springer. https://doi.org/10.1007/978-981-13-9996-1_15

Venturini, F. (2009). The long-run impact of ICT. *Empirical Economics*, *37*(3), 497–515. https://econpapers.repec.org/article/sprempeco/v_3a37_3ay_3a2009_3ai_3a3_3ap_3a497-515.htm

Vu, K., Hanafizadeh, P., & Bohlin, E. (2020). ICT as a driver of economic growth: A survey of the literature and directions for future research. *Telecommunications Policy*, *44*(2). https://ideas.repec.org/a/eee/telpol/v44y2020i2s0308596120300148.html

Vu, K. M. (2011). ICT as a source of economic growth in the information age: Empirical evidence from the 1996–2005 period. *Telecommunication. Policy*. https://www.sciencedirect.com/science/article/pii/S030859611100022X

Yakunina, R. P., & Bychkov, G. A. (2015). Correlation Analysis of the components of the human development index across countries. *Procedia Economics and Finance*, *24*, 766–771.

Yousefi, A. (2011). The impact of information and communication technology on economic growth: Evidence from developed and developing countries. *Economics of Innovation and New Technology*, *20*(6), 581–596. https://econpapers.repec.org/article/tafecinnt/v_3a20_3ay_3a2011_3ai_3a6_3ap_3a581-596.htm

Chapter 18

The Effects of the COVID-19 Pandemic on the Microeconomic Development of Czech Exports

Petra Růčková and Tomáš Heryán

Silesian University in Opava, Czechia

Abstract

As Czech export is widely considered the key to the economic development of Czechia, this chapter explores the relationship between microeconomic profitability among companies in selected TOP10 export industries and the macroeconomic development of the export itself. An investigation was carried out to compare the differences caused by the COVID-19 pandemic. In addition, the comparison is developed according to the size and concentration of ownership among exporting companies. Annual data are obtained from the Bureau van Dijk Orbis database to analyse profitability among 4,283 companies in 10 NACE industries from 2012 to 2021. We have obtained encouraging results, demonstrating that not only those less profitable companies affected export development. However, in general, our results emphasise the importance of those less profitable medium-sized companies for Czech export, within the manufacture of machinery and equipment, and the manufacture of motor vehicles in particular.

Keywords: Exports; performance of enterprises; return on assets; return on equity; COVID-19 pandemic; generalised method of moments

18.1 Introduction

Czechia is one of the largest exporters of goods in Europe, and the Czech economy has a large trade surplus. That is exactly why this country is very attractive to foreign investors. Furthermore, there is a very developed manufacturing sector, and many multinational corporations have established their businesses here

Modeling Economic Growth in Contemporary Czechia, 281–297

Published under exclusive licence by Emerald Publishing Limited
doi:10.1108/978-1-83753-840-920241018

(International Trade Administration, 2023). If one looks at the ownership concentration of companies exporting goods from Czechia, it is possible also to better understand the importance of foreign investments in the Czech economy investigated by Kosova (2008), as well as the potential risks and opportunities associated with them. Despite interest in the macroeconomic development of export in Czechia, few authors have also considered microeconomic issues among the various NACE industries (Roubíčková & Heryán, 2014). Nevertheless, to our knowledge, so far no one has compared the main business industries among Czech exporters and further, the impact of the COVID-19 pandemic.

However, companies of different sizes will have different concentrations of the optimal ownership structure. Larger companies require a lot of capital and a lot more industry expertise, and they will spend more money than smaller companies (Shleifer & Vishny, 1997). One could assume that it makes more sense for them to have a strong leader and a small group of investors who are very well informed, with one shareholder taking the final decision. It would be optimal to have an experienced individual or small group running a large firm with the ability to make quick decisions based on market knowledge, which represents a high concentration of ownership. To break a company up into a lot of small shareholders would mean a lot of people with different ideas, and you would end up having to debate every possible decision the company could make, which would be inefficient. On the other hand, the opposite argument holds that many small shareholders create some sort of democratic system with a dispersed concentration of ownership (Al-Najjar & Kilincarslan, 2016; Setiawan et al., 2016; Udin et al., 2017). Therefore, this chapter aims to estimate which industries have the greatest impact on Czech export, focusing on the size and different ownership concentrations of the companies.

18.2 Overview of Czechia's Export

The Czech economy is a strongly pro-export economy. Its strategic location in the centre of Europe is one of the main reasons why its traditional trading partners are mainly neighbouring and European Union (EU) countries, but goods are exported to a lesser extent to the whole world. The development of exports and the balance of foreign trade between 2009 and 2021 are documented in Fig. 18.1.

Fig. 18.1 shows that the sum of exports between 2009 and 2019 has an increasing trend, which is positively reflected in the foreign trade balance, which showed a surplus in the period under review, and the surplus in 2019 was a record according to the Czech Statistical Office (CZSO). A surplus was also achieved in 2020, despite a significant decline in exports, although 2020 was very significantly affected by the COVID-19 crisis. This crisis had the effect of limiting or temporarily halting production and reducing foreign demand, which was inevitably reflected in the foreign trade of Czechia's main export partners. The reason for the trade surplus was mainly due to the fall in oil and gas imports, which offset the losses from the high export shortfall with France and Spain in particular, and the losses caused by the fall in exports to the United Kingdom as a result of Brexit.

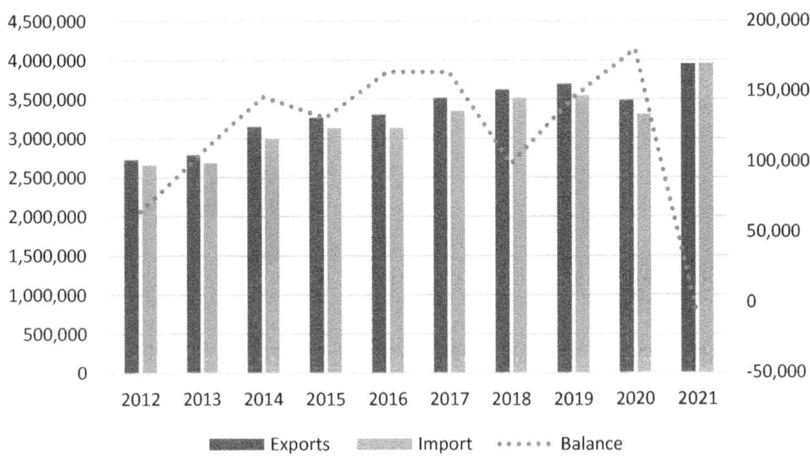

Fig. 18.1. Development of Exports, Imports and Foreign Trade Balance of Czechia Between 2012 and 2021 (in Thousands CZK). *Source:* Authors' Calculations According to Data from CZSO.

The balance with motor vehicles and electrical equipment, which, as shown in Fig. 18.3, represents the bulk of Czech exports, showed an unfavourable impact. By 2021, exports had already grown again and, according to CZSO data, reached a growth rate of 16.5%. However, it should be noted that this is based on a lower comparative base from 2020 when exports were affected by the COVID-19 pandemic. At the same time, it should also be noted that the foreign trade balance ended in deficit this year. In the last 10 years, a deficit in the external trade balance has been achieved. Trade in oil and natural gas has affected this balance due to the rise in the price on the world market. Czech foreign trade is strongly linked to European countries in particular, as also shown in Fig. 18.2. The graph on the right shows that 89% of the total exports of Czech companies are to European countries. Only 6% goes to Asia, 3% to North America and the remaining 2% to other countries (left).

If we analyse the structure of the European countries (right), it is clear that the key trading partner in terms of exports is Germany, to which a full third of exported goods go and which maintains a very dominant position over other countries. Slovakia is second with 8.3% of Czech exports and Poland third with 7%. The shares of the other European countries in the top 10 then range from 4.6% to 2.2%. In this respect, it may also be interesting to note that, while overall foreign trade ended in a deficit in 2021, trade with EU countries showed a surplus, especially in trade with Germany and Slovakia. Interestingly, trade with Poland showed a negative balance. It may also be interesting to note that the territorial structure of imports differs from exports. Germany remains first, but China has the second-largest share of imports.

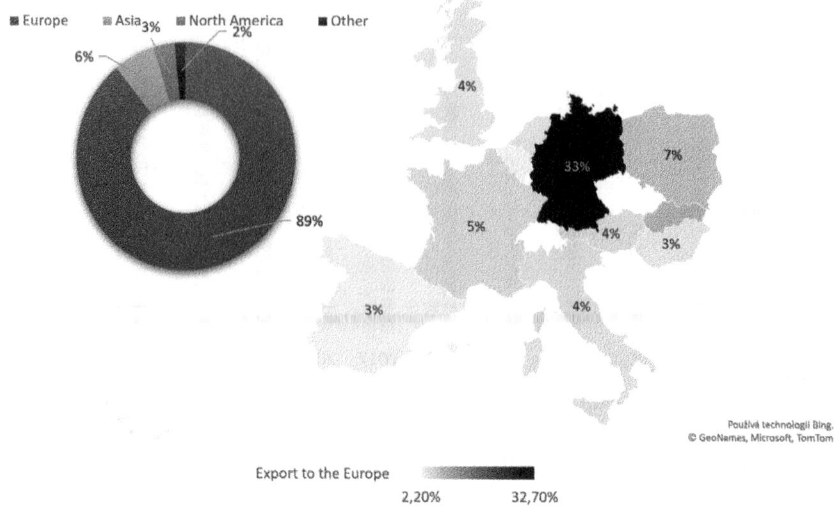

Fig. 18.2. Territorial Structure of Exports of Czechia in 2021 (Smaller on the Left) and the Share of European Countries in Exports of Czechia (Map). *Source:* Authors' Calculations According to Data from CZSO.

According to CZSO data, 93.7% of exports come from manufacturing. Data from the CZSO show that motor vehicles and accessories account for a significant share of Czech exports, representing a full quarter of total exports in 2021. This is followed by machinery and equipment, and electrical equipment. Together, they account for half of Czech exports. Exports of all groups, except machinery and transport equipment, increased in the last year under review. Given the share of these groups of goods, the negative balance of payments result is understandable.

Automobiles and their accessories are one of the most important exports from Czechia to Germany. According to the CZSO, cars represented 24.5% of total goods exports to Germany in 2020, the highest share of any EU country. The value of car exports to Germany reached CZK 264 billion, 14% less than the record result recorded in 2019. The decline was mainly due to the impact of the COVID-19 pandemic on demand and production. Automotive exports from Czechia to Germany have a long history and are supported by strong trade and investment ties between the two countries. German car companies such as Volkswagen, BMW and Daimler have subsidiaries or suppliers in Czechia, where they benefit from skilled and cheap labour, good infrastructure and a favourable business environment. Czechia is also a transit country for German car exports to other EU countries or world markets. For Czechia, automobile exports to Germany are a key factor in economic growth and employment. The automotive industry accounts for around 10% of the Czech GDP and employs over 150,000 people. Car exports to Germany also contribute to balancing Czechia's trade balance, which showed a surplus of CZK 293 billion in 2020. In the future, Czechia's car exports to Germany are expected to continue to grow but will face new challenges and opportunities. These include digitalisation, electromobility, autonomous driving, environmental standards or competition from other regions. Czechia will need to invest in innovation, qualification and diversification of its automotive industry to maintain its competitiveness and attractiveness to German partners.

The influence of the automotive industry is also evident in other business sectors in Czechia, for example, in the production of plastics or the production of rubber (there is a significant influence on tyre production). According to data from the Czech Ministry of Industry and Trade, products from the rubber and plastic products manufacturing sector are among the products that are used in other parts of the manufacturing industry, especially in the automotive and electrical industries, which are important exporters to Germany. It should also be noted that in the last year under review, sales in the medium-high technology sector, which includes most of the leading Czech export sectors, decreased, which may potentially affect profitability in future periods. Combined with external economic factors such as energy price developments and inflation rates in Czechia, this may mean that investment will decrease and this could potentially negatively affect both exports and GDP.

Currently, there is no comprehensive study of the relationship between exports and the profitability of enterprises in Czechia. However, a similar study can be found in the data of German export enterprises. For example, Eickelpasch and Vogel (2009) examined the determinants of the behaviour of German service firms. Based on panel data analysis between 2003 and 2005, they examined the impact of size, productivity and national market experience on firm performance. Based on the results, they concluded that a positive effect on export behaviour can be observed for these firms only from the position of firm size. Similar research on Swedish companies can be found in Falk and Hagsten (2015). The research was carried out on small and medium companies between 2002 and 2010. However, their studies primarily addressed the impact of human capital on export levels, with profitability only marginally. At the same time, in their studies, some authors argue that exporting firms are more productive than the same firms without exporting, although they have to bear more additional costs related to the adoption of products in foreign markets. This has been shown, for example, by Bernard et al. (2007) on US companies or by Mayer and Ottaviano (2008) and Wagner (2007) on European companies. Fryges and Wagner (2015) showed a positive effect of exporting on firm profitability between 1999 and 2004 using data from German manufacturing firms. The focus was on firms that employed at least 20 employees and the sample of firms contained around 18,000 firms. This study also showed that it is not profitable for German manufacturing firms from a profitability perspective if most of their production goes abroad. It was the absence of studies on the conditions of Czechia and the obsolescence of data in previous studies that motivated this analysis.

18.3 Performance Among Exporters and Its Impact on Export From Czechia to Germany

From the above, it is clear that Germany is a key trading partner. It is not only the largest importer for companies from Czechia, but it is also a very stable trading partner, as most companies that export to Germany have been exporting there for at least 5 years. It is therefore interesting to see how the performance measured by the profitability of Czech and German companies affects Czechia's foreign trade with Germany. Attention will also be paid to the structure of companies in terms of individual industries and services. The aim is to estimate the differences in the Czech impact of performance in selected business sectors on the development of Czech exports. Information on enterprises in Czechia and Germany is obtained from the Orbis database, and the period 2013 to 2021 is analysed.

The analysis is also broken down by sector, size of the enterprises and ownership structure. Table 18.1 shows that a total of 4,283 enterprises were analysed in the sectors that make up the bulk of Czechia's exports to Germany. The largest share of the number of companies analysed was held by companies in the metal products sector, which represents 39.8% of the total sample of companies. The second largest group of enterprises is in the Machinery and

Table 18.1. Number of Enterprises in the Analysed Sample by Enterprise Size.

NACE	Medium	Large	Very Large
24	70	43	19
25	1,847	344	42
26	171	47	15
28	616	213	35
31	130	17	1
221	42	18	8
222	270	139	7
267	4	3	1
291	16	13	8
292 + 293	53	54	37

Source: Orbis Database.

Note: 24 Manufacture of basic metals, 25 Manufacture of fabricated metal products, except machinery and equipment, 26 Manufacture of computer, electronic, and optical products, 28 Manufacture of machinery and equipment, 31 Manufacture of furniture, 221 Manufacture of rubber products, 222 Manufacture of plastics products, 267 Manufacture of optical instruments and photographic equipment, 291 Manufacture of motor vehicles, and 292&293 Manufacture of bodies (coachwork) for motor vehicles; Manufacture of trailers and semitrailers & Manufacture of parts and accessories for motor vehicles.

Equipment sector, and the third largest group in terms of the number of enterprises is in the Computers, Electronic, and Optical Equipment sector. Motor Vehicle Manufacturing, which accounts for the largest share of exports to Germany, is represented by the smallest number of companies in the sample. Therefore, it is clear that the number of companies represented in a given sector is not a decisive factor for the volume of exports realised. The analysis also focused on the size of the companies (Table 18.1) and their ownership structure (Table 18.2).

The companies in the sample are divided into medium, large and very large enterprises. The breakdown of enterprises is different from the usual practice for the breakdown of enterprises according to the EU methodology. The Bureau van Dijk uses a different methodology. Companies on Orbis are considered to be medium-sized when they match at least one of the following conditions: Operating revenue > = 1 million EUR (1.3 million USD), Total assets > = 2 million EUR (2.6 million USD) and Employees > = 15. Companies on Orbis are considered to be large when they match at least one of the following conditions: Operating revenue > = 10 million EUR (13 million USD), Total assets > = 20 million EUR (26 million USD) and Employees > = 150. Companies on Orbis are considered to be very large when they match at least one of the following conditions: Operating revenue > = 100 million EUR (130 million USD), Total assets > = 200 million EUR (260 million USD) and Employees > = 1,000. Table 18.1 indicates that medium-sized enterprises are the most represented group in terms of size, accounting for nearly 81% of the total sample analysed. In terms of size, enterprises of all sizes are most represented in metal products, with the second largest group being machinery and equipment enterprises. Interestingly, although automobile manufacturing accounts for the largest share of Czech exports, it is

Table 18.2. Number of Enterprises in the Analysed Sample by Ownership Structure Concentration.

NACE	High	Low
24	111	21
25	1,683	550
26	184	49
28	667	197
31	110	38
221	56	12
222	325	91
267	8	
291	33	4
292 + 293	126	18

Source: Orbis Database.

the second smallest group in the sample. It will be interesting to see whether the numerical representation of companies by size shows up as statistically significant in the regression analysis performed.

The ownership structure is divided into two groups for this study (Table 18.2). Enterprises with a fragmented ownership structure, that is, the absence of a majority owner, are labelled LOW in the study. Companies with concentrated ownership and the existence of a majority owner are labelled HIGH. In terms of ownership structure, it can be noted that the sample is dominated by companies with concentrated ownership, as 74.71% of the total sample falls into this category. It can also be seen from the table that the breakdown in terms of ownership narrowed the sample from the original 386,900 observations to 369,050 observations since it was not possible to determine the ownership structure of 17,810 observations. The number of enterprises in each sector by ownership concentration naturally follows the number of enterprises by size. The category with the most concentrated ownership structure is the most numerous and, as mentioned above, it is the manufacture of fabricated metal products. An interesting feature of this type of breakdown is the fact that in the optical and photographic equipment manufacturing sector, we do not find enterprises with a fragmented ownership structure, that is, with a low concentration of ownership shares.

Given the objective of the analysis, two indicators were chosen as independent variables to measure the performance of firms in terms of microeconomic data. Return on total assets (ROA) is characterised as the ratio of earnings before interest and tax to the total assets of the company. The indicator was chosen to provide a comprehensive assessment of the company's ability to use its assets efficiently. The second indicator, which is chosen primarily concerning the ownership structure, is the return on equity (ROE). This indicator is constructed as the ratio of net profit to equity. The dependent variable is the gross domestic product and the value of exports within each sector. Macroeconomic export data are taken from the CZSO database, and the gross domestic product is taken from the OECD database.

18.4 Methodology

The two-step system GMM estimation is the Blundell and Bond (1998) technique deployed with the robust bias-corrected variance-covariance matrix for standard errors, recommended by Windmeijer (2005), and the STATA *xtdpdgmm* command, further described by Kripfganz and Schwarz (2019). Due to the high correlation between covariates and the rejection of their strict exogeneity, profitability is treated as predetermined, with both lagged levels of instruments. The main estimation is further described by Eq. (18.1):

$$y_{it} = \sum_{j=1}^{p} \alpha_j y_{i,t-j} + x_{it}\beta_1 + v_i + \varepsilon_{it} \quad i = 1, \ldots, N t = 1, \ldots, T_i \tag{18.1}$$

where α_j indicates the total number of p parameters for the estimation of the explanatory variable, particularly the Czech export on GDP, x_{it} means $1 \times k_1$ vector of predetermined variables and β_1 is $k_1 \times 1$ vector of parameters to be estimated, particularly return on assets (ROA) and return on equity (ROE), v_i represents panel effects that can be correlated with regressors, and ε_{it} is the residual component, that is, the panel of idiosyncratic estimation errors, having a variance σ_{ε}^2. Arellano-Bond test for zero autocorrelation in first-differenced errors is used to test whether the moment conditions in the model are valid. According to Windmeijer (2018), first, the problem of underidentification has been verified by both Cragg and Donald (1993) robust CUE-based (LM version) and Kleibergen and Paap (2006) robust LIML-based (LM version) tests. Second, the problem of overidentification has been verified with techniques developed by Sargan (1958) and Hansen (1982). According to the non-linear relationship among the means within our data, it is obvious that among several NACE industries, the number of linear as well as non linear moments have been used among the GMM estimations. Furthermore, less than 30 moments are models with collapsed instruments due to the orthogonality issues further discussed by Hansen and Lee (2021).

In Fig. 18.3, we can see whether a positive (or negative) coefficient based on the convex (or concave) curve would have been expected via the exponential trend between the means of the data. Apparently, among the selected TOP10 industries of exporters, those curves depicting microeconomic profitability, either wider return on equity (ROE) or return on assets (ROA) in the middle, and its impact on the macroeconomic variable, particularly the export on GDP, lead us to different results. For both types of profitability, the positive impact according to the convex curve would be expected among industries 24, 25, 222 and 221 companies, though with a low concentrated ownership structure, while the negative impact according to the concave curves would be expected among 26, 28 and 267 companies though with a low concentrated ownership structure, vice versa.

In Figs. 18.4 and 18.5, we see the distribution of both profitability variables, before and during the COVID-19 pandemic. Fig. 18.4 clearly illustrates the ex ante distribution of darker ROA and lighter ROE, also together with the median value for all NACE industries (vertical lines) before 2020.

In terms of comparing the median of observed profitability with the median value for the whole sample in the period 2013 to 2019, we can state that for companies with a more concentrated ownership structure, a higher median value of the profitability of total capital employed was observed only in the business sector Manufacture of rubber products. The situation is different for the profitability of equity. There, the highest median values refer to three business sectors: 221: Rubber product manufacture, 291: Motor vehicles and 292&293: Manufacture of parts for the motor vehicle industry. This may be mainly since companies in these business lines distribute profits and do not retain the full amount for reinvestment, which is positively reflected in the magnitude of the indicators. With rising profit values and unchanged or only slightly rising equity values, ROE growth is natural. The return on total capital employed for the low-concentrated ownership structure shows no difference from the median values of the full sample of companies in either line of business. Thus, again, we find differences, especially in the return on equity. As with concentrated ownership, we find a higher median

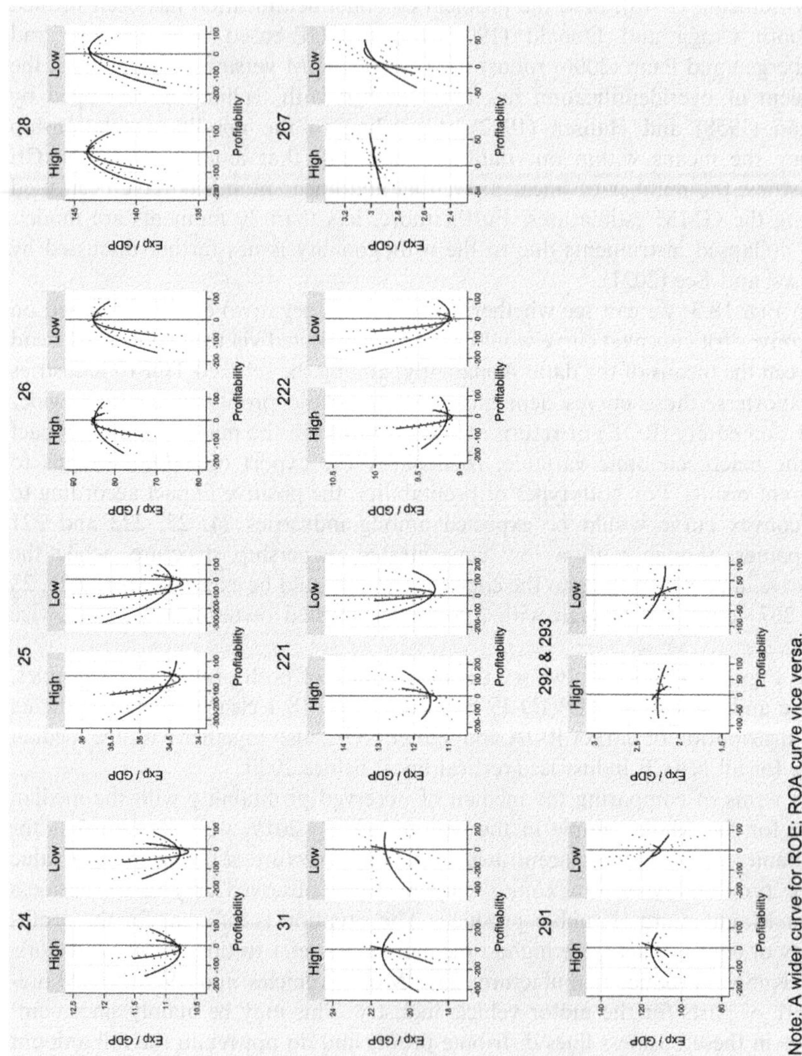

Fig. 18.3. Expected Impact of Profitability on the Macroeconomic Export on GDP. *Source:* Authors' Calculations.

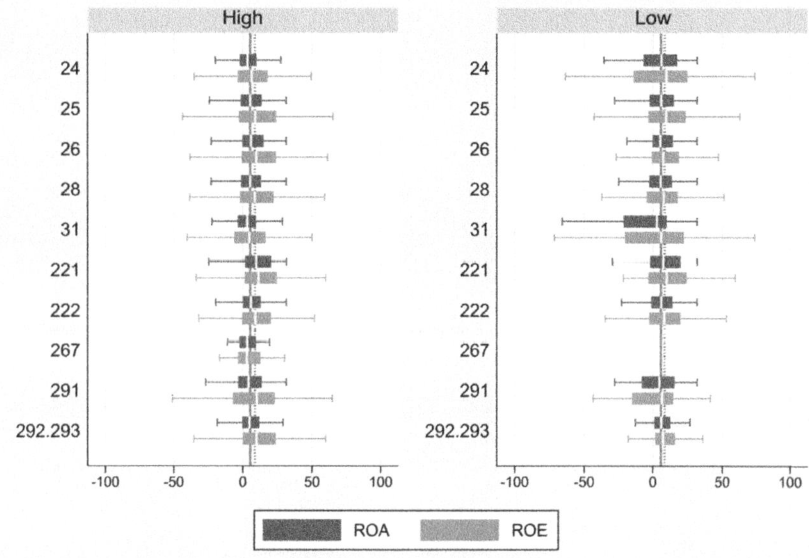

Fig. 18.4. Profitability Distribution Against Median Values Before the Pandemic COVID-19. *Source:* Authors' Calculations.

value in industry 221. The other two business lines, 24: Manufacturing of basic metals and 25: Manufacturing of fabricated metal products, also show ROE values higher than the median of the whole sample.

Fig. 18.5 clearly illustrates the ex-post distribution of darker ROA and lighter ROE also together with the median value for all NACE industries (vertical lines) during the pandemic years 2020 and 2021.

The situation changed when we included both pandemic years in the analysis period. The median values for both indicators have decreased and the distribution within each business sector has also changed. The situation changed most significantly for the highly concentrated ownership in industry 267 – Manufacture of optical and photographic equipment. In this industry, both the median ROA and ROE were higher than the industry median, and throughout this industry, most firms performed better than the median. This may be due to the representation of exports of microscopes, which grew during the period of COVID-19. These products were already the main driver of this industry during the pre-pandemic period, but the need for these products increased significantly during the pandemic. The second industry with a higher median ROE than the median of the whole sample is 25 – Manufacture of fabricated metal products, which even according to the data of the Ministry of Industry and Trade of Czechia became the driver of exports between 2020 and 2021 (export growth of

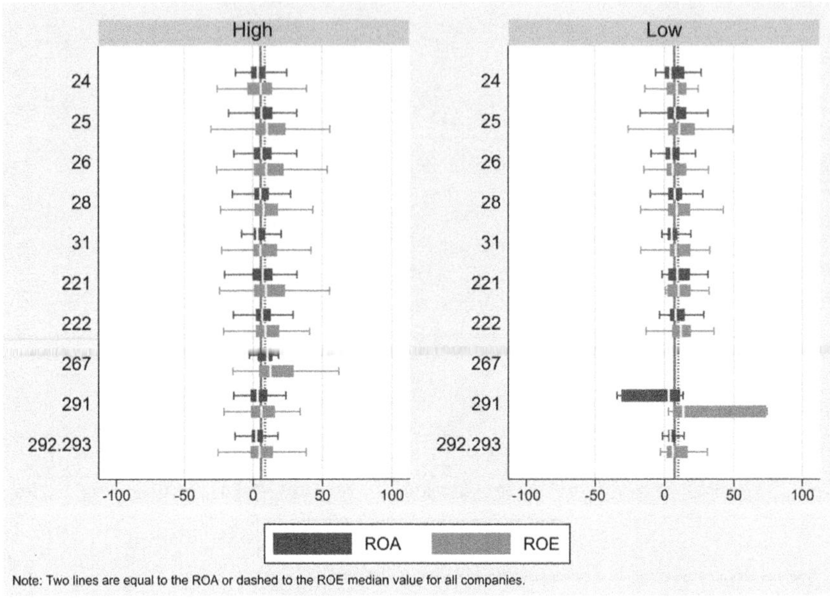

Fig. 18.5. Profitability Distribution Against Median Values During the Pandemic COVID-19. *Source:* Authors' Calculations.

8.8%). If we have evaluated higher medians, we must not overlook the lower medians than the whole. The latter can be observed for industry 292.293 – Manufacture of parts and accessories for motor vehicles. This industry has suffered significantly from the decrease in automobile exports and the decline in motor vehicle demand during the pandemic period. For the less concentrated companies, we find higher median ROEs for the business sectors 222 – Plastics manufacture and 291 – Manufacture of motor vehicles. It is also interesting to note for the business industry 291 that most of the companies in this business have a median ROE higher than the median of the whole. Equally interesting, however, is the fact that most businesses in the same industry have a median ROA significantly lower than the overall median. The median value of industry 24 – Basic metal manufacturing is also lower, but the distribution of ROA values for most enterprises cannot be assessed as negatively as in the case of industry 291.

18.5 Discussion on Empirical Results

Although they are generalised and do not vary between companies according to their size, our expectations simulated through exponential relations of the mean data in Fig. 18.5 have not been efficient. Only two expectations are correct when comparing GMM estimation output and are included in Table 18.3. Correct

Table 18.3. GMM Estimates (the Czech Export-to-GDP Ratio as the Dependent Variable).

NACE	EX ANTE (2013-2019)						INCLUDING PANDEMIC (2013-2021)					
	HIGH			LOW			HIGH			LOW		
	Middle	*Large*	*V.large*	*Middle*	*Large*	*V.large*	*Middle*	*Large*	*V.large*	*Middle*	*Large*	*V.large*
24												
a.	0.8372^{a}	0.0000	0.0000	0.8809^{a}	0.9574^{a}	0.9356^{a}	1.0115^{a}	0.0000	0.0000	0.9626^{a}	0.9834^{a}	0.9170^{a}
b.	-0.0139	-0.0103	0.0000	**-0.0147^{c}**	**-0.0298^{b}**	0.0164	-0.0186	-0.3361	0.0000	-0.0051	-0.0019	0.0115
c.	-0.0010	0.0377	-0.0328	-0.0008	0.0019	0.0026	0.0005	0.1700	0.0627	-0.0028	**-0.0065^{b}**	0.0012
25												
a.	1.0550^{a}	0.1129	0.0000	1.0576^{a}	1.0038^{a}	0.9697^{a}	1.0315^{a}	0.0158	0.0000	1.0217^{a}	0.7428^{a}	0.6592^{a}
b.	**-0.0443^{a}**	0.0035	0.0000	**-0.0418^{a}**	0.0214	0.0752	**-0.0434^{a}**	0.0045	0.0000	**-0.0464^{a}**	0.0085	0.0795
c.	-0.0042	*0.9655^{a}*	0.2842	**-0.0058^{b}**	**-0.0129^{c}**	-0.0005	**-0.0050^{c}**	*0.7553^{a}*	0.2842	**-0.0044^{b}**	**-0.0076^{c}**	-0.0032
26												
a.	1.0624^{a}	0.0000		1.0585^{a}	1.0556^{a}	1.0627^{a}	1.0441^{a}	0.1746		1.0369^{a}	1.0240^{a}	-0.9400
b.	-0.0610	0.0000		**-0.0822^{c}**	0.1016	0.0239	-0.0529	-0.6146		**-0.0909^{b}**	**0.1583^{c}**	0.9391
c.	-0.0364	-0.5527		-0.0121	-0.0472	-0.0044	-0.0395	-0.9834		-0.0039	**-0.0484^{b}**	0.2095
28												
a.	1.0368^{a}	0.6209	0.0000	1.0450^{a}	1.0142^{a}	0.9937^{a}	1.0368^{a}	0.4809	0.0000	1.0478^{a}	1.0155^{a}	1.0000^{a}
b.	**-0.3395^{a}**	-0.1539	0.0000	**-0.2243^{a}**	0.1447	0.3157	**-0.3209^{a}**	-0.1161	0.0000	**-0.2037^{a}**	0.1075	0.2540
c.	0.0489	*0.9859^{a}*	0.0000	-0.0078	-0.0655	**0.0820^{c}**	0.0392	*0.9869^{a}*	-0.9946	-0.0126	-0.0431	0.0549
31												
a.	1.0479^{a}	0.0000		1.0782^{a}	0.9273^{a}	0.1165	1.0580^{a}			1.0925^{a}	0.9546^{a}	-0.3355
b.	**-0.0335^{a}**	0.0000		**-0.0201^{c}**	**0.3196^{c}**	-0.0965	**-0.0326^{a}**			**-0.0226^{b}**	0.1981	0.1078
c.	-0.0037	-0.4105		**-0.0106^{a}**	**-0.1110^{a}**	0.0000	-0.0041			**-0.0106^{a}**	**-0.0851^{c}**	-0.0965
221												
a.	0.8656^{a}	0.0000		0.8529^{a}	0.9052^{a}	0.9843^{a}	0.9034^{a}			0.8745^{a}	0.9261^{a}	0.9134^{a}
b.	0.0343	0.2316		0.0131	**0.0639^{c}**	0.1669	0.0393			0.0113	**0.0421^{c}**	0.0569
c.	**-0.0221^{c}**	0.1538		-0.0068	0.0005	-0.1335	**-0.0238^{c}**			-0.0050	-0.0008	-0.0233
222												
a.	0.9258^{a}			0.9193^{a}	0.8899^{a}	0.3397	0.2699^{a}	-0.0041		0.4064^{a}	0.9236^{a}	0.3821
b.	0.0005			**-0.0212^{a}**	**0.0773^{a}**	0.0807	0.0060	-0.0068		-0.0071	**0.0431^{b}**	-0.0376
c.	-0.0122			-0.0013	**-0.0102^{c}**	0.0045	-0.0123	1.1285^{c}		0.0005	-0.0065	0.0098
267												
a.		-0.0009		-0.2188	-0.5163	-0.0099				-0.5237	-0.7356	-0.0099
b.		-0.0115		0.0300	0.1118	-0.0356				0.0156	0.0000	-0.0230
c.		*0.8511^{b}*		-0.0012	0.0166	0.0000				-0.0003	0.0000	0.0000
291												
a.	-2.3798	0.0000		1.0364^{a}	0.0002	0.9411^{a}	1.2982	0.0000		1.0319^{a}	0.0531	0.9340^{a}
b.	-9.2989	0.0000		0.2774	0.0134	1.2232	2.5790	5.7301		0.3244	-0.0047	0.6195
c.	2.2632	0.0000		**-0.2171^{a}**	-0.0744	-0.1194	-0.4314	0.0000		**-0.2098^{a}**	*-0.1268^{b}*	0.0311
292,293												
a.	0.6733^{c}	0.1076	0.0000	1.0575^{a}	1.1168^{a}	1.1789^{a}	0.8859^{a}	-0.0007	0.0000	0.9335^{a}	1.0113	1.0042^{a}
b.	0.0403	-0.0427	0.0000	0.0013	**-0.0103^{c}**	-0.0132	0.0223	0.0000	0.1858	-0.0003	0.0000	0.0048
c.	-0.0226	*0.7678^{c}*	-1.1408	-0.0001	-0.0016	-0.0032	-0.0131	-0.7234	0.0376	-0.0015	0.0001	0.0008

Source: Authors' Calculations.

Note: 24 Manufacture of basic metals, 25 Manufacture of fabricated metal products, except machinery and equipment, 26 Manufacture of computer, electronic, and optical products, 28 Manufacture of machinery and equipment, 31 Manufacture of furniture, 221 Manufacture of rubber products, 222 Manufacture of plastics products, 267 Manufacture of optical instruments and photographic equipment, 291 Manufacture of motor vehicles, and 292&293 Manufacture of bodies (coachwork) for motor vehicles; Manufacture of trailers and semitrailers & Manufacture of parts and accessories for motor vehicles. HIGH ownership concentration with majority power vs. LOW with minority power to affect financial management. Symbols (a) (b) (c) stand for three GMM covariates: (a) dependent variable (share of the Czech export on GDP) lagged by one year, (b) ROA and (c) ROE. Furthermore, the small letters ^{a}, ^{b} and ^{c} denote significant coefficients at levels 0.001, 0.01 and 0.05. The two-step system GMM estimation is the Blundell and Bond (1998) technique deployed with the robust bias-corrected variance-covariance matrix for standard errors, recommended by Windmeijer (2005), and the STATA *xtdpdgmm* command developed by Kripfganz (2019). Due to the high correlation between covariates and the rejection of their strict exogeneity, profitability is treated as predetermined, in both cases with lagged levels of instruments. The Arellano-Bond test for zero autocorrelation in first-differenced errors is used to test whether the moment conditions in the model are valid. According to Windmeijer (2018), first, the problem of underidentification was verified by the Cragg-Donald robust CUE-based (LM version) and the Kleibergen-Paap robust LIML-based (LM version); then, the problem of overidentification was verified by the Sargan-Hansen test.

expectations have been reached only for NACE 28 and 222, or partially for 31 and 291. However, through further detailed analysis, it has been proved that even non-linear moments should have been included within a few cases. Otherwise, the Arellano-Bond serial autocorrelation post-estimation technique has not indicated any significant first-order coefficients. Just in these particular cases, those non-linear moments have been included in our models.

According to estimated coefficients, the most influential are those less profitable middle-sized companies within both the lower and higher concentrated ownership structures of NACE 28 and their ROA in Table 18.3. Neither companies of different sizes nor the COVID-19 pandemic affected the share of export on GDP in this particular industry. The other influential case are those less profitable middle-sized companies in NACE 291. However, only these companies with low ownership concentration, and not ROA but ROE, had the impact on our macroeconomic dependent variable. The extreme difference between the ROA and ROE values in industry 291 may be largely influenced by the fact that the median value is made up of 16 firms where the effect of covariance measures is more apparent than in industries where more firms are represented. The assets of the companies showed an increasing tendency and the results of economic performance were decreasing, which caused a drop in these indicators. As already mentioned, this business sector, in particular, has returned to export recovery very quickly, so the falls in the export-to-GDP ratio have not been as large. In addition, these are medium-sized enterprises that are more sensitive to changes in the external economic environment than large or very large enterprises. Therefore, even though enterprises have not performed as well in terms of profitability, a rapid return to exports, which provide a significant part of effective sales, has been highly desirable. Conversely, ROE is largely influenced by a non-zero dividend policy, which causes a non-growing item in equity. Therefore, the loss in profits does not represent a drop in the indicator, as it did for ROA. Similar arguments apply to business line 28: manufacturing of machinery and equipment.

Two specific ROA coefficients are also detected for large companies with low-ownership structures in NACE 26 and 31 in Table 18.3. However, the more profitable exporters in NACE 26 have the impact only during the period affected by the COVID-19 pandemic, though not ex ante. On the other hand, even though those large more profitable companies in NACE 31 and their ROA have affected our dependent ex ante, this relationship disappeared during the pandemic. The ROE coefficient is negative, so those less profitable companies have affected the export on GDP throughout the period and even ex ante, on the contrary. Business area 26 includes the manufacture of computers, peripheral equipment, telecommunications equipment and similar electronic products, including their components and parts. A characteristic feature of the manufacturing processes included in this division is the design and use of integrated circuits and highly specialised miniature technologies, which are mostly purchased by European companies in Asian markets. For this business sector, the failure of the Asian market has brought export opportunities, as the demand for computers and electronic products has increased significantly in the current era, which has had a positive effect both on the export of these companies' products and their profitability.

18.6 Conclusion

This chapter aimed to estimate which industries have the biggest impact on Czech export, focusing on the size and different ownership concentrations of the companies. The analysis was carried out using the GMM method, the dependent variable being the share of exports in GDP and the independent variables the lagged value of exports in GDP, return on assets and return on equity. The focus was on selected manufacturing industries. The data, which were sourced from the Orbis database, covered the period 2013 to 2021. It represented 4,283 firms in 10 industries.

If we focus on firms with concentrated ownership structures, the analysis showed that for very large and large companies, the profitability of the companies did not affect the share of exports in GDP, as no significant effect was observed for either sector. However, it is observed when the return on assets of medium-sized companies in the sectors Manufacture of fabricated metal products, Manufacture of machinery and equipment and Manufacture of furniture decreases. Furthermore, companies in these industries were found not to show the effect of the COVID-19 pandemic. The declining return on the total capital employed by companies with declining profitability was driven by the increase in the share of exports in the gross domestic product. The decrease in profitability was mainly due to the increase in assets, which in the case of these business sectors boosted the productivity of the companies. At first glance, it is interesting to note that the return on equity did not have a significant effect on any of the industries studied.

Nevertheless, this is not the case for firms with a low concentration of ownership; here the results are different and differences are evident between the ex ante COVID-19 period and the inclusion of the pandemic period. Industries in which a significant effect of profitability can be traced on the dependent variable are also different. The industry with the same effect in medium-sized firms is the Manufacture of fabricated metal products. In the Manufacture of plastics products, it is interesting to observe the effect of total profitability on the growth of exports to GDP, also in large companies. If we look at the total period that includes the pandemic period, the effect of return on assets is no longer statistically significant. Interestingly, the Manufacture of motor vehicles is the only sector that shows an impact of return on equity. This can be explained by the nongrowing value of equity, that is, the nonzero dividend policy. However, the effect remained the same as that observed in the other sectors: declining profitability had a positive effect on the growth of the export-to-GDP ratio. The analysis carried out suggested that different concentrations of ownership structure do not necessarily imply different analysis results, but there are sectors where ownership structure is significant and it would be interesting to focus attention on more detailed structuring within the sector. Another possible analysis is to focus attention on the behaviour of firms before and after the pandemic period.

References

Al-Najjar, B., & Kilincarslan, E. (2016). The effect of ownership structure on dividend policy: Evidence from Turkey. *Corporate Governance*, *16*(1), 135–161. https://doi.org/10.1108/CG-09-2015-0129

Bernard, A. B., Jensen, B. J., Redding, S. J., & Schott, P. K. (2007). Firms in international trade. *The Journal of Economic Perspectives*, *21*(3), 105–130. https://doi.org/10.1257/jep.21.3.105

Blundell, R. W., & Bond, S. (1998). Initial conditions and moment restrictions in dynamic panel data models. *Journal of Econometrics*, *87*(1), 115–143. https://doi.org/10.1016/S0304-4076(98)00009-8

Cragg, J. G., & Donald, S. G. (1993, June 14). Testing identifiability and specification in instrumental variable models. *Econometric Theory*, *9*(2), 222–240. http://www.jstor.org/stable/3532477

CZSO. www.czso.cz

Eickelpasch, A., & Vogel, A. (2009, June 14). *Determinants of export behaviour of German business services companies*. Discussion Papers of DIW Berlin, 876. DIW Berlin, German Institute for Economic Research. https://econpapers.repec.org/paper/diwdiwwpp/dp876.htm

Falk, M., & Hagsten, E. (2015). Export behaviour of micro firms in the Swedish computer and business service industries. *Economics*, *9*(1), 1–24. https://doi.org/10.5018/economics-ejournal.ja.2015-32

Fryges, H., & Wagner, J. (2015). Exports and profitability: First evidence for German manufacturing firms. *The World Economy*, *33*(3), 399–423. https://doi.org/10.1111/j.1467-9701.2010.01261.x

Hansen, L. P. (1982). Large sample properties of generalized method of moments estimators. *Econometrica*, *50*(4), 1029–1054. https://doi.org/10.2307/1912775

Hansen, B. E., & Lee, S. (2021). Inference for iterated GMM under misspecification. *Econometrica*, *89*(3), 1419–1447. https://doi.org/10.3982/ECTA16274

International Trade Administration. (2023, May 15). *Czech Republic – Country Commercial Guide*. https://www.trade.gov/country-commercial-guides/czech-republic-market-overview

Kleibergen, F., & Paap, R. (2006). Generalized reduced rank tests using the singular value decomposition. *Journal of Econometrics*, *133*(1), 97–126. https://doi.org/10.1016/j.jeconom.2005.02.011

Kosova, R. (2008, May 15). *Do foreign firms crowd out domestic firms? Evidence from the Czech Republic*. https://doi.org/10.2139/ssrn.891776

Kripfganz, S. (2019, September 5). *GMM estimation of linear dynamic panel data models. STATA conference in London*. https://www.stata.com/meeting/uk19/slides/uk19_kripfganz.pdf

Kripfganz, S., & Schwarz, C. (2019). Estimation of linear dynamic panel data models with time-invariant regressors. *Journal of Applied Econometrics*, *34*(4), 526–546. https://doi.org/10.1002/jae.2681

Mayer, T., & Ottaviano, G. I. P. (2008). The Happy Few: The internationalisation of European firms. New facts based on firm-level evidence. *Intereconomics*, *43*(1), 135–148. https://doi.org/10.1007/s10272-008-0247-x

Ministry of Industry and Trade of the Czechia. www.mpo.cz

Roubíčková, M., & Heryán, T. (2014, May 15). Impacts of selected NACE industries' foreign ownership on the Czech economy. *E+M Ekonomie a Management*, *17*(4), 58–69. https://dspace.tul.cz/handle/15240/7134

Sargan, J. D. (1958). The estimation of economic relationships using instrumental variables. *Econometrica*, *26*(3), 393–415. https://doi.org/10.2307/1907619

Setiawan, D., Bandi, B., Phua, L. K., & Trinugroho, I. (2016). Ownership structure and dividend policy in Indonesia. *Journal of Asia Business Studies*, *10*(3), 230–252. https://doi.org/10.1108/JABS-05-2015-0053

Shleifer, A., & Vishny, R. W. (1997). A survey of corporate governance. *The Journal of Finance*, *52*(2), 737–783. https://doi.org/10.1111/j.1540-6261.1997.tb04820.x

Udin, S., Khan, M., & Javid, A. Y. (2017). The effects of ownership structure on likelihood of financial distress: An empirical evidence. *Corporate Governance*, *17*, 589–612. https://doi.org/10.1108/CG-03-2016-0067

Wagner, J. (2007). Exports and productivity: A survey of the evidence from firm-level data. *The World Economy*, *30*(1), 60–82. https://doi.org/10.1111/j.1467-9701.2007.00872.x

Windmeijer, F. (2005). A finite sample correction for the variance of linear efficient two-step GMM estimators. *Journal of Econometrics*, *126*(1), 25–51. https://doi.org/10.1016/j.jeconom.2004.02.005

Windmeijer, F. (2018, June 14). *Testing over- and underidentification in linear models, with applications to dynamic panel data and asset-pricing models*. https://www.bristol.ac.uk/efm/media/workingpapers/working_papers/pdffiles/dp18696.pdf

Chapter 19

Impact of Working Capital Management of Czech Companies on Their Performance

Markéta Skupieňová, Tetiana Konieva and Ivana Košturíková

Silesian University in Opava, Czechia

Abstract

The amount of current assets and the structure of their financing within working capital management define the level of risk, liquidity and profitability of any company. This chapter identifies the type of working capital investment and financing policies and reveals their influence on the financial performance of Czech firms.

The type of investment policy was defined, based on the structure of current assets and the working capital-to-sales ratio, followed by the share of different liabilities in assets, used to determine the financing policy. The Orbis database provided the chapter with indexes of manufacturing, agricultural, construction and trade companies for the period of 2012–2021.

The results obtained revealed the liquidity and financial independence of all selected industries. Flexible investment and conservative financing policies in agriculture were accompanied by low profitability. The decrease of the working capital-to-sales ratio and the attraction of the current debts for assets financing provided a higher return on assets in the manufacturing, agricultural and trade sectors.

Keywords: Working capital; investment policy; financing policy; liquidity; financial independence; return on assets

19.1 Introduction

The development of the economy of a given state is closely linked, among other things, to the development of the business sector. Factors such as a decrease in consumer demand, a decrease in the investment activities of business entities, reduced interest in debt financing or an increased number of companies in

Modeling Economic Growth in Contemporary Czechia, 299–313

Published under exclusive licence by Emerald Publishing Limited
doi:10.1108/978-1-83753-840-920241019

insolvency can lead to a deterioration in the financial condition of a given economy. Small and medium-sized enterprises represent an integral part of the national economy and are also an important source of employment. These companies are interconnected with large companies, where the deterioration of the competitiveness of large companies and their investments is reflected in the economic situation of small and medium-sized companies, which act as suppliers of individual goods and services.

In connection with foreign sources of financing, these enterprises are considered by financial institutions as a risky group of borrowers due to their weak financial strength. No less important is the division of enterprises by sector. The manufacturing industry participates to the highest extent in the production of capital goods and significantly influences the level of the entire economy of a given economy. It is an important segment of the economy, which is an important carrier of the development of technology, knowledge and job opportunities. Among the key sectors in Czechia is also construction, which is considered an important indicator of economic development. Agriculture and the trade sector also represent a significant part of the national economy of modern economies. A different level of working capital and its financing, including the impact on corporate profitability, will be characteristic for each of the above-mentioned sectors.

The aim of this chapter is to identify the type of investment and financing policy of the working capital and reveal their influence on the financial performance of Czech companies in selected economic sectors. When the information about the structure of the working capital of selected companies operating across the selected sectors and the investment and financial policy applied by the companies in the analysed sectors has been determined, attention will be focused on how the type of investment policy and financial policy of working capital management can affect the development of the profitability of companies operating in selected industries. This part will focus on the comparison of return on assets and the share of working capital on sales and current liabilities on total assets.

19.2 Theoretical Basis of Working Capital

Working capital represents the capital that companies have tied up in current assets, because it constantly 'works' (circulates) in the company. The problem of working capital management is mainly the determination of the optimal level of investments in current assets, and the associated search for ways to finance them appropriately. In this context, business management decides between the achievement of profitability and the level of risk. Of course, businesses demand the highest possible profitability with the lowest possible risk. The size of working capital then depends not only on internal influences but also on external influences. In this context, companies should consider the volumes of individual sales, production programs, production technology in relation to its organisational and time arrangement, supply and sales corporate policy, access to risks, costs related to production or, for example, the seasonality of production and sales and other factors. It is therefore clear that both the management of the capital structure of the company and the management of the working capital of the company can have a significant impact on the company's performance, among other things.

According to Failback and Krueger (2005), the main objective of working capital management is to maintain an optimal balance between each component of working capital. The optimal level of working capital can be considered as a state in which a balance between risk and efficiency is achieved. This requires constant monitoring to maintain adequate levels of the various components of working capital, that is, cash, inventory and liabilities. The business success of any business thus depends heavily on the ability of managers to effectively manage accounts receivable, inventory and payables.

Effective management of working capital and capital structure can ensure the success of a business, while their inefficient management can lead to its bankruptcy. Working capital management enables a business to obtain sufficient liquidity needed to pay payables. Especially nowadays, companies, regardless of their size and industry, need operating cash flow and liquidity. On the other hand, the way in which working capital is managed has an effect on the profitability and creation of the economic added value of the enterprise.

Alvarez et al. (2021) believe that working capital management is an important part of business management and thus represents the ability of the business to ensure adequate coverage of short-term liabilities with short-term assets. In fact, working capital management has become one of the most important issues within the business, where many financial managers are trying to identify the basic determinants of working capital and its optimal level. By understanding the role and determinants of working capital, a company can minimise business risk and improve overall business performance. The primary objective of working capital management is to demonstrate a sustainable level of current assets and liabilities of the company so that the company does not have a problem with profitability and liquidity. Lower inventory levels increase liquidity risk due to reduced working capital.

Working capital management involves a trade-off between profitability and risk. According to the theory of risk and return, investments with higher risk can generate higher returns. Businesses with higher liquidity and higher working capital will take fewer risks to meet their obligations, but at the same time, they will achieve less profitability. In short, working capital management primarily focuses on ensuring an optimal combination between profitability and risk. This goal can be achieved through continuous monitoring.

According to Küster (2022), the idea that working capital management affects the profitability and risk level of every business entity and has a significant effect on the value of the business itself has recently received considerable attention. The lower the investment in working capital the company has, the higher the profitability it should achieve. Additional investments in inventory or receivables are usually associated with higher sales; therefore, a positive relationship between working capital and profitability can be expected. Larger inventories can prevent disruptions to the production process and loss of business due to product shortages and can also reduce supply costs and prevent price fluctuations. The provision of trade credit also stimulates sales, as it allows the receiving companies to verify the quality of products and services before payment. However, these additional investments in working capital may also adversely affect operating performance if the cost of a higher investment in working capital outweighs the benefits of holding more inventory or extending more trade credit to customers. Maintaining inventory involves certain costs such as warehouse rent, insurance and security costs, etc., which tend to increase with increasing inventory levels. On the other hand, a situation may arise in a company where lower investments in working capital may have a negative effect on the company's profit. If businesses invest less in working capital, there may be disruptions in the production process associated with low levels of working capital and consequently sales may decline.

The investment policy is about how many resources the company invests into the current assets (inventories, accounts receivable, cash, financial investments) in order to provide the targeted sales. Working capital investment policy can be relaxed, moderate and restrictive.

Within the relaxed policy, the estimation of current assets for achieving the targeted revenue is prepared after carefully considering uncertain events such as seasonal fluctuations, a sudden change in the level of activities or sales, etc. After the reasonable estimates, a cushion to avoid unforeseen circumstances is left to prevent the maximum possible risk. Companies with relaxed working capital policies assume the advantage of almost no risk or low risk. This policy guarantees the entrepreneur the smooth functioning of the operating cycle. On the other hand, there is a disadvantage of lower return on investment (ROI) because higher investment in the current assets attracts higher interest costs, reducing profitability.

Within the restricted policy, the estimation of current assets for achieving targeted revenue is done very aggressively without considering any contingencies and provisions for any unforeseen event. Adopting this policy would benefit the lower working capital requirement due to the lower level of current assets. This saves the interest cost to the company, which produces higher profitability, that is, higher ROI. On the other hand, there is a disadvantage in the form of high risk due to a very aggressive policy.

The moderate policy balances the two policies, that is, restricted and relaxed. It assumes the characteristics of both policies. To strike a balance, moderate policy assumes the risk to be lower than restricted and higher than conservative. In terms of profitability, it lies between the two.

De Almeida and Eid (2014) argue that additional investment in working capital reduces firm value. Similar conclusions were also reached by Zaiden and Shaper (2017), who believe that companies that invest excessively in working capital are economically inefficient. They believe that shortening the cash conversion cycle related to working capital management and its elements will lead to higher corporate profitability, higher stock prices and increased cash flow.

Gill et al. (2010) believe that slow debt collection is related to low profitability. Managers can improve profitability by shortening the credit period extended to their customers. The turnaround time of the liability also has a negative effect on the company's profit. It can be stated that the management of working capital and its elements has a significant impact on corporate profitability. Thus, operating profit appears to be determined by the extent to which managers act in terms of receivables management. Managers can create value for their shareholders by reducing accounts receivable turnover. Additionally, the negative relationship between receivables and firm profitability suggests that less profitable firms will seek to reduce their receivables in an attempt to reduce their cash gap in the cash conversion cycle. Business profitability can be increased if firms manage their working capital more effectively.

According to Howarth and Westhead (2003), there is evidence that most small companies focus their efforts on one area of working capital management and resources for working capital management are limited. They believe that the return on expended resources can have a major impact on the scope and focus of working capital management. The dynamics of working capital management are complex, and the links with performance are bidirectional and difficult to disentangle. Small companies can invest resources in managing a certain area of working capital in which they are not performing well in order to eliminate problem areas where higher returns can be expected. If the direction of causality is not understood, in this case, an overly simplistic conclusion may be drawn that investing more resources in an area leads to poorer performance. The complexity of causality makes it difficult to determine the effect of working capital management routines on firm performance. We can infer that firms with a lower propensity to perform working capital management routines are not significantly associated with increased cash flow problems or reduced profitability.

Afzal and Nazir (2008) argue that working capital investment policy is interconnected with working capital financing policy. The first principle concerns the structure of current assets, where attention is focused on the volume of inventories, receivables, cash or financial investments. The company can reduce its financing costs and increase the volume of available funds for potential projects by reducing the volume of investments tied up in current assets. In general, current assets are considered one of the most important components of a business's total assets. A company may be able to reduce investment in fixed assets by, for example, renting or leasing machinery and equipment, while the same policy cannot be applied to working capital components. A high level of current assets can reduce liquidity risk associated with the opportunity cost of foregone funds that could have been invested in long-term assets. The second principle focuses on what type and amount of capital the company needs to finance current assets.

Working capital financing policy is about what type of capital and how much of it we attract in order to finance the company's assets. Financial policy can be conservative, moderate and aggressive. Within the conservative strategy, long-term funds will finance fixed assets, permanent working capital and part of temporary working capital. Short-term funds will finance the remaining part of temporary working capital. Within the aggressive strategy, long-term funds will finance fixed assets and part of permanent working capital. Short-term funds will finance the remaining part of permanent working capital and temporary working capital.

According to PR's (2020), in addition to profitability and liquidity, working capital management also has an impact on the risk, solvency and value of the company. Effective working capital management has an impact not only on profitability as short-term financial performance but also on maximising shareholder value as long-term financial performance. Working capital management is critical to the day-to-day operations of any company and often changes form as part of day-to-day business.

Top management and other interested parties are therefore looking for answers to the question of how to ensure the creation of profit and economic added value in the longer term. As part of financial management within the company, attention is paid in particular to capital budgeting, working capital management and capital structure management. The management of the capital structure is important mainly because of the search for the optimal combination of own and external sources of financing and the optimal level of indebtedness in comparison with own sources of financing. Too high a level of indebtedness can reduce the profit and economic added value of the company and subsequently lead to bankruptcy.

19.3 Data and Methodology

The aim of this chapter is to identify the type of investment and financing policy of the working capital and reveal their influence on the financial performance of Czech companies in selected economic sectors. In order to fulfil the objective, companies operating in agriculture, manufacturing industry, construction and trade in Czechia were included in the analysis. The data sample included annual data for the period 2012 to 2021. The data were drawn from the Orbis database. The data sample included 2,813 enterprises operating in agriculture, 10,520 enterprises in manufacturing industry, 5,380 enterprises in construction and 12,899 enterprises in trade.

As part of working capital management, it is first necessary to find out the structure of the working capital and also to find out what part the individual components of the working capital contribute to the working capital as a whole. The following Eq. (19.1) can be used for such a finding:

$$\text{working capital structure} = \frac{(\text{selected component of working capital})}{\text{working capital}} \tag{19.1}$$

As mentioned above, a number of authors also focused on defining a conservative and aggressive working capital policy (investment policy) and working capital financing (financial policy) in connection with working capital management. As part of the working capital management policy, businesses can apply conservative working capital management (conservative investment policy) or aggressive working capital management (aggressive investment policy). An aggressive investment policy leads to a minimum level of investment in current assets compared to fixed assets. Conversely, a conservative investment policy represents higher investments in current assets, which can have a negative impact on profitability.

Many authors who have dealt with defining the influence of a conservative or aggressive working capital management policy on business activity consider the following Eq. (19.2) for measuring the degree of investment policy (IP) of working capital:

$$IP = \frac{\text{working capital (WC)}}{\text{sales (S)}} \tag{19.2}$$

The higher the value of this indicator, the more conservative working capital management policy is applied in the company. On the contrary, the lower the value of this indicator, the more the company applies a more aggressive working capital management policy.

In addition to the working capital management policy, it is also important to examine the working capital financing policy. Following the financial policy (FP) of working capital, we distinguish an aggressive financial policy and a conservative financial policy. The following Eq. (19.3) and Eq. (19.4) can be used to determine the degree of financial policy:

$$FP_1 = \frac{\text{current liabilities (CL)}}{\text{total assets (TA)}} \tag{19.3}$$

$$FP_2 = \frac{\text{non current liabilities (CNL)}}{\text{total assets (TA)}} \tag{19.4}$$

The higher FP_1 is than FP_2, the more aggressive working capital financing policy is applied. Aggressive financial policy uses, on the one hand, higher levels of short-term liabilities and, on the other hand, a smaller volume of indebtedness.

19.4 Characteristics of Working Capital Management in Selected Economic Sectors of Czechia

The selected sectors greatly influence the Czech economy, in that they represent half of the value generated by producing goods and services (51% in 2012 and 49% in 2021). Thus, in 2021, the value-added share of manufacture, trade, construction and agriculture, respectively, is 23.2%, 17.9%, 5.59% and 2.03% (OECD, 2012–2021).

While the average annual growth rate of the entire economy during 2012–2021 was 1.9%, the agricultural sector grew annually by 2.7%, the trade and manufacturing sector – by 2.1% and 1.9%. After the economic decline in 2020, when the annual growth rate of Czechia was negative (−5.3%), only some of the selected industries showed positive changes in 2021. The index mentioned in the entire economy was fixed at a level of 3.4% in 2021, in trade and manufacture, respectively, 6.3% and 4.9%.

The importance of the analysed industries is also evident in their contribution to total employment. In 2021, 1.36 million people were employed in the manufacturing sector, 413.4 and 132.9 thousand people in construction and agriculture. From 2012, these numbers had not changed significantly. The total number of people employed in these three sectors increased only by 1.7% (OECD, 2012–2021).

The manufacture, agriculture, construction and trade relate to the material production process, for which investments in working capital as well as structure of its financing define liquidity, financial stability and financial results of the companies.

19.4.1 Type of the Working Capital Investment Policy

The type of investment policy can be determined by the structure of the working capital. The corresponding data for the selected sectors are presented in Fig. 19.1.

During 2021–2021 on average 43% of working capital in agriculture is formed by stocks, saving of which usually demands special storage conditions, that generates a lot of additional costs for companies. This sector has the biggest share of stocks (less liquid part of current assets), compared to manufacture, construction and trade. The peculiarity of agriculture is almost the same share of cash and account receivable (debtors) in the working capital during the investigated

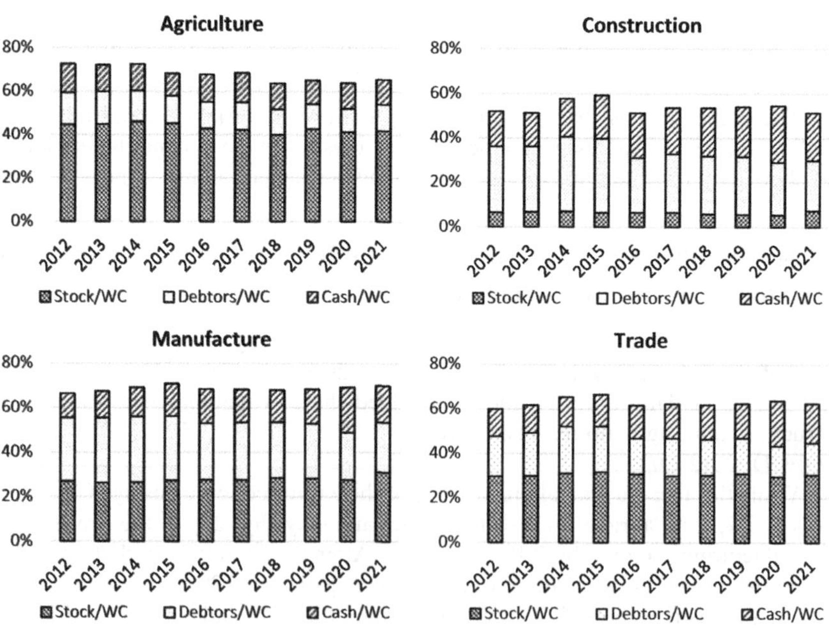

Fig. 19.1. The Structure of the Working Capital of Companies in Selected Sectors From 2012 to 2021. *Source:* Authors' Calculations Based on Data from the Orbis Database.

period, respectively, 12% and 13% on average. Despite the flexible investment policy, agriculture tries to control the payment discipline of customers. This, along with cash reserves, improves liquidity.

The structure of working capital in manufacture is more liquid, compared to agriculture, due to the lower ratio of stocks and the higher ratio of cash to current assets, respectively – 27.5% and 15%. During the analysed period, the liquidity of working capital was improved by positive change of the shares of accounts receivable and cash. The share of debtors decreased from 28% in 2012 to 22% in 2021, and the share of cash increased from 11% to 16%.

Obviously, construction has the lowest share of stocks and the highest share of cash in current assets among compared sectors, respectively, 6% and 20%. Furthermore, the cash-to-working capital ratio increased from 16% to 22% during the period. This peculiarity can be explained by the specifics of the operating activity. It is about a period between the moment of funds being collected from investors and the moment the permission documents are received to start the construction process. That is why during this period companies can accumulate additional liquidity in the form of cash. The third part of working capital is made up of debtors' liabilities (on average 27%). In addition to the production cycle, the sale process in the construction sector can also be long. Considering the price of its finished production, customers can get a payment delay that provokes accounts receivable. However, the share of such risky part of working capital is falling from 29% in 2012 to 22% in 2021.

Towards the specifics of the trade, the third part of the current assets has the material form due to the stocks. The payment discipline provided during 2016–2021 inside trade companies leads to that share of cash, which year by year is the same or even higher than the share of accounts receivable. In 2012, the ratio of the cash-to-working capital and debtors-to-working capital were, respectively, 12% and 18%. In 2021, they changed to 18% and 14%.

To provide the operating activity, agriculture maintains the highest working capital-to-sales ratio among the analysed economic sectors, on average 78% (Fig. 19.2). Over 10 years, this ratio changed from 71% in 2021 to 79% in 2021. It means that the increase in sales was followed by a change in the amount of working capital, which was growing faster, especially during 2012–2016. From 2012 to 2021, the volume of sales in agriculture increased by 36%, while working capital changed by 41%. This investment policy refers to the flexible type. It ensures the stability of the production process, which is extremely important, considering the specifics of agriculture. Also, it allows for covering an unexpected increase in demand, provides favourable credit policy and attracts customers.

Manufacturing companies maintain the amount of working capital on an average level of 40% to provide sales during 2012–2021 (Fig. 19.2). Such a ratio is a sign of moderate policy as a middle type between flexible (relaxed) and restrictive investment policy. However, the dynamics have a negative tendency. Similarly, to agriculture, the ratio of working capital-to-sales increased from 38% in 2012 to 44% in 2021. This means that the turnover of current assets is slowing down as sales grows. From 2012 to 2021, the volume of sales increased by 40%, while working capital by 58%.

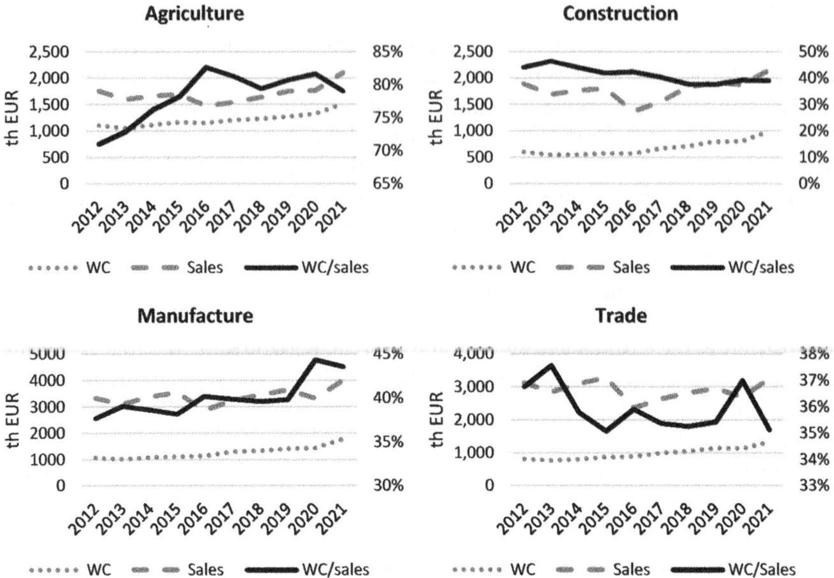

Fig. 19.2. Development of the Working Capital Investment Policy of Companies in Selected Sectors From 2012 to 2021. *Source:* Authors' Calculations Based on Data from the Orbis Database.

The construction sector also has a moderate investment policy, the average ratio of working capital-to-sales during the analysed 10 years being 41%. Growing revenue of the companies in the sector does not provoke a bigger amount of current assets, because the mentioned ratio is decreasing from 44% in 2012 to 39% in 2021. During 2012–2021, the volume of sales in construction grew by 61%, while working capital by 59%.

If the average ratio of working capital-to-sales in agriculture is 78%, in construction – 41% and in manufacture – 40%, trade has the lowest value – 36%. This ratio has a slight fluctuation during the analysed period, it decreases from 37% to 35%. The observed level, compared to other sectors, is close to a restrictive investment policy of working capital.

19.4.2 Type of the Working Capital Financing Policy

According to Fig. 19.3, the financing policy of the agricultural sector is conservative. Firstly, the stability of the capital structure should be mentioned. The share of equity and borrowed resources in total capital is stable for the 10 years analysed. Secondly, agriculture is characterised by financial independence. The equity-to-assets ratio is on average 72%. Thirdly, debts are divided almost equally

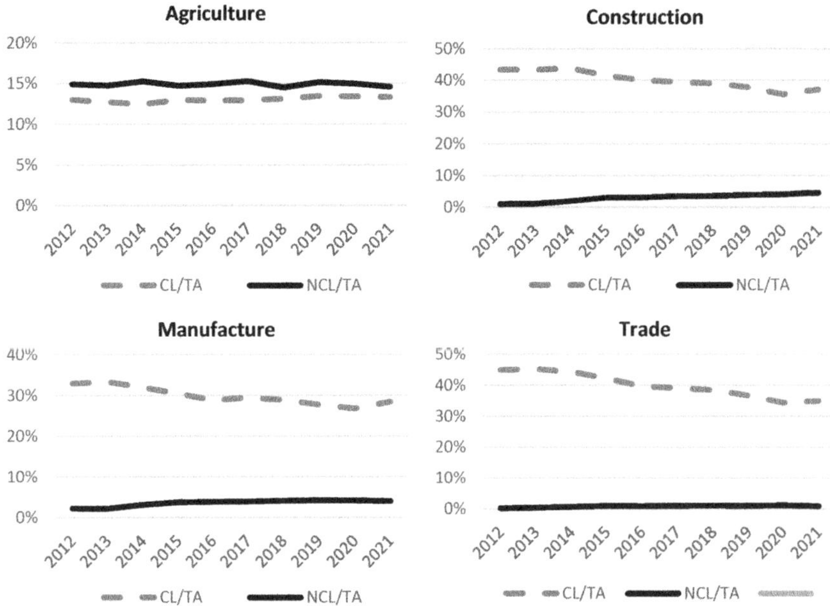

Fig. 19.3. Development of the Working Capital Financing Policy of Companies in Selected Sectors From 2012 to 2021. *Source:* Authors' Calculations Based on Data from the Orbis Database.

between current and long-term liabilities. Their shares in the assets financing are, respectively, 13% and 15%.

The stable and low share of short-term borrowed capital positively affects the sector's liquidity. Therefore, the average level of the current ratio (current assets-to-current liabilities) is 2.8 during 2012–2021. Predominantly based on long-term resources (equity and non-current liabilities), agricultural companies provide the stability of financing of their seasonal process of production and selling.

Manufacture and agriculture are financially independent sectors, where only 33% (on average) of the capital was formed with the help of borrowed resources. However, within conservative financing policy, manufacture gives a clear advantage to current liabilities, which make up most debt sources. Short-term borrowed capital on average finances 30% of assets. Furthermore, this share is decreasing from 33% in 2012 to 28% in 2021. Manufacture always had a high level of current ratio – on average 1.9, which was increasing during analysed period.

The financing policy of working capital in construction and trade can be considered as moderate, so far as the debt share is, respectively, 43% and 41% on average for 10 years. The rest is formed by equity. Both sectors prefer current liabilities as a borrowed source of assets financing. However, it should be mentioned that their share is decreasing from 43% in 2012 to 37% in 2021 (construction) and from 45% to 35% (trade). Such moderate policy, which has insignificant long-term debts, is safe for trade because of permanent cash flows and short operating cycle. In case of construction with a long and specific production process, the attraction of mostly current liabilities can be risky for the liquidity level. The average current ratio in this sector (1.7) is lower, compared to trade (1.8), manufacture (1.9) and agriculture (2.8). Nevertheless, it is sufficient and increases over time, as long as the amount of working capital in construction changes much more quickly than current liabilities.

19.4.3 The Influence of Working Capital Management on Company Profitability

The flexible investment policy and conservative financing policy of agriculture can be expensive (Figs. 19.4 and 19.5). In the first case, it relates to storage costs for stocks saving, in the second case – with high cost of equity and long-term debts. Agriculture is the only sector where losses can be observed. Thus, in 2013 and 2014, return on assets (using profit before taxation) is negative, respectively, 0.5%

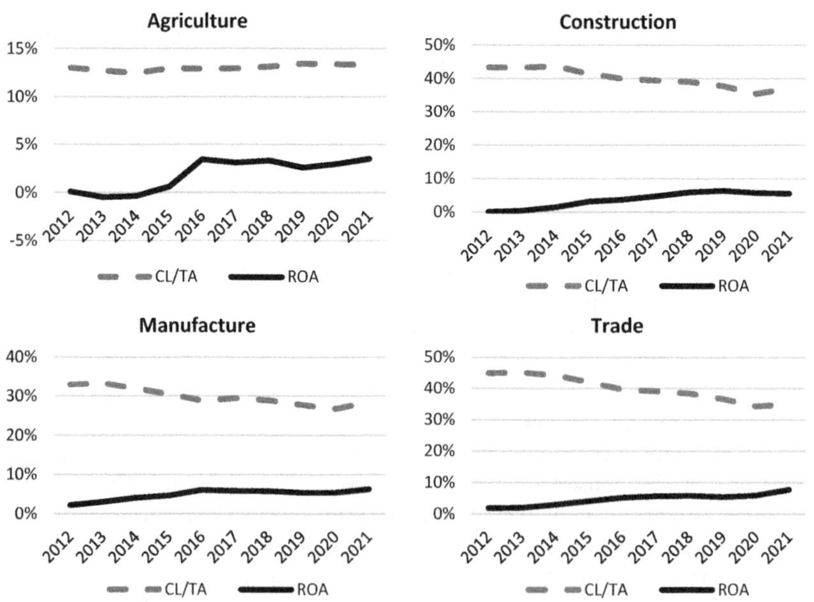

Fig. 19.4. The Influence of the Working Capital Financing Policy on the Profitability of Companies in Selected Sectors From 2012 to 2021. *Source:* Authors' Calculations Based on Data from the Orbis Database.

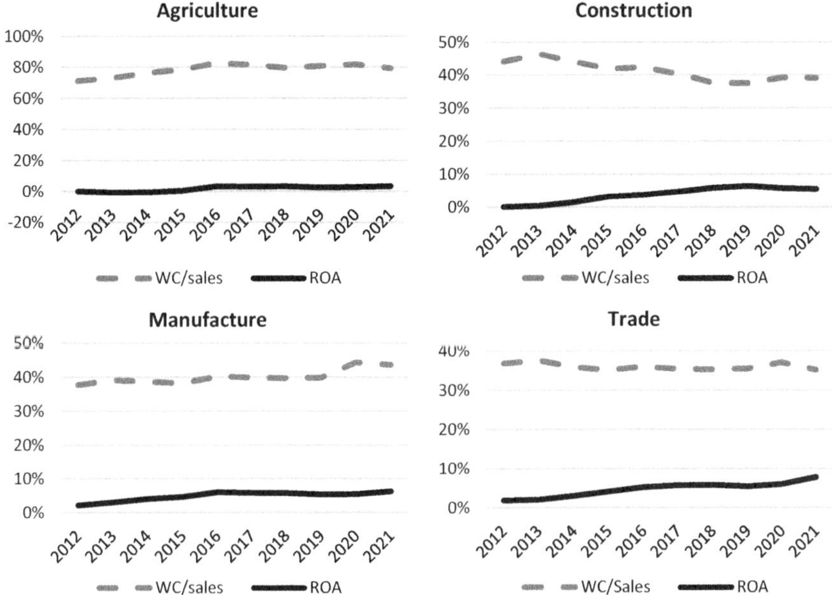

Fig. 19.5. The Influence of the Working Capital Investment Policy on the Profitability of Companies in Selected Sectors From 2012 to 2021. *Source:* Authors' Calculations Based on Data from the Orbis Database.

and 0.3%. Moreover, even during profitable years, the level of ROA is, on average, 2.5%, which is lower, compared to other sectors. In addition to this, from 2017 to 2021, any tide connection between the type of investment/financing policy and ROA cannot be fixed. The working capital-to-sales ratio and the share of current liabilities in total capital during this period are stable. However, there is an obvious fluctuation of the profitability of assets.

In the case of manufacture, the increase of the working capital-to-sales ratio within moderate investment policy is followed by the strengthening of the conservatism degree of the financing policy due to the decrease of the role of current liabilities. Both tendencies encourage the growth of the return on assets. ROA tripled from 2% in 2012 to 6% in 2021.

Moderate investment and moderate financing policies of the working capital in construction are accompanied by a growing return on assets. Within this sector, some opposite tendencies, compared to agriculture and manufacture, can be observed. In construction simultaneously, both ratios (current liabilities-to-assets and working capital-to-sales) are decreasing. Nevertheless, it does not interfere with the positive change of ROA from 0.11% in 2012 to 5.62% in 2021.

Like other sectors, trade is characterised by a falling share of current liabilities into assets financing. It is accompanied by the lowest working capital-to-sales ratio among the analysed economic sectors. Thus, the restrictive investment policy of working capital in trade coexists with a moderate policy of its financing, which provides increasing ROA from 2% in 2012 to 8% in 2021.

Thereby, the most conservative investment and financing policy during 2012–2021 is observed in agriculture, which has the highest share of working capital to provide sales and the lowest share of current liabilities to finance its activity. Manufacture combines conservative financing policy with moderate investments in working capital. Construction is characterised by a moderate level of current assets compared to annual revenue, and a moderate level of current liabilities compared to assets. The trade due to the short operating cycle can afford the restrictive investment policy of the working capital; however, it tries to reduce the role of short-term debts in its capital. Unlike agriculture, where borrowed capital is equally distributed between current and long sources, manufacture, trade and construction prefer liabilities, attracted for periods of up to 1 year. Despite this, all selected economic sectors have a high level of liquidity. The provided activity influences profitability in different ways. The highest ROA can be fixed within the trade sector – on average 5%, then manufacture – 4.8% and construction – 3.8%. The lowest return on assets is in agriculture, on average 1.9%.

19.5 Conclusion

Working capital management aims to provide a smooth production and sale process as well as timely coverage of current liabilities of the company, which defines the efficiency of its operating activity. Thereby, this chapter identifies the type of investment and financing policies of the working capital and reveal their influence on the financial performance of the companies in manufacture, agriculture, construction and trade as the most important sectors for Czech economy.

The results revealed that agriculture is the only sector characterised by a flexible investment policy between 2012 and 2021. Compared to manufacture and construction, which implement moderate policy, the trade sector affords relatively restrictive investments in the working capital, attracting a lower amount of current assets to provide the sales. All industries have a high level of financial independence, as equity forms more than half of their capital. Along with this, manufacture and agriculture finance their operating activity in a conservative way, at the same time, construction and trade provide moderate financing policy of working capital, preferring current liabilities. Despite this, all analysed sectors support a sufficient level of liquidity.

Accumulating significant working capital compared to sales and attracting mainly long-term financial resources negatively influence the profitability of agriculture. Its flexible investment policy and conservative financing policy are accompanied by a low return on assets and even losses. The predisposition to moderate investment and moderate financing policy of working capital in construction and manufacture improves their financial results. The return on assets of these sectors grew steadily during the analysed period. The highest profitability can be observed in trade that combines moderate financing policy and restrictive investments in working capital.

References

Afzal, T., & Nazir, M. S. (2008). Working capital approaches and firm's returns in Pakistan. *Pakistan Journal of Commerce and Social Sciences*, (1), 25–36. http://hdl.handle.net/10419/187978

Alvarez, T., Sensing, L., & Vazquez, M. (2021). Working capital management and profitability: Evidence from an emergent economy. *International Journal of Advances in Management and Economics*, *10*(1), 32–39. https://managementjournal.info/index.php/IJAME/article/view/689

De Almeida, J. R., & Eid, W. (2014). Access to finance, working capital management and company value: Evidences from Brazilian companies listed on BM & FBOVESPA. *Journal of Business Research*, *67*(5), 924–934. https://doi.org/10.1016/j.jbusres.2013.07.012

Failback, G., & Krueger, T. M. (2005). An analysis of working capital management results across industries. *American Journal of Business*, *20*(2), 11–20. https://doi.org/10.1108/19355181200500007

Gill, A., Bigger, N., & Mathur, N. (2010). The relationship between working capital management and profitability: Evidence from the United States. *Business and Economics Journal*, *10*, 1–9. https://citeseerx.ist.psu.edu/document?repid=rep1&type=pdf&doi=4fbaa2174386ee0cc6e90de5d098b9e36962f2de

Howarth, C., & Westhead, P. (2003). The focus of working capital management in UK small firms. *Management Accounting Research*, *14*(2), 94–111. https://doi.org/10.1016/S1044-5005(03)00022-2

Küster, D. (2022). The impact of working capital management on profitability: Evidence from Serbian listed manufacturing companies. *Economic Themes*, *60*(1), 117–131. https://doi.org/10.2478/ethemes-2022-0007

Zaiden, R. M., & Shaper, O. (2017). Cash conversion cycle and value-enhancing operations: Theory and evidence for a free lunch. *Journal of Corporate Finance*, *45*(C), 203–219. https://doi.org/10.1016/j.jcorpfin.2017.04.014

Index

Printed and bound by CPI Group (UK) Ltd, Croydon, CR0 4YY

02/06/2024

14509089-0003